THE
PRICE
OF
MERCY

THE
PRICE
OF
MERCY

Unfair Trials, a Violent System,
and a Public Defender's Search
for Justice in America

EMILY GALVIN ALMANZA

CROWN
NEW YORK

CROWN
An imprint of the Crown Publishing Group
A division of Penguin Random House LLC
1745 Broadway
New York, NY 10019
crownpublishing.com
penguinrandomhouse.com

Page 78: Graph © 2021 by Gallup, Inc.

Library of Congress Cataloging-in-Publication Data
Names: Galvin Almanza, Emily, 1983– author.
Title: The price of mercy / Emily Galvin Almanza.
Description: New York : Crown, 2026. | Includes bibliographical references and index. |
Identifiers: LCCN 2025013313 | ISBN 9780593799116 (hardcover) |
ISBN 9780593799130 (trade paperback) | ISBN 9780593799123 (ebook)
Subjects: LCSH: Criminal courts—United States. | Criminal justice,
Administration of—United States. | Public defenders—United States.
Classification: LCC KF9223 .G35 2026 | DDC 345.73/01—dc23/eng/20250326
LC record available at https://lccn.loc.gov/2025013313

Hardcover ISBN 978-0-593-79911-6
Ebook ISBN 978-0-593-79912-3

Editor: Aubrey Martinson
Production editor: Terry Deal
Text designer: Amani Shakrah
Production: Heather Williamson
Proofreaders: Taylor McGowan, Ruth Anne Phillips
Indexer: Ina Gravitz
Publicist: Josie Roberts
Marketer: Kimberly Lew

Manufactured in the United States of America

1st Printing

First Edition

The authorized representative in the EU for product safety and compliance is Penguin Random House Ireland, Morrison Chambers, 32 Nassau Street, Dublin D02 YH68, Ireland, https://eu-contact.penguin.ie.

This book is dedicated to every person
I have had the privilege of representing.

Contents

Part Two

Solutions

Part One

The
Problem

Chapter One

Outsiders on the Inside

The Power of Public Defense

When I was a teenager, my life fell apart. I fell into substance abuse, and, ultimately, ended up getting arrested at the age of sixteen, thousands of miles from home. I was cuffed, crumpled into the back of a Boston PD cruiser, taken to booking, photographed, searched, and put in a holding cell until a responsible adult could come and get me. Two days later, I was standing in an austere Suffolk County courtroom, waiting to find out what would happen to me. It was not a great time.

I remember very little about that day. There is only one person I remember clearly—Judge Leslie Harris, a juvenile court judge who had dedicated his time on the bench to seeing potential in children instead of seeing threat. I didn't know at the time how lucky I was, or that my life was about to be saved by this man's commitment to helping kids rather than doing harm. I remember clearly when he asked me to approach the bench, where he could speak with me alone. He asked me why I was in his courtroom when I had a college admission letter in hand. I don't remember what I said, but I remember his reply.

"I'm going to dismiss your case," he told me. "And this arrest will not stop you from going to college. But I don't ever want to hear from you again, unless you've done something good with your life." With those words, he let me go.

This story is a mixture of heroism and privilege. Obviously, I carried the incredible privileges of whiteness, education, involved parents, and future prospects into the courtroom. But also, I was standing before a Black jurist who had decided that in a system designed to punish, he would continually insist on offering children protection.

A decade later, because Judge Harris gave me that chance, I was able to land a job at the Los Angeles County Public Defender's Office and show up to work, during my first summer of law school, at the Eastlake Juvenile Courthouse, which was, at the time, the busiest court for children in Los Angeles. Day in and day out, I was hurrying through the rabbit warren of hallways behind the courthouse, meeting kids who had made the same choices I had once made. But unlike me, these kids were largely Black and brown and had been born in a hyper-policed, hyper-surveilled L.A. neighborhood that punished all and protected none. As a young public defender, my practice of law was deeply personal. I saw kids whose futures were going to be thrown away when mine was preserved. As a lawyer, I could fight for those futures. I could try to pay forward the chance I had been given.

I worked on cases of people whose lives were set to be discarded for crimes as small as stealing a pair of socks. Over the years, I met a lot of people who were just plain not guilty, because the state of investigation in our streets is often closer to lazy bureaucratic box checking than any recognizable form of real inquiry. I also met innumerable people who were overcharged, meaning that while they might have done *something,* they certainly didn't do what they were accused of. I spent my energy on litigation and winning trials while knowing full well that many of these cases were arising from addressable, or even avoidable, underlying circumstances: the fallout of entrenched poverty, lack of opportunity, constant police surveillance, structural racism, lack of health care, and the desperation and nihilism these circumstances breed. As public defenders, we are in solidarity with our clients, and standing together to face down a system that hides information, conceals misconduct, chooses efficiency and finality over the harder work of getting it right, and, even when right, is still deeply wrong, because all it can do is punish.

———

A third of Americans have had a loved one represented by a public defender.[1] Public defenders are free lawyers. In America, we only get free lawyers in one context, which is criminal court—if your liberty or your life is on the line, the U.S. Constitution says you have the right to counsel. For that reason, every jurisdiction in America has the ability to appoint a lawyer in a criminal case if a person cannot afford to pay for one themselves.

This looks different from place to place—in some places, public defenders are government attorneys working in a governmental agency, while in others they may work at a nonprofit public defender that holds a contract with the jurisdiction, while in yet other places they might be part of a network of local lawyers who get assigned to public defense cases. Across America's 5,900 defender agencies, both the nature and quality of practice vary.[2] A public defender's office with more resources will be able to do stronger work than an under-resourced, overworked agency. And a public defender with a culture of commitment to client-led service and creating an empowering, high-quality defense for each person they serve will do better than an office where the lingering power dynamics of poverty lawyering have taken over and created cultural toxicity. So like anything else, defenders are not all alike. But they are all dedicated to the zealous, skilled defense of low-income people who stand accused, and they are also a last bulwark against government overreach and the intractable impulses of law enforcement to trample our Constitution.

At some point, every defender will be asked how we can represent "*those* people," meaning "criminals." I don't love that word. I've represented people who have made devastatingly bad choices. I've represented people who had found themselves in a state where they could no longer control their behavior, for one reason or another. I've represented people who were operating under circumstances that I cannot personally imagine surviving. I've represented a lot of people who were innocent, a fact that I have noticed often surprises laypeople, because television tells us that most people who get arrested are guilty, while in real life most people who get arrested are poor, and may or may not be guilty.

The system looks very different from the inside than it does on the outside. The laws are not applied as they are written, they're *interpreted,* letting all manner of human bias and opinion seep into the decision-making of courts. Exhaustion, jadedness, nihilism, and secondary trauma are everywhere, and since the court system isn't just a machine—all these human emotions, irritations, and traumas come into play. The "law," often perceived as objective, is applied so subjectively from place to place that two neighboring counties may in fact have unrecognizably different charges, procedures, and outcomes. People getting offered support and recovery in one town might have received hard time in the next town over. Even the language varies: an arraignment in New York might be magistration in Texas or callout in Louisiana.

So like everyone else who works in the criminal court system, we spend all day, every day, watching the law as it is practiced turn out to be nothing like the law you see on TV. But unlike everyone else in the legal system, we aren't there to uphold the machine. We're there to argue against the grinding of the machine's gears, find flaws in the machine itself, object to it, and, sure, okay, sometimes rage against the machine. When we do this, we usually start by saying, "Judge, I have to make my record," meaning that we know we're getting shut down now, but we want to preserve all the wrongness we're witnessing for a higher court, one that will review the transcripts from this day.

I spent ten years practicing in various Halls of Justice from Cali-

fornia to New York, including at the legendary holistic defense practice
the Bronx Defenders. After representing thousands of people, it became
clear to me that there was a fundamental need in public defense that
was, often, not being met. To truly defend someone, one must equip
the defense team with the means to deal not only with the criminal case
but with its drivers and fallout: loss of housing, employment, educational opportunity, health care. In 2018, I left trial work to start Partners for Justice (PFJ), a nonprofit supporting defenders around the
country in filling that need. Our approach, termed Collaborative Defense, quickly took off, growing from two pilot locations in 2018 to
more than forty locations by 2024 and has managed to eliminate over
eight thousand years of incarceration in that time.

In the early days of Partners for Justice, I was on the phone with a
potential funder, standing in front of a laundromat in Laramie, Wyo-
ming, where I had gone to visit my dad. The person on the other end
was considering joining in the mission to expand public defense, but
wasn't so into resourcing a government service. I realized, then, how
many people don't understand the key factor that makes defenders a
different part of the legal system: we are lawyers provided by the government, indeed, but we're put there precisely to *fight* the government.

This also means that we are, in many ways, your best protection
against government overreach—even if you think you will never break
the law. The rights you think you have—the right to remain silent, to be
safe from unreasonable searches of your home, car, or person, to speak
privately with a lawyer if you're in trouble, to be safe from unlawful interrogations, to have a fair trial—aren't ironclad. They are under attack
almost every day, because in an adversarial system it is the government's
prerogative to argue about why a judge should lessen or set aside an individual's rights to give the government a little more leeway. When they
do this, it erodes the Constitutional protections we all expect. The people standing between you and that erosion are public defenders, whose
daily fight to preserve those rights for others will directly benefit you or
your loved one, should you ever need those protections.

So that's where we stand. Part of a system, but also trying to dismantle that system's power, and carrying an almost sacred duty to fight that system at every turn. We are, essentially, outsiders operating on the inside.

———

The idea that if the government takes it upon itself to accuse you, it must also take it upon itself to defend you, or else justice cannot be found, has been alive among us since the 1960s. In 1963, a man named Clarence Earl Gideon was accused of stealing some beer and loose change from a pool hall in Florida. He asked the judge in his case for a lawyer, and the judge said no, because at that time in Florida, people only got lawyers if the death penalty was on the line. So (predictably) he got convicted, and (astonishingly) he handwrote a petition to the U.S. Supreme Court, in careful pencil script, arguing that people shouldn't be deprived of their liberty without the right to counsel. The Supreme Court agreed, and now, decades later, people are still reaping the benefit of Gideon's pencil, as 80 percent of people in the criminal court system[3] use the free lawyer provided courtesy of Clarence Earl Gideon and the U.S. Constitution.[4]

What I just told you, though, is not the whole story. Like many stories, this is a story where a guy gets credit for something a woman did. In this case, something a woman did seventy years before the Court decided Gideon's case.

Clara Shortridge Foltz was just fifteen when she left home to elope with a Union soldier. She bore five children, moved across the country, and got left there by said soldier, suddenly a single mom far from family.[5] Like many women at the end of the nineteenth century, Clara was interested in change—she had fought for the right to vote, and her fellow suffragettes helped her land a job working for an attorney in California. Clara was sharp and soon decided that instead of working *for* a lawyer, she'd like to *be* the lawyer.[6] Which, of course, took some doing—she literally had to change the law. She proposed an amended bill that took a law allowing any "white male" to be a lawyer and changed it to allowing any "citizen or person" to be a lawyer. The bill passed, but the governor refused to sign it. So Clara showed up in person at his office, retrieved the bill from the discard pile, and made him sign it right there and then.[7]

The law itself allowed her, but the legal community was another matter. She was bullied out of law school at Hastings and promptly sued the school. During the suit, she had to sit there and listen to the school's lawyers talk about how, as the *San Francisco Chronicle* recounted, women lawyers were a terrible idea because "an impartial jury would be impossible when a lovely lady pleaded the case of the criminal." These arguments didn't land, apparently, because Clara won, and attended Hastings for two years, until her growing legal practice required the entirety of her attention.[8]

Clara was a lot of firsts. Not just the first woman lawyer in California, but also the first female district attorney.[9] She seemed to recoil, though, from the power imbalance inherent in our legal system even then, because at the 1893 World's Columbian Exposition in Chicago, Clara got up and gave an absolute barn burner of a speech, in which she took down the hypocrisy of the government representing one side in criminal court but not the other.[10] To quote just part of it, she pointed out how the prosecution is incentivized to convict at all costs, while the rights of the accused are trampled:

> Not only is machinery for prosecution provided, but it is most effectively operated. The prosecuting attorney is usually imbued with the idea that he must convict at all hazards, and this idea takes deeper root because, in many instances, the State pays him a money bonus for each conviction. . . .
>
> For the conviction of the accused every weapon is provided and used, even those poisoned by wrong and injustice. But what machinery is provided for the defense of the innocent? None. Absolutely none.[11]

Clara closed by calling upon our nation to do better: "Let the criminal courts be re-organized upon a basis of exact, equal and free justice; let our country be broad and generous enough to make the law a shield as well as a sword; let the citizen understand that his flag is his protection in his own home as well as when his foot is on foreign soil." Two decades later, her vision came to fruition when the Los Angeles County Public Defender's Office opened its doors.[12] Clara would ultimately work to legislate the idea of the public defender into existence in thirty states,[13] decades before *Gideon.*

———

Thanks to these visionaries, if a person is accused of a crime and they cannot afford a lawyer, they are assigned one by the government. If you found yourself in this position in San Jose or the Bronx during certain years, that lawyer might have been me. I spent the first half of my professional life inside courthouses and jails, fighting for my clients. First in L.A., then in Santa Clara County, then at the Three Strikes Project, helping end the appalling life sentences of California's darkest tough-on-crime era, and later as a Bronx Defender.

Under California's Three Strikes law, enacted in 1994, thousands of people were sentenced to life for exceptionally low-level crimes—stealing a piece of pizza or a pair of socks, for example. The horrifying aspect of this legal scheme was its immunity to context. The law threw people into prison for life on the technical basis of their prior offenses, no matter how old that history or how minor their new misconduct. In one of my own cases, a man who stole about $30 worth of plumbing supplies from a hardware store was sentenced to life in prison because a decade before, when he was around nineteen years old, he had (twice) drunkenly entered garages. He was accused back then of attempting to steal VCRs, but hadn't actually stolen anything, because he had passed out on the floor. But he pled guilty to both instances as burglaries, received a short sentence, and went on his way. The Three Strikes law is "retroactive," meaning the two burglaries this kid got in the early 1990s were now "strike felonies"—crimes that, if he was ever again accused of a felony, would send him away for life. Around the state, untold numbers of Californians became "walking lifers" overnight. And when my client had a young family to take care of, and a home, and was dead broke, between jobs, and had a leak in the house he had to fix but no supplies to do so, he tried to shoplift from a chain supply store. He was charged with "petty theft with a prior" (the 1990s cases), which, in California at that time, turned a petty theft into a felony. He was sentenced to life in prison.

My job, throughout much of law school and again afterward, was to try to undo the viciousness of the state one person at a time. With Stanford's Three Strikes Project, and under the tutelage of extraordinary attorneys, my task was to attack these convictions through state or federal processes, often having to be creative, because courts are largely built for finality, not justice. To even find a way to properly raise the issue of the man languishing in prison over $30 in plumbing supplies is a challenge, because the law is set up to give judges multiple reasons to set aside or dismiss such a petition, and a very narrow, difficult path to actually considering the claims of a sentenced person in prison. And once one had secured the ability to even be heard, success was highly dependent on my ability to force a judge to encounter the humanity of the person I represented. As the Three Strikes law evolved, it became allowable to present the "background, character, and prospects" of the person whose life was on the line. To do so well has almost nothing to do with a juris doctorate and everything to do with attending to the details of each person's story—and, of course, their potential.

Unlike private attorneys, who may visit a given court system from time to time, I spent most of my waking hours inside the system, getting to know the people who work there, the incentives they labor under, the weird corners that can be cut, and the slippage between what the law says and what's actually going to happen on any given day.

As public defenders, we see it all: how one-fifth of people confined to solitary stay in darkness for years on end;[14] that 90 percent of children waive their right to a lawyer when in police custody,[15] and, once interrogated without protection, over a third will falsely confess;[16] that about a quarter of new prison admissions in this country aren't due to new crimes, but to *technical violations of parole.*[17] We bear witness to and do battle against the consequences of benighted public policy, because when voters mistake punishment for safety, they make policy choices that actively take us further from the kind of nation (or neighborhood) we want to live in.

It is *exhausting.*

Around the country, defenders are generally representing more people than we should—our caseloads are so high that studies, lawsuits, and strikes[18] are all accumulating into an urgent chorus of calls for change. Our resources are also scarce. While prosecutors can review 100 percent of the evidence, use the police force and forensics labs as their investigative branch, and essentially create the cases they litigate, defenders are often dealing with "trial by ambush," where courts can shove us—and our clients—out to trial when we've only been given much of the crucial evidence hours or even minutes beforehand.

Defenders and prosecutors also operate under wildly different incentives. Defenders are rewarded for standing up for fundamental rights, and for doing our best work to defend both the individual and the Constitution, whether we win or lose. We don't come to this job for the money—there isn't much—or the prestige—even less—but rather because we believe in the Constitution and we feel passionately about standing up for others and doing good. A lot of the feedback we receive is immediate, coming from the person we serve, and, at its best, can be a constant source of growth and moral alignment (at its worst, it's getting yelled at by a sovereign citizen).

Prosecutors may face very different incentives, including pressure to secure convictions or risk their own advancement, as you'll hear from some former prosecutors in the chapters ahead. I recognize that the people in this book do not represent 100 percent of their profession, just as I do not represent or speak for all public defenders. I also recognize that there's a lot of variance within this line of work: there are prosecutors who callously seek to advance themselves by stepping on the necks of the wrongfully convicted, and there are prosecutors who are actively and even heroically fighting for a safer and more just society. There are public defenders who dedicate their lives to free and equal justice, and there are public defenders who burned out long ago and are falling short of their duty of representation. There are police who pose a lethal threat to the citizenry, and there are police who genuinely just want to keep people safer. But these caveats aside, the rampant inequities of the criminal courts are largely not because of "bad" individuals, but rather arise from the system in which these individuals operate, and the incentives and beliefs that shape their actions.

That being said, bad incentives do not excuse oppression. The reason many of the ideas in this book—proven, exciting solutions that don't just make us safer but might also have great side effects like more-hospitable neighborhoods or stronger public health—aren't already implemented at scale is because there are powerful figures at play, whose power was gathered through the violent oppression of historically marginalized people and whose vested interests lead them to use their power to fight change.

There are things we need to tear down, in other words. This book is an attempt to highlight the worst, so that we can think about how we can build something worthy of justice. On any given day, public defense work is a study in grief, recovery, agility, improvisation, and deep knowledge of the systems around us. We've got clients all over the courthouse, maybe ten cases set to be heard on an average morning, appearances on every floor, and that doesn't even touch the jail visits, investigations in the field, or trips to talk with our clients and their families, wherever they may be. Defense is also, at its core, a service profession, meaning that if you're a good defender, you're delivering the kind of legal counsel and support that doesn't just keep your client out of jail, but also takes into account their specific life circumstances. If a kid wants to go into the military, for example, a good lawyer isn't just offering a one-size-fits-all deal but recognizing that 99 percent of case outcomes short of dismissal and expungement will destroy this kid's dream, so we, as lawyers, have to do the extra work to not only end the case but do so in a way that keeps their hopes for the future alive. If you're doing the job right, you're learning a vast amount about each person you serve and, of course, the community in which they live.

This is one of the most misunderstood aspects of being a public defender. While we are publicly perceived as criminal defense counsel (which is true), the fact that we're operating inside a system that can touch so many aspects of a person's life—from housing to employment to health to children and families—means that we're also doing a lot of other work. In holistic defense offices like Bronx Defenders, or in the collaborative defense offices I support in my current role, that other work may be quite overt; public defender attorneys may be collaborating with housing lawyers, civil rights lawyers, social workers, mental health treatment professionals, community organizers, employment advocates, and more to make sure that we, as a team, can fully address the fallout from a criminal case. But even in "regular" criminal defense, the role of the defender goes astonishingly far beyond litigation.

For example, when a defender helps secure a dismissal of charges, wins a trial, helps a client get their record expunged, or even negotiates a plea to a less damaging charge, they're not just potentially preventing incarceration, but also doing direct economic mobility work by keeping their client more employable. Not to mention how often we find ourselves on the phone with someone's boss, asking them not to terminate this person's employment for having to come back to court again and again, explaining that the repeated days off are a feature of an overburdened court system rather than willful absenteeism by our client. When we prevent an unaffordable fine or fee from being imposed, or have a hearing that enables a client to keep their driver's license, we're keeping money in the pockets of people who can least afford to lose it. And, of course, incarceration itself is expensive, to the state, the incarcerated person, and their family. Public defenders play a vital role in preserving the economic well-being of low-income families and limiting the out-of-control government spending on incarceration.

When we help a client find a mental health or substance use treatment program that's actually a good fit for their goals and needs, that isn't just criminal defense, it's the provision of health care. Every good defender has fielded those late-night calls from a person in crisis, ready to quit the program, and spent the hour it takes to talk our client through the moment of panic and support them in a decision to stick with recovery. Incarceration is so damaging to health—via trauma, creating and exacerbating chronic conditions, addictions, relapses, and exposing people to communicable disease without adequate access to medical care—that preventing incarceration may, in some cases, be as important to lifespan as quitting smoking. Yet few people ever talk about the role defenders play in improving and protecting public health.

All of these interventions aren't just serving the individual client, but the public at large. Many of my clients have indeed done harm. If there's some reason why they've done that (as there usually is), solving the problem—and helping them be less likely to engage in that harm again—doesn't just benefit them, but everyone around them who might have been negatively impacted by their actions. Safety, after all, is collective. If I'm not doing well and I act on it, it impacts everyone around me. I cannot be individually "doing well" when my neighbors are unhoused, or unable to feed their kids, because their state of desperation will inevitably impact us all.

The system touches everything, and that pushes a lot of defenders to end up doing work in areas we never expected. We have to figure out whether we have the bandwidth and expertise to litigate school suspension hearings when our kid client will otherwise be alone against a government lawyer. We have to decide whether we have time before court to go through our client's résumé and help them figure out how to talk about their open case in a job interview. There are more than forty thousand documented "collateral" consequences of having a criminal case.[19] That's a lot of complexities to heap onto the shoulders of under-resourced, overloaded defenders. The stakes, obviously, are highest not for us but for the person we've promised to protect. It's amazing how often we manage to do so, against all odds.

This is not to say that there is nothing beautiful or worthy to be found in our legal system. If anything, this book is a love letter to some of the best ideas of justice writ large, and to the future we could have, if we were willing to do the work of reimagining our legal infrastructure. This critique is an act of love. There is something touching, brave, and profoundly human about a nation that chooses to leave the finding of truth in the hands of an assemblage of strangers. A nation that gives ordinary people the franchise of jury service, and places, in the hands of our communities, so much power to determine what we collectively believe is right and wrong. There is wisdom in the testing of a story, in the cross examination of witnesses to try to highlight, for those finders of fact, any flaw that might crack the facade of credibility. Our adversarial system—were it able to actually include and represent the people it most impacts, and if it had the resources to offer people solutions instead of punishment—could be powerful, effective, and humane. If we want to make it better, we can choose to do so. I hope, after reading this, you'll make that choice.

———

After all that, I have to break it to you: this book is not about public defenders. It's about you, and your legal system, and the things you should know about it. The American people deserve to know what their legal system is doing—and not doing—in their name and on their dime. Being a public defender affords a lot of access to the men behind the curtains of the court system. It also offers access to the people we should listen to the most in this conversation—people who are personally impacted by arrest, prosecution, and imprisonment. Many of the people I have served would also like you to know the truth about their experiences, and I'm so grateful to have had their partnership in telling these stories.[20] To be entrusted with their stories also means doing the work of placing those stories in context, marshaling the available evidence on how this system is harming not just them and their families but all of us. After all, safety is not individual; it's a shared state. Happily, many of these problems are problems for which there already is an available solution, we just need the political will to fully implement it. And if more people see the inner workings of this machine, the will to fundamentally change it will grow. So I'd like to take you with me on a tour, down and through some very dark places, but, ultimately, emerge into some transformative light.

Chapter Two

All Rise

Judges, Bail, and Being Human on the Bench

On August 29, 2005, Hurricane Katrina nearly leveled the city of New Orleans. According to more than a thousand testimonials gathered by the ACLU,[1] as the Orleans Parish Prison filled with toxic, waste-filled brackish water, the people confined inside were forced into cells by fleeing jail staff, the doors handcuffed shut. Every single person was held there on the order of a local judge—who had not changed their orders in light of the coming storm. Some people locked inside hung signs out broken windows begging for help. Others claim that they saw their fellows shot when trying to flee. The waters rose. For days, without power, food, or water, people confined in jail were left to stand in the dark, water up to their chests, with no way to send word to their families. Without hope of rescue.

Less than a month later, John G. Roberts sat before the United States Senate, seeking confirmation as the next chief justice of the U.S. Supreme Court. In his opening remarks, he delivered one of the most famous quotes to date about what it is to be a judge in a court of law: "Judges and Justices are servants of the law, not the other way around.

Judges are like umpires. Umpires don't make the rules, they apply them. The role of an umpire and a judge is critical. They make sure everybody plays by the rules, but it is a limited role. Nobody ever went to a ball game to see the umpire."[2]

Here's the problem: no one has ever given an umpire the right to decide if their fellow man should be left to die in a fetid, flooded jail cell. Which is why we need to talk about what judges really are, and take a good hard look at the people behind the curtain.

Many defenders would argue that arraignment is the most important moment in a criminal case. It is when the person learns what they are being accused of, and usually when a judge will decide whether the person is sent to jail while the case proceeds. This is not a minor factor. If a person is in jail, every day that goes by could be lethal. Not just because of the chance of being abandoned in a hurricane, but because of every jail's daily mixture of violence and neglect. While jails subject people to overcrowding, illness,[3] freezing temperatures and out-of-control heat, contaminated or rotting food, lack of basic sanitation,[4] and insect and vermin infestations,[5] people enduring these conditions are also often threatened or abused by jail and prison staff.[6] Violence is daily. One study found that nearly all people in jail witness or experience violence behind bars, leading to trauma, anxiety, depression, and other psychological or emotional wounds that persist long after they come home.[7] What's more, it's hard to communicate this reality back to the outside world. Phone calls are unaffordable and eavesdropped upon.[8] If your mom comes to visit you, there is a nonzero chance she'll be strip-searched.

In jail, any source of physical or mental health support a person might have had outside prison walls is cut off. Jails can refuse to honor a person's existing medication regimens when they are detained, so they often decompensate with dangerous withdrawals of all kinds while waiting to be re-diagnosed and re-prescribed medications that may or may not work as well. And that's if they get them at all. In my own practice, I would often take down a list of medications my clients needed and read it into the record at their arraignment, asking the judge to order Rikers to honor the list or at the very least get people to a doctor immediately. You can guess how well that worked. And it's not just my clients, and it's not just mental health meds. Take, for example, Dexter Barry, who, after he was arrested in Florida, died because the jail refused to give him his transplant rejection medication.[9] Or the fact that people in jail are much more likely to have diabetes, asthma, hypertension, hepatitis, depression, or severe mental illness, and much *less* likely to be given any prescription medication to manage their condition.[10]

And of course, in a state with weak speedy trial provisions, the length of detention can seem indefinite. For example, an average jail stay around the country is about one month of detention,[11] but in New York the average stay is still over one hundred days.[12] In the United States, prolonged solitary confinement—where a person is confined alone without human contact for as much as twenty-two to twenty-four hours a day—is commonplace, with around one in twenty confined people held in solitary.[13] In jails specifically, about 6 percent of people are in solitary at any given time, but almost 60 percent of them have been there for more than fifteen days, meeting the international definition of torture.[14] The result is lasting psychological harm, as evidenced by the tragic case of Kalief Browder, who was wrongfully accused, languished at Rikers Island for three years *awaiting trial,* was detained in solitary, and died by suicide after being released.[15]

He is not alone. The strongly damaging effect of solitary confinement on physical health and mental well-being is well documented and, in addition to all its other deleterious impacts, results in a situation where the suicide rate inside New York's jails, for example, is five times higher for those in solitary.

What's more, the harm follows people home. People who were in solitary are 78 percent more likely to die by suicide once released.[16] It's no wonder people will plead guilty to almost anything if the result is that they'll be allowed to go home, to experience human contact—or simply daylight—once again.

Even without solitary, to be in jail at all is to already have lost the job you had, the housing you had, the access to your kids you had, and also to wake up every day without access to any of the things that can give comfort in a dark time: family, health care, diversions, the outside world. The single leading cause of death in jail is suicide, accounting for almost one out of every three jail deaths.[17]

This is why it is so easy to get people who are already suffering in this environment to plead guilty, when that guilty plea opens up a path to homecoming. In her book *Punishment Without Trial,* Carissa Hessick explains that the courts often use pretrial detention as a punishment for being belligerent or being late to court. "Judges and law enforcement *know* that pretrial detention is no different from actual punishment. And so they intentionally use it to punish people for behavior that they find annoying or disrespectful, even if it isn't a crime."[18] The numbers bear this out: people behind bars plead guilty 2.86 times faster than people fighting their case from home do.[19] A study from Harris County, Texas, the third-largest county in the United States, found that people detained pretrial were 25 percent more likely to plead guilty.[20] And research examining the opposite—the impact of pretrial *release* on guilty pleas—sheds an equally important light: one study found that being released pretrial decreases a person's likelihood of pleading guilty by almost 20 percent.[21]

When a person is sitting in a cell, having their daily existence crushed into compliance by the carceral system, every day weighs heavily and the prosecutor's ability to dangle a light at the end of the tunnel—release—is dramatically enhanced. Plead guilty and get out in three months instead of possibly years. Get out in two weeks. Get out tomorrow. Who can resist, when they haven't been able to hold their child in their arms for months or years?

From a strategic perspective, going home is essential, because it means fighting against the full power of an over-resourced police-and-prosecution apparatus (a huge lift even for the most innocent person) from the outside. From the comfort of their own home, an accused person can assist their lawyer by getting supportive letters from friends and family about their good character. They can help track down witnesses, meet freely with their legal team and talk through options as much as they need, seek—or not interrupt—substance use treatment, not lose their job, and tuck their kids in at night.

In jail, a person's life is stripped away: they can't see anyone, including their lawyer, without restriction. It's harder to look at documents or evidence together. But not only will your ability to assist your counsel be curtailed; your ability to withstand the phenomenal coercive power of our legal system will also be all but eradicated.

So who is it that makes the call about whether you get to remain in your life or are forced into a living hell? In American courts, it's a judge—often a judge who will never see the individuals before them again, a judge who appears just for the limited purpose of determining initial liberty. At a life-altering moment, an individual is asked to stand, handcuffed, in front of a total stranger as a prosecutor presents the worst possible version of that individual's actions or life to the stranger. In the best cases, that individual will also be defended by an insightful and persuasive defense attorney who has been able to take the time to get to know them, their life, their work, their family, and their challenges. In the worst cases, they may stand completely alone, because no lawyer is provided, or a lawyer is provided only to people who can fill out lots of paperwork in English or pay a $400 fee.[22] Alone and bewildered by the legal jargon filling the air. The whole thing takes about ninety seconds. And then their fate is sealed.

One of the most stressful things about being a public defender is that your workday is often filled with not one or two of these encounters with judges but dozens. A normal day may involve two or three painful sentencings in which people you have come to deeply care for will accept preposterous guilty pleas that solve nothing and cost them everything, separating families for years. It may involve doing all of that before going into a hearing in which a police officer is clearly, demonstrably lying, and yet probable cause is found because of a judge's innate trust in law enforcement. But in an arraignment shift, you are asked to meet dozens of frightened, unhappy, angry, unwell, or despairing people, none of whom have any reason to trust you after being funneled through arrest and booking and meeting innumerable system employees whose primary job is to lock them up. And then ask them to trust you enough to give you the information you need so you can stand up in front of a judge and ask for every single one of those people to go home.

It's a strange feat: to stand up and convince a judge that your client is so unusual, so compelling, so innocent, so worthy, that they are the "exception" to the rule of pretrial detention[*] and therefore should go home . . . and then to convince them that the next person is the same. And the person after that. And again and again, until, ideally, the cells behind the courtroom are empty. It's usually impossible.

---

[*] Legally, of course, this is more complicated. At arraignment, the presumption of innocence still applies, but the judge isn't deciding guilt. Instead, they're usually asked to give the prosecution's version of events some level of credit and then decide, based on that (as well as anything the defense can offer to undermine that), whether a person is (1) a risk of flight—meaning they might not come back for their court date—or (2) dangerous to the community. Different jurisdictions handle this decision differently, but the bottom line is that pretrial detention, in most places, *isn't supposed to be the norm;* it's supposed to be the *exception.* Bail is supposed to be an amount a person can pay to be free, but still be financially motivated to come back to court and face the music. If the bail is so high that a person cannot pay it and have that freedom-plus-motivation, it's failed its actual purpose. The idea of bail being a way to hold people in jail—rather than a way to safely set people free—is a gross mutation of its actual legal and historical intent, which has, unfortunately, evolved into another toxic norm of our modern system.

Unless you really, really know your judge.

The judge, as it turns out, is in no way an umpire. For one thing, to conflate the fate of a human soul with the outcome of a baseball game is the kind of metaphor credible only to a person who has never directly felt the weight of the criminal system. The difference in stakes, though, isn't just about how important the decisions are, it's also about *how possible it is to be neutral*: after all, to be neutral about whether the Phillies beat the Nats is pretty doable. To be neutral when you are trying to decide whether the person in front of you is a dangerous gang member who is a threat to society or a wrongly accused family man who needs to be present for his three kids? That's a little different.

The subject matter of the criminal system itself is almost exclusively fodder for bias, fear, and pre-built ideologies. Our criminal legal system emerges from our legacy of slavery. In large part, it was evolved to capture and re-enslave Black men after the passage of the Thirteenth Amendment,[23] which included an exception allowing slavery to continue so long as it was punishment for a crime.[24] Slaveholding states immediately wrote laws known as Black Codes, which created pretexts to arrest, convict, and re-enslave the Black people of those states.[25] To this day, our system operates in a way that continually targets not only Black families and neighborhoods but also other groups who have, historically, been shut out of power in America—people with little access to money, power, education, or the means to get ahead. And even when the system seems to get better, its tendency to magnify and weaponize our societal biases remains. For example, in 2025, researchers released a study that found "educational inequality is now much greater than racial inequality in prison admissions for all major crime types."[26] Whether it's dividing us along race or class lines, the prison system is consistent in its ability to impact groups with less power more harshly.

What's more, criminal cases are, well, *criminal* because they involve allegations of behavior that most people really don't like. Sometimes, it's just annoying behavior: a person who gets arrested for riding a noisy motorbike, for example, or the neighbors who cannot stop quarreling, culminating with one destroying the other's mailbox or peeing on their doormat. Sometimes—albeit much more rarely, because about 80 percent of criminal arrests are for misdemeanors[27]—the stories are genuinely frightening, or even traumatizing: burglars in the night, gunpoint robberies, domestic violence, murder. These are all patterns of fact that push some of the most ancient and fundamental buttons in our limbic system: fear, anger, outrage, and the desire to protect a helpless community. Judges, as it turns out, have limbic systems too.

There's a chasm of background and experience between judges and the people they judge. Race is a deeply imperfect proxy for life experience, but in a system that disproportionately impacts Black people, it's an unavoidably relevant topic. And the legal profession is notoriously white. In fact, Bureau of Labor Statistics data shows that as of 2023 it is among the top 15 percent of occupations with the highest percentage of white employees.[28] As of 2023, 76 percent of sitting federal judges are white. About 80 percent of lawyers are white, and only 5 percent are Black—a number that hasn't changed significantly in a decade.[29] Ninety-five percent of prosecutors are white, meaning the people who make the calls about whom to charge, and with what, are not, statistically, the people who most directly feel the impact of those charges.[30] And my own side of the aisle isn't exempt: a survey of recent law school graduates found that of the public defender jobs taken in 2021, 72 percent of job takers were white.[31]

I am, personally, the beneficiary of two phenomenal Black judges who used their unique perspectives and life experience to be fairer, better, and more transformative on the bench: Judge Leslie Harris, who gave me a chance to succeed when I was sixteen years old and in crisis, and Judge Thelton Henderson, the judge I was lucky enough to clerk for and one of the great shapers of my mind and spirit. Their brilliance wasn't merely a product of their identity, but rather a complex product of hard-won insight, intellectual acumen, a moral compass, and an unshakable interest in truly understanding the cases and controversies before them.

The career that led a judge to the bench, of course, has a tremendous impact in shaping their perspectives. For the most part, judges are former prosecutors or corporate lawyers. Data is hard to come by for state court judges, but federally more than a quarter of judges were once prosecutors, and almost 70 percent were corporate lawyers of some kind.[32] This means that very, very few judges have ever had the experience of standing up on behalf of an individual—in their own careers, they chose to represent companies or governments, and that's who they became accustomed to fighting for.

So who are they judging? Well, it's not usually the companies they once represented or people who live in their neighborhood. We know that about 80 percent of people facing criminal court judges are so poor as to be given a public defender,[33] but also Black people are much more likely to be noticed by police and ultimately detained.[34] People of privilege are less likely to live in hyper-policed neighborhoods.[35] Controlling for all other factors, including behavior, Black participants in one study were still seven times more likely to be arrested than their white counterparts.[36] Once through booking and in front of a judge, white people were much less likely to be held in jail, and got lower bail.[37]

There are endless, seemingly race-neutral statistics a judge can point to for why they set bail lower or let someone go home, like whether a person has a home, or a job in the community, or a good education—but in our country many of these factors are *still* influenced by race, as Black people are more likely to be unhoused,[38] Black and brown jobless rates remain higher than those of white people,[39] and the factors involved with educational attainment are similarly racialized.[40] Even as concerted efforts to rebalance our legal system may be starting to close this racial gap, new class and educational gaps are becoming more acute.[41] Many judges will never have the chance to see how these gaps influence their decisions and how the repackaging of biased factors shrouds our legal system in the appearance of neutrality.[42]

So here you have judges, raised in the same bias-filled, fraught American miasma as the rest of us, and then plunked into a courtroom where they are told they are supposed to be suddenly cleansed from bias, and able to hear inflammatory stories without ever allowing themselves the luxury of relatedly inflamed passions. Almost all of the people brought in front of them come from a background very different from their own, which is inherently more difficult for them to empathize with, especially if they are operating in a court system that does not actively offer support to overcome existing structural biases.[43] They are given plenty of training in the law but little, if any, training in overcoming implicit bias, structural inequality, or the natural and unnoticed assumptions of the human brain. And they are expected, somehow, by virtue of their office and special robe, to suddenly transform into an umpire.

Well, John Roberts, good luck.

It's dangerous to pretend that judging is an act of independent impartiality. As it is conceived, our system is supposed to let all actors function as checks on one another, with adversarial testing of evidence acting as a constant stabilizer against runaway assumptions and unconscious instincts. Humans, at the end of the day, are human. But in a system overrun by plea bargains, where few cases ever make it to the crucible of trial, these checks have been weakened. And at a stage as early as bail—a highly consequential, sometimes outcome-determinative decision, with overwhelming discretion concentrated in the judge's hands, and so early in the process that essentially no adversarial testing is yet possible—you have a recipe for disaster. The best judges know this, and wrestle with their own innate preconceptions and biases constantly. This makes for better, fairer decisions, but also makes their job exponentially more difficult.

One of the things that gives public defenders an edge in criminal court is that we're native to it: we spend all day, every day, in the same courthouse, working with the same judges and prosecutors. As a defender, I quickly came to understand the personalities of the bench. You have to know which judge wants to get to lunch as fast as possible and which judge will be irritated if they feel rushed. As a woman defender, you also have to know who is rooting for you and who thinks women belong in the kitchen (yes, I was, at times, in front of a judge who didn't really think I should have that big ol' law license in the first place). One judge had been a Golden Gloves boxer in his youth, and could be relied upon to seek mentorship and opportunity for our young clients, even if it meant making a bold choice from the bench—but you had to tell him a little bit about the kids in his court, something to make him feel he had the full picture. Another judge had been a police officer early in his career, and could almost never bring himself to see problems with police testimony, no matter how clearly it was laid out, and was really only going to rule against the cops if given no alternative. One judge confessed to me once, early in her tenure on the bench but late in the evening at a cocktail party, that she often felt overwhelmed and was terrified she didn't know what she was doing—for her, presenting options that offered an ironclad, highly justifiable path to the right decision was what she needed. She needed safety. A very charismatic judge, who, like many performers, was attracted to dynamism and energy, came down with crushing harshness on lawyers who seemed tentative but always rewarded one who could show some bravado.

Sometimes the details had nothing to do with character, but just biology: I practiced before a wonderful judge who would make great decisions—if he was paying attention. But he often struggled to retain focus on the bench (he had been known to nod off). To keep him alert enough to give my client a second chance, I would stack my arms with plastic or metal bracelets, using bangles to become a one-woman liberty bell. It worked. We had a great time, and he fostered a great deal of success in my clients, who were able to return to work or school and get supportive treatment as needed, because their judge was able to recognize their potential through the cacophony. For another judge in that same courthouse, who was notoriously sadistic and truly enjoyed torturing defense lawyers, I had a much less dignified strategy: a particularly aggressive push-up bra, which, depressingly, meant that I was never subject to that judge's diatribes—and my clients didn't suffer the violent consequences of his moods.

One of the hardest things to get laypeople to see, when you operate daily in the criminal court, is how mundane the injustice is. Rarely are there lofty differences of legal interpretation or arcane theory. Usually, the heartbreak stems from such horrifying things happening for such stupid, simple reasons. Take, for example, the case of Ken Oliver, who, at the age of twenty-nine, was sentenced to life in prison for being a passenger in a stolen vehicle. The year was 1997, and California was in the fever of the Three Strikes era. Ken ended up doing twenty-three years behind bars. Those twenty-three years started with a judge, an offer, and a devastating combination of impatience and power.

The transcript of Ken's case reveals that on May 1, 1997, he was brought before Judge Stephen O'Neil in Torrance, California. The judge made Ken an offer: plead guilty on the spot, and he would give Ken a sentence of twelve years rather than life imprisonment. Judge O'Neil knew little about Ken—he noted, "I honestly, I don't know how old you are"—but, brushing off the lack of detail he held about Ken or the case, he asked Ken to consider pleading guilty on the spot. Ken, seemingly taken aback by the question, took a moment to explain his hesitation:

> It has come on rather quickly, and I feel very uncomfortable about the amount of time I've been given to make the decision. I asked to come in earlier before lunch to possibly ask could I sleep on it, or spend the night on it, and you mentioned yourself it is a very serious case. I don't know anybody who likes to make serious decisions shooting from the hip, emotionally or reactionary. So I kind of wanted to have the night to weigh out the options, to think out my personal situation. I have children, I have a wife, I have a family life out there.

Thinking back on it years later in a 2023 conversation with me, Ken remembers feeling strong-armed. "I had three young children at the time that were five, four, and three. . . . I just wanted twenty-four hours to process what was happening, and . . . he was basically telling me he'd give me five minutes in the holding tank to decide."

And in that moment, Ken refused. "You know what?" he told me. "It was just a moral decision that I made. It felt extremely restrictive. It felt oppressive. It felt extraordinarily heavy."

But after thinking on his situation, Ken changed his mind. After the Thursday offer, he was back in court on Monday. "I thought about it, and I had a chance to talk to my folks, and I said, 'I'm sure I pissed him off, but then he's not going to go from twelve to a hundred years to life.' So I went in and pled guilty."

It was a trust fall onto a judge's mercy. And it was an understandable one; after all, just two business days earlier, the judge had expressed that twelve years felt fair. Theoretically, if twelve years was justice on Thursday, it should still have been justice on Monday.

This was Ken's thinking when he walked into the courtroom on May 5, 1997. "I went in and pled guilty. And he turned around and gave me fifty to life."[44]

Other biases can be as cruelly, irrationally decisive as personal animus. In the Bronx, we once had a judge colloquially known around the courthouse as "Bad Santa," a moniker earned by the juxtaposition of his cheery white beard and jolly face with his harsh treatment of our clients, as well as his choice to publish a children's book about the dangers of immigration,[45] in which dandelion seeds invade and take over a carefully tended hothouse garden. (Which didn't inspire confidence for those of us representing immigrants in his courtroom.) But the problem is not restricted to individual xenophobes. Black people, on average, receive sentences that are 20 percent longer than white people's, even accounting for criminal history and background.[46] A 2019 study found that judges appointed by Republicans were more likely to give longer sentences to Black defendants (three more months than non-Black defendants accused of similar crimes) and shorter sentences to women (two fewer months than men accused of similar crimes).[47] One study found that judges are more likely to associate Asian people and Jewish people with immoral traits ("greedy," "dishonest," and "controlling") but see white and Christian people as "trustworthy," "honest," and "giving" . . . and they gave the Jews longer sentences than similarly situated Christians.[48]

Professional history, too, feeds directly into bias on the bench. Because many judges are former prosecutors, and because many self-select into the judiciary because of a "tough on crime" worldview, many judges are understandably biased in favor of the prosecution.[49] The ratio of federal judges who are former prosecutors to former defense attorneys is four to one, and of the judges appointed during Trump's first term, ex-prosecutors outnumbered former public defenders and other defense attorneys by more than ten to one.[50]

On the state court side, data is harder to come by, but what data there is suggests this disparity is a constant. A 2024 study from Scrutinize, a nonprofit dedicated to making data about judges available to the public, noted that "similar disparities exist in the state supreme courts. Approximately 40% of state supreme court justices have a background in prosecution, while only 11% have experience as public defenders or non-government civil rights lawyers. The disparity becomes even more pronounced when examining specific state supreme courts. The judiciaries of 19 state supreme courts are composed of 50% or more former prosecutors. In contrast, only two states have 50% or more former public defenders in their courts of last resort."[51]

Research indicates that former prosecutors are, unsurprisingly, more likely to impose jail and prison time than former public defenders on the bench. The researchers concluded that if every former prosecutor on the bench were a former public defender instead, twenty thousand fewer prison sentences would be handed down over a ten-year period.[52] New research shows the professional background of judges is deeply influencing crucial release decisions in New York, resulting in about $4,000–$5,000 more bail per case. Ultimately, the authors concluded that swapping out a single former prosecutor for a judge with no prior criminal system experience at all could save New York taxpayers $460,000–

$1.6 million. Because many judges are appointed by the mayor for a ten-year term, this means that each judge with no criminal court experience is currently saving taxpayers $4.6 million to $16 million during their term when compared with former prosecutors, and during that time will set $3.67 million–$10.3 million less cash bail.[53]

It should not be surprising that a career as a prosecutor often results in much more punitive views on the bench. Prosecutors have a role whose emotional weight is so unbearable that much of our system is designed to shield them from confronting the true nature of their decisions. After all, a defense lawyer's job is to bring people home and shield them from harm; even if our clients themselves have engaged in harm, defense lawyers are always free to seek harm reduction, therapeutic paths forward, reconciliation, mediation, change making, anything in the world they can imagine to help their client move forward successfully. Prosecutors, meanwhile, have less autonomy, and essentially one tool: the threat of punishment. When they "win," a human being is separated from their life, family, and community, and often confined under dangerous, violent, and inhumane conditions. This is why the language of the system creates softening euphemisms: We are *sentencing* the *offender* to the *custody* of a *secure housing unit* rather than *locking a young mother in a cage.*

Prosecutors need that linguistic shield in order to carry out the system's punishment objectives, and they also need other things in order to feel comfortable with the work they do. They need, for example, to believe that the police officers they work with are largely telling the truth rather than pursuing biased, easy, or more profitable arrests.[54] They need to believe that the system is fair, and that punishment is justice.

If one has needed to make these mental and emotional commitments in order to do the work of prosecution, perhaps for decades, how can one suddenly be expected to set those ideas aside and become skeptical of the system and its assumptions when ascending to the bench? It's not reasonable to expect such a shift, which is why changing the makeup of the bench—experientially, professionally, racially, economically, academically—is so essential to seeking real justice. When we do, we see change: a 2024 study found that people whose cases were assigned to judges who were former public defenders were less likely to be incarcerated and, in some cases, were given shorter sentences,[55] which may actually be better for public safety.[56]

How people get on that bench matters, too. For example, what does it do to justice when we make judges cater to voters to secure their job? On the one hand, letting people vote judges off the bench who do not agree with the values of the community seems like a wonderful democratization of justice, but how does it play out in real life? A Brennan Center for Justice analysis of ten empirical studies found that upcoming reelection campaigns make judges more likely to give harsher sentences. Trial judges in Pennsylvania and Washington sentence people to longer and longer sentences the closer they are to reelection, and the more frequently rival candidates' television ads air during an election, the less likely state supreme court justices are, on average, to rule in favor of criminally accused people. We see similarly distressing results when death is on the line: appointed judges are more likely to reverse death penalty sentences than judges who have to be reelected. Though no judges reverse death sentences regularly, a study looking at thirty-seven states over fifteen years found that appointed judges reversed death sentences about a quarter of the time, while judges who had to run for office reversed only 15 percent of the time, and just 11 percent of the time if their race was hotly contested.[57]

There are also just some aspects of putting humans into positions of inhuman neutrality that cannot be made perfect. Judges, for example, have been found to be more lenient after they've had a break, or some lunch.[58] There is a relationship between sentence severity and judges inflicting public shame on accused people: a study demonstrated that "the average period of incarceration for offenders where there was some form of humiliation in the reasons for sentencing was 2.6 years less than offenders where there was no humiliation present."[59] Unlike the authors of this study, I wouldn't suggest that judges are getting off on the humiliation, though maybe some are, but I do think that the systemic pressure against mercy is so strong that judges feel pressured to verbally humiliate people to "make up for" an "easy" sentence. As a defender, whenever a judge was about to make a crucial decision and started off by saying things that sounded good for my client, I knew we were headed over a cliff—but if they started off incredibly harsh, we had a shot, because maybe the scolding would substitute for a sentence.

As a defender in the Bronx, I would often have night shifts, when I would come to court from 5:00 p.m. to 1:00 a.m., powering New York City's nearly twenty-four-hour arraignment cycle. We would have a dinner break at 9:00 p.m., and exhaustion would palpably grow in the courtroom for the hours that followed. Toward the end of the night, there was always the chance of something wild happening: a fabulous case disposition handed out simply to get everyone out of there and home to bed, for example. A surprise release when an exhausted judge realized that I was not going to shut up and let this all be over until she set bail my client's mother could pay. As defenders, we instinctively leverage our shared humanity—but it also means that sometimes two people do the exact same thing and get wildly different outcomes because one person's judge was hangry and the other's wasn't.[60]

Perhaps the worst example of the animal brain playing out in courtroom acts of power comes, like many of the saddest and most worthless aspects of our system, from juvenile court. In a sphere where the youngest lives hang in the balance, one might hope that judges would exert the utmost care—or at least be subject to the strictest form of oversight, preventing careless and impetuous decision-making. But a study of juvenile court data spanning sixteen years found that when a judge's favorite sports team loses, they give harsher sentences to children. An unexpected loss by a judge's favorite sports team led to longer sentences in juvenile court for the entire week following the game, with worse impact when the game was particularly important. The effects were stronger when the accused child was Black.[61]

Ken served twenty-three of the fifty years he was sentenced to in state prison, eight of them in solitary confinement.

After winning release a few years ago, Ken became an accomplished executive, working at a background check company that—unlike most players in that industry—actively advocates for folks with records in the workplace. He got a settlement for his time in solitary and became a philanthropist as well, using his means to advance causes of liberation.[62] I think about this a lot—how much talent, including his, has been locked away from us for decades. And in many cases, not because of a real public safety concern or genuine need for incapacitation, but perhaps because of something as simple as a vindictive judge's need for immediate compliance.

The sooner we start trying to see through the role and catch a glimpse of the real person underneath, the sooner we move away from a world in which judges are locking up kids over lost football games, giving fifty years to life to an adult for being a passenger in a stolen vehicle, or leaving their own constituents to die in a flooded jail.

Chapter Three

The Grind

The Maze of Court Dates and Their Consequences

If you've been lucky enough to never have to interact with the criminal legal system in America, you might envision a case process as something straightforward: a person gets arrested, they report to the courthouse and appear in front of a judge, they take a plea or assert their right to trial, and ultimately the case is finished with exoneration or punishment. In actuality, it's nothing like this. It is hell, and sometimes it goes on forever.

A few years ago in the Bronx, my client Jannell found herself navigating this web of leverage and neglect. A family support specialist with the New York Department of Education, Jannell loved her job and did it while raising three kids of her own. One morning, Jannell woke up and realized that her car was gone. She had been having trouble with the payments, so she assumed it had been repossessed. But after calling tow lots and the bank, it became clear that no one had any idea where her car was.

She waited endlessly on hold, was bounced from department to department, and spent days trying to figure out the proper next steps. The bank told her to call a local tow lot, and the tow lot actually quoted her a price to get her car back, but she couldn't pay it, so she decided to just try to get her belongings back out of the car. But when she tried to set up a time to go get her belongings, she found the lot didn't have her car after all. So she was back to square one, calling the insurance company and the bank, and even the police, all to no avail. And then a pivotal thing happened: when she told one of the customer service people from her repo company that police hadn't taken the report, the rep told her to just give the date the car was stolen as the date of her call. So she did, and it worked.

But unbeknownst to her, someone *did* actually know where the car was—the Baltimore Police Department, which had found the car, burned out and abandoned, a few days prior.

Because the date she gave as the date of theft was a few days after when the car had been found—making it clear that it had actually been stolen earlier—the NYPD decided that Jannell wasn't just a confused victim of car theft but rather the architect of an elaborate insurance scheme. When Jannell explained the days she had spent trying to find the car, her explanation was rejected.

Jannell experienced what happens when police take hold of a piece of your life and create their own narrative. Instead of looking at Jannell's records and weighing her story equally with their own assumptions, they took their version of events to the prosecutor, who promptly wrote up a complaint for felony insurance fraud. The theory? That Jannell had orchestrated the theft of her own car, then had it driven to Baltimore and set on fire, in an attempt to get an insurance payout. Was there any evidence of this, perhaps communication between Jannell and a car thief or a scheme between Jannell and her husband to get rid of their car and earn a profit? No, they had nothing. They had Jannell's incorrect date of the car's disappearance—and nothing more. Still, the prosecutor listened to the police as they spun this story, and Jannell found herself arrested, torn away from her job and her kids, waiting to find out what would happen to her next.

———

Let's start with something as straightforward as court dates, and what they do to a person's life. At the start of her case, Jannell had a job and kids to take care of. She had already missed work because she was in jail waiting to be arraigned, but now she's out. In Jannell's case, she was instantly suspended from work, but even if she hadn't been, she would have had to take another day off and find child care and transportation every time she needed to come back to court. Because she did not live near the courthouse, either transportation took hours—and she had to be present in court at 8:30 a.m.—or else it was very expensive. The courtroom is always busy, so every court date inevitably means missing the entire day of work waiting for one's case to be called; there's no way to make it to the office in the afternoon. For most people, their boss is either immediately or eventually furious about these absences, if they haven't been fired outright for getting arrested. They will have to do this each and every time they come back to court. So how many times do they have to come back to court?

For a typical misdemeanor (the majority of cases in the legal system), the first date is to come to court for, essentially, nothing at all. Nothing happens because the prosecutor has not yet had time to decide on a plea offer, nor to make the defense attorney any copies of the evidence against the person. Then, a date when we come back to see if there's an offer, which there is, but still no "discovery" (the packet of papers setting forth the evidence, to which the accused person is entitled and which is necessary to prepare for trial). A demand for discovery is filed, and we have another date to come back and see if the discovery has been handed over—it has, but only partially, we are missing crucial documents, like witness statements or lab tests. So we get another date for that. Meanwhile, the offer was horrible, so on the next date we talk about what offer the accused person might be willing to accept. The prosecutor in the room has no authority to change the existing offer on the case, so we pick another court date to receive that offer. We come back to court again, and the prosecutor (who has been incommunicado in between court dates) announces that their boss will let them change the offer to something less punitive, but only if the accused person completes a series of classes. We set a new court date to get enrolled in the classes. The classes, as it turns out, are expensive, so at the next court date we ask if we can do an alternative class. The prosecutor says they have to go ask their boss again, who is out of the office that day. When we come back, the prosecutor's boss has said no: either find the money for the original class or go to jail.

In the meantime, I've filed suppression motions because the search of my client was illegal, but the prosecutor hasn't replied to the motion yet, and requests an extension, explaining that they've been distracted by this class business. So we set a date for their response to my motions. They do file a response, and I file a reply, and we come back for a decision from the judge on the motions. The judge has decided that we get a hearing on those motions, so we set a date for the hearing. We show up to the hearing date, but the police officer doesn't show up . . . turns out he took PTO that day. We come back for another crack at the hearing, and are actually able to do the hearing—the officer testifies about the search in the case, and we present evidence demonstrating that the officer couldn't have seen what he says he saw from where he was standing. The judge wants to think about it, so we set a new court date.

Before the next court date, we get a written opinion from the judge saying that the police officer must have been able to see what he said he saw, so we are setting a date for trial. My client will have to come back every day for trial, probably for about a week or so—can they make it? I request the missing lab reports again. We get the lab reports before the next court date, but at that time my client also gets their tax refund, and thinks that now maybe they can pay for the classes. So on the trial date, we ask to do the classes after all. The prosecutor's boss—now pulled down to the courtroom finally—agrees, so we set a date to check in on class progress. At that next date, my client has a letter detailing their progress, but still needs another few weeks to finish the whole class.

Almost done, maybe just one more date. They finish the class and come back with a certificate, but the prosecutor is now on parental leave, and the case has been transferred to another prosecutor. I throw a fit about how long this has taken and insist that someone come down to the courtroom with the authority to resolve this case. No one is available. Finally, a few weeks later, my client takes off work again, and comes back to court for the privilege of pleading guilty to an infraction and paying a fine. Sixteen court dates over almost two years. For a misdemeanor.

And this is considered a good outcome.

———

On any given day in America, millions of people are undergoing a process like this. Every minute of every day, American courts resolve about forty felonies and one hundred misdemeanors as eighteen million cases churn through our state court system, usually lasting six to nine months each.[1] Every single one of them has the potential not only to utterly destroy the life of the accused person, but also to upend the stability of their families, colleagues, and whole communities.

So how do all these cases hit the courts in the first place?

When a person gets arrested, the system professionals defining their charges are, initially, police. Police identify the crime they claim has been committed and write up the paperwork to go along with the charges they think should be brought. Most people imagine that police write down a fairly complete account of what they know, to whom they spoke, what those witnesses said, and what evidence they gathered. And in some jurisdictions, they do, but in many they write down as *little* as possible, so as to make sure a defense lawyer who receives the arrest paperwork in discovery has almost nothing to go on, and to create maximum freedom for police to alter or adjust their stories later. This means that the initial police paperwork for one case might be as detailed as this:

Oakland Police Department

455 - 7th Street   Oakland, CA 94607

Crime Report - Continued

OCCURRED	DATE	TIME	DAY	PREMISE TYPE	CAD INCIDENT	RD #	
ON OR FROM	04 AUG 17	0000	FRIDAY	Residence / Home	LOP170804000320	17-040665	
TO	04 AUG 17	0800	FRIDAY	ADDRESS / LOCATION		BFO	BEAT
REPORTED	04 AUG 17	1257	FRIDAY	5404 5404 Holland St. ST, Oakland, CA 94621 (At: PC 247(B) – Sgt. M. Melham 8879)		2	27Y

☑ PHOTOS TAKEN	☐ PRINTS OBTAINED	TECHINICAN	H. Allemani 4590

Narrative

Summary:

On 04 Aug 17 at about 1257 hour I was working as 1A27 with Ofc. W. Tjhia 9670. Ofc. Tjhia was driving fully marked OPD Patrol SUV # 1470 and I was riding in the front passenger seat. Ofc. Tjhia was wearing full OPD Wool Uniform and I was wearing full OPD BDU Uniform. We were dispatched to a call regarding a possible shooting at an inhabited dwelling at 5404 Holland St.

When we arrived on scene we made contact with ▮▮▮▮▮▮ (V-1) who stated that this morning ▮▮ residence sustained a strike mark from what appeared to be a firearm.

▮▮▮▮▮▮ showed us the location of the strike mark in the entrance way to ▮▮ residence. There were two holes in the sheet rock of the residence that appeared to be roughly in line with each other at an upward angle. There were no strike marks on the exterior of the residence. It appears that the round came from the east, went through the first wall and terminated in the west wall of the residence. There was no apparent slug in the sheet rock of the residence.

The east wall of the apartment is a shared wall with 5406 Holland St. It appears that the damage could only have come from the residence at 5406 Holland St. due to the strike marks and the residue on the ground at 5404 Holland St.

I spoke with ▮▮▮ who stated that last night ▮▮ went to that part of ▮▮ residence around 0000 hours and did not see the damage to ▮▮ wall. ▮▮▮▮▮ stated that ▮▮ observed the damage around 0400 hours walking back and forth to there van. ▮▮▮▮▮ also believes that the main renter at 5406 Holland St. is Clair.

▮▮▮▮▮ also stated that there has been lots of ongoing issues with the residence at 5406 Holland St.

OPD Technician H. Alemani 4509 arrived on scene and took photos of the residence.

We made contact with the female occupant at 5406 Holland St. and located a previous report with a ▮▮▮▮▮, ▮▮▮▮▮▮ ▮▮▮▮▮▮ who resides at 5406 Holland St. I conducted a CRIMS check on ▮▮▮▮▮ and it appears to be the subject that we made contact with. I conducted a W&W check on ▮▮▮▮▮ and ▮▮ was not on probation or parole and did not have a warrant.

There were two younger MB's located with ▮▮▮▮▮ who I was not able to identify.

I conducted a LEAP search on the residence and determined that a ▮▮▮▮▮▮, ▮▮▮▮ ▮▮▮▮▮▮) used to live at this residence. It appears that ▮▮▮▮▮▮ is in pre-sentencing status for attempted murder. On W&W it appears that ▮▮▮▮▮ no longer lives at 5406 Holland St. as of 2017.

▮▮▮▮▮▮ did not match the description of anyone at the residence.

Ofc. Tjhia check Shot spotter and did not locate any activation that matched the time and location of the incident.

I gave ▮▮▮▮▮ an OPD Blue Resource Card and Marcy's Law Card.

No further known witnesses.

No force used or observed.

In the above document, we know everything down to Officer Tjhia wearing *wool*. And to be clear, the Oakland Police Department is not historically a bastion of progressive practices—at the time of this writing, it remains under federal oversight because officers were beating and framing Oakland residents.[2] If even the Oakland Police Department can write a fairly thorough narrative, you'd think that any department could. And yet, let's look at the NYPD:[3]

Supervisor On Scene - Rank / Name /Command :	Canvas Conducted: NO	Translator (if used):
NARRATIVE: AT T/P/O MOS REPORTED A TASTE F BLEACH IN HIS DRINK (SHAKE), AIDED REPORTED NOSYMPTOMS ON SCENE AND WAS REMOVED TO BELLEVUE HOSPITAL FOR EVALUATION.		

Who called for help? Who was aided? Who else was there? What type of establishment is this? Did anyone else smell the drink? Did they visit the kitchen? Was there a video camera in the kitchen? Was the drink taken for testing? Were the kitchen staff interviewed? This report[4] is taken from a case where several police officers accused Shake Shack staff of poisoning their drinks with bleach—allegations that later turned out to have been unfounded.[5] It's often good for police when they don't fully record their investigations, but it's bad for the seeking of actual truth in a court proceeding.

Whatever the nature of the report, if police make an arrest, they must then submit their report and usually communicate with a prosecutor about the case. The prosecutor will likely review the police report, perhaps hear verbally from an officer about their impressions of the case, and, in some cases, speak with a victim or witness before deciding what charges to file.

Prosecutors are unique among lawyers—instead of representing an individual, they are tasked with representing the people of a given jurisdiction, and given the unique nature of their role they are also given a unique ethical obligation. All lawyers are governed by a code of ethics that requires us to not mislead the court and not tell our clients' secrets or act against their interests. But prosecutors are given an additional duty, since they represent not one individual but the community: they carry an ethical obligation to do justice. It is, perhaps, the single most important aspect of their role and what differentiates them from ordinary attorneys. At its best, this duty should protect prosecutors who want to use their discretion to offer creative, restorative strategies instead of imposing yet more jail time.[6]

But in practice, we rarely see prosecutors' offices recognize that duty. Rather, we see prosecutors at all levels of an agency pushed to secure as many convictions as they can—mostly in the form of plea bargains. I spoke with a prosecutor I had once gone up against, who has since left prosecution and asked to remain anonymous so that he could speak freely about his experiences—I'll call him Michael. It's a system, he said, that rewards people "who will cut corners and try to win, even if that's not how we're supposed to do it." Management's wide discretion to accept or reject bail requests, plea offers, trial strategies, and even discovery decisions makes it incredibly challenging for line prosecutors—the people handling cases day to day—to do anything besides seek to maximize convictions, if that is management's goal. "You get in because you care about people, and then you're just part of the system that doesn't give a shit about anybody."[7]

In order for the courts to handle the sheer volume of people who are arrested in this country, the vast majority of cases *must* end just like this, in plea bargains. If they all went to trial, the system would collapse under its own weight. A system that requires a lot of plea bargains to operate at scale has, over the years, vested prosecutors with more leverage, ensuring that they have a stunning array of tools to promote plea bargains from the very beginning of a case. About 90 percent of federally accused people and 94 percent of people in state court take plea bargains.[8] The record-setting level of incarceration in this country simply wouldn't be possible otherwise. It takes a great deal of time to do even the simplest jury trials, and a significant amount of public participation as well. After all, every case needs a jury, alternate jurors in case something goes sideways, and a pool of people from whom those jurors can be chosen. In a system that processes millions of people every year, the beauty of finding truth is set aside in almost every case because it's inconvenient.

How is this possible? The U.S. Constitution protects each and every one of us by affording us an unassailable right to a jury trial. So how are we persuaded, in all but a handful of cases, to give that right up, admit guilt, and even take prison time?

It starts with charging. And "charge stacking." Prosecutors have absolute discretion in deciding what charges to bring and what bargains to offer. At the time the prosecutor wrote up a complaint against Jannell, she hadn't heard Jannell's version of events. This is both a flaw in the system and a safeguard: prosecutors don't meet with the accused person for good reason, because the person doesn't yet have the guidance and protection of counsel and might say something that could be misunderstood or inadvertently worsen their legal situation (if you take one thing from this book, please let it be the lesson that no one, no matter how smart or how innocent, should ever talk to a cop or a prosecutor without a lawyer present, should a cop seek to speak with you). This means that the prosecutors are entirely reliant on police—or a witness chosen by police—when they are determining what the charges will be. And by the time the facts—as law enforcement has constructed them—are contained in legal papers, they have been filtered through multiple intervening players (possibly multiple police officers, their report, a prosecutor, their charges as written). They are then usually sent to an arraignment court, where a judge looks at this narrative and makes a decision about a person's liberty. In many places, the person facing this wildly one-sided determination still doesn't have a lawyer.

A prosecutor could have looked at Jannell's case, decided it was just too thin—after all, there was no connection found between Jannell and the burned car, merely the wrong date given—and decided not to file this case at all, but let the insurance provider figure this out civilly, deny the claim, or find some other noncriminal consequence. She could, alternatively, have charged Jannell with a misdemeanor. And of course, she could choose to charge Jannell with a felony. So what does the prosecutor do? Some charge what they think is right (even declining to file weak cases), but many will go for the felony, feeling it gives them more "leverage." Leverage to do what? To secure a plea.

Why is that so important? For one thing, the prosecutor's advancement at work may hinge on how many convictions they can secure, or how high their conviction rate is. And if they have political ambitions, this helps toward a reputation of being "tough on crime." For others, there may be a feeling of doing good—forcing someone to take a plea, for example, that mandates them to do something the prosecutor feels is necessary, like mental health or substance use treatment. Unfortunately, even the most beneficial therapeutic process can lose its potential when done under threat of being thrown into a cage, which is how most diversionary pleas work: get better or we'll throw your future away.

Further adding to the prosecutor's capacity to exert power is the fact that at the moment of arraignment, when a case formally begins, the accused person may not even *have* a lawyer,[9] and likely will not know what the evidence is against them. Prosecutors do have to turn over their evidence to the defense eventually, but this doesn't stop them from offering favorable bargains *before* the person fully knows what the evidence is against them, with the threat that if a person holds out to examine their case or test that evidence, the offer will get worse. In our practice, this is known as a trial penalty, meaning the likelihood that a person will be sentenced to much more time if they exercise their right to a jury trial instead of capitulating and pleading guilty. This means that the initial evidence brought by police, as flawed as it may be, will never be tested, inspected, or challenged. It is perfectly legal for a prosecutor to insist a person plead guilty without ever seeing the evidence against them.[10]

It's a phenomenon that hasn't been studied nearly enough by people outside the criminal court system, because it takes place largely in informal plea negotiations—conversations over the phone or in the hall outside a courtroom, rife with quiet threats. Sometimes the threat comes directly from a prosecutor, along the lines of "tell your client that if he doesn't take this deal, I'm going to ask for the max after trial," but sometimes it doesn't need to; mandatory minimum laws, which mandate that judges impose a certain amount of prison time for specific offenses, do the work for them.

With a mandatory minimum, it is the charge itself that defines the amount of time a person could get. For example, there may be a mandatory minimum law saying that anyone who commits a "commercial burglary" gets at least two years in prison, but there's no such law for grand larceny. If a person goes into a Best Buy store and pockets a cellphone, the prosecutor could "charge stack" and bring both charges. After all, the grand larceny is the stealing of something worth over a certain amount of money, and the commercial burglary is going into a structure (the store) with the intent to commit a felony (the grand larceny). One crime was committed, but multiple charges can be brought. Setting up the law this way enables prosecutors to use their choice of charges to create a lot of leverage, resulting in fewer trials, more guilty pleas, and a higher-volume (if not more just) system.

Looking at those stacked charges, the mandatory minimum on the commercial burglary means that if the person goes to trial and loses—even by fluke—they will absolutely do prison time. Even a judge who thought the accused should *clearly* remain in the community would have tied hands and no ability to secure their freedom. The prosecutor's control over the charges, though, means that *they* can offer to drop the burglary charge and give a person probation on the larceny, guaranteeing the ability to stay with their family, or, if the person is in jail, offering them the option to get out today.[11] Even the most innocent person has a hard time refusing to plead guilty when there is a chance a jury will get it wrong, giving them years in prison on an overinflated charge.[12]

Beyond the severity of the initial charges, prosecutors have other huge advantages when it comes to securing guilty pleas. One of the first is the timeline of representation. At the early stages of a case, which shape every moment that plays out thereafter, prosecutors have an informational advantage: they know what the police know—the accused person does not yet know what the evidence is against them—and they know not just what the evidence is now but also what new facts or areas are still under investigation. They know where the evidence might be leading. They are attorneys, experts in criminal law and the jurisdiction, and the accused person is, at the early stages, still unrepresented.

Laypeople often think that there is something good or right about police being able to interrogate citizens without a lawyer present—in the cop shows, we get used to it, and sometimes even cheer for police who use illegal tricks to score a confession. But in real life, what most people don't know is that the interrogation tactics of police are not designed to get the truth; they're designed to get a *confession.*[13] Although only about 4 percent of people believe that they themselves could ever falsely confess to a crime, in one experiment almost half of young adults falsely confessed when interrogators used the classic police technique of minimizing the seriousness of the misconduct and offering a deal in exchange for a confession.[14] This is, perhaps, why the National Registry of Exonerations shows that almost 13 percent of exonerations from 1989 to 2024 involved people pleading guilty to crimes they were later proven not to have committed.[15] If you're wondering how on earth that could happen, remember that police are allowed to lie to subjects, tell them that if they just confess they can go home, minimize the degree of trouble they're in, and interrogate them for hours on end, using techniques that are intended to cause normal adults to capitulate.

When these techniques are applied to children, the result is even more striking: in a study of wrongful convictions caused at least in part by false confessions, 42 percent of people eighteen and under had falsely confessed, compared with 13 percent of adults.[16] The younger kids are, the readier they are to falsely confess: one look at children who were wrongfully convicted revealed that a whopping 86 percent of the kids under fourteen falsely confessed.[17] This is a big risk, because children rarely have anyone in the room to stop them—children waive their *Miranda* rights about 90 percent of the time,[18] meaning that they're usually alone when subjected to adult-caliber police interrogation techniques.

Once a confession—false or true—is in place, people are more likely to plead guilty[19] because a confession seriously hurts one's chances at trial, even if the confession is completely false. Juries believe confessions—true or false—about 88 percent of the time.[20]

⸻

The only version of a story a judge sees of the person in front of them is the version contained in the criminal complaint—that narrative curated by police and prosecutors. They are missing the huge body of knowledge necessary to grasp who this person is in front of them.

Who are they really? Who do they take care of at home? Who are they responsible for? Who takes care of them? What have they struggled with? What have they overcome? What have they achieved? What are they committed to? With this kind of representation, their counselor may not just push back on holes in the allegations—like pointing out the total lack of evidence that Jannell was conspiring with car thieves. They can also introduce a more vivid picture of the accused person's life into the courtroom, making better judgments possible. A lawyer knows how to bring in detail: a client who participates in his kid's school is fine, but a dad who coaches seventh-grade basketball and makes it to every Pancake Tuesday is unforgettable. With a lawyer at arraignments, the accused person is much less likely to ultimately plead guilty.[21]

When Jannell got in front of the judge, she was lucky, in that she had a lawyer by her side and a judge on the bench who was willing to look skeptically at the charges. Jannell recalls, "When I came out, they wanted a $10,000 bail. The judge looked at the paper. She says, 'No, this just looked like she messed up on the paperwork.'"[22] Jannell was released, but it would take prosecutors years to see what that arraignment judge recognized after a five-minute review of Jannell's case. Because unlike the arraignment judge, the system doesn't incentivize prosecutors to look skeptically at their own charges, nor is it geared to seek out evidence of innocence.

Every day a case drags on is a normal day for a prosecutor. With the exception of certain cases in which they have a complainant who is very active in pushing for resolution of a case, or need to act quickly so as not to lose a key witness, prosecutors have little to fear from a long-pending case. Sure, a judge might get salty with them for taking their time, but there will be no real consequences. Police memories also magically never seem to fade; as any defender can tell you, they regularly and reliably take the stand to testify that they remember every detail of an encounter or investigation from 458 days ago as if it were this morning. In short, to a prosecutor, though there may be reasons to rush in some cases, usually you've got a lot less on the line than the other guy.

This is because the other guy is actively losing everything with each day that goes by. Even the fact of an arrest can and often does cause a person to lose their job; though arrested people are legally considered innocent, employers aren't required to treat them as such.[23] Finding a new job with an open case is incredibly difficult, not to mention finding a job when you may be required to take time off from work to come back to court again and again and again.[24] An open case might also mean certain "protective orders," which bar a person from being around others in their case or other accused people—even if the other people involved are family or neighbors.[25] A person may find themselves functionally evicted from their housing overnight.[26] Finding a new place to live with an open criminal case (again, still while legally innocent) is not any easier than finding a new job. In short, from the very moment of accusation, a person is at a much higher risk of losing their income, their housing, and even their access to their kids, because criminal court involvement can trigger family police interventions. And that's if a person is lucky enough to be out of custody.[27] If they're in jail, of course, they have already lost many of the most crucial things in their lives—a place to call home, a job, access to their kids, meaningful access to their lawyer—and, as the case drags on, are likely just trying to survive.

———

For Jannell, not being in jail was a small comfort. She was suspended from the job she loved with the Department of Education while facing felony charges. The evidence against her was weak. There was no evidence suggesting she had any connection to the people who stole her car. Jannell, for her part, remained consistent about her initial mistake in thinking the car was repossessed, and the time that had cost her. "I did call the repo people, and they said they had my vehicle, and told me an amount I had to give in order to get the car back. It was before Christmas. I called back the next day and said I'm not going to get my car back, we were just done with it. I just want my belongings back. And I remember they told me which lot it was in, Phantom Towing company. She gave me the number to Phantom, and I called to say I was coming to pick up my property out of the vehicle, and they said they don't have my car." She went back and forth with Phantom, who called around trying to find her car, and ultimately a representative from the company that held her car loan told her to call 911 and make a police report. Which she did.

"I called the precinct. The precinct said to call 911. I called 911. The first time, it took three hours. I explained the situation to them, and they told me to give it another day or two, because sometimes the car turns up in the system, or they'll find it in the lot. They had this happen before. I called the other person back and told her what 911 told me, and she said, No, no, just try calling again tomorrow. So I called 911 again. They took four hours the next day. I called and explained it to them. I explained the whole story three times. And on the fourth time, when the officers came out, I just said, 'My car got stolen.' That was it. And all hell broke loose."

The prosecution's case against Jannell was rooted in this problem of her report coming in days after the stolen car had been found in Baltimore; this was their key evidence that Jannell was actually orchestrating an intricate plot. The truth was simpler: she wasn't a criminal mastermind; she was a person who lost her patience for bureaucracy. But given the lack of evidence in the case, there was one thing that would be crucial: the recording of Jannell's phone call with the mysterious bank representative who told her to call 911 and report the car stolen. Without that piece of evidence, it was her word against the cops.

In Jannell's case, getting that crucial piece of evidence—and then getting a prosecutor to pay attention to it—took years. She was assigned different public defenders, each of whom pursued the recordings, but the process was slow. Jannell's court dates were every few months. She was out of work, calling regularly to let the Department of Education know she was still fighting. Again and again she would come to court. "I remember, every time they said, Case number whatever whatever, docket number whatever they say, Jannell Spikes. . . . When I stood up, I just wanted to fall back down. I was so nervous. They're all looking at me like, Oh, *you're* Jannell Spikes. It's so horrible. It's not a place that I ever wanted to be, or saw myself being, standing in front of a judge. It was the worst. I'm not upper class, but I hold certain standards to myself. I worked. I raised three kids. It was difficult, and I was scared, and sometimes the judges weren't so nice. There were times I left out of there and just threw up because my nerves were so bad."

Month after month dragged on. Jannell's three kids were seven, eleven, and twenty years old. While the littlest ones were at school, she would drag herself back to the courthouse, but the grinding of her case was beginning to impact her home life. "It takes away from really being a parent, coming home. You had another court day. I was told I have to come back again. I just wanted to go on with my life, go back to work, and do what I was doing, being at my best. It took that from me. It took a lot from me."

In the courthouse, Jannell's lawyers were fighting for time—the time they needed to get the exonerating evidence so she could walk away from the courthouse with a clean record. But the time they needed was extracting an enormous price. "I was so depressed that I had family members having to come and get me out of bed, open my curtains. I didn't even want to look at the world." The night before every court date, she couldn't sleep. She started to self-medicate just to get to sleep.

"I picked up drinking, and when I say I picked up drinking, I picked it up so bad. I used to only occasionally drink wine, and then all this happened, and I'm drinking hard liquor, no chaser. I got to the point where I was waking up drinking." These days, Jannell describes what she was doing as a kind of slow-motion suicide attempt, combining medications and liquor until she ended up in the hospital. "The arrest," she says, "took everything from me."[28]

Jannell is not alone. People called to come to criminal court almost universally experience a process that ranges from unpleasant to outright violent, depending largely on whether they are in custody or out. The court system is overloaded.[29] Police are incentivized to make arrests much more than they are asked to engage in solving problems—meaning that situations reasonable people might choose to handle with de-escalation, negotiation, or collaborative problem-solving just get dumped into criminal court with the idea that once an arrest is made, the underlying problem is someone else's to solve.[30]

The result is chaos. Prosecutors have too many cases, and often work in systems where the assigned prosecutor isn't even in the room when the case is being heard, sending the file down with their notes instead. This creates a situation where the person in the room knows very little about the case in their hand, and has almost zero authority to take key actions on it—like adjusting a plea offer, or finding missing evidence.

And in this bloated system, defenders *also* have too many cases, which makes it hard to ensure that every case is rapidly and thoroughly investigated, researched, and prepped. Meanwhile, judges are told that they need to "move the calendar," meaning get through these cases and prevent lawyers from causing delays. In the words of Michael, the former prosecutor, "It's all about the system. Keep this moving, counsel, keep this moving. But sometimes you actually have to talk about things. Kicking this person out of their house because of a restraining order is going to have real repercussions. Not saying a restraining order isn't appropriate, but we should still talk about what that means, and it shouldn't be in thirty seconds."[31]

But when the delays are quite legitimate, due to missing material, ongoing investigation, or other causes, judges can't force cases forward, which of course means that courtrooms are places where at any given moment someone is either not getting what they want or being forced to do something they think is wrong, and that's just among the courtroom professionals. You will be unsurprised to hear that this leads to a bad atmosphere in most courts, and that's just as a starting point, before the public is even involved.

Into this morass walk those members of the public who have been arrested, accused of crimes, and forced to take time off work and find child care and transportation, entering a building where they are treated as if they were criminals, forced to sit silently in the crowded courtroom, at attention while case after case is called, waiting for hours without being allowed to read anything or look at their phones, punished if they're late, and then subjected to the humiliation of having their case called in front of a group of strangers—all pretrial, when they have not been found guilty of anything at all.[32]

For people forced by a judge to stay in jail, each court day is even worse. They are usually woken up in the dark and the cold, sometimes as early as 3:00 or 4:00 a.m. Whether there's any breakfast is a toss-up. Some people say they do not want to go to court and can be violently forced or "extracted" from their cell by guards. Others are simply left to skip their court date—delaying progress in their case and hampering communication with their lawyer. As an attorney, I've had incarcerated clients tell me regularly that they actually *did* want to go to court, but no guard came and got them. And then the guards told me that my client "refused." These were often clients who were highly participatory in their cases, and whose absence at court was surprising. On balance, it was clear that my client wanted to come to court and was forgotten, neglected, or deliberately ignored by a guard.

If people do make it out of their cell, they are shackled, put on a bus, and brought to the holding area of the courthouse. Usually they're left sitting in a blank, fluorescent-lit cage. Or maybe they're shackled to a hard bench in the bowels of the courthouse. While people who are not in custody can discuss their case with their lawyer in the hallway and talk about their options, people who are in custody have a much harder time communicating with their lawyer at all during a court date. The lawyer has to go down to a meeting booth area, ask guards to bring their client out, and, since many buses per day come to the courthouse, manage to time their visit right so that the client is actually in the building at the time of their request. They may be stuck in line behind dozens of other attorneys, all hoping to speak with their clients, all using maybe three to six interview booths. The wait can be hours long, and it isn't uncommon for the guards to require counsel to be present while waiting to get put into a booth with their client—meaning that these lawyers cannot go see other clients or appear on other cases in the meantime.

An alternative to these rushed meetings in the courthouse is to find time with one's client in advance of the court date. This isn't always possible; if an overloaded prosecutor only chooses what offer to make on the day of, there is no way to convey the offer sooner. But there are a million other reasons why one needs to speak deeply and at length with one's clients: to learn more about what areas of the case to investigate, to find out who potential witnesses are and how to reach them, and to delve into this person's background and life story so as to write persuasively about why they should receive a dispensation in this case, just to name a few. It's functionally impossible to represent someone without talking with them, but jails are seemingly built to prevent that kind of right from being exercised.

Many jails are inconveniently located, placed outside the community or far from the courthouse. For example, detained people in New York City were held at either Rikers Island or "the boat," which was literally a floating prison barge docked in the Bronx. The boat—officially the Vernon C. Bain Center—closed in 2023, which is cold comfort when the alternative is Rikers Island, a jail notorious for its violent, dehumanizing conditions and frequent deaths.[33] To get to either requires a lawyer to take a lengthy bus ride—sometimes as much as two hours in transit each way—and then be stripped of one's belongings (no phones, laptops, or other things essential to getting work done while waiting to see a client). How long would we wait to see a client? Who knows, it was up to the jail staff to decide when and how we could meet. And what was I interrupting for my client? Did the timing of my visit prevent them from joining a particular class or program? Would it cost them a missed meal? Because I had little control over the timing, I had little ability to be sensitive to the impact of my visit. In New York, instead of being able to visit my jail clients at a moment's notice, I needed to set aside an entire day and prepare for any number of things to go wrong. This is just the basic package of challenges, by the way, that apply to all attorneys. If you're an attorney who wears women's clothing, your appearance will be constantly policed. Is your shirt strap too thin? Your skirt too close to your knee? Is your underwire setting off the metal detector? Ripping out your own underwire or hem to get into a jail is a core public defender experience.

As you might imagine, the need to have a meaningful conversation with a client comes up all the time—and often unpredictably. A new offer may hit my inbox unexpectedly, and I may want to have time to discuss its implications with my client; after all, there are more than forty thousand[34] documented collateral consequences of conviction in America, and no one should plead guilty without being told what the real consequences of that choice are. Will my client lose their job? Be unable to get a license to practice their career? Will they be barred from student loans, unable to get certain types of apartments, unable to live in certain neighborhoods? Will access to their children change? What about access to other loved ones? People plead guilty to things all the time without having a chance to discuss the plea in depth with their attorney, crushed between the rush of the court to "move the calendar," high caseloads for lawyers, and the circumstances of confinement, which seek to stifle meaningful conversation at every turn.

To be clear, people out of custody experience this crunch as well, but people in jail experience it more acutely. Receiving crucial information from their lawyer requires hours instead of minutes. Jails are built to stifle communication rather than foster it. All phone calls are recorded, and lawyers whose conversations are protected by attorney-client privilege—and must have that assurance of confidentiality in order to allow for discussion of difficult, sensitive things—have to rely on claims that their calls, though recorded, will not be listened to. If, like me, you don't trust the phone calls, you can arrange a video visit, but often the video visit booths are broken, or maybe there are only one or two booths for the hundreds of lawyers trying to reach their clients during any given week, or maybe the cameras are set up to capture only the air above a person's head.

On busy days, or for matters the lawyer thinks are small, the lawyer may try to shortcut these barriers by quickly chatting with their client about a new plea offer up in the courtroom, right before a client is brought out to appear before the judge—giving the jailed person dramatically insufficient time to consider their options or think meaningfully about a plea.

It wasn't just the grind of the court process that was harming Jannell. She had been suspended from her job, a common consequence of an arrest. Sometimes it's the fact of the arrest itself that costs someone their livelihood, but other times it's purely the time commitment required by an open court case. As a defender, I would routinely walk into arraignment booths where the first request from my client was to please call their boss or help get their shift covered so that their absence due to arrest wouldn't get them fired. Even if we could get them past that first hurdle, having to repeatedly take time off to return to court is much more than even the most patient employers will allow. Many of my clients struggled to take a day off every month or two to come and sit in the courthouse, waiting for nothing to happen yet again. But it was also not uncommon for me to have a judge—who has been told by their boss to "move the calendar and get these cases done"—insist on having my client come back to court multiple times in just a few weeks, missing as many as three or four days of work in a month, using this continual disruption in my client's life as a forcing factor to make them more likely to plead guilty just to end the case.[35]

Losing a job is a huge financial burden, but it isn't just the loss of income that forces people with court involvement deeper into poverty. Court debt itself has become a national epidemic.[36] A legally innocent person might already have had to pay hundreds or thousands of dollars in bail money just to get out of jail,[37] or pay pretrial services as much as $5,000 per year for an ankle monitor.[38] An open case can render a person ineligible for benefits programs that help them stay afloat.[39] Taking part in diversion programs—seen by the public as a fast track out of trouble—can cost thousands of dollars as well. The cost is such a huge factor that one Alabama report found one out of every four low-income people was turned down for diversion because they couldn't afford it.[40] And none of this even touches the other legal financial obligations people take on, like fees to have a public defender (to which one is Constitutionally entitled), fees for one's own jailing, fees to use expert witnesses, and more.[41] In Florida, the law has gone so far from sanity that people are forced to pay for the entirety of their incarceration, even if they're released early for good behavior—leading to situations like that of Shelby Hoffman, who was sentenced to seven years but released after ten months for completing a boot camp program. When she returned home and began working toward a college education and career in the health-care field, she found out she was more than $120,000 in debt, charged $50 per night for the full seven-year sentence she never served.[42]

Debt drives desperation, and desperation drives poor choices. The Alabama report also found that not only were 83 percent of formerly incarcerated people giving up paying for necessities such as rent, food, medicine, transportation, and child support to pay their court debt, but 50 percent of those surveyed had also been jailed for failure to pay their court debts, and 44 percent had been forced to rely on predatory pay-day loans to make the court payments.[43] Even children aren't excused—contact with the legal system can saddle kids with debt, whether through court system fines[44] or simply fines from their school.[45] The same report showed that almost 40 percent of people crushed under these debt burdens had committed a new crime . . . just to pay back the debt they owed to the court.[46]

It's not just debt; jailing itself may be making people more likely to engage in future crime.[47] Researchers have found that jailing exacerbates recidivism in multiple studies, and the effect size may grow with continued exposure to jail.[48] Holding people for only two to three days in jail made them almost 40 percent more likely to commit new crimes before trial than similar people held for less than twenty-four hours.[49] And the longer someone was in pretrial detention, the greater the chance they would later miss court appearances, have new arrests, or even have new arrests for violent crimes.[50]

Housing, of course, is a key source of stability for most people, without which it is incredibly hard to keep food and medicine, sleep safely, or apply for legitimate jobs. Most people don't know that the court system itself regularly forces people into homelessness even before they have been tried for a crime.

All it takes is an arrest to cause a person to get evicted. As the Bronx Defenders put it, "In criminal court, a person is 'innocent until proven guilty,' but in public housing, proof of guilt is not required to start eviction proceedings against a household."[51] This is because private landlords and public housing authorities alike still evict people for arrest, even without conviction,[52] despite guidance from the U.S. Department of Housing and Urban Development asking public housing institutions not to evict tenants solely because of an arrest.[53] A drug-related arrest doesn't even have to be in the home to cause eviction, and the eviction, of course, isn't limited to the individual, but includes the entire family.[54] Cities like New York and Philadelphia allow housing authorities to "permanently exclude" the arrested person, putting families in the position of deciding between seeing their loved one—or child—and keeping their apartment.[55] And lest you think my use of "seeing" is an exaggeration, this form of permanent exclusion applies to all forms of contact with the premises; the person (even a child) is not allowed to enter the apartment for any reason. No holidays, no birthdays, no caring for an elderly relative. This, unsurprisingly, often forces excluded people into homelessness.[56] One mother even had to kick out her fifteen-year-old child because of his marijuana possession arrest, and still lost the home for the whole family when she allowed him to attend Thanksgiving dinner.[57]

It's not just arrests that cause homelessness—court orders that prohibit contact between two people can cause one of them to become homeless.[58] "Crime free" ordinances cause people to be kicked out of housing for even having *contact* with police, including when they themselves are the victims of crime.[59] In some places, like Tampa, rules requiring police to notify landlords of contact result in hundreds of people losing housing over even unfounded accusations or incidents that didn't take place on the property, like a complaint about a teenage girl accused of stealing hair extensions seven miles away from the complex.[60] Even if landlords don't want to take part, some jurisdictions will fine them or pull their license if they do not evict tenants who are arrested, are suspected of crimes, call for help because of an overdose, or even violate city ordinances like having grass that is too long.[61] Sometimes the exclusions aren't just from one housing complex but from neighborhoods—cities like St. Louis and Seattle will ban people from returning to entire neighborhoods where they were accused of misconduct, limiting where they can look for housing, cutting them off from any services located in that neighborhood, and denying them access to friends and family who might help them survive housing instability.[62] Trying to find housing once kicked out, of course, is incredibly difficult in a world where 90 percent of landlords conduct background checks that disqualify anyone with an open criminal case.[63]

Most people outside the legal system have no idea how much lasting harm it does even before a person has been convicted of a crime. They often reward political candidates who run on "tough on crime" platforms, all because they think that this system makes us safer. And at every step of the process, people are told they can end the pain and move on with their lives if they just "wrap it up" and accept a guilty plea. They are often not told about the lasting consequences of a conviction on things beyond the courthouse doors; while the law requires that people be accurately advised about the immigration consequences of a plea or conviction, it does not require that they be advised of what might happen to their job, home, education, or access to their kids.

At its heart, one of the most damaging failings of our pretrial process is the failure to incentivize prosecutors to look first toward restoration instead of conviction. As Michael told me, "You have to have policies in place for people to respond to and act under. I would advise [prosecutorial agencies] to reconsider what is considered a 'win,' because that determines whether staff are 'successful.' Is it a win to put somebody away or clear your docket? Or is it a win to ensure that this community still has members who are functional? I would advise DAs to have a hard look at what they consider a 'success story' and how they reward those success stories." I asked Michael what a win—or a success story—had been for him, personally, on the job. "Not wasting time on something stupid. Meaning you're in for two days over a turnstile hop? Get the fuck out of here. And spending time on stuff that mattered. . . . For me, a win wasn't putting somebody away or lowering my case[load]. It was, all right, well, this person's life wasn't ruined . . . over something that white people don't have to deal with."[64] Indeed, if prosecutors were rewarded for restorative ideas and outcomes rather than promoted on the basis of conviction rate, we might see smarter problem-solving from their side. And absent that, if judges were incentivized to dismiss junk cases—and to serve as a more skeptical eye on prosecutorial filings—the volume of cases in the courts could go down, enabling everyone to focus on more serious matters.

For Jannell, even a great outcome in court couldn't save her from the consequences beyond the courthouse doors. After years of her case being transferred from one prosecutor to the next, and defender after defender, she finally landed on my desk, with the simultaneous good luck of going to a prosecutor who was willing to listen. We used the recording of her call with the customer service person who told her to report the car stolen, and the prosecutor assigned went to great lengths to get us the full dismissal we were fighting for. When the charges were finally dismissed, we celebrated. But when she returned to her job, she was told she had been terminated. "I would've been thirty-two years with the Board of Ed," she told me. "I most likely would have been able to retire at fifty-five. I'm on unemployment right now. I've been putting in applications, sending my résumé. I want to go back to the Board of Ed. One of the interviews I did, they wanted me to come on board. They nominated me, I went downtown, I did the paperwork, the fingerprinting. And then of course it came back that I got arrested, and they withdrew. I've been on a few interviews . . . a lot of them, actually. Every time this arrest comes up, they don't pick me."[65]

Chapter Four

Bad Incentives in a Bad System

How the Structure of Policing Enables Misconduct

When I ask you to imagine the leading causes of death for young men, what do you think about? My guess would be that accidents come to mind (yes, there are innumerable videos of men in their twenties doing unbelievably stupid things, enough that you start to wonder if they might be made out of sawdust and old tires). Suicide, perhaps, or cancer, or heart disease. These are, indeed, some leading causes of death for men between the ages of twenty-five and twenty-nine.

Another is the police.

As of 2019, police use of force is a leading cause of death for all young men in America. And for young Black men, this cause of death is exceedingly common, competing with accidents, suicide, homicide, heart disease, and cancer.[1] Every Black man in America steps out into his daily life with a one-in-a-thousand chance of being killed by police during his lifetime.[2]

This country asks people to go about their daily lives, their jobs, to care for their children and do the shopping and get gas and take their moms to medical appointments while operating in a space of constant, unremitting, and, in substantial part, government-created and government-sanctioned risk. A risk that is enhanced and sustained by many of our current public policies—policies that people who have the privilege of not living with this particular and exhausting background radiation may well support and vote for, unaware of their impact.

We have spent years in protest repeating the names of people whose lives were stolen from them by their own government. You, as a taxpayer, will almost certainly pay out of your own pocket for police killings and misconduct this year, as you do every year.[3] There is no other context in which the citizenry will accept widespread, unjustifiable, lethal abuse by a public employee. If bus drivers or firemen were killing more than a thousand people each year[4] and only 2 percent of these killings ever resulted in charges,[5] can you imagine a world in which they would be continually, relentlessly let off the hook?

———

Anyone, under the right circumstances, can make a bad choice at work, but in policing the incentive structure of the institution itself only serves as a driver of bad behavior. Policing, after all, is a job. And most people on the job will choose to do the tasks that offer the least risk and the most efficient way to meet their metrics for the day. Trespassing and related low-level, non-dangerous crimes are a low-risk and high-arrest-rate way for NYPD officers to fill their shift time, and this means they are forms of enforcement that have a lot to like for your average beat cop.

Alex Vitale, a professor of sociology at Brooklyn College and the CUNY Graduate Center who has spent thirty years studying police and consulting with everyone from governments to human rights organizations, told me this isn't just the NYPD: "We tend to labor under this illusion that police are primarily spending their time getting the super bad guys, chasing bank robbers, finding hidden serial killers, and what-not. But in fact, most policing, especially patrol policing, is incredibly mundane."[6]

A *New York Times* look at three major jurisdictions showed that police spent only about 4 percent of their time on violent crime in the first half of 2020.[7] Which, on the one hand, is a very heartening reminder of how rare violent crime actually is. But it's also a reflection of incentives: chasing down someone violent or armed is dangerous and difficult and may result in only one arrest. But kids wandering around their friends' and relatives' apartment buildings is incredibly common. Kids also tend to hang out in groups, meaning that if you nab one kid for trespassing, you can probably nab two or three others as well.

So what are they doing with the other 96 percent of their time? According to Professor Vitale, "Mostly what they're doing is micromanaging the lives of the most vulnerable and alienated parts of the community. If they're in a small town, they're going to stake out the place where poor people go to buy beer, the convenience store. . . . Some officers get a knack for identifying unregistered vehicles, which is a misdemeanor that can result in arrest. Other officers are good at spotting street-level drug transactions and run up on people hoping to find some dime bags. This increases the crime numbers and makes the department look productive."[8] The crime numbers that most of us see— even when we diligently go looking for real data—are, on some level, a reflection of where police choose to closely surveil a community, looking for any detectable transgression. They're not a pure reflection of the actual harm impacting our neighborhoods.

Beyond this kind of surveillance patrolling, there can be proactive ways of creating crime—when police departments choose to send out undercover officers to persuade unlucky drug users to score an extra dose to share. Narcotics units are a great investment for police departments that want to show high arrest numbers but keep on-the-job risk low, since going after street users isn't as risky as, say, trying to bring down large-scale trafficking operations.[9] It doesn't do much for safety.

It's not just that these time-filler arrests make departments look good; they can also be personally profitable for police. As public defenders, whenever we'd see a *really* stupid arrest (think a guy named Alejandro giving his name as "Alex" and being charged with "false personation" or a local mechanic charged with "possession of burglary tools" because he still had a screwdriver in his pocket as he walked home from work), the first thing we'd want to know was what time the officer's shift ended. Because each and every arrest *begins* with handcuffs and a ride to the precinct but then *continues* with a great deal of paperwork and follow-on tasks. The officer has to fill out an arrest report, a complaint report, and booking sheets, submit substances for lab testing, and carry out any number of related bureaucratic tasks. They have to not just take the individual they arrested to their precinct, but then, after completing all the paperwork, head on over to the DA's office and talk with a prosecutor about the case so that the prosecutor can write up and file charges. This means that every arrest an officer carries out will potentially involve hours and hours of paperwork and meetings, and if the arrest was carried out at the end of an officer's scheduled shift, these hours will be paid out as overtime,[10] typically compensating the officer at 150 percent or more of their regular pay. In some places, there aren't even limits on what kind of activity can garner overtime pay, allowing one officer in Kansas City to become the highest-paid city employee by taking it upon himself to renovate the local jail.[11]

This means that in almost every city around the United States some of the highest-paid public employees aren't mayors or commissioners or public attorneys but ordinary cops who made a *ton* of money on overtime.[12] Examples include New York Port Authority police, who were averaging $43,778 per officer in overtime in 2023,[13] with some making extra hundreds of thousands of dollars per year,[14] and the Chicago Police Department, which racked up almost $300 million in overtime in 2023.[15] It's not just the big cities, though—searching for overtime records in almost any region yields news reports about overtime payouts.[16]

The roots of this problem aren't exactly mysterious: police, after all, like every other piece of this system, are human. Like those in any other profession, some of them will be ethical, upstanding people who do their best to foster good in the world. Some may, of course, just be people who wanted a decent-paying job, and who are standing on the street at three o'clock in the morning, exhausted, and being screamed at by a harmless but deeply irritating member of the public. Do they tap into their higher self and let it slide? Or do they make up an excuse to arrest the screamer and get paid time and a half for their troubles? Bad incentives can make decent people do awful things.

—

Recognizing that human beings are susceptible to positive and negative incentives, American public policy embraces the idea that being sent to prison is a disincentive that will prevent ordinary people from committing crimes, and that the extraction of wealth through civil settlements will disincentivize corporate misbehavior. Whether this is true is up for a lot of debate—the current research suggests that people care a lot more about whether they get caught than they do about how long a sentence is.[17] Regardless, our legal system is a forest of harsh disincentives. Police, though, get to stand in a very special clearing.

If your neighbor pulls their car out of their driveway and backs into your kid, you can sue your neighbor or even have them criminally prosecuted. If a police officer backs their cruiser into your kid, you may have no recourse. In my own practice, I can tell you that most of the harm I saw from police was essentially a blend of intentional violence and lazily delivered wrongful accusations. A school police officer beat my client bloody inside an unseen corner of his own school (no charges brought against the cop). A cop claimed my client injured him, when the only injury he sustained was a sprained wrist on his punching hand (my client was charged with assault and resisting, apparently for resisting a fist with his face). A woman was accused of prostitution and arrested because she was waiting at a bus stop and when she walked, the (male) cop decided that she was "moving her hips in a suggestive manner." A young man was accused of a murder he did not commit, but police hated him so much that they threatened a local teenage runaway with prison time for drugs if he didn't lie and implicate my client. The witness sat on the witness stand, crying and apologizing, explaining that he had lied and was scared he'd never see his mom again. To my knowledge, none of these cases resulted in charges against police, or even a civil judgment against them.

Where is the accountability for police? In part, it's buried under a special set of rules shielding police and prosecutors from liability: qualified immunity. Qualified immunity is a rule, created by judges, that says government officials cannot be held liable for actions carried out as part of their official duties, as long as "their conduct does not violate clearly established statutory or constitutional rights of which a reasonable person would have known."[18]

In other words, it's a racket: police can break the rules six ways to Sunday, and if the exact way they broke the rules hasn't already been considered by a court, the civilian who was harmed is out of luck. When you consider the fact that police unions further restrict whether police can even be held accountable by their own departments—98 percent of police union contracts contain at least one provision protecting police from being held accountable for misconduct[19]—it becomes clear that life as a police officer is almost a mirror world of life in the most police-surveilled communities. While some people are being jailed for walking into the wrong apartment building or selling fruit without the right license, others are able to quite literally kill and experience few if any consequences.

The judges that created qualified immunity, originally, were trying to minimize four things: "(1) 'the expenses of litigation,' (2) 'the diversion of official energy from pressing public issues,' (3) 'the deterrence of able citizens from acceptance of public office,' and (4) 'the danger that fear of being sued will "dampen the ardor of all but the most resolute, or the most irresponsible [public officials], in the unflinching discharge of their duties." ' "[20]

But here's the thing: when lawsuits are brought against police officers, they essentially *never* bear "the expenses of litigation" or have anything to fear from being sued or functioning as public officials. As UCLA professor Joanna Schwartz explained, "I looked at 81 law enforcement agencies across the country and looked at lawsuits that were successful and paid out over a six-year period. What I found was that 99.98% of the dollars came not from the officers but from the local governments or their insurers. The fact that officers virtually never contributed anything into these cases was not a result of qualified immunity protections, but instead what are called indemnification agreements or statutes that provide that when an officer is sued, any settlement or judgment will be paid from government funds."[21]

So when a cop gets sued, taxpayers and insurers cover the cost, meaning that the officers accused of wrongdoing have essentially no personal disincentive to misconduct stemming from civilian lawsuits.[22] If we got rid of qualified immunity as a legal notion, individual officers who engage in misconduct wouldn't likely go bankrupt, but perhaps municipalities would do a better job of ridding themselves of bad cops and cultures of misconduct if the price tag for bad apples was steeper.

Or would they? Elected officials, after all, are motivated by what works with voters. Most voters are unaware that they are personally footing the bill for every bad cop in their town, and so elected officials have more to fear from being seen as "anti-police" than from being seen as paying out millions of dollars annually so bad cops can stay on the street.

And the cost is not minor. A majority of states and the federal government deny the public access to police officers' disciplinary records,[23] and perhaps because the public is left in the dark about how bad things are in local law enforcement, officers with prior complaints— even *multiple* priors—are often kept on the force.[24]

As Professor Vida B. Johnson at Georgetown pointed out, "The officer who killed George Floyd had eighteen complaints against him and was disciplined for two. The NYPD officer who was responsible for Eric Garner's death had seven misconduct complaints at the time. A police officer in Little Rock, Arkansas, had a significant number of complaints against him before he killed an unarmed child. Tamir Rice's murderer was in the process of being fired for a 'lack of maturity' when he was hired by the Cleveland Police Department where he killed the twelve-year-old. He was then rehired by a Pennsylvania police department. The officer who shot Walter Scott in the back on videotape had previously been in trouble with his department for killing an unarmed person. The officers who killed Alton Sterling in Louisiana also had a history of excessive-force complaints. The police chief who hired the officer apologized and admitted he never should have been hired or kept on the force as a result of his treatment of others he had arrested and personal interactions he had had with other officers."[25]

Police budgets are massive, often the single biggest cost a city incurs.[26] Police misconduct costs cities billions of dollars, with forty thousand payments across twenty-five departments costing more than $3 billion over the past ten years.[27] Yet no government agency tracks and publishes the issue of crime by police officers,[28] making this a region one could think of as "invisible crime"—crime that never enters the public imagination, because there are strong disincentives to reporting it and little public accountability.

The question of how much misconduct is perpetrated—and then rendered invisible—by police officers is important, but incredibly difficult to answer. Even with the mix of essentially no reporting agency or requirements and strong (even terrifying) disincentives to disclosure, some studies claim officers are four times as likely to engage in domestic violence as the general public.[29] This is the tip of the iceberg of potential harm perpetrated by police, but it's rarely disclosed to the public or brought into court. There's sexual misconduct on the job—for an unfortunately not uncommon example, a burglary victim is rendered even more vulnerable when police find drugs in the home, and is then pressured for sexual favors in exchange for the officer's looking the other way. "In many jurisdictions, there's no specific or automatic prohibition against police officers having sexual relations with people who are in their custody. Even here in New York City, up until a few years ago, if the officer claimed that it was consensual, it was not considered an illegal act. Therefore, that puts the onus on the victim to have to *prove* that it was nonconsensual, even if they were handcuffed," Professor Vitale tells me. This of course creates especially heightened danger for people who are rarely treated as credible complainants in our tilted legal apparatus, like sex workers, who are subject to both frequent arrest and surveillance and list sexual assault by police as the number two hazard of their job after physical assault, according to Professor Vitale.

And then, of course, there's what police are routinely allowed to take from the people they encounter. This can be done illegitimately—police pocketing money they find at a scene, or stealing cash from people they see as legitimate targets, like drug sellers. "This is such a widespread problem," Professor Vitale explained, "that many departments have auditing procedures where they set up sting operations, dispatching a patrol unit to an apartment that's been set up with drugs or money lying out"[30] and telling the patrol officer that there was a prowler or a domestic violence call; they then watch to see whether officers attempt to pocket the money or drugs. But there is also a completely legitimate form of police theft, called civil asset forfeiture.

Asset forfeiture is a vestige of the war on drugs.[31] The original idea was that law enforcement should be able to seize the proceeds of crime, like the fancy cars or cash or flat-screen TVs of drug dealers. "Some people remember *Miami Vice*," Professor Vitale reminded me, "where we saw the police confiscating fancy cars and boats and then using that to facilitate further undercover drug sting operations. This made the process seem appropriate, glamorous, and in the service of some greater good." Unfortunately, that belief in a greater good allowed this body of law to evolve with almost no checks on police power, and as of 2024 civil forfeiture has become, essentially, "an additional cash cow for departments, and also another mechanism by which officers sometimes just pocket the money individually in a corrupt manner."[32]

Police are able to legally go so far as to engage in a pretextual traffic stop, stopping someone for a small reason like an overly large air freshener hanging from the rearview mirror[33] (I have represented people on far too many cases that started with fuzzy dice). Their true intent isn't to ticket the person for the small issue but to investigate them for some larger suspicion. And then, without the targeted person ever being convicted of a crime, they can seize the belongings they *suspect* may have had an illicit origin. This is not a process governed by criminal court.[34] Unlike in a criminal case, where a person stands accused and the burden is on the government to prove their guilt, in a civil forfeiture case the police's supposition that a large amount of cash *must* have been from drug dealing puts the onus on the person whose goods were seized to find a lawyer, file suit, and try to get their possessions back. The police often get to keep what they seize, whether it's cash or a new fridge for the break room.[35] People are so rarely successful fighting back that since the year 2000, states and the federal government have seized more than $68 billion worth of goods from Americans[36]—often with no criminal conviction at all.[37]

———

Where *is* the accountability? One huge problem is that it's not coming from prosecutors. Prosecutors work closely with police, relying on them to build the case that the prosecutor will ultimately bring in court.[38] Professor Stephanos Bibas of the University of Pennsylvania Carey Law School has pointed out that prosecutors are strongly motivated to attain a high number of courtroom wins, not only because of ego and competitiveness, but also because of the need to see themselves (and be seen by others) as good at their jobs. This influences promotion and even the ability to seek future political office, as prosecution is often (inappropriately) treated as a major stepping stone to power.[39]

So all of these powerful incentives—self-image, dreams for the future—rely, for prosecutors, on the willingness of police to collaborate with them to help them win their cases.[40] As Professor Johnson explains, "For prosecutors, winning at trial requires police. Police investigate prosecutors' cases and then testify at their preliminary hearings, grand juries, motions hearings, and trials. In some cases, police may be the only witnesses for the prosecution."[41] And making matters worse, prosecutors interact with police vastly more than with constituents. While they may be building their cases with officers every day, their exposure to the general public comes more from the odd town hall or community meeting, oftentimes more unpleasant than collegial.[42] For all of these reasons, the closeness of police and prosecutors lessens the likelihood that the legal system will create disincentives to police abuse.

Even with so little data on how often police are prosecuted, we can draw a few conclusions. First, that arrests of police are rare—about a thousand per year, for all manner of charges.[43] Second, the data is so scarce that it's hard to tell to what degree this is "the tip of the iceberg."[44] When we try to extrapolate how much of a disincentive the risk of prosecution is for police, though, it's important to understand that even when police shoot civilians, they're charged less than 2 percent of the time.[45]

Even if police are *technically* prosecuted, prosecutors can use grand juries to insulate themselves from criticism for failing to indict police. In the grand jury proceeding, selected members of the public are chosen to be grand jurors and presented with information about a given police incident by prosecutors. These presentations are kept secret—the general public doesn't get to know what the prosecutor told the grand jurors. The public isn't allowed in the room, nor is the media, nor is there a judge or defense lawyer present.

Because prosecutors have total control over what is presented to the grand jury and zero outside scrutiny, it is relatively easy to get a case indicted. Yet when you look at how few police officers actually get indicted,[46] it's clear that prosecutors become suddenly and mysteriously less able to indict when the accused person has a badge.[47] Essentially, prosecutors can shift responsibility for the decision to indict or not indict police onto the grand jury members, and utterly evade visibility about how hard they fought (or didn't fight) for indictment. Indeed, indictments for civilian killings are commonplace, but indictments for police killings are rare.[48]

It's not just about failure to prosecute police who commit crimes, but also about ways prosecutors can cover up police misconduct. Any prosecutor or prosecutorial agency could, if they so chose, create a list of officers who are known to have engaged in misconduct, and refuse to call those officers as witnesses, discouraging police departments from using those officers. Prosecutors could then routinely reveal an officer's past to the defense, meaning all juries would be allowed to decide an officer's credibility with a full picture of both their present testimony and their history. In other words, if prosecutors wanted to create an immediate, effective disincentive to police misconduct, they could do so *tomorrow.*

——

But in most places, they don't.[49] Instead, we see prosecutorial choices that are actively increasing the ability of police to engage in misconduct with impunity. For one thing, have you ever considered why the rules around what police are allowed to do when interrogating or investigating civilians are so broad? For example, how weird is it that we have certain rights that don't exist until we "invoke" them by using magic words to speak them into existence?

The right I'm referring to, of course, is the right to remain silent. As anyone who can recite *Miranda* warnings will tell you, we all have the right to remain silent, and the right to an attorney, when we're being accused of a crime. This isn't just the right to safely refuse to open your mouth, but the right to be free from nonconsensual interrogation. But in 2010, the right became weirdly eroded by a case called *Berghuis v.*

Thompkins, in which the Supreme Court, at the urging of prosecutors, held that if you want to remain silent, you have to *invoke* that right by speaking aloud that you're choosing to remain silent.[50] If a person chooses to simply remain silent, nothing stops the police from continuing and continuing to interrogate them until they break; only speaking the right "magic words" will let the person *utilize* the right they supposedly incontrovertibly hold.

Similar "magic words" hurdles have also been placed on the right to counsel. In the "lawyer dog" case—wherein a man said, "If y'all think I did it, I know that I didn't do it so why don't you just give me a lawyer, dog, 'cause this is not what's up"—the court decided that this request for a lawyer was too ambiguous, saying that "the defendant's ambiguous and equivocal reference to a 'lawyer dog' does not constitute an invocation of counsel that warrants termination of the interview."[51]

The "lawyer dog" case may be funny, but it's a terrifying example of what courts will do to accept bad police behavior (continuing to interrogate a suspect who has asked for a lawyer, in this case). These erosions of the right to counsel, this focus on the specific *words* of invocation, are myriad—at this point, allowing any uncertainty into the request for counsel at all, as in "Oh, gosh, I feel uncomfortable, maybe I should have a lawyer for this?" is likely not good enough to allow a person to actually *utilize* their Fifth Amendment rights.

It's not just the Fifth and Sixth but also the Fourth Amendment that prosecutors have made available for police violation. Decades of prosecutorial appeals to high courts have resulted in ruling after ruling that trims away at civilian protections against police intrusions.[52] At one time, police needed probable cause to stop and talk to a civilian, but after *Terry v. Ohio*[53] police could stop civilians with a lower level of suspicion, directly creating the stop and frisk policies that have wrongfully detained millions of primarily Black and brown people.[54] At one time, police could not enter a person's home without a warrant, until prosecutors persuaded the Supreme Court to allow police to enter under what they deemed "exigent circumstances" in *Kentucky v. King.*[55] Not only did prosecutors in thirty-four states advocate for police power, but, according to Professor Johnson, "they argued that courts should not be able to question police motives in their creation of the exigencies that allow the warrantless search of a home."[56]

This is a small portion of cases in which prosecutorial appeals have created more leeway and less accountability for police. As a criminal defense attorney, I have to engage in constant and continuing study to keep up with all the new cases tweaking how many rights Americans actually have. At the urging of prosecutors, appeals courts continue to remove yet another incentive to keep police honest: the threat that the fruits of bad behavior will not be used in court. Every time a court says evidence can be used at trial even though it was wrongfully obtained, pressure on police to act right is relieved. In so doing, courts further and further dilute our Constitutional rights.

What's more, prosecutors have also found ways to push their sphere of authority beyond the criminal courthouse, finding things they can do that actively shield police from civil consequences. Specifically, in the case of *Town of Newton v. Rumery*, prosecutors were caught parlaying a relatively bogus arrest by police into a release of civil liability— a promise not to sue. Specifically, Bernard Rumery, after hearing that his friend David had been indicted by a grand jury for sexual assault, went to their mutual acquaintance to find out more about what was going on. She, as it turned out, was the *victim* of that assault, and she quickly turned Mr. Rumery in to the town's chief of police, claiming that he was trying to make her drop the charges. After Mr. Rumery was hauled into court, the prosecutor agreed to dismiss the charges against him . . . "if he would agree to release any claims he might have against the town, its officials, or the victim for any harm caused by his arrest. Three days later, he signed the 'release-dismissal agreement,' and the criminal charges against him were dropped." When he later did bring a civil rights suit, the Supreme Court said that agreements like this—where prosecutors agree to dismiss cases in return for promises not to sue—are allowable, if evaluated on a case-by-case basis.[57] The problem? In a world where police disciplinary records are secret and prosecutors don't officially record or reveal who the bad cops are (and almost never prosecute them), civil cases are often the *only way* the public still has to find out who the bad cops are, and what they've done in the past. By using their office to prevent even civil cases from going forward, prosecutors have further assisted in shielding police misconduct from accountability—or even any form of public scrutiny at all.[58]

So let's go back to our aforementioned exhausted officer, considering whether to make a little overtime by arresting a dingus who, though a dingus, hasn't *actually* broken the law. In my job or your job, where we might get caught and fined or even fired for breaking the rules, and could certainly get prosecuted if we broke the law, the incentives are rather clear. But that officer, who's to stop him? He will likely not be disciplined, and if he is, he can always get a job at the department one county over.[59] He certainly won't get sued if he has a *Rumery*-style prosecutor friend, but even if he does, he won't pay out of pocket. He *will* get to keep the overtime money, though. And the odds of his being arrested for perjury are essentially zero.[60] So why not teach the asshole a lesson, and, at the same time, be able to afford to rent a bouncy house for his daughter's birthday?

Chapter Five

What We Talk About When We Talk About Crime

How Media Obscures the Truth About Safety

Reading the news, you'd think that crime is something naturally occurring, universally observable, and perhaps a little bit subjective, like a groundhog's opinion of seasonal change. This arises from an incredibly weird juxtaposition where most of the national and local news we receive tells us only about the most shocking, memorable, or horrifying crimes and then turns around and takes a poll wherein ordinary people are asked whether they *think* crime is rising.

Now, to be clear, crime *is* either rising or falling, in ways that usually make a bit of sense if you think about humans. Interpersonal violence, for example, appears to have risen after the pandemic lockdown, suggesting that bad things happen when we're cooped up, under historic-scale anxiety, losing our jobs, unexpectedly homeschooling our kids, maybe drinking more to cope, and separated from our friends, with limited access to both the things we enjoy and the medicines we need (and, well, toilet paper).[1]

There's a great example of how our perception of crime is more political than realistic in a poll from Gallup that reveals that for the last twenty years if you ask Americans whether they think crime in their locality is higher or lower than it used to be, their answer doesn't reflect the crime rate; it reflects whether their preferred political party is in or out of power.[2]

Percentage Saying There Is More Crime in Area Than a Year Ago, by Party ID

Is there more crime in your area than there was year ago, or less? (% More)

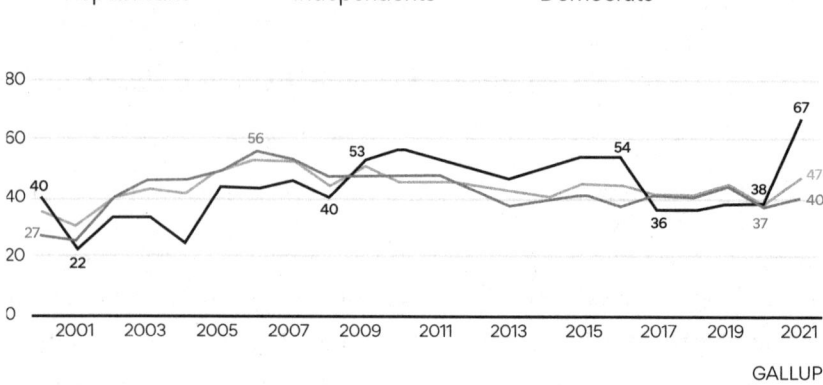

GALLUP

Most people do not experience crime regularly, or even bear witness to it on a daily or weekly basis, nor do most people spend much time thinking about the underlying drivers of crime (except for you, of course, since you're reading all about it here). Which means that when a pollster calls up a randomly selected citizen and asks them whether crime is up or down in their community, they probably don't know. So they repeat what they've been told, usually by reporters, police spokespeople, or politicians[3] who may be offering more ideology than information and taking us further from the possibility of having a shared news-based reality.[4] So, for example, as crime fell in 2023,[5] the majority of Americans would still swear up and down that crime was rising.[6] This is what happens when we're fed a carefully curated (often misleading) mirage,[7] seemingly real safety data operating as highly legitimized clickbait.[8]

In the Bronx arraignment court, the handful of attorneys staffing the court on any given shift saw *all* the arrests and arrested people in the period of time for which we were there, giving us a regular sample of local criminal accusations. A substantial chunk of our cases were arrests for driving on a suspended license and trespassing, both of which involved little harm to the public. The suspended license folks were almost always stopped for a small traffic infraction like failing to signal or rolling through a stop sign, and often had no other matters in their record. The trespassing folks were often young, and mostly only hauled into court because New York's "Clean Halls" program allowed landlords to sign up to have NYPD prowl the halls and stairwells of apartment buildings, demanding ID of anyone in those spaces and then arresting them if they weren't a resident of the building and couldn't get a resident to claim them as a guest[9] . . . which meant that if you went to a friend's apartment to see if they wanted to hang out and your friend happened not to be home, you were going to jail.

The accusations we would fight day in and day out were a good reflection of what the data tells us about crime: most crime is boring. Misdemeanors.[10] Schoolyard scuffles, neighbor disputes, low-level drug use, injury-free DUIs. Very little of what we see is the kind of crime covered on the news. Violent crime is much less common than property crime, but on the news we see roughly equal amounts of news about the two.[11] Unsurprisingly, the more people watch local crime news, the more frightened they report being, even if crime is not prevalent locally.[12]

As described in the last chapter, there is a world of invisible crime the general public is simply not seeing, hearing about, or being protected from. So what are we encountering when we do hear about crime on the local news?

When we talk about crime, what we're actually talking about is crime *that police tell us about*. They're not telling us about any of the stuff in the last chapter. And they're also not telling us about things happening in places they never choose to go, inspect, or attend to. Crime, in this way, is often a reflection simply of where police choose to be.

Take two communities—let's call them Uptown and Downtown. Both have drug use and sales, wage theft in the local businesses, and environmental crime by industrial companies in the area. In Downtown, police concentrate their forces and set quotas for arrest, using a "stop and frisk" policy that subjects ordinary citizens to constant searches of their person. This drives up the number of low-level arrests for drug possession that police are able to make, sends more people to jail for substance use problems, and establishes Downtown as a "high crime" neighborhood. The jailing doesn't fix addiction, and hardly anyone reaches recovery. Adults who should be home caring for their children are constantly being removed, fracturing families through continual arrests. These constant arrests drive higher rates of eviction and joblessness as well as deepening poverty through the imposition of steep court fines and fees, leading ultimately to higher violent crime as economic mobility withers and people suffer from higher rates of untreated mental health conditions and substance dependence, fueled by the weakened access to care that comes with entrenched poverty.

In Uptown, though, police do not come unless called upon by the residents. In this gated suburbia, drug purchasing and use continue at the same initial rate as Downtown, but behind closed doors. Instead of being subjected to arrests and jail to stem addiction, the residents of Uptown, who remain housed and employed, are able to privately seek out medical help and substance use treatment, leading to higher rates of recovery from addiction. Because arrests in Uptown happen only if police are called in by residents—usually only in cases of real violence or threat—Uptown is seen as a low-crime neighborhood. Inside the houses of Uptown there is no less domestic violence, child abuse, or date rape than in Downtown, but residents of Uptown are allowed to choose when to bring in an outside party and when to deal with matters privately, giving them a greater ability to choose when they want to engage with the court system and when they want to use private, therapeutic, or other means to respond to or recover from harm.

Designation as "high crime" or "low crime" isn't just branding for these regions, but materially changes the way police are allowed to enforce the law. In the case *Illinois v. Wardlow*,[13] the Supreme Court weakened the right to be left alone—but only in "high crime" neighborhoods, where they decided that a citizen's unprovoked flight from a police encounter was sufficient to legally justify seizure of that person by police, and that a police officer's assertion that a person was being "evasive" was enough to create "reasonable suspicion" and allow police to stop someone.[14] This ruling had a massive impact on low-income neighborhoods, which were suddenly subjected to a separate system of law, curtailing residents' rights[15] more sharply than their wealthier, whiter counterparts'.

And yet people living in hyper-policed neighborhoods may have much better reasons to run from police. As Justice John Paul Stevens himself pointed out in *Wardlow,* "Among some citizens, particularly minorities and those residing in high-crime areas, there is also the possibility that the fleeing person is entirely innocent, but, with or without justification, believes that contact with the police can itself be dangerous, apart from any criminal activity associated with the officer's sudden presence. For such a person, unprovoked flight is neither 'aberrant' nor 'abnormal.' Moreover, these concerns and fears are known to the police officers themselves, and are validated by law enforcement investigations into their own practices."[16]

These erosions leak into other areas of law. Let's say the state in which Uptown and Downtown are found has "castle doctrine" and "stand your ground" laws that allow people to defend themselves and their homes with violent force. The law, specifically, says that a homeowner does not need to retreat from an intruder before using self-defense, but can rather use lethal force to defend themselves and their property. Because police can claim to the local judiciary that Downtown is a "high crime" area, they are able to get a judge to sign off on "no knock" warrants, which are a type of warrant allowing police to forcibly enter a civilian's home without announcing themselves or identifying themselves as police. No-knock warrants set up some of the most lethal encounters between police and ordinary people, as evidenced by the case of Breonna Taylor, a twenty-six-year-old medical professional who was killed by police during an error-ridden no-knock raid in 2020.[17] They also enable the indelible biases of the legal system to reign supreme, because a homeowner who attempts to use the castle doctrine to defend his home against intruders will face grave felony charges if those (unannounced, unidentified) intruders happen to be police.

In Downtown, people are now living in greater fear—poverty and desperation, as well as substance dependence and worsening mental health, have driven up interpersonal conflict in the neighborhood and depressed home values, leaving more properties and lots vacant or derelict. More people are interested in carrying guns to protect themselves, but because police have chosen to concentrate enforcement so profoundly on Downtown, most people have also, by this time, been arrested at least once. This means that many people cannot legally own a firearm, but out of fear for their safety or their families' they choose to carry one illegally anyway. But because the law allows police to search people more readily in "high crime" areas, people in Downtown are routinely stopped and frisked, leading to high rates of arrest for weapons possession. This, in turn, deepens the impression of Downtown as a dangerous place.

In Uptown, meanwhile, people keep their unregistered guns quietly in their homes. Many Uptown residents visit gun shows out of state and bring illegal weapons home for fun, unchecked by police. As Uptown becomes wealthier and Downtown becomes poorer, a greater concentration of local business leaders and powerful leaders chooses to live in Uptown. At work, these residents of Uptown are engaging in all manner of crime, but they are choosing forms of crime that are difficult to investigate and are therefore de-prioritized by police.

Wage theft, for example, is booming. This is a crime in which an employer illegitimately refuses to pay workers to whom wages or benefits are owed, such as by directly refusing to pay, paying less than minimum wage, withholding tips, not paying for benefits like Social Security, Medicare, or unemployment insurance, or misclassifying an employee as an independent contractor—and it's *incredibly* common, not just in Uptown, but in all of America.[18] In 2017, the Economic Policy Institute estimated that just *one* form of wage theft (paying below minimum wage) resulted in minimum wage workers having more than *$15 billion* stolen from them every year, a number that exceeds the value of all robberies, burglaries, larcenies, and car thefts combined.[19] This is a crime whose lack of enforcement arises cleanly from what police are willing to do, and whom they are willing to respond to. Because of course if a low-wage worker whose paycheck has been withheld decides to take money from the till, and their boss calls the cops, they are going to be arrested for larceny.

But if the boss is the one taking money from the employee, they are almost never dealt with by police or criminal courts.[20] Instead, accountability for the powerful is shoved over into the civil rather than criminal court system.[21] If an employee calls the cops, they can declare this outside their area of responsibility entirely, and leave it to local nonprofits or public interest groups to bring lawsuits against these companies. They can say this is a department of labor matter, meaning that the very same low-wage workers, in addition to potentially having to work multiple jobs to survive, must also figure out how to navigate the complex bureaucracy of an administrative agency, or find a lawyer for themselves and engage in civil litigation, just to get the same kind of recompense for theft that others can seek by calling 911.

Wage theft isn't the only widespread crime you probably aren't hearing much about. Crime by powerful entities against marginalized people has always been minimized in our law enforcement apparatus. American policing, after all, is an institution that emerged originally in the wake of the end of slavery and in the emergence of industrial capitalism in the mid-nineteenth century to protect the interests of the powerful against the interests of the poor. There is no reason why we, as a country, *need* to have police who fervently arrest people for jaywalking[22] and prosecutors who ignore the chance to stop the leaders of companies that pollute entire towns[23] or give thousands of children cancer. Nevertheless, big companies that get prosecuted are likely to get "deferred prosecution agreements," in which prosecutors agree to essentially put prosecution on hold to give the accused time to comply with certain conditions.[24] These are made available even when the companies themselves may be repeat offenders.[25] How many get them? It's hard to say. The government doesn't measure corporate crime rates.[26]

In our example above, I expect that when you picture Downtown, you're picturing run-down public housing complexes and people sitting on grimy street corners. Far too often, we see these vignettes of American poverty without recognizing them for what they really are: an image of the crimes of landlords who keep tenants in unconscionable conditions but prevail in court because tenants have no right to a lawyer in housing court. An image of public entities failing to comply with the law about lead paint, hazardous trash collection, or other public hazards. An image of people suffering because they cannot afford the price of a medicine they need, which has been unconscionably jacked up by a guy in a suit (or a hoodie) somewhere.

———

Of course, most people, looking at the image above, do not see the invisible crimes of powerful entities. Instead, they see poverty as a proxy for criminality, a falsehood that flattens the real public safety problems we face. Substance use, for example, is happening all the time behind closed doors, but the people whose substance use we are, collectively, shown the most by the media are those who don't have the privilege of a door to close.

I spoke with Stephen Murray, an overdose survivor, researcher, and program implementer, who explained the problem:

Because drug use is criminalized, you have to be really, really marginalized in some way in order to come to the surface about your drug use. What I mean by that is, when you think of a drug user, the first thing that's going to come into your head is someone who's experiencing homelessness. Why? Because whatever they're doing is happening out in the open. It's being photographed. Anytime the news does an article, if you're going to tell a story about a new drug like Xylazine impacting people, well, you're going to want footage and pictures of people experiencing that drug or adulterant. So what are you going to do? You're going to go out to the street where people have no privacy and you're going to film them in what may appear to be a stupor.

And what does that do? For the general public, which includes police and nurses and my mom, watching the local news, what are they doing? They're saying "this is drug use" and they're showing a very, very marginalized portion of that—people who are in that situation mostly not because of drugs, but because our system is terrible and they don't have housing. . . . Now, this could be any of us—most Americans are one paycheck away from losing our housing. So what they're showing is a condition that many problems have contributed to, and saying drugs are evil. But what they're missing is that the vast majority of folks who use drugs are not unhoused. They are working. Almost all of our callers are "regular" members of society. They have jobs, they're engaged in their community in some way. They volunteer, they love their cat. All normal stuff, right? And those people are never going to go public with their story because why would they? They would be criminalized.

This constant association of a health condition—using substances—with other things people find frightening or troubling—being unhoused—has a profound impact. Stephen, who spent close to a decade working as a first responder, pointed out how his fellow paramedics were being conditioned to treat people with substance use problems as fundamentally different from people with other health problems. "There was one older lady in our community who had in-home help during the day, but overnight she had no help. She would hit her button at three in the morning because she'd be stuck on the toilet when she'd go to the bathroom. So I would go help her up. I [saw] her three nights a week, for four years. She was like my grandmother. But as a paramedic, I could look at that and say it's an abuse of the system. She had a family that obviously had enough money to provide overnight help. If I'm tied up with her and some other emergency comes in, I'm the only ambulance within 265 square miles. But you would never hear people complaining about that burden, because she's a cute little lady. If a paramedic has to go to the same person who's overdosed twice in the same week, you'll never hear the end of it."[27]

The more the news shows a type of person and tells us we should be afraid of the *type of person* instead of the crime or the form of harm, the more bias is fomented, impacting our jury pools and even our judges. Lack of housing isn't the only way in which people who are historically marginalized are more at risk of "representing" crime in the news. A white middle-class male manager who places harassing phone calls to his ex-wife all night isn't going to make the news unless he murders her. The people whose mug shots are shown on the news for minor crimes like shoplifting, dirt bike riding, and drug involvement are much more likely to be disproportionately Black. In the news, Black Americans are more likely to be negatively depicted as perpetrators, and white Americans are more likely to be positively depicted as victims and police officers.[28] Moreover, some studies show Black Americans are overrepresented in crime stories than actual crime rates would render reasonable. In fact, a 2021 study showed that 45 percent of images in news articles were mug shots of Black people accused of crimes, while only 9 percent of images in news articles were mug shots of white people accused of crimes. White victims of crime, meanwhile, were four times as likely to be shown in humanizing photographs with friends and family than Black victims of crime.[29]

It's not just the news. Police departments often report crime on their own via social media, and a Stanford study looking at these posts from 2010 to 2019 found that in every region of our country except for Hawaii and heavily Black regions of the South, Black people were substantially overrepresented in these posts, creating a false impression about the racial breakdown of crime and arrestees.[30]

Whether we're getting our news from Facebook (please don't) or news clips, nuance is often hard to come by these days. The very nature of TV news, for example, which is short and episodic, makes complex storytelling difficult. And because many more people consume news than have real experience with the criminal legal system, there isn't a great deal of public knowledge out there to serve as a counterweight against sensationalist coverage.[31]

———

Uptown and Downtown are *everywhere*. How a person perceives police, and the role of police in creating safety, will differ substantially depending on what type of policing they get, determined in part by who they are and where they live.[32] It's unclear whether the residents of Uptown are actually safer from crime, but it is clear that they enjoy vastly greater control of their own level of contact with the criminal legal system, and because of that control they are less likely to see that system as abusive, intractable, counterproductive, and illegitimate. They may simply credit police with the overall state of their streets, whether or not police are actually responsible for that state of well-being.[33]

Kingston Farady, who has spent almost two decades as a defense investigator and now works as a special assistant for investigations at the Statewide Appellate Support Center in New York, noted how individuals who experience crime have to do the difficult calculus of deciding whether they're safer with or without police—and whether police will add value.[34] Kingston recalled a horrifying incident in his own life in which his best friend was shot. "They were shot three times by an unknown group who drove up and shot into their car. And the police just didn't investigate. My friend was in grad school getting their master's. But they are dark-skinned Black, they are masculine presenting, queer, and the police saw that and didn't investigate. There were surveillance cameras everywhere. They didn't get the surveillance camera footage." Kingston, an accomplished investigator, accompanied his friend to meet the police on the case. To his shock, they admitted they had done nothing—and apologized. "That's how we found out that they didn't investigate. Their apology was, 'We're so sorry. We thought this was a drug deal gone wrong.' This just speaks to how so much of policing is based on how the police are *perceiving* somebody."[35]

When we talk about crime, we are really talking about two timescales of policy choices: where police choose to carry out enforcement in the present, and what long-standing policy choices (including health care, housing, education, economic, and environmental policy) have done to a place over generations.

Of course, members of the general public aren't usually seeking out FBI arrest data in their spare time (that's reserved for weirdos like me). Instead, they're hearing about crime from the media, which, in turn, has long been ensnared by an existential problem: people pay more attention to news stories that are more shocking, meaning that journalistic outfits can get more clicks, readers, and ad revenue when they cover stories that attract more attention.

Though "clickbait" is a new word, the idea isn't new at all. In the early days of American print journalism, newspapers commonly understood the concept that gory stories from police with a lot of insider details about crime were more likely to sell papers (and also, as Khalil Gibran Muhammad has pointed out, to advance false linkages between

Blackness and criminality).[36] It was so common that the expression "if it bleeds, it leads" is attributed to William Randolph Hearst, who embraced sensational stories about war and crime to outcompete rival newspapers.[37] As Dr. Matthew Guariglia, a historian on race, policing, and technologies of governance, explained, "It was a time when crime reporters and police had an incredibly chummy relationship, in part because reporters needed access, and in part because of the history of extremely partisan politics in cities in the United States in this period. In those places, if you had a newspaper, the political machine that was in power—the mayor and the mayor's police commissioner, all of one party—your newspapers had to be chummy with that party in power. A paper that supported those partisans had a vested interest in making their police department look good, in showing that they were good at preserving law and order, and also in hyping the threat of crime and the necessity of this hard-line policing. Because a paper also had a vested interest in showing what the city might *become* should the other side take power: chaos and crime and violence."[38]

The natural upshot of this approach to coverage is that the crimes that got covered in the paper—as in our modern media—tend to be those that are the most shocking or creepy (hello, entire "true crime" industry) rather than those that best educate the public about the real risks they face.[39] It also deepens the reliance of journalists on police, because police are the most ready source for the gory details of crime stories. Survivors and witnesses often have partial information, or may be too emotionally devastated to participate in media, and defense attorneys have little incentive to make public statements early in a case, when they may not want to commit to a theory of the case or alienate prosecutors who hold so much leverage in the plea bargain process. This means that for a journalist trying to break news before anyone else, working on a tight deadline and looking for powerful information no one else has yet about a given incident, staying friendly with the police force may be essential. This reliance on police sources, of course, gives police "privileged status in the marketplace of ideas"[40] and makes it easier for police to set the narrative about what happened in a given crime—and what's happening generally in public safety.[41]

Police are able to do this, of course, because of how they are funded. If a budget is a statement of values, most localities value their police above all else.[42] Beyond the vast sums dedicated to paying out that over-time and those settlements, police departments often have sizable strategic communications departments working full time to "control the narrative"[43] and portray police positively.[44] Alec Karakatsanis, founder of Civil Rights Corps, noted San Francisco's police budget items in 2022 "included a nine-person full-time team managed by a director of strategic communications who alone costs the city $289,423; an undisclosed number of cops paid part-time to do PR work on social media; a Community Engagement Unit tracking public opinion; officers who intervene with the families of victims of police violence and who are dispatched to the scenes of police violence to control initial media reaction; and a full-time videographer making PR videos about cops." In L.A., the same sheriff's department that's under seemingly endless investigations for its own criminal activity has "forty-two employees doing PR work in what it calls, in Orwellian fashion, its 'Information Bureau.' The Los Angeles Police Department has another twenty-five employees devoted to formal PR work."[45]

By contrast, it is rare for public defenders or private law firms to have any communications professionals at all within their ranks—and certainly not departments of this magnitude. Certainly, the community members most impacted by both policing and crime do not have social media experts and spokespeople at their disposal. This means that police have tremendous capacity to control the narrative about what "crime" is happening in a jurisdiction—directing media attention toward the offenses and neighborhoods they wish to amplify in the public imagination. Plus, in a world of constantly emergent news, it's just very tempting to rely on police sources instead of investing more time into community relationship building.[46] In 2024, even the Associated Press had to take note of the issue, releasing new guidelines for how journalists cover police. The new guidelines urge journalists to remain skeptical of police reports, noting that "accounts by police, especially in the hours just after a crime, are very incomplete and can be inaccurate, whether about specific details or about motivations behind the crime."[47]

The heart of the PR effort, usually, is to get the public to agree with the police on matters of policy. One example might be fentanyl: any medical doctor or drug intervention specialist will tell you that touching fentanyl is harmless.[48] Yet police have repeatedly claimed that fentanyl is dangerous to touch and can cause overdose through the skin.[49] This has been disproven time and again—indeed, many of the officers who suffer symptoms after fentanyl proximity may be having panic attacks brought on by their own departments' counterfactual communications efforts.[50] In spite of a chorus of doctors explaining that fentanyl does not bear this type of lethality when handled,[51] these communications efforts increase public fear of fentanyl and demonize drug users, who are implicitly to blame for putting whole communities at risk. As a community becomes more afraid of and angrier about fentanyl in particular, people become more likely to support harsher enforcement measures (for example, longer sentences for drug users) and less likely to speak up for more restorative measures[52] like expanded access to treatment (which, in actuality, is effective at reducing drug use as well as more cost efficient and likelier to reduce recidivism).[53]

This is a great type of enforcement for police to highlight: after all, police don't perform equally well across all types of crimes. Every jurisdiction, for the most part, tracks police "clearance rates," which are the proportion of cases of various types of crimes that police are able to close by any means. This doesn't necessarily mean they *solved* the case, just that they *closed the file*. So a case can be "cleared" by an arrest, or by "exceptional means," a category that is supposed to apply to situations where police have done all the work—identified a suspect, gathered evidence, and so on—but could not close the case because of extenuating circumstances, such as the death of the suspect.[54]

A little more than a third of violent offenses (37 percent) known to law enforcement were cleared by police according to 2022 FBI data, the lowest level since 1993.[55] Property crime is faring worse, dropping from almost 20 percent of cases cleared in 2013 (not so great) to 12 percent in 2022 (even worse).[56] So that gives us a sense of how successful police actually are at "solving" cases (not very).

Clearance rates on crimes that are, in essence, initiated by a police officer (like an undercover cop offering a drug user $20 to go buy themselves their drug of choice, as long as they buy some for this kind stranger as well) are quite high. They can also abuse the "exceptional means" category to close way more cases than they're actually solving, like Baltimore County police did in 2016, the year that they "closed" 70 percent of rape cases but made arrests in only 30 percent. These are tactics that make police performance look good.[57] They can be a PR win for police departments like those in California, which attorney general data reveals are otherwise clearing, in 2023, as few as 27 percent of rape cases, 10 percent of burglary cases, and only about 6 percent of motor vehicle thefts.[58]

The result is that you, as a citizen, have likely seen copaganda: adorable stories about police pulling people over, only to give them ice cream, or fixing someone's car, or buying a meal for a person living on the street. What you haven't seen is the truth about how many officers in your local department have engaged in misconduct (and how often), how many have lied under oath, how many have hit, punched, or kicked a person they were arresting, how many have executed wrongful arrests, what all these lawsuits are costing you, as a taxpayer, what they're charging you for their overtime hours (and how they're spending those hours), and, of course, whether they're actually succeeding at solving crimes. Are clearance rates abysmal in your town? Probably, and you can and should look it up today. No matter what you find, you won't have seen your local nightly news reporting on how police are solving only 6 percent of thefts.

As cellphone cameras, body-worn cameras, and security cameras have become ubiquitous in the United States, police narratives on crime have started to fall apart. Police-worn body cameras and civilians with cellphones have shown us the truth much more often than we used to be able to see it—videos of police planting evidence, assaulting teenagers and the elderly, and even engaging in extrajudicial killings.[59]

But the problem is that visibility hasn't yet equated to transformation. Police budgets remain largely unchanged or even increased,[60] without meaningful changes in police practices. These funding choices have consequences in a world of finite resources. Dollars spent on body armor are dollars not spent on housing or mental health care. For people who live in areas more like Uptown, where intrusive and even violent policing tactics are not visible on a daily basis, the obfuscation of police misconduct and their failure at their primary function (solving crimes) may create a feeling of safety. It also creates less interest in alternative public safety solutions that would be much more effective than what we have now.

And for people who live in places more like Downtown, where police abuse is visible and constant, and the problems that drive crime are worsened rather than ameliorated by law enforcement, these videos only serve to substantiate what people already know: that police don't bring *safety*, they bring *enforcement*. Safety is a thing that takes place before the bad stuff happens—preventative measures, access to resources, giving people the kind of care and opportunities that direct them away from engaging in harm. Enforcement is unrelated to safety, because it takes place after an incident of harm, prevents nothing, and often spurs cycles of future danger. And importantly, it is also affirmatively and actively dangerous to the people who are its usual targets.

Annelise Finney is now a reporter for the Bay Area NPR station KQED. But when I met her, she was a ferociously energetic criminal defense investigator, finding truth in some of the unlikeliest places in the Bronx. Annelise's work could make or break a case.

We often underestimate how much misconduct is just normal,

sloppy mistakes made by people not paying attention while at work. Annelise herself witnessed innumerable instances of sloppy mishandling of investigations. Like the time police accidentally let an eyewitness into the room where she was standing with our client, giving them a sneak peek at the "right" person to pick out of the subsequent lineup. Or, more commonly, having a witness do an "ID procedure" that consisted of the cops driving by in a cruiser with the person they just arrested in the back, asking "is this the guy?" instead of bothering with a proper lineup. Or the ways they routinely speak to witnesses that could hopelessly impair accuracy in an investigation—"just suggesting things to an eyewitness, like 'This person was wearing a long-sleeve shirt, right? This person was really tall, right?' Even something as simple as creating a closed list of possibilities. 'This person, were they wearing a red or a blue shirt?' When you're dealing with memory, you have to be aggressively attentive to not being suggestive. And police, even when they are trying to do things right, will be suggestive, as if by default."[61]

But this kind of minor misconduct can radically impact a person's life. An eyewitness whose memory is influenced by suggestive questioning could almost single-handedly cause a wrongful conviction, if they testify with great confidence. And research on memory suggests a person feels more confident in their recollection according to how cohesive their story is, regardless of the accuracy of the memory itself.[62]

This is a category of police misconduct that is even more difficult to detect than police violence, because it is insidious and subtle, and, without an Annelise there, would likely never come to light. Police themselves have no reason to reveal the truth about their day-to-day shortcuts to prosecutors, and prosecutors are unlikely to be present at the time these shortcuts take place, choosing instead to litigate against defense attorneys who raise a red flag about police investigatory problems. A witness like Annelise is sometimes the only person standing between a deficient criminal court apparatus and two different categories of civilians who stand to be harmed: the wrongfully accused person and the crime survivor who has had the wrong person arrested on their behalf.

To people in Uptown, these daily sloppinesses that cost lives are unlikely to be visible. But to the people in Downtown, who see their loved ones harmed by police on cellphone videos, subjected to wrongful arrest, or having their entire future altered by a sloppy investigation that taints evidence and witness memory, it is another story. For these families, the question of whether to call the police is a very real quandary: if police might kill you and probably won't solve your problems, why call them in the first place?

Annelise affirmed that many people she spoke with as a defense investigator were more comfortable speaking with her than with the police themselves. "We don't consider police violence a crime often. But that is a huge part of what impacts our clients and that has the result of invisibilizing other crimes. People don't feel like they can turn to the police for help because they've never received that before. And people in the community don't believe that they will receive any help. And so the potential to develop insight or systems of knowledge about crime in the community is just buried in this massive distrust of the legal system."[63]

Distrust, of course, is allowed in some places, but not in others. This means that in a neighborhood with a ShotSpotter system, residents may choose not to invite police into their community every time they hear a loud bang, but loud bangs will automatically result in a call to police from the technology installed without their consent. Dr. Guariglia pointed out ShotSpotter as a particularly problematic substitute for community consent, because it can set keyed-up police loose on any number of unsuspecting civilians: "There are a number of things wrong with this, obviously. One is that the technology doesn't really work. You have police showing up armed for a gunfight and finding kids with firecrackers in the street. It creates incredibly dangerous situations. Two is the fact that one of the biggest questions that needs to be asked, which police don't seem to be asking, is, *Why is nobody calling us?* And the answer is because, I think, after living what we've lived through the last thirty years, the idea that, if you were to call the police on what you thought was a gunshot, and it turns out to be, like what we're seeing with ShotSpotter, kids with firecrackers, you are then somehow responsible for putting those children in harm's way and potentially deadly violence."

This effect is then compounded by technology like "predictive policing." As Dr. Guariglia points out, "Rather than ask people, 'Hey, what streets do you fear walking down at night? How can we improve those streets? Can we put up streetlights? Can we encourage more mixed-use zoning so that there are more people walking to and from restaurants at night?' they are seeing where people are being arrested, and they're mapping that. And those maps, based on police statistics, are shaping patrols. And so you have police going not necessarily where people in communities feel less safe but where police *already* had an overwhelming presence, because how otherwise would you get a database of tickets and arrests from that exact area?"[64] The result is a heavier, undesired police presence and yet another dilution of the citizens' ability to consent to the manner of their own governance.

Chapter Six

A Game of Telephone

Favoring Expediency over Transparency,
and Precedent over Fairness

When people imagine the law, they often think of it as a heavy book. Black letters on white paper, setting forth a series of rules. In some countries, that *is* how law works. But in ours, the law as it is written is just a starting point, because what the law "is," and how it is applied to human beings, are never fully contained in the law as it is written.

Instead of imagining the law as a book, it might make more sense to imagine each point of law as a room full of pages of text-covered paper hanging from the ceiling so that they brush your face a little as you walk through. At the back of the room, yes, you find the original piece of paper with a rule written on it, but the vines of paper surrounding it comprise every single time a judge *interpreted* that law in a published decision, branching out into interpretations that might vary from place to place, making the very same rule wildly different in Indiana than it is in New Mexico. The interpretations layer—each new one discusses the one before, quotes from it, and then builds on it a little bit—and add new pieces of understanding (or complexity) to the growing body of jurisprudence evolving from the original law.

Where the rubber meets the road—in the trial courtrooms of America, where ordinary people try to assert their rights—the rules that are imposed are these distillations of the original rule, called *case law* because the rule that decides a case comes from other cases interpreting the original law. This is where lawyers really get to roll up their sleeves, because judges, of course, can disagree, and no two cases are ever exactly alike. So the lawyers on each side find the cases that most agree with their side. Then they go in front of a judge and argue in court about how *this* case is much more like *these* cases that came before rather than *those* cases that came before. You say this raven is like a writing desk and I say the raven is a prophet, a thing of evil, prophet still if bird or devil, and then we each give reasons, and the judge gets to decide what the raven is.

So, for example, the Sixth Amendment to our Constitution says, "In all criminal prosecutions, the accused shall enjoy the right to a speedy and public trial, by an impartial jury of the State and district wherein the crime shall have been committed, which district shall have been previously ascertained by law, and to be informed of the nature and cause of the accusation; to be confronted with the witnesses against him; to have compulsory process for obtaining witnesses in his favor, and to have the Assistance of Counsel for his defense." Zoom in on the part that says an accused person has a right to "be informed of the nature and cause of the accusation" and "be confronted with the witnesses against him," and a reasonable person might argue that accused people have the right to be presented with the evidence against them prior to trial.

But then the reasonable person would read the case law.

Brady v. Maryland, a landmark decision, pointed out that the government has an obligation to hand over material evidence that is favorable to the defense.[1] This really feels like it should be a floor. Yes, if the government is accusing you of a crime, and they also have evidence you didn't do the crime, they should have to hand that over—at minimum. And since the only people who have that evidence are the prosecutorial team, it's up to the prosecutor to decide what is or is not *Brady* evidence.

Some prosecutors are pretty ethical about this; they understand the truth-seeking function of disclosure, and they use something like what Michael, our former prosecutor, describes as his "shit test": "If you say 'Shit' when you see it, you hand it over."[2] In other words, if it is something that doesn't help the prosecution's case, it gets sent to the other side for a closer look.

But there's an immediate expertise problem with this: a defense lawyer, who thinks about these things all day, might see six different ways in which a seemingly bland or neutral fact might be exculpatory. Eli Northrup, my former Bronx Defenders colleague, recalls representing a man who had been in a car with his friend. In Eli's case, police were claiming that his client had "Jamaican beads" hanging from the rearview mirror, and that's why they stopped him. Eli's defense hinged on the fact that police were lying about the stop: the car hadn't actually been moving at all, but rather parked in a driveway. The case dragged on, and in the middle of the trial Eli found out that the other guy in the car—who had been charged in a separate filing, and who had his own lawyer—had police documents in *his* case saying that the stop had been for an illegal turn, with no mention of any "Jamaican beads." The prosecutor had overlooked this difference, but to a defense lawyer it was like a flashing neon sign reading POLICE MADE THIS UP. Though this is clearly *Brady* evidence, the person deciding whether this inconsistency was "material" to the case was someone with a vested interest in finding it immaterial, and the result was that, without months of insistence and fighting from a good defense lawyer, two men could have been ground down into guilty pleas without ever knowing there was documented evidence of law enforcement wobbling about the reason for the stop.

Sometimes, case law holds true to certain core principles. And sometimes, a series of cases, laid out over the years, operate more like a game of telephone, each one muddling—or riffing on—the one before. This is what happened with *Brady:* American courts steadily winnowed down the idea of what an accused person was entitled to.

With *Brady,* courts can find themselves arguing over what evidence is "material." In a case called *Strickler v. Greene,* for example, the 1999

Supreme Court required the government to turn over evidence that directly contradicted the testimony of the one eyewitness in the case . . . but said they *wouldn't* have had to turn it over if they had other evidence strong enough to get their guilty verdict without that witness. Prosecutors get to replay an imaginary other trial in their head, and make decisions accordingly.[3]

And *Brady*, of course, applies only to evidence that a court can clearly see suggests the accused person isn't guilty ("exculpatory" evidence) or shows that a witness may be lying ("impeachment" evidence). But what about the rest of the evidence? Is there any right to see that, if you're accused of a crime?

The Sixth Amendment says that an accused person gets to know the nature and cause of their accusation. But over the years, courts have not adopted the simplest interpretation of that clause (which would be that a person gets to see the evidence against them in full before trial). Instead, the rules of "discovery" in state courts—the rules that define when and how a person gets to see the evidence against them—mutated slowly into a convoluted pile of interpretations and opinions.

Take the discovery rules of New York, for example. A 1973 Supreme Court decision arising out of Oregon[4] noted that the due process clause (which says no one may be deprived of life, liberty, or property without *due process* of law) is pretty vague as to discovery rules, but also noted that you can't force a defendant to give the government notice of their alibi if the government doesn't have to hand over "reciprocal" discovery to the defense. Turnabout is fair play, right?

Four years later, in 1977, the Supreme Court references that decision, but only for the point that "there is *no general constitutional right to discovery* in a criminal case, and *Brady* did not create one. And as the Court wrote recently, 'the Due Process Clause has little to say regarding the amount of discovery which the parties must be afforded.'"[5] Wait! This case isn't just about alibis! Instead, it goes on to say that if a government witness *lies* to the defense about whether they're not going to testify, well, too bad, because the defendant doesn't even have a right to know who will testify against them at trial.

Over a decade later, in a 1988 New York case, the New York Court of Appeals (the highest court in the state) decided that this meant it got to go a whole huge step further, establishing that there is simply "no general constitutional right to discovery in criminal cases."

Mind you, we have ventured into a completely different set of facts by now. The original call here was about whether a defendant has to tell the prosecutor whether they're going to say they have an alibi, when the prosecution doesn't have any parallel duty to disclose evidence. Now we're somehow in a situation where a guy was accused of speeding and had requested (as discovery) "certain documents and information pertaining to the type of radar used, and its associated testing and operating procedures."[6] Seems reasonable—he wanted to be able to cross examine the traffic cop with decent information about the tool the cop used to zap his car. Which—when we go back to the Sixth Amendment—seems to have everything to do with whether he can adequately "confront" the witness against him. But the court says no, turning a decision about alibi evidence into a justification for stripping the entire right to discovery in New York criminal court. And that "no," contained in a scant two-paragraph opinion, has been referenced in sixty-four subsequent cases about whether a person has a right to see and test the evidence against them.

It's easy to get lost in this forest of opinions and interpretations and lose track of where these decisions are coming from. In the end, it resulted in a bit of a weird rule nationally: the government has to hand over material, exculpatory evidence to accused people, but whether they have to hand over anything else is kind of up to the individual states, which can make whatever scheme they want.

When you look at what evidence accused people have a right to see before trial around the country, it's wildly different from place to place.[7] In California, an accused person has the right to receive a list of witnesses who will be called at trial, statements from any and all defendants, "all relevant real evidence seized or obtained as a part of the investigation of the offenses charged," felony convictions of any witnesses on whose credibility the case might hinge, exculpatory evidence, prior written or recorded statements of trial witnesses, including experts, and of course the results of any scientific tests used at trial.[8] But in South Carolina, the government need only turn over (at the defendant's request) any of the defendant's *own* statements, documents, and prior record, as well as other documents, lab tests, experimental results, or objects that will be used in the case, but *not* statements from witnesses who will testify . . . until *after* the witness has testified on direct examination.[9] If you're accused of a crime in South Carolina, you have essentially no way to know what to probe a witness on before the moment of cross examination, and since we know more than 90 percent of cases will never make it to trial,[10] this means that the vast majority of people will plead guilty without ever getting to check whether the witness against them has made contradictory statements about the crime. When I went from defending the public in California (where we had "open file" discovery, and—usually—I got the evidence I needed well before trial, allowing me to properly prepare) to New York (where the overall vibe was, "let's play a fun game where you go to trial with almost no information and see what happens"), I almost couldn't believe that New York could get discovery law so wrong. It was the legal equivalent of thinking you're going to Brooklyn and winding up somehow playing croquet with the Queen of Hearts.

You may, at this point, feel you've followed me down a lawyerly rabbit hole. And you're right: criminal court discovery rules are convoluted and contradictory, headache inducing, and often surprisingly unusable. We probably shouldn't call them "discovery" at all. In civil court—as opposed to criminal court—where disputes do not land one side in prison, you get to see the other side's goods before trial. You get to actively interrogate their witnesses, wield artful subpoenas, and *demand* information from your opponent. This kind of access is required; some of it has to be turned over early on even if the other side hasn't asked for it, so they can get a basic picture of the facts and figure out what they do need to ask for.[11] And unlike *Brady*, where only exculpatory evidence must be turned over even if it isn't requested, in civil cases you've got to hand over whatever you think is helpful to your case. What we have in criminal court is so far removed it could more accurately be called plain old secrecy.

We didn't get here by accident. Ion Meyn, a law professor and expert in discovery, procedure, and its history, has written extensively about how modern criminal court discovery rules emerged from a singularly American miasma of punitive urges and racist ideas. Criminal and civil court procedures didn't used to be so far apart—from about the year 1400 until the 1930s, there was generally one set of rules for all court proceedings. But in the New Deal era, broad agreement arose that these rules were clunky and not working well, so Congress asked the U.S. Supreme Court to appoint a commission to write new rules for both systems.[12] These rules—the Federal Rules of Civil Procedure—were finished in 1938. A signature feature was the creation of "broad, open-handed discovery." Although there has been some trimming in recent decades to make civil discovery more efficient,[13] it remains true that more civil rules are dedicated to achieving "mutual knowledge of the relevant facts"[14] before trial than any other part of civil litigation. After they were adopted in 1938, a committee was established to write rules for federal criminal courts. Ideally, rules for state courts to use as a model.

We could easily have just kept on keeping on with all court rules—civil and criminal—matching. The committee's first instinct was to do just that. But one notable prosecutor on the committee made it his mission to strip the defense of the usual powers of pretrial discovery. Alexander Holtzoff, DOJ prosecutor, was a deeply political creature. In the meetings of this commission, "he contradicted himself for days with one sole purpose, which was to ensure that the defense would be worse off. If you look at everything that was preserved and everything that was rejected in the drafts, you can see a through-line of increasing prosecutorial advantage," according to Professor Meyn. His goal was evident in

his choices, where, at every turn, he "preferred existing common law practices over [new] civil rules, unless the civil rule better facilitated prosecution."[15]

Holtzoff got his way, winning a set of rules that bore little resem-
blance to what counts as "fair play" in civil court, and, after the fact, described his thinking: "Criminals should not go unwhipped of justice
because of technicalities having no connection with the merits of the
accusation. . . . Any form of criminal procedure that unnecessarily hampers and unduly hinders the successful fulfillment of this duty must be
discarded or radically changed."

The "whipped" language was not accidental: in a world where 99 percent of litigants in civil court were white, the disadvantage of Black defendants in criminal court was a clear, essentially overt intention. "The
committee published comments that asserted it was a white burden to
represent Black defendants because Black defendants, when they speak,
only implicate themselves and are not the best witnesses. These racial
stereotypes were used to help justify the lack of discovery, as if it was to
protect Black defendants from tripping themselves up in their incompetence," said Professor Meyn.

The rules of the game were rewritten to maintain white power. The
result is that nearly a century later, we're still using rules designed to
ensure Holtzoff's vision of "expeditious prosecution."[16]

Discovery isn't the only space in criminal law where the laws have
been evidently written to create separate and unequal rules for Black
and white defendants. Gang designations and injunctions are a striking
example of how police and prosecutors have been allowed to designate
entire swaths of the community for heightened surveillance and disfa-
vorable rules in court.

Gang injunctions, for example, can be issued on reentry or pretrial—
a person is ordered not to associate with (or live with, or take a work shift
with, or share parenting duties with) anyone police have designated as a
gang member. The problem is, police designation of gang membership
is notoriously flawed. California police, for example, were revealed to

have put babies into gang databases,[17] utterly undermining public credence in the police's ability to identify who is and is not a real threat.

Gang designation also, like all other forms of policing, is not equally distributed. Although gang laws are often so broadly written as to encompass essentially any group (even three people) with a unifying symbol who break the law together, six white fraternity brothers drunk in public and breaking mailboxes with a baseball bat will essentially never be designated a gang. Yet it's common to meet Black and brown kids who were designated gang members purely because they were seen with the "wrong" kid, or have a "wrong" relative, or were present—as a bystander—at the scene of a gang crime. There's a reason that only 1.5 percent of people in New York's gang database are white, and the reason is not that white people never engage in criminal activity as a group.[18] After all, Irish, Italian, and Russian mobs are routinely prosecuted using RICO statutes or other criminal conspiracy laws. But, conspicuously, rarely under gang statutes.

This difference is significant. Conspiracy laws, for example, require a more rigorous showing from prosecutors; they require that prosecutors prove, beyond a reasonable doubt, that a conspiracy to commit a crime existed and that the prosecuted individuals took steps to carry out that plan. Gang prosecution, on the other hand, offers a much lower bar. Most gang laws require only that prosecutors prove the existence of a gang, the association of the accused individual with that gang, and some kind of assistance (or even just "promotion," a word whose definitional stretchiness abounds) of the gang's felonious activity. Which means that if a gang is out there doing awful things to people, and there's a kid associated with the gang only through a friend, who does no awful things but drives his friend around sometimes, this uninvolved kid can be prosecuted under gang law . . . but not conspiracy statutes. The conspiracy law would require the prosecutor to show that he was actually working toward a criminal plan with the gang. The gang statutes? Not so much.

Moreover, it also enables prosecutors to present all kinds of evidence that would never normally be allowed in court. For example, in an ordinary, non-gang prosecution, a prosecutor could never admit evidence that the accused was *friends* with a Very Bad Dude who did all kinds of (unrelated) crimes (which the accused never participated in). But in gang prosecution, proving the existence of the gang allows prosecutors to put unrelated crimes by other people in front of juries, amping up prejudice against the person who currently stands accused but who might have had nothing to do with these other, unrelated crimes, other than being friends with the wrong people.

The result of these designations and surveillance is that Black and brown families are disproportionately torn apart. Defenders have seen gang injunctions force a mother to choose which of her children can live at home, or compel a father to leave his family so that his kids can stay. These orders further intrude into every area of a family's life: one fellow defender came back from juvenile court shaken by having witnessed a judge bringing a young mom to tears over gang injunction rules. She had been told her child was not allowed to wear red, blue, purple, or green, so she had spent money she didn't have to buy the kid gray clothes, only to be told the money was wasted, because those weren't allowed either. Like many rules of supervision, the dictates aren't tailored or responsive to a person's actual life, challenges, or merits—they're applied with the same blunt force as DMV rules, just with much more devastating, pervasive consequences.[19]

It's truly hard to justify a process that sets up an adversarial system to find truth and then keeps one half of that adversarial equation in the dark or creates separate rules for people depending on race, culture, and police perception. A person accused of a crime should have simple, universal rights, such as the right to inspect the evidence against them. The state comes up with evidence of a crime, the accused person gets to stress test that evidence and try to poke holes in it, and if the evidence is strong, the person is convicted. And if the evidence is weak, perhaps the person *shouldn't* be convicted.

Most laypeople have been kept in the dark about the real aftermath of a wrongful conviction. Yes, there are multiple episodes of *Law & Order* in which a wrongful conviction is discovered and the lead character, Prosecutor Jack McCoy, must grapple with the system having put an innocent person in prison, but in almost every case the situation is quickly remedied. "I voided the conviction," Jack says, and we all move swiftly on with our lives. In truth, the horror of wrongful conviction is far less easily undone.

In 2006, a law professor named Mary Prosser wrote an article about a case she had worked on as a young lawyer.[20] In that case, a group of young men committed two armed robberies on Halloween. The scene was violent: a victim was robbed, pistol-whipped; a shot was fired, which grazed the victim's foot. After the first robbery, the group went into a shop, pointed the gun at the owner, demanded money, and shot the owner in the leg when he resisted. The group took money from the register and left.

Both victims were taken to the police station and shown mug shots. Reportedly, they both picked the same photograph as the man with the gun, but gave different descriptions; one victim said this man had been dressed in tan, the other said dressed in blue. There are many, many factors in a case like this that can profoundly affect the memory of witnesses, leading to recollections that are high in confidence but low in accuracy—a topic we'll get to in a minute. But first, who was the man in the photograph?

The man in the photograph was an individual Professor Prosser pseudonymously refers to as Mr. Williams. He was arrested a few weeks after the incident, and immediately gave an alibi: on Halloween, he had been at home, having a party with his mother, wife, child, and other relatives. The officers' reply? "Tell it to the court."

He tried. Mr. Williams denied participating in the robberies again and again. The prosecutor still charged him; the case still went to a preliminary hearing. At the hearing, Mr. Williams's lawyer spoke with the police, who "let slip" that there was another "suspect or suspects" but refused to give any further information. So the lawyer tried to ask these officers about the other suspects when the officers got on the witness stand—but was stopped by the prosecutor, who objected to the questions because it was an "ongoing investigation." The judge agreed, and the defense wasn't allowed to ask the questions.

The store owner testified that he'd seen the robbers around the neighborhood, and said there had been other people in the store right before the robbery—two girls—but couldn't say who they were. Both victims identified Mr. Williams, from the witness stand, as having been the man with the gun.

It took many months for Mr. Williams's case to go to trial. During that time, the defense tried to find out more about what was going on with these other suspects, but police and prosecution revealed nothing. The defense filed motions with the court, asking for information about alternate suspects, and also asking for the names and addresses of the other witnesses. The judge ordered the prosecution to provide discovery, but the prosecution "dragged his heels." More motions were filed, a new prosecutor was assigned to the case, and the new prosecutor then handed over information, which finally allowed the defense to further investigate.

What they found was deeply troubling. A young woman who went to high school near the store had spoken to her school counselor days after the robberies, saying that she had seen the robbers going into the store as she was leaving and that she recognized them from school. She was afraid, because they had seen her there, and asked to be transferred to another school. She gave the names of the robbers to the principal and vice-principal of the school. Crucially, Mr. Williams was not one of the names she gave; indeed, he was not a student at the school, not a teenager at all, didn't live in the neighborhood, had no record, didn't know these girls, and had an alibi.

The school called the police and told them everything. The police said that they already had a suspect in custody. They were not interested in this new information.

The police never investigated the new information, spoke with the girl, or looked at any of the suspects she identified. They never showed her a lineup or photographs that included the people she named. They never made a report about any of this. They never attempted to confirm or discredit Mr. Williams's alibi—that he was having a party with multiple people present, an easily verifiable claim. And by the time the defense learned of this information, after months of delays, any potential school witnesses had largely forgotten what they knew. A school year had gone by, the key girl was gone, they couldn't remember her name or where she might have transferred to. They did remember the names she had given, though, and it turned out that those three people went to the school, lived near the store, fit the description of the robbers, and had violent priors.

This, of course, isn't just a discovery problem; it's a *Brady* violation. The material that the defense was denied wasn't just any old evidence, but evidence that was material to the case and tended to indicate Mr. Williams was innocent. The delay in revealing this information to the defense resulted in irreparable loss of memories and a key witness. The prosecutor, to his credit, said that he would not appeal a dismissal, if the judge chose to dismiss the case because of the *Brady* violation. After all, he wasn't the original prosecutor on the case, it wasn't his doing, and he also didn't think that Mr. Williams matched the victims' initial description anyway—one victim had said the robber had markings on his face, and Mr. Williams didn't have any markings.

At this point, the decision about whether the case against Mr. Williams—a husband, father, young man with a future—goes to trial is in the judge's hands. But the prosecutor has *prosecutorial discretion,* meaning that they get to choose which cases to pursue and which to drop, based on their legal ethical obligation to *do justice.* A prosecutor's job isn't, technically, to pursue all possible convictions, but to do what is right. Yet again and again in the real world, the incentives of the system seem to push prosecutors to do things more like the first and second prosecutors in Mr. Williams's case. The first one failed in his duty to adequately investigate the charges (to say the least), and the second one came clean but didn't exercise his prosecutorial discretion to drop the case. Instead, he said he didn't think Mr. Williams was the guy, and said he'd be fine if the *judge* dismissed the case.

But the judge did not dismiss it. Instead, saying it was a close call, the judge allowed the case to proceed. At this point, the prosecutor *still* could have dismissed the case. After all, he didn't believe he had the right guy, and he was now aware of this growing mountain of evidence suggesting that the real robbers were on the loose. And yet, after all that, he did not dismiss. He went to trial. Mr. Williams's defense counsel could not produce the unnamed girl. Her evidence, for legal purposes, had vanished.

Mr. Williams was convicted and sentenced to state prison.

Professor Prosser concludes her story: "And that's the end. There is no subsequent exoneration in this story. As with many crimes, no physical evidence was collected. Perhaps none ever existed that could have been tested then (or later) by better scientific methods. This was not a high-profile case that might have drawn witnesses to come forward to give new evidence. This was, in many ways, a very ordinary case."[21]

In the real world, there is no Jack McCoy "voiding" wrongful convictions like this. And in many cases, there is no DNA evidence or late-discovered videotape that solves the case and frees the innocent. Unfortunately, most wrongful convictions look more like Mr. Williams's case: official misconduct (or even laziness), bad eyewitness testimony (a factor in nearly 70 percent of wrongful convictions),[22] and the permanent loss of crucial evidence through bad investigation and police inaction. The system prioritizes expediency over accuracy; both state and federal systems have legal rules in place that sharply limit when a person can try to reopen their case and argue that the trial court got it wrong.

President Bill Clinton signed a law cleverly called the Antiterrorism and Effective Death Penalty Act (AEDPA), which sounds as if it protects you from terrorists but which, in actuality, cuts back the ability of people in prison to ask courts to take a second look at their convictions.[23]

In the 1990s, when the rise of DNA exonerations was revealing to the American public how fallible our courts really are, this law forced federal courts to defer to state court rulings, even when those rulings were largely wrong, and even if the ruling was so wrong a judge probably shouldn't be on the bench anymore. AEDPA put in place sharp and arbitrary deadlines that have, over the years, denied thousands of people access to meaningful habeas corpus.

If we were to have a contest for what the worst criminal law on the books is, AEDPA would be a strong front-runner. AEDPA is just one of many statutes and legal schemes restricting the right to have a bad conviction reviewed, meaning that it can prevent higher courts from undoing the mistakes of lower courts. To quote a prominent law textbook on the topic, the combination of AEDPA and existing doctrines created by judges over the years amounts to "a maze of requirements through which almost no petitions successfully emerge." While about 3–4 percent of people in state prison who filed petitions in federal court were able to get relief back in the 1970s and 1980s, that number dropped to 0.6 percent by 2004 for people not sentenced to death. For people sentenced to death, AEDPA also lowered their chances of finding relief in the federal courts—while about 40 percent of death-sentenced people got relief between 1973 and 1995, by 2002 that number had dropped to 9 percent.[24]

Some of this might have been because of AEDPA's requirement that the state court have wrongly applied "clearly established" Supreme Court precedent. But what if the Supreme Court hasn't clearly established any law on a given point? So, for example, in a case like *Lockyer v. Andrade,* where a guy stole some videotapes and was sentenced to two consecutive sentences of twenty-five years to life under California's Three Strikes law, the Court found that the sentence could not be undone as violating the Eighth Amendment's ban on cruel and unusual punishment, because it failed to fully and unequivocally violate clearly established Supreme Court precedent. Yet Justice Sandra Day O'Connor, writing for the majority, admitted that the existing case law was not a "model of clarity," suggesting that even though there wasn't much clearly established law to consider, Mr. Andrade was *still* required to prove that the lower court had violated "clearly established" precedent—a hopeless Catch-22.[25] The highest court in the land couldn't undo a horrifying sentence because of a Congress-created technicality.

There are many justifications for this law, such as the idea that finality is a part of due process, or the argument that many petitions are frivolous; the idea that federalism requires federal courts to defer to state criminal process; or the argument that plenty of cases might have had mistakes, but that doesn't mean the person is factually innocent, so they shouldn't get their case reversed. And if finality and lower case volumes were the only legitimate goals, these justifications might make sense. But they can't justify blocking courts from meaningfully *considering* a claim. How can one justify the risk that a person who has been subject to a life-altering error might not be able to find a legal path to reconsideration and relief?

In recent years, the Supreme Court has tightened access to relief even further, holding that AEDPA says people cannot get their conviction overturned because of a wholly inadequate defense (*Shinn v. Martinez Ramirez,* 2022), or because of failure to present exonerating medical evidence (also *Shinn v. Martinez Ramirez*), or because their judge actually misinterpreted the law and convicted them for conduct that wasn't actually a crime (*Jones v. Hendrix,* 2023). As Arizona's lawyer Brunn Wall Roysden III said to the Supreme Court in *Shinn,* "Innocence isn't enough."[26]

⸺

If innocence isn't enough for reconsideration, then getting things right the first time seems even more important. And of course, time is of the essence: in a country where only about 5 percent of cases ever make it to trial,[27] keeping people in the dark, without discovery, until the eve of trial means that millions of people are being asked to plead guilty without ever seeing the evidence against them. And of course, some plea deals involve asking the person pleading guilty to also give up their right to appeal, so convictions arising from these discoveryless, flying-in-the-dark guilty pleas may never see the sunlight of an appellate court's review. As Professor Prosser points out in her article, this kind of one-sided informational disadvantage would seem insane in any other area of law. "Imagine a person's reaction to a lawyer counseling his client in a divorce case about the issue of a property settlement":

> Your husband has made an offer, which he says is a generous offer. It would be nice to know what assets he has, but we can't force him to disclose his assets and you have always let him handle the finances. If we go to trial, we might learn [this offer is] more than the law requires or that the judge would award you, or we might find out he's been holding out on us and you [were] better off [refusing the offer and] going to trial. Of course, I can't guarantee we'll actually be able to prove he has more than he claims. What do you want to do?

The example above feels laughable, but only because it removes the stigma of criminal accusation. Unfortunately, criminal courts ask lawyers to provide advice to their clients based on strikingly incomplete information every day.

Furthermore, as Mr. Williams's case makes so appallingly clear, delayed revelation of evidence means delayed investigation, and evidence is harder to come by after time has passed and memories have faded. If we want a system that seeks truth, the evidence of a crime should be disclosed at the outset of a case, in each and every case.

So why isn't that the rule across the fifty states?

Historically, discovery practices have sprouted from some pretty bad ideas. First is the assumption of guilt. Even though our system is supposed to presume every accused person innocent until proven guilty (and, of course, an innocent person would be unaware of the evidence against them . . . because they're innocent), discovery practices are often rooted in an assumption that the accused person must *already know* the evidence, because, of course, they're guilty and they were there at the time of the incident. Just look at *McCleskey v. Zant*,[28] in which a man in prison brought a habeas petition, claiming that the prosecutor in his case had withheld a lengthy statement from a jailhouse informant who said Mr. McCleskey had confessed to him. Mr. McCleskey said this conversation never happened, and also wanted to argue that the statement reflected a kind of quid pro quo between the prosecution and the jailhouse informant—favorable treatment in exchange for fingering McCleskey, a common feature of cooperation agreements. Mr. McCleskey was just asking the judge to order the prosecution to hand over the statement. The judge refused, based on the assumption that Mr. McCleskey "participated in the conversations" (which of course were the very conversations McCleskey claimed had never even *happened*) and therefore "he knew everything in the document." Habeas denied.

Another bad assumption is the implicit assumption that nasty defense lawyers are getting up to some nasty tricks. Yes, there are cases where witness intimidation may be a very real risk—organized crime matters with a track record of intimidation, for example. But these are cases that can be easily distinguished and dealt with on a case-by-case basis, and don't justify the weird idea that, perhaps, if the prosecution is asked to reveal who their witnesses will be at trial, the defense might routinely go out and intimidate the witnesses into changing their stories.[29] In the words of Professor Prosser, "This view assumes bad faith solely of the criminal defendant. It does not acknowledge that police and prosecutors exercise considerable power to influence witnesses by threats or rewards for particular testimony and that sometimes they have knowingly presented perjured testimony to secure a conviction."[30] In reality, defense lawyers are largely subject to the same ethical rules and restrictions as prosecutors, and risk losing their license if they engage in misconduct—an accountability structure that has justified the choice to give broad latitude for prosecutors, but somehow doesn't have the same effect for the defense.

A lot of these assumptions have been shaped by prosecutors offering their perspective to lawmakers. Prosecutors, in general, have a fair amount of success lobbying for bills, especially with Republican legislatures.[31] And recall that the federal rules were directly influenced by a prosecutor. Still, it's puzzling why someone interested in justice would want to shield crucial evidence from testing. After all, handing things over early lowers the chances of an (even accidental) *Brady* violation, protecting the integrity of the whole case (and meaning that, if they secure a conviction, it's less likely to be overturned on appeal).

One would also think that most prosecutors would *personally* not want to cause a wrongful conviction, and that there would be a certain sense of a safety net against that outcome in letting the defense investigate and double-check the work of the police.

In a class I teach at Stanford Law School, I often ask students to engage in exercises where they take the part of prosecution and defense lawyers. In one exercise, I was struck by a student's actions in her role, which was the role of the prosecutor. She had gone off script, becoming more punitive than the rules of the game suggested she should, and at a certain point declined to negotiate further with her counterpart. When I asked her, during our debrief, about how she had been feeling during the negotiation, she expressed how worried she'd been about being *tricked* somehow by the defense. In just a one-hour class exercise, she had somehow already replicated a theme in the prosecution/defense dynamic, where some prosecutors seem to believe that early and complete disclosure of the evidence might give the defense too much of a chance to pull some sneaky lawyer magic. (I wish I had sneaky lawyer magic; the best I've ever been able to do is hard work and good one-liners.)

Yet concerns about stupid lawyer tricks can almost always be assuaged by having discovery be "reciprocal," meaning that *both* sides disclose their witnesses, experts, and certain legal claims early. Studies on open discovery have found that instead of allowing guilty people to evade conviction, "participants' access to discovery information, including exculpatory information, significantly influenced both ratings of the strength of the evidence against them and their perceived probability of conviction at trial."[32] A little sunlight, here, is healthy for the innocent and the guilty alike.

The bigger concern among prosecutors, though, is far more mundane: handing over complete discovery early in a case is a lot of work. Nowhere has this been more clear than in New York. In a state with a progressive reputation, the discovery rules, for decades, were startlingly medieval: only select materials had to be handed over to the defense, and many incredibly important pieces of evidence (like the statements of witnesses) only needed to be delivered in time for cross examination. People were being arrested, held on Rikers Island, indicted by a grand jury, and allowed to languish while their case dragged on for years, all without their attorney having a full understanding of the evidence against them. In 2019, all that changed.

Under a new law, prosecutors in New York were required to hand over the evidence that was in their possession. Not *some* of the evidence, not only what they thought was important or exculpatory, not only materials *requested* by the defense. All of it. Automatically. And crucially, right away. No more letting people sit at Rikers with no sense of the evidence against them. Things they could previously withhold until trial—witness statements, recordings of 911 calls, contact information for people with information about the case—were now to be handed over within fifteen days of arraignment. And blind guilty pleas were off the table—if a person was offered a plea, they must be given full discovery before the expiration of the plea offer.

It sounds simple. If you're going to bring the full weight of the government, and its capacity to punish, down on an ordinary person, you need to have evidence and you need to hand that evidence over right away. Get used to the scanner at your office, it's your friend. But in the wake of the new law, prosecutors started appearing in the press, claiming that these obligations were so difficult they could no longer function in their jobs. Headlines claimed that New York prosecutors were leaving their jobs in droves,[33] driven out by endless photocopying of witness statements. Given that the New York law was roughly similar to the statutory scheme that California prosecutors have managed to work under for decades, the reaction of the New York DAs drew something like a collective eye roll from the defense bar.

The most common argument against open and immediate discovery is that it's too hard. That prosecutorial caseloads are too high, and the police are uneven enough at actually providing material to prosecutors, making robust discovery rules unduly difficult. One prosecutor I spoke with pointed out that not everything in their file is discoverable; there are notes and outlines and lawyerly impressions in those files, too, which must be taken out before the file is handed over. And certainly, one must acknowledge that yes, sifting through a file and handing over the right things, promptly and thoroughly, does create work for prosecutors. But their lives are not on the line. And in many conversations about discovery reform, this is where we land: that the liberty interest of the ordinary person is far more important than the comfort of a prosecutor's workload.

Morally, that is probably sensible. Practically, it doesn't lead to great results—burned-out, stressed, overwhelmed prosecutors don't make great decisions, and as we saw in Mr. Williams's case, healthy, equitable decision-making ability is also a crucial check on the system's ability to slide toward carceral chaos. They also make more mistakes, and prosecutorial mistakes cost lives.

The right answer is to lower the workload for everyone involved, defense and prosecution alike. With 80 percent of cases in the criminal court system being misdemeanors, it's clear that the bulk of the cases weighing everyone down are things that might not need to be in the legal system in the first place: driver's license problems, trespassing, fare violations, petty crime, small amounts of drugs, disorderly conduct. In cities that have added a separate line of first responders equipped to deal with mental health concerns, these teams have managed thousands of civilian contacts with zero fatalities (unlike police),[34] shepherded in lower reported crime, and substantially dropped 911 costs overall.[35]

Another answer is to address the "decision fatigue" that limited discovery creates for the prosecution. When, in the heat of trial preparation, the only person making judgment calls about what the evidence will be, what is "material," and, of course, what is *exculpatory* is the prosecutor, their workload is increased, and the weight of the entire accuracy of the process may be falling on a lawyer with hundreds of cases. They may not even have all the evidence, because police might have neglected to turn over crucial things, leaving the prosecution unable to fully assess what needs to be turned over. Affording prosecutors stronger technological processes and support staff to make the sending of material to the defense essentially automatic could reduce and shift the work of disclosure, removing one of the primary objections to open discovery.

Looking back at New York, things have settled down. After an initial negative reaction to the more expansive discovery rule, prosecutors changed their minds, and just asked for more funding to implement the new rules.[36] The defense asked for the same; after all, with reciprocal discovery should come reciprocal funding. The results, so far, have been strong: 92 percent of defense attorneys surveyed said that the new rules have improved their ability to investigate their cases, 93 percent said they improved their ability to advise their clients, 81 percent said they improved their ability to negotiate with the prosecution, and 77 percent said they were better able to write meaningful motions. Nine out of ten defense attorneys surveyed said that the reform had a positive impact on their ability to prepare for hearings and trials, and that they now spent more time reviewing the evidence in their cases. While 79 percent said that they now had to spend more time on each case, 80 percent still agreed that the reform had made criminal case proceedings fairer in New York.[37] Other researchers have found that the reforms have increased court efficiency by reducing needless pretrial motions, shortening the pendency of cases overall (since no more time is being wasted trying to get ahold of discovery, and people can more accurately and rapidly assess plea offers made to them), and reducing lengthy appeals arising from discovery problems.[38] Perhaps, for once, a system of laws is beginning to shake off its adherence to its years and roomfuls of hanging paper, looking not to the most recent rulings of the legal world but to the Sixth Amendment right they are supposed to protect.

Chapter Seven

Weird Science

How Bad Forensics Leads to Bad Convictions

For decades, people have watched shows like *CSI* and *Bones* and excitedly followed along as a team of brilliant, dedicated, deeply moral scientists with ample resources and cutting-edge technology figures out who done it based on a funny smell detected on the tip of a pencil, or the DNA of a rare particle of plant leaves found at the scene. They can take blurry video and magically render it HD just by saying, "Enhance that!" It's enormous fun. It's also complete fantasy, leading the public to believe that most forensic science is strong, neutral, and fair. The truth is far more depressing.

To begin with, we have to consider *what* gets to come into court and wear the cloak of being "science." You might think that scientists would be in charge of deciding what practice or field of study is robust and reliable enough to meet that bar—and you'd be wrong. It's judges.

Science can't walk into court by itself; in order to be "admitted into evidence," it has to be talked about by a witness, who can authenticate any reports and be examined in front of the jury, explaining it all for a lay audience. "Expert" witnesses get treated differently from lay witnesses; for example, they're allowed to express their opinions, while lay witnesses are only allowed to talk about the facts. Understandably, they're also highly persuasive to juries, who are told all about the background of the expert, their credentials, and how carefully they analyzed the evidence.

But who gets to be an expert, and what methods and scientific approaches they can testify about, is up to the judge. A lawyer who wants to bring in an expert witness and scientific evidence has to present these experts and methods to the judge, who then applies the correct legal standards (we're back to that room full of case law hanging in your face). First off, the witness has to have some kind of qualifying expertise, but what qualifies as "expertise"?

Back in the nineteenth century, courts took a "sporting" approach to expert testimony, letting in almost any expert who could make a living in their field and setting up a situation "where quality control was exercised not by judges in excluding testimony, but by the parties through cross-examination and the adversarial process."[1] But of course, because people will inevitably make cottage industries of almost anything, this resulted in partisan experts who were as "effective in producing obscurity and error, as in the elucidation of truth."[2] It got so bad that the public was losing faith in the courts altogether, and judges were saying things like "opposite opinions of persons professing to be experts may be obtained to any amount"[3] and "there are three kinds of liars: the common liar, the damned liar, and the scientific expert."[4]

So they did something about it. A 1923 case called *Frye v. United States* set a standard that expert testimony should be "deduced from a well-recognized scientific principle or discovery, [and] the thing from which the deduction is made must be sufficiently established to have gained general acceptance in the particular field in which it belongs."[5] And later, *Daubert v. Merrell Dow Pharmaceuticals* affirmed that judges should be the gatekeepers of scientific reliability in court, and asked them to consider things like whether a given method has been generally accepted in the scientific community, whether it has been peer-reviewed, whether it can be (and has been!) tested, and what the known error rate of the practice might be.[6] With these two decisions, the days of the sporting approach were basically over, and judges were tasked with figuring out what science was reliable enough to bring into the life-or-death context of criminal court.

———

Think about what it might be like to be a judge faced with a tricky scientific question. You have spent your career parsing statutes and reading case law. You were a history major in college. You are a completely decent human who fears making a bad decision that will cause an unjust outcome in court. And you are being asked to decide the admission into evidence of an expert whose field you know nothing about. You have no training on this. All you have is the information the parties have given you in their briefing—the prosecutor has cited the lengthy résumé of the expert and all her publications, and the defense has given you a corresponding briefing on new research coming out suggesting her methods *may* have flaws—but if the defense literature is correct, these flaws are incredibly serious and impugn the credibility of her larger field.

This is the decision faced by judges across the country every day. In a system clogged with millions of cases per year, though, a lawyer's ability to spend time doing research and building a strong briefing is curtailed, making it more likely that judges have to make these tricky scientific decisions based on residual feelings of confidence about the field and its intuitive trustworthiness rather than by taking a hard look at the most current data. Worse, the volume of cases in the system means that judges themselves are often incentivized to keep their calendar moving quickly. The result? Court systems may be pressuring judges to make *any* decisions rather than offering support for *good* decisions.

The result is, as you would expect, not great for truth or justice. In a survey of four hundred state court judges, 94 percent had little understanding of the falsifiability of research, and 96 percent did not clearly understand what an error rate is—an incredibly big problem when you consider that these are the factors on which they're supposed to make a decision. In fact, 96 percent of these judges ultimately "reported that they had not received instruction about general scientific methods and principles."[7]

When people don't really know what they're doing, they're more likely to rely on vibes.[8] A 2005 study noted an "entrenched judicial unwillingness to review expert evidence at all in criminal cases, much less to assess reliability and restrict expert testimony that is unreliable."[9] This might be why in the five years following the *Daubert* decision, trial courts accepted 96 percent of the experts offered by prosecutors but only about 8 percent of the experts offered by defense attorneys.[10] Junk science has flowed into courtrooms, with a snowball effect: because of our case-law-based system, the more times a type of evidence comes into court, the more likely future courts are to let it come in again. Law journals are filled with analyses of the "*CSI* effect" growing among American jurors, wherein juries place far too much faith in forensic experts, and remain unwitting about the shortcomings of the science.[11] This might be why about half of our growing number of wrongful conviction cases involve bad forensic science.[12]

So what *are* the bad sciences that keep pouring into court? It's hard to list them all, because humans are incredibly inventive and keep coming up with more ideas. Just ask the Iowa College of Law professor Alison Guernsey, who had to fend off a prosecutor's attempt to present a "pimpologist" as an expert at trial—not a social scientist of any kind, mind you, but just a police officer who wanted to testify about what he believed pimps often, or sometimes, or perhaps, do.[13] An appellate court found that this cop could testify as an expert on pimps because a cop with even less relevant experience was previously allowed to testify as an expert on pimps. Precedent![14]

My personal favorite faux-science memory was when I had an officer tell me that he had decided my client was intoxicated because he had measured his pupils with a "pupillometer" and determined that they were dilated. What was this scientific device he used? It turned out it was nothing more than, essentially, a kind of bookmark with circles of different sizes printed on it, which he held up next to my client's face, enabling him to guess which size of circle best matched my client's eyes. That was the "pupillometer."

In response to tactics like this, scientists have been waving massive red flags for more than a decade. In 2009 the National Academies of Sciences' National Research Council put out a report (the "NAS report") detailing the horrifying state of science in the courtroom, listing all the gaps in research and weaknesses in each one.[15] It was met with resounding yawns from criminal courts around the country, and cited in only about 150 decisions in the eight years following its release, many of those citations not grappling with the flawed science but just acknowledging the report or wondering if, in a conviction appeal, this report counts as "new evidence."[16]

But the report—and other analyses of bad science's greatest hits—is damning. It literally concluded that "with the exception of nuclear DNA analysis . . . no forensic method has been rigorously shown to have the capacity to consistently, and with a high degree of certainty, demonstrate a connection between evidence and a specific individual or source." A President's Council of Advisors seven years later (in the "PCAST report") raised the same question: Is any of the stuff courts routinely treat as science . . . actually science?[17]

Probably not.

Let's take bite mark evidence, for example. This is a type of analysis where an expert looks at marks on a body, says those marks came from teeth, and then claims that you can match the imprint of one set of teeth to a particular person. But the PCAST report found that there is no scientific basis for this as science. It's unclear whether, when tested, these experts can even accurately say whether something *is* a bite mark— and when they try to link whatever the mark is to a given person, error rates are as high as 64 percent,[18] meaning that this "science" can be wrong more often than it is right. This might be why PCAST found that "bite mark analysis does not meet the scientific standards for foundational validity and is far from meeting such standards" and that it likely "may not be salvageable."[19]

Hair analysis is in the same disgraceful bucket. The FBI itself has admitted that in cases involving microscopic comparisons of hairs, intended to link a person to hairs found at the scene of a crime, 90 percent of the trial transcripts they analyzed contained erroneous statements about the science.[20] One man targeted by this type of testimony was Santae Tribble, who was accused of murder and linked to the crime by thirteen hairs found on a stocking mask. As it turned out, *none* of the hairs belonged to Santae, and one wasn't even human; it was a dog hair, which "experts" nonetheless used to wrongfully convict Santae of murder. He spent twenty-eight years in prison before being exonerated, and died in 2020, after just eight years of freedom.[21]

Santae isn't alone. According to the FBI, thirty-five people got the death penalty because of hair analysis. Errors were present in 94 percent of those cases. Nine human beings were actually executed. Another five had died in prison by the time the FBI issued its press release.[22]

Junk science doesn't show up out of nowhere; it emerges from deep tragedy. There is perhaps nothing more horrifying than the loss of a child, and allegations that parents murdered their children via shaken baby syndrome have grown exponentially, resulting in the imprisonment of thousands of parents.[23] The idea that certain signs and symptoms can be conclusively linked to shaking a child (rather than an accident or other cause) developed originally from a tenuous interpretation of a triad of symptoms: bleeding in the brain and retinas, and brain swelling. The problem with linking these symptoms to shaking is that the cause behind them is not always obvious—there are numerous accidents, diseases, and even genetic disorders that can cause similar symptoms and death, and because many of these disorders are rare, physicians asked to make a judgment call on the cause of death might never have seen such a disorder in their practice.[24] The linkage between these symptoms and a finding of abusive shaking is so weak that Dr. Norman Guthkelch, the author of the paper that gave rise to this "syndrome" idea, has actively spoken out against the use of his work for this purpose:[25] "I am frankly quite disturbed that what I intended as a friendly suggestion for avoiding injury to children has become an excuse for imprisoning innocent parents."[26] He later served as an expert in defense of wrongly imprisoned parents.[27]

Yet even as the scientific basis for "shaken baby syndrome" is widely criticized, junk science becomes more admissible the more it is repeated.[28]

Nothing may be more widely repeated in forensics than fingerprint evidence. Fingerprint analysis, often treated as golden in the media, has no uniform, objective standards governing it. Rather, fingerprint "analysts" look at two prints, find points of similarity, and decide individually whether they consider these prints a "match." As Jennifer Mnookin, chancellor of the University of Wisconsin–Madison and former law professor at the University of Virginia, explains:

> There is simply no uniform approach to deciding what counts as a sufficient basis for making an identification. Some fingerprint examiners use a 'point-counting' method that entails counting the number of similar ridge characteristics on the prints, but there is no fixed requirement about how many points of similarity are needed. Six points, nine, twelve? Local practices vary, and no established minimum or norm exists. Others reject point-counting for a more holistic approach. Either way, there is no generally agreed-on standard for determining precisely when to declare a match. Although fingerprint experts insist that a qualified expert can infallibly know when two fingerprints match, there is no carefully articulated protocol for ensuring that different experts reach the same conclusion.

A 1995 study indicated that 34 percent of fingerprint test takers made a mistake.[29] More recent research is mixed: The Miami-Dade police performed research where they claimed false positive rates as low as 4.2 percent,[30] but a group of researchers in 2020 working on close non-match fingerprints (which are on the rise) found false positive error rates for two tests administered to 125 fingerprint agencies to be 16 percent and 28 percent.[31] The PCAST report itself put the error rate somewhere between 1 in 306 prints being wrong and 1 in 18, adding, "We also note it is conceivable that the false-positive rate in real casework could be higher than that observed in the experimental studies, due to exposure to potentially biasing information in the course of casework."[32] In other words, who knows.

This is a form of forensic accusation that dates back hundreds of years, having, like many questionable forensics, become established at a time when there was little expectation of skepticism. As modern technology allows analysts to do weird things like picking up two fractions of prints and assembling them into a mélange for analysis, that lack of skepticism becomes ever more troubling. At this point, the gateway to this kind of evidence making it into court is the *Daubert* standard above, and as Professor Mnookin points out, "the judges who are assessing fingerprinting most likely believe deeply in fingerprinting."[33] The forensic tail, maybe, is wagging all the dogs.

The seduction of history permeates modern forensic admissibility, meaning that some things get accepted as "science" even if they're just one guy's untested idea. Blood spatter analysis, like fingerprints, is more about "pattern matching" than science, and can have error rates as high as 11 percent, often driven by different analysts having totally different understandings of common terminology and classifications, which also makes it really difficult for any one analyst to accurately reproduce the results of another one.[34] It's a free-for-all of interpretation, making blood-stain analysis, like other "pattern matching" processes, subject to the criticism that they are "not really sciences at all, in that they were not invented and validated in academic laboratories and then subjected to peer review in scientific journals, but rather were developed by police as an investigatory tool to solve crimes."[35] Bloodstain pattern analysis didn't take hold until the 1980s, when a man named Herbert MacDonell, who considered himself a modern-day Sherlock Holmes, began impressing juries with in-court demonstrations on the interpretation of spattered blood. MacDonell's nearly single-handed championing of bloodstain pattern analysis resulted in a kind of case-by-case, state-by-state adoption of this untested "science" until it was ubiquitous in American courts.

MacDonell was not a trained forensic scientist; he was a chemist at a glassworks company. But he had a personal interest in analyzing the pattern of bloodstains, and after a report he published on his process garnered some attention (even though MacDonell himself admitted that the accuracy of the method "could not be quantified"), he quit his job "to work full time as an instructor and forensic expert for hire. He branded his unaccredited basement lab with an impressive title, The Laboratory of Forensic Science, and named himself its director. In time, MacDonell would testify and publish books and articles using this official-sounding moniker. Few realized the limited scale of the operation."

Indeed, that operation became a cottage industry as MacDonell insisted that any investigator with a "natural scientific attitude" could engage in this kind of analysis with great success. He made his way across the country, testifying in cases and training police departments, managing to administer "exams" to determine proficiency in these groups for thirty-eight years and failing only five students. He got weirder, shooting dogs to examine their spatter and keeping his own fingernail clippings to try to develop "fingernail identification" as a field. But with his accreditation, his students were able to gain admission into courts through judges who, likely, didn't understand the basement origins of this field. State by state, case by case, his methods spread across the country, until they had been deemed acceptable in so many legal cases that it was hard to push back against their legitimacy.

The 2009 NAS report did try to push back. It noted that "the uncertainties associated with bloodstain pattern analysis are enormous," and that its proponents' conclusions were "more subjective than scientific," but to little avail. Nancy Gertner, a legendary judge in Massachusetts and professor at Harvard Law School, also tried to push back, establishing a practice of holding a hearing in her court on the admissibility of any evidence listed in the NAS report, but few other judges followed suit. In an interview, she spoke out against the rote practice of judges admitting things into evidence simply because they had been admitted before, with little skepticism or new scrutiny. "Precedent is like a child's game of telephone," she said. "You start off saying something. You whisper it down the line and you continue to whisper it even though it no longer makes sense."[36]

MacDonell, for his part, was still teaching his homemade blood spatter course in 2011, and police officers with just forty hours of training in analyzing droplets continue to be treated as legitimate modern-day Holmeses in their own right. His own career ended in ignominy, with allegations of sexually abusing children (albeit allegations that were never proven in court).

Other researchers who have tried to carry bloodstain pattern analysis forward have noted that MacDonell's research failed to account for crucial factors in fluid dynamics—like gravity. Daniel Attinger, whose research revealed these issues and has continued to push the field into more scientific territory, also acknowledged that "there's been no change" in law enforcement techniques, in spite of his research. But he thinks that's okay. "I have trust in the U.S. justice system," he said.[37]

Attempts to figure out who or what started a fire aren't much better. Alex Kozinski, a former Ninth Circuit Court of Appeals judge, pointed out that "many defendants have been convicted and spent countless years in prison based on evidence by arson experts who were later shown to be little better than witch doctors."[38] One victim of the witch doctors was a man named Cameron Todd Willingham who experienced the ultimate nightmare: His wife and daughters were killed in a house fire. He became "hysterical" at the scene, saying, "I couldn't get my babies out." He tried to run back into the flaming house, and had to be tackled and handcuffed by police to prevent his suicidal rescue mission.[39] But the local arson investigator became convinced that the fire had been started with an accelerant, and testified that Cameron Todd Willingham was guilty of murdering his family by arson, telling the jury, "The fire is telling me this. The fire tells a story. I am just the interpreter. I am looking at the fire, and I am interpreting the fire. That is what I know. That is what I do best. And the fire does not lie. It tells me the truth."[40]

The evidence the Texas arson investigator relied on was "not based on scientific testing, but on heuristics consistent with practices employed in the 1980s and, in some cases, still relied upon today," but his testimony was persuasive to the jury and the appellate courts alike. Even though multiple reports were issued—by arson experts, by journalists, by the National Fire Protection Association—discrediting the forensic testimony that had put Mr. Willingham on death row, his appeals were all denied, and he was executed.[41]

Fire analysis is an ancient field. It began in ancient Rome, where the *Quarstionarius* was assigned to determine the cause of all fires.[42] It persevered into 1950s America, including the 1955 book passage titled "How to discover whether a female caused the fire," which details the "fairly recognizable traits or techniques in common" one must look for to figure out if a female is responsible—you know, things like how female fires "tend to be a bit 'childish,' 'silly,' hasty, poorly planned[,] . . . [and are] often spur-of-the-moment, impulsive, and ill considered jobs." Any form of forensic science that has ended up describing itself, in modern times, as "a mixture of art and science" should get serious and extreme side-eye, and arson investigation is squarely in this box.[43] Practices evolved without testing: One investigator would teach his protégé what "alligatoring" or scorch marks meant, without anyone actually confirming that these suppositions were correct. The touchstones and myths of the arson investigation community became so widespread that the National Fire Protection Association started putting out reports and guidelines detailing which approaches were sufficiently reliable as to be appropriately used, and yet, "even though the Guide has existed for over a decade, many fire investigators still employ scientifically disproved techniques to locate fire origins." John Lentini, a noted fire expert who has testified for both prosecutors and defense attorneys in criminal cases, "estimates that currently 100 to 200 people are in prison serving long sentences, or even facing the death penalty, for setting fires that were actually accidents."[44] Gerald Hurst, a chemist with a doctorate from Cambridge University, also believes that many innocent people have likely been convicted over the past fifty years—likely based on the expert testimony finding, erroneously, that the fire was arson. "You've got tons of holdouts—good old boys who've investigated 5,000 fires and they are doing it the same way they've always done it."[45]

A rigorous analyst who is up to date on the most supportable methods may be an incredibly valuable aid in finding truth. But a good old boy who thinks the fire is talking to him can cost hundreds of people their freedom or even their lives. If there were a neutral scientific authority governing who was allowed to testify in court, we might not be in this position; we actually might avoid this position if defense lawyers were given equal access to scientific and forensic resources so that any assertions by experts whose expertise lies outside the ken of your average lawyer could be well confronted, tested, and verified. But in the current criminal legal system, police oversee the majority of crime labs.[46] Most crime labs will look at evidence only upon a prosecutor's request, and much of the time the defense does not even have access to the physical evidence, which may remain solely in the prosecutor's control until trial. This means that to bring in a forensic expert of their choosing, prosecutors usually need only ask their lab employee, who may be "subject to significant unconscious bias by experts seeking to help their bosses, the prosecutors."[47]

Sometimes there isn't even a lab involved; sometimes the science is being done on the street by police officers. "Field tests" to detect whether a given substance is an illicit drug are incredibly common in the United States, where more than 700,000 arrests happen every year on the basis of these "presumptive" tests. The cheap, portable test lets a police officer take a sample of a substance and, using a small chemically reactive strip, test the sample. The problem is, these field tests have a massive error rate; a 2023 report suggests that as many as 30,000 people *per year* may be falsely arrested based on bad tests.[48] There are a few memorable instances of this, such as when a Georgia cop arrested a star quarterback for possession of cocaine (it was actually bird poop)[49] or when Florida cops arrested a man for possession of methamphetamine (it was crumbles of Krispy Kreme doughnut glaze, which you would think cops would be able to recognize).[50] In a system where over 90 percent of people plead guilty, the vast majority of these allegations may never be tested at trial—or even tested at all.[51] The report revealed that 89 percent of prosecutors surveyed were willing to take a guilty plea based on field-tested drugs without any follow-up or confirmatory testing, and 67 percent of labs wouldn't even test a sample where there was already a guilty plea in place. A quarter of labs surveyed just accept the field test and do no confirmatory testing, even though the field test may have a false positive rate as high as 38 percent.[52]

Under the current scheme, while a prosecutor can simply seek confirmatory testing or not, ask a lab expert to explain a report to them or not, or check in with any number of outside junk science peddlers, a defense attorney would need to (1) request access to the relevant evidence (and perhaps get a judge involved if the prosecutor refuses), (2) find the right expert to do the testing or analysis, (3) schedule that examination so that it can take place within the window of time available pretrial, (4) find a way to pay for this expert, likely having to once again file motions before a judge to request the court allocate indigent defense funding to this endeavor (and having to call the whole thing off or privately fundraise if the court says no), and only then (5) be able to secure an independent expert analysis of the evidence.

If the crucible of truth is cross examination, defense lawyers can't realize the promise of this crucible without equal access to expert support. I went to law school, not medical school, and as much as I love watching *House,* I'm not qualified to cross examine a medical doctor on medical records unless I have my own medical expert looking at the records, finding questionable spots, and telling me what to look for. For example, I once took a case to trial in which an individual was accused of injuring a man in a fight. The man had ended up hospitalized with internal bleeding, which made no sense based on what appeared to have happened in the fight: the injured man had been swinging my (much smaller) client around like a rag doll. Because we were able to have a doctor look at the medical records and educate us about the man's preexisting conditions, I was able to cross examine the prosecutor's medical witness on possible alternate causes of this man's internal bleeding—causes that were, in fact, much more likely than the injury having been caused in the fight. Because I had access to these records ahead of time, the ability to prepare, and my own expert to guide me, the jury was able to hear not just the prosecutor's version of the medical evidence but all the holes in that version as well. And because of that, the jury acquitted (and actually gave my client hugs in the hallway outside the courtroom when it was all over).

This isn't a defense advantage; it's a justice advantage. There is no reason why ordinary people would have read the NAS report, or know whether lab analysts in court see themselves "not as neutral fact-finders, but as police in lab coats . . . seek[ing] test results that match the prosecution's goals."[53] There is no reason why your average, *Bones*-watching juror would know that crime labs are, themselves, also underfunded and subject to error due to lack of resources, poor training, and high caseloads.[54] They probably would not have heard of the crime lab investigation in Minnesota that found "major errors in almost every area of the lab's work," including "sloppy documentation, dirty equipment, faulty techniques and ignorance of basic scientific procedures . . . lab employees [who] mistakenly classified at least one-third of all fingerprints as unidentifiable and destroyed them . . . case files [that] 'were largely unintelligible' . . . [and a] lab [that] lacked any clean area designated for the review and collection of DNA evidence."[55] The equipment was so badly ventilated that it sprayed drugs into the air, contaminating other samples.[56] Police had known about these conditions for years.[57] People might have heard of Annie Dookhan, the forensic specialist who contaminated (or made up results for) as many as tens of thousands of samples,[58] but likely assume she's a rarity. In March 2024, a new crime lab scandal erupted: a lab analyst in Colorado cut corners that might have impacted more than 650 DNA analyses.[59] Without meaningful oversight, cross examination, and defense access to experts to inform that examination, the danger of business-as-usual terrible lab practices may never see the light of day.

We live in a world full of imperfection and complexity. Every form of science in the courtroom—including DNA analysis, which, though more advanced certainly than hair inspection and bite marks, is still subject to contamination, degradation, bad lab practices, and the error rate inherent in small sample sizes—has its strengths and weaknesses. A system concerned with fairness would invariably resource each side in every case to test the other side's experts, methods, and conclusions, and would offer judges ample scientific support and training to suss out junk science. A system concerned with punishment, efficiency, and a stolid business-as-usual embrace of the status quo does none of that, relying on what is familiar rather than what is true.

The prioritization of the familiar and efficient over new, and perhaps better, forms of inquiry or analysis isn't set in stone. Rather, it has grown from myriad decisions by myriad judges, building over the years into this room full of interpretive paper that is case law. These papers, of course, comprise only a small fraction of the decisions of judges around the country; the vast majority of legal decisions in America are "unpublished," meaning the judge who wrote the decision chose not to present it for public scrutiny nor make it available to use as precedent in subsequent legal arguments. One recent analysis of New York legal decisions found that "only 6 percent or so of written decisions in criminal cases have been published in recent years, and that of the 600 criminal court judges who published at least one decision between 2010 and 2022, 20 of them (just 3 percent) were responsible for 28 percent of all published decisions; 356 judges (59 percent) published three decisions or fewer."[60] Leaving a decision unpublished gives a judge the option to rule a particular way in *one* case, without worrying that this decision will instruct other judges to make the same choice in other, similar cases. Because of this, as practitioners we often find that decisions that follow the status quo (including all of its junk science and restrictive discovery rules) will be published, while more inventive decisions, decisions that push back against the status quo or reject commonly accepted but bad science, are more likely to be unpublished, meaning that even if future lawyers and judges can *read* the decision, they can't use it to argue for the same outcome in their case. It also means that, as one can see above, certain judges dominate the world of published decisions. When fewer voices become precedent, the impact of a diversity of views and experiences on the bench is sharply curtailed.

Like many problems in the law, the root of this issue is fear and poor incentives. Judges, like anyone else, want to be good at their jobs and respected by their peers (though whom they consider "peers" may vary widely). We have built a system in which it is safer to "move the calendar," "dispose of cases," and stick to accepted interpretations of the rules and evidence, stymieing progress and the evolution of ideas. Resourcing defense lawyers to investigate cases more thoroughly, better educate the bench, put more effective and informed experts in front of judges, and push back against the defaults of a prosecution-minded legal apparatus is a crucial step. But giving judges the resources they need to engage in more informed skepticism is equally important, as is not assuming that the adversarial nature of the system itself will tend toward justice.

Chapter Eight

Finders of Fact

Juries: Who Wields Power, Who Is Excluded,
and What They're Allowed to Know

For public defenders, there is one moment that will always be more horribly filled with anxiety—and, worse, hope—than any other. A moment that, no matter how many times you go through it, always feels as if you were standing on the roof of a skyscraper, looking over the edge and thinking about what it might feel like to just take one step into free fall. I have a good friend who has to take a Zofran just to survive it. For me it's always an interesting tour of how hard my heart can beat without actually killing me.

It comes at the end of a jury trial. You've done everything you can, and the jury has been sent out to deliberate. Eventually, you get the call: "They have a verdict." You return to the courtroom, you and the person who has entrusted you with their protection and fate stand side by side, and the jury files back in. You stare at them as they sit down, trying to read something from their posture, expressions, eye contact. Everyone else is seated except the foreperson, who will read the verdict, and your client, who is asked by the judge to rise. You rise with them. The foreperson is asked to read.

To be clear, the nausea *starts* when you get the call and only intensifies until you find out what this group of strangers has chosen as their collective version of the truth. American faith in the accuracy of random people in small groups is astonishing.

Ordinary people don't usually have a lot of power in this system. For the entire life of a criminal case, the people exerting power over the accused are experts: judges and prosecutors. But for a very specific set of staggeringly large decisions—guilt, innocence, life, death—fate lies in the hands of twelve of our fellow citizens. If anyone ever told you that voting is your most important civic duty, well, you can go tell them they're off by one: it's your second most important duty after coming in, when called, to personally act as a safeguard against injustice.

A life, after all, is on the line. Even in cases where the penalty may be small—because our legal system has tied itself to our employment, our health, our educational access, our housing, our custody of our children— every jury is making a choice with potential lifelong repercussions.

But who gets to make which decisions in the courtroom? Yes, most of the time, the benevolent or malevolent ruler of the courtroom is the judge. The scope of decisions that judges get to make is technically limited: they get to interpret what they think the law says and how it applies to different sets of facts in their case. In practice, this means they are deciding almost everything that matters right up until the moment a person reaches a jury: they start off by making the single most important decision, which is whether this person will fight their charges from home or from a jail cell. And then they get to decide whether police broke the rules, whether evidence gets to be actually used against a person or thrown out, and, often, what the punishment should be for a crime. But what they don't get to decide—most of the time—is what actually happened. That's what juries are for.

America is an anomaly. Most countries stick with judges as the decision-makers. The majority of jury trials in the world occur in the United States.[1] What's more, other countries that do utilize juries often reserve them for specific types of cases, rather than making the ruling of ordinary people the default mechanism of every criminal case.[2] But in our quirky, arcane system, the intent was not that 95 percent of cases end in a plea bargain, as they do now, but rather that the community serve as a check on the authority of the government to prosecute and condemn.[3]

Of course, whether juries serve as a check or a rubber stamp depends entirely on who, exactly, these strangers are. It depends on their education, their life experience, the media environment in which they are steeped, how much they know about their community, cops, and legal apparatus, and what they've been led to believe. So when it comes to the search for justice in a punishment system, the question of who is getting put on these juries is a huge one.

———

There are two kinds of juries a person can serve on in the U.S. system. One is big and comes together at the beginning of a case (a grand jury), and the other is smaller and shows up more on TV (a petit jury or trial jury). Let's start with the big, secretive one you probably haven't been told much about.

You see, our system was not built to be one that imparted blind faith in government. It was supposed to have *multiple* levels of safeguards. Things like the presumption of innocence and the right to a lawyer are two ways in which our system—at least nominally—is seeking to ensure that ordinary individuals are somewhat protected when facing down the full force of their government. Of course, these safeguards were always pretty flimsy and have been further weakened through years of our nation using this system to marginalize and oppress specific groups. When you use the system to go after people you don't like, generally the safeguards get dialed down a whole lot, rendering them less effective than they were meant to be. But before we talk about their real-world impact, let's take a look at what they were *supposed* to be.

A key safeguard is the idea of a probable cause determination at the beginning of a serious criminal case. "Probable cause" is one of several different standards of proof in our legal system. A "standard of proof" is basically the legal rule for how sure you have to be that something did or did not happen. The lowest standard is (predictably) how sure a cop has to be to walk up and talk to a person; to do that, cops need only "reasonable articulable suspicion," meaning that they have to be able to say a reason why they want to talk to someone, something more than a hunch.[4] As you might imagine, the requirement that police actually have a good reason to talk to someone is only as strong as judges make it, and years of judges accepting things like "the individual matched the description of a Black male suspect in the area" or "he looked nervous" or the omnipresent "he gestured furtively" have essentially ensured that whom police are allowed to talk to is rife with bias, and police continue "speaking" to Black men in hyper-policed neighborhoods while ignoring crime among the privileged.[5]

But reasonable suspicion isn't enough to actually search or arrest someone, or charge them with a crime: to do that, police need *probable cause.* Probable cause is often thought of as a "probably" standard: enough evidence that a reasonable person could believe that a crime *probably* happened, and that this person *probably* did it, or that the area to be searched *probably* contains evidence of the crime.

———

This is where the first jury comes in. Interestingly, if prosecutors want to move forward with a serious case—a felony,[6] often defined as matters where punishment is a year or more in prison—they usually can't just do so of their own accord. Our system is supposed to question prosecutorial discretion when the stakes are high. So in most serious cases, prosecutors have to run their evidence by someone else first and make sure that person or group agrees that there is probable cause.

So, whom do they run the evidence by? They get choices. The first option is a "preliminary hearing" in front of a judge, where they present their case and witnesses, let the accused person be present, have the defense cross examine the prosecution's witnesses, and then let a judge decide if there's probable cause. As Brendon Woods—the first Black Chief Defender of Alameda County, California, and a noted expert on racial bias in the makeup of juries who practices in a jurisdiction where "prelims" are the norm—pointed out, prelims are a healthy dose of sunlight. "We can test the evidence, the DAs can see if the witnesses hold up in a cross examination, we have a preview of what's going to happen at trial. It's good for clients to see it. It's good for me as a lawyer to see it. Across the board, it makes sense. I honestly think that every person who is facing time in prison should get a preliminary hearing automatically. Automatically. Before a person goes to prison for X amount of years, they should be able to see what the evidence is against them without being punished for it."[7]

And then there's the grand jury, which is pretty much the opposite of sunlight. Instead of presenting their case and letting a defense lawyer kick the tires and allowing the accused person to see the evidence against them, prosecutors get to pull together a roomful of about twenty-three citizens, and present their evidence in total secrecy, *without even a judge present*. This is a "grand jury," called grand not because it's fabulous but because it's got more people in it than a twelve-person trial jury. The accused person isn't there (unless they choose to testify and be cross examined by the prosecutor), the defense lawyer isn't there (unless their client is getting grilled), nobody gets to find out what's happening in the room until months later at trial, and the only info that comes out is an "indictment" or non-indictment: in other words, a finding that there is or is not probable cause from the grand jury.

This is the first way in which juries have a huge influence on a case, whether or not it ends up going to trial. Members of a grand jury are left alone with a prosecutor, without any competing perspective to help them see holes in the evidence or problems with the case. So a jury that is highly trusting of authority, has few personal experiences with bad policing or corrupt systems, and generally thinks that anyone who has been arrested must have done *something* wrong, well, they're going to find probable cause pretty quickly and credulously.

In the Bronx, though, people aren't so credulous. They have experienced street harassment, lived through stop and frisk, driven down the boulevards knowing that at any moment they can (and will) be stopped for driving while Black. They have been prosecuted on police lies, have had family members prosecuted on police lies, and, unlike most Americans, know that lying is actually an accepted part of policing; even at the investigative level, police officers are trained, and encouraged, to lie[8] if it elicits useful information from their interlocutor.[9] People who are unfamiliar with policing in America are often surprised at how integrated false information is into the work of a government actor, and are hesitant to believe that the culture of useful dishonesty trickles up from the investigative stage and permeates every part of the process, creating what people in the legal profession often call "testilying," or comfortable, accepted, and unchecked dishonesty under oath to serve the goal of conviction. But in the Bronx, hyper-policing has given rise to familiarity, meaning that the jury pool isn't just willing to believe that police *could* lie; they walk through the door basically expecting half of anything a cop says to be untrue. This has a real impact on the grand jury.

Take, for example, a client I had who decided to hold her head up and walk into that grand jury room. Most of the time, having to put their own statements on the record without much protection from their attorney, and be cross examined, on the record, by a prosecutor, long before they even know what the full evidence is against them . . . well, the risk is insane. Reasonable people avoid testifying in the grand jury, choosing to fight the case after the inevitable indictment is handed down. But in places like the Bronx, where jurors are ready to really listen to their fellow citizens and ready to send some serious side-eye toward the prosecutor, that risk is slightly more acceptable.

This is what happened to my client (let's call her Mary) who had a shitty boyfriend. When she let him stay at her place, unbeknownst to her he hid his stash of drugs inside her home, in a place he knew she'd never look. And she never did. Until the cops busted through her door in the wee hours, terrifying her and her child, ransacking her place, finding the drugs, and charging her—a law-abiding single mom—with drug felonies.

The probable cause they had was that the apartment was in her name, and the drugs were in the apartment. They even tried to hold her house keys as evidence, claiming the keys themselves linked her to the drugs. Sure, the lease agreement in her name also linked her to the apartment, but taking the keys ensured that she and her child remained locked out. They also charged the boyfriend, but in a prime example of prosecutors choosing a scattershot, wide-net, logically untethered approach to ruining people's lives with criminal accusation, they went forward with a theory that the clean-as-a-whistle single mom was somehow an important part of the drug operation to which she had no apparent ties.

If we'd had a grand jury full of people who reflexively believe law enforcement, I would have thrown myself between Mary and the door to the grand jury room. Mary had been through hell. When I talked with her about it later, she recalled layers upon layers of terror from this incident—from sitting in the police van from 4:00 a.m. (when she was arrested) until 1:00 p.m. (when the van was "full" enough of accused people to go to the station) to the way the investigating cop kept ceaselessly and weirdly calling her on her personal cell phone, even after she had a lawyer. In most places, I'd never want her to take the horrible risk of telling her story openly to strangers and having them indict her anyway because a prosecutor told them to.

But this was the Bronx, one of those places in the United States where juries carry so much more of their own hard-won deep insight into what police are really like. Mary and I both felt pretty sure that ordinary people could relate to both having a shitty boyfriend and living in a world where cops arrest first and ask questions later. So we decided that she would go to the grand jury and tell her story, all of it: how they had been dating only a little while, how he had been staying with her not because they were leveling up their couple-hood into cohabitation but out of necessity, how she never went to the area of the apartment where he had hidden his stash, how she had no idea what was happening when the cops busted in, in the middle of the night, terrifying her child. As her lawyer, I was forced (by the rules of the grand jury proceeding) to sit silently behind her, unable to help but ready to object if the ADA asked improper questions. The whole thing took about half an hour, and then we left to sit in the cold, white-walled courthouse anteroom, waiting to find out whom these twenty-three strangers would believe.

This, by the way, is similar to the verdict kind of nausea, but tempered a little bit by the ability to share the moment—and reassurances, bits of hope, good facts—with one's client, who really has it all on the line. I remember Mary and me agreeing that everyone in there must have dated someone, at some point, who wasn't who they said they were. That they would probably understand. In a recent conversation, Mary reminded me that as we sat on hard plastic chairs waiting for an answer, my father-in-law had happened to call, and we had ended up praying together in Spanish for these strangers to see the truth.

And they *did.* The grand jury rejected the indictment, and the charges against Mary were dropped, saving her job and her apartment, as well as her mental health. She was able to trust her community, and it paid off.[10] Because of that, Mary was able to move forward with her life, and recently finished sending off her applications to law school. She hopes to become a public defender.

The impact for Mary was, of course, immediate, but also says something larger about how much the legal system can do harm to citizens of the Bronx. There will always be a great number of prosecutors who bring any charges they think they can get away with rather than contemplating what they *should* charge if they want to truly do justice. And in most jurisdictions, the grand jury will rubber-stamp that decision.[11] Grand jury indictment rates have been reported to be as high as 99 percent, and elsewhere in the world—in England, where grand juries originated, as well as in Canada, Australia, New Zealand, Ireland, and more—grand juries are no longer used because they are "putty in the hands of the prosecutor."[12]

This is where we get the saying "you can indict a ham sandwich." The Bronx is one of a handful of anomalies, where prosecutors have picked the process more likely to rubber-stamp their choices and less likely to seek truth, but the citizenry's ability to spot and reject lies, half-truths, weak connections, and wild assumptions nevertheless creates a powerful protection for their community. Here, a grand jury who doesn't believe everything they hear has the potential to be an actual safeguard rather than a rubber stamp on the conveyor belt toward prison.

———

In most places, frustratingly, communities are not so universally well informed.[13] In thinking about how my Bronx days differed from grand jury realities around the United States, I turned to my colleague Ashley Payne. These days, Ashley works with me to help empower public defense agencies around the country and bring more of their clients home—work that we think of as prison abolition in action, building proof of concept for accountability without prisons and jails. But, like those of all mysterious heroes, Ashley's past has a hidden chapter: she used to be a prosecutor in DeKalb County, Georgia.

Ask Ashley about a grand jury, and you can almost see her blood pressure rise. "I wish this topic could be discussed more," she told me. "While grand juries were designed to ensure that prosecutors tested their cases with the community before formal charges were filed, they've devolved into little more than a routine spoke on the wheel of mass incarceration."

"In practice," she told me, "what happens is, prosecutors with heavy caseloads and little patience for the burdensome process run through presenting cases like contestants in a marathon. When I was practicing, prosecutors signed up for a grand jury rotation. People *hated* it. It took all day, you were presenting everyone's cases—not specifically your own, unless it was a specialty case—and the pressure to get them done quickly was enormous."

The result, she explained, was that prosecutors just started using every tactic they could to get it over with. "A prosecutor would typically call one witness—usually law enforcement—swear them in, and limit themselves to five or six questions about what happened and who they believe to be responsible. With no judge in the room, these are often *leading* questions. Once they've concluded those questions, they'll ask the grand jurors if they have any questions for the witness.

"But that's not really an invitation for inquiry," she continued. "Grand jury service is extremely disruptive for jurors. Where I worked, grand jurors were summoned twice a week for a *month*. People are missing work, school, scrambling to find child care, and prosecutors are *keenly* aware of this. They use it to their advantage. They remind jurors over and over that *things will take even longer if you ask too many questions.*"

With long service obligations, little compensation, and constant reminders that everybody gets to go home as soon as the prosecutors get what they came for, grand jurors start pressuring *each other* to just get through these cases as fast as they can. The result, Ashley says, is "a prosecutorial free-for-all"[14] in a room without oversight, with too many cases, crushing pressure to bring in indictments, and a vulnerable pool of citizens. Ham sandwiches are getting indicted every day.

⎯⎯

When we move from a grand jury to a petit (trial) jury, though, the same questions—who is on the jury and what do they know—become infinitely more important, because the result of this group decision will not be a continued process but potentially a conviction and a sentence. For the (very) small proportion of people who withstand the crushing pressure to accept a plea bargain, the matter of how the twelve strangers carrying their fate will be called upon to serve, screened, and selected may mean the difference between a fair outcome and a shattering miscarriage of justice.

At the outset, there are things about the trial jury that make it feel a lot more fair than the grand jury. For one, the jury is the "audience" for a trial. Furthermore, the system lets both sides choose that audience through a process called voir dire, which are the French verbs for "to see" and "to speak," but which apparently comes from an old Norman form of French and may mean "to speak the truth."[15] Either way, it's the only opportunity for the jurors themselves to speak in court before their ultimate announcement of a verdict, and it's the only chance the two sides have to see their potential audience members speak about themselves, their lives, their views, and their biases.

The conceit, of course, is that if both sides are afforded an opportunity to hear the jurors and weed out the people with serious biases, the remaining group will be able to listen fairly to the testimony presented, look at the evidence, and, using their unique human instincts about what's true and who's lying, suss out the truth. We often hear the phrase "a jury of our peers." But in Woods's words, "A jury of your peers would be great, but it doesn't really exist in the law. We don't get a jury of our peers. If we got a jury of our peers, there'd be a lot more Black and brown people serving as jurors as opposed to the jurors we have today."[16] Once again, the system in theory and the system in practice diverge massively. There is no cross section of the community coming to jury service, but rather a pool of people who are whiter and wealthier than the people who stand accused.

———

It all starts with who gets called to jury duty. You might think that everyone gets summoned to jury duty at some point, but you'd be wrong.[17] Jury "pools" are drawn from things like DMV records and voter registration rolls. This necessarily filters out people who, for one reason or another, do not have a driver's license or have not registered to vote.[18]

And at the outset, it whitens the jury pool. After all, because of policies lingering from the Jim Crow South, forty-eight states still strip people of their voting rights due to a felony conviction. In a system that targets Black people in particular, this means that in a state like Tennessee as many as one in five Black people will not be on the voter registration rolls by law.[19]

Jurisdictions *could* call many more people using resources like utility bills, tax records, local governmental records (like transit or toll tracking accounts), and even the National Change of Address database. But they don't. So if you're not in this particular in-group, you don't even get asked to come to the courthouse.

The next filter is who can answer that summons. A day of jury service means, at the very least, one day off from work, and if a person is actually placed on a jury, they will have to miss multiple days of work while also arranging for transportation and child care, if necessary. All of this costs money. But a 2022 study found that on average jurisdictions compensate jurors only $16 per day to serve.[20] "In California," Woods tells me, "we only pay people $15 per day to serve as a juror. That will not cover your parking in San Francisco or Oakland for a day. So you have to be in a position in your life where either your employer will pay for you to serve, or you have the income to *afford* to serve. And that in itself removes a certain class of people, mostly low-income people. Those are mostly Black and brown people, especially in the location where I work."[21] The median white American in their early thirties in 2022 had $29,000 more wealth than the median Black American of the same age. And the median white American in their late fifties had $251,000 more wealth than the median Black American of the same age.[22]

In addition, the whitening of the jury pool has extreme consequences: in a system where Black people are over-targeted in the first place, research has demonstrated that white jurors tend to make harsher decisions against Black people who stand accused,[23] while more diverse juries are better at sorting out the truth.[24]

Yet instead of acting on the evidence, most jurisdictions cling to even *more* racially biased limits on the jury pool. The next filter is the criminal record. People with criminal records are often excluded from jury service altogether. Now, you might be thrilled that Charles Manson won't be sitting in a homicide trial, but that's not really who we're talking about. We're talking about people who are home, having paid whatever the price was for their prior misconduct. It then saddles people with records for a lifetime, largely impacting low-income communities of color.

This isn't theoretical. In California about 30 percent of Black men were excluded from jury service until a 2020 law eliminated the blanket prohibition of people with felony convictions on juries.[25] About twenty million people nationwide (roughly 8 percent of the population) were locked out of jury service in a 2021 assessment.[26] Just as Black Codes were used in the South after the Civil War to turn the law into a tool for re-enslavement, our system's current targeting of primarily Black and brown men enables it to strip them of two of the most powerful forms of civic participation an American has, voting and jury service—which Abraham Lincoln is often quoted as calling "the greatest service of citizenship."

But even if a jurisdiction lifts one restriction and, for example, permits people with records to serve on juries, they won't get called to serve if they're still kicked off voter rolls, nor would they have the ability to vote for people who might address the problem of their exclusion from fundamental civic participation. The result is a system in which people who have lived through prosecution aren't allowed to use that perspective in analyzing the reliability of prosecutorial accusations.

———

Juries, from the outset, are not "peers." In most places, the juries, having less personal experience with the machinery of American punishment, are more pro-police and prosecution-minded[27] than the people who are sitting to be judged, with the exception of certain communities where the legacy of over-policing has made deep marks. When I started practicing law in San Jose, California, it was common to try to suss out how pro-police a juror was by asking about how they would judge a police witness—something like "We all know that people don't always tell the truth, but sometimes we're more likely to assume someone is telling the truth because they are a police officer. Would you be able to hold a police officer to the same high standard as everyone else, and be able to decide a witness is untruthful in spite of them being a police officer?" Who knows if anyone answers that particular question honestly, but the asking itself is important, because by asking the question, I have introduced into the jury pool the idea of unthinking overreliance on police witnesses. In a pro-police jury pool, I really needed my jurors to ask themselves if they were maybe a little too ready to be credulous toward anyone in a uniform.

When I got to the Bronx, though, I was flabbergasted. Just like in the grand jury, trial juries' personal experience of policing made them sharper and more skeptical about the evidence and witnesses they were offered. Instead of defenders asking whether potential jurors could countenance the idea of imperfect police veracity, you saw prosecutors humbly asking whether jurors could believe a witness "in *spite* of her being a police officer." Being a cop on the stand—a credibility advantage in the vast majority of jurisdictions—is a huge liability in the Bronx, where jurors actually know what cops are like. The whole power dynamic and preset assumptions of credibility were reversed, all because the human beings who made up our jury pool were walking through the door with a different set of experiences, and, therefore, expectations.

———

Most places, though, aren't the Bronx. In most places, the jury pool has already become whiter and wealthier by how jurors are called. So by the time we get to questioning the potential jurors, the voir dire process can't dig us out from what's already been built. However, it absolutely can advance the winnowing of the jury pool even further.

The primary purpose of voir dire is to weed out people who, seemingly, cannot be fair in a case. Lawyers get to ask jurors questions about their perspectives, and if a person says something that reveals a hopelessly biased perspective on the facts of the case, they can be removed "for cause." Typical examples include people saying things like "I just believe that if a person was arrested, there must have been a good reason, and so I can't really imagine this person here is innocent," but more fun examples come from the case of Martin Shkreli, the famously smirking pharma don who jacked up the price of insulin. As unsympathetic as Mr. Shkreli was, our system demands that everyone who stands accused get a fair and impartial jury, which is incredibly challenging for someone whose case has been splashed all over the news. For Mr. Shkreli, the result was a voir dire that went like this (as published in *Harper's Magazine*):

THE COURT: The purpose of jury selection is to ensure fairness and impartiality in this case. If you think that you could not be fair and impartial, it is your duty to tell me. All right. Juror Number 1.

JUROR NO. 1: I'm aware of the defendant and I hate him.

BENJAMIN BRAFMAN, SHKRELI'S LAWYER: I'm sorry.

JUROR NO. 1: I think he's a greedy little man.

THE COURT: Jurors are obligated to decide the case based only on the evidence. Do you agree?

JUROR NO. 1: I don't know if I could. I wouldn't want me on this jury.

THE COURT: Juror Number 1 is excused.[28]

While it might be easy to laugh at this reply in the case of Mr. Shkreli, if a defendant in need of a public defender has been in the media, it's because they are accused of something highly inflammatory. Police are far more likely to issue comments to the media, to issue them quickly, to release relevant evidence and footage selectively, and to have strong, well-staffed communications departments,[29] while defense lawyers are more likely to caution their clients to remain silent until they've seen the full scope of the evidence and its weaknesses. This means that the ability to use "for cause" challenges (requests to a judge to remove a juror for clear bias that could impede their ability to judge a case fairly) in a tainted jury pool isn't usually protecting the Martin Shkrelis of the world. It's protecting ordinary folks with no money and their life on the line.

And let's be real: for-cause challenges also aren't usually as clear-cut as the examples above. In a system that is trying to process way too many cases much too quickly, judges are under massive pressure to "move their calendar" and get cases finished as fast as possible. This means that they generally don't want to spend too much time on jury selection, and want to get as many people as possible from the initial venire (group of summoned jurors) into the twelve-person jury box. So when a person says something like "Oh, gosh, it would be very hard for me to be fair on a trespassing case, I really hate trespassers," a judge may choose to "rehabilitate" the witness by asking them a pointed question along the lines of "But if I, the judge, *ordered* you to be fair, you could do it, *right?*" The power dynamics in the room strongly encourage the juror to agree, and the accused person ends up with a juror who is struggling with her own admitted bias.

But another tactic remains! Let's say this exact thing (which I have seen play out about a hundred times in court) happens. The juror said she probably can't be fair, and the judge pushes her into taking it back. A lawyer can still use "peremptory challenges," which are essentially a limited number of get-rid-of-this-person-for-free cards that each side has. They allow the prosecution or the defense to kick a person off a jury without giving a reason—so the person above, rehabilitated by the judge, could still be eliminated by the defense if they used a peremptory challenge. Which seems great, right? Well, it is. Until you consider what it allows in terms of baked-in racism.

You will likely be unsurprised that in America's illustrious history with race and equity, prosecutors have (pretty regularly) been accused of using peremptory challenges to get rid of certain groups they think won't favor them on a jury. Prosecutors using reason-free peremptory challenges to get rid of Black jurors in particular happened so much that in 1986 the Supreme Court had to weigh in. In *Batson v. Kentucky*,[30] the justices said that when a litigant suspected the other side was eliminating jurors on the basis of race, they could object, and then the burden was on the other side to offer a race-neutral reason why they were kicking jurors off the panel.

The result has been a whole stable of race-neutral cover reasons hiding the systematic exclusion of Black people from juries. "I didn't like the way Juror No. 4 looked at me when I was speaking with her" or "she seemed sleepy" or "she said she had had a bad experience with police" or (with racism alarms ringing in full force) "he seemed to be of low intelligence" or "he looked like a drug dealer." These excuses and many more have resulted in a world where, in Jefferson Parish, Louisiana, the Equal Justice Initiative found that there was no Black representation on 80 percent of juries. Prosecutors were even being trained, they found, to eliminate certain racial minorities from juries and then cover it up. The results were not only universally bad but also lethal. Houston County, Alabama, for example, a 27 percent Black county, removed 80 percent of eligible Black jurors from service on death penalty trials, meaning that half of death penalty case juries were all-white and the rest had only one Black member.[31]

It's not just the South. Brendon Woods, our Oakland defender, has experienced it personally. "I was trying a case," he told me, and was at a point in jury selection where "this was the second Black person the DA had kicked off. And I made my objection, tracking really closely who had been kicked, the reasons for kicking them, and the answers given by this juror in particular. All their answers were such that they were a fair juror. They would be able to handle the evidence in a fair way, and they were similarly situated to the other answers given by other jurors. So there wasn't anything that made her an outlier." But once the DA used a peremptory challenge and Woods objected, a "race-neutral" reason had to be given. In this case, "the DA's response when the judge asked him why he removed that juror was . . . she was wearing a puffy coat."

At this point in his story, I interjected. "A puffy coat? Did the judge at least make the DA articulate what relationship there is between a puffy coat and jury service? What the coat *signified* to the DA?"

"No."

So there it is, our "race-neutral" reasoning, approved by a judge and telegraphing to other DAs that this kind of ploy works, and will work again.

This means that peremptory challenges are a terrifyingly double-edged sword—sometimes letting accused people evade a judge's plastering over of clear bias, but much more frequently allowing for the systematic, intentional silencing of Black and brown voices from core civic participation. And the result is an even more distilled form of privilege in the jurors whose decision ultimately impacts our lives.

So what's the answer here? Do we do away with peremptory challenges altogether, as some advocates have suggested? Woods cautions not to go so far so fast. "I think peremptories are important because it's one of the few places where our client has a direct say in the process. So, I am the final decision-maker, but I make sure that my client is very involved in the selection of the jury. Before every challenge, we discuss, and I'll give my reasoning—if they have strong reasoning why they want to keep a person I would challenge, we go through my notes and discuss. If they feel strongly, we're going to keep that person. I have my expertise. I have my thoughts. But at the end of the day, it's not my life."

This perspective is common among defenders. I myself always make sure my client has their own jury chart and notebook to track juror answers during voir dire, and check in about every peremptory challenge we're going to make, often huddling with my client. We decide together, as a team, who stays. Why? Because it's their life, yes, but also their instincts might be much sharper than mine when it comes to who will or will not be a fair juror. Woods talked about this very phenomenon playing out in his puffy coat case, where there was a juror he was ready to dismiss, but his client gave him pause, urging him to keep her. Woods agreed. "A few passes later, the DA kicked her off. And as she left, she went out of her way, walked over to our table, literally put her hand on my shoulder, and said, 'Good luck, Mr. Woods. I hope you and your client do well.'"[32]

As Woods told me this story, I realized it felt deeply familiar. In one of my own cases, a juror I had doubted had gone on to acquit my client, and then, after the trial was over, embrace him and urge him to join her for Sunday services. I can have all the legal expertise in the world, but there is something to be said about instinct.

A lawyer cannot always luck out enough to serve the community one knows best; those of us who come from other places need to spend the extra hours visiting the streets whose names appear in our papers, and really *listening* to our colleagues, clients, and witnesses about their lives. But the degree to which the law filters out the people who already carry this proximity is staggering. The law, as a profession, is massively white. At the time of this writing only about 5 percent of lawyers are Black and only about 6 percent Latin,[33] meaning the people most impacted by the criminal legal system are least represented in its operation, least able to access its power. It also means that, all too often, the lawyers practicing in the community don't come from it, and obviously coming from the community your jury pool shares is a massive home-field advantage.

Representation isn't a DEI checkbox. It's a path to the kind of insight that increases effectiveness—and when the jury pool is shifted so as to exclude people from the community most impacted by our court system, the power of representation in the law is also eroded.

———

There are layers upon layers of impact that lack of representation can have in the prosecutorial world, from charging decisions—after all, prosecutors charge, basically, things they're afraid of and things they're mad at, and culture influences both of those reactions—to the way prosecutors understand witnesses, survivors, and juries. For example, I once watched a prosecutor stand up at trial and tell the jury that the streets were empty on a given occasion, with no witnesses to be seen, because the day was hot and so everyone had stayed inside. To a Bronx jury, this is worth a good laugh—air-conditioning is generally weak or missing, and on a hot day people are just as likely to go outside seeking relief from a cramped, hot apartment. This prosecutor's version of reality revealed both his privilege and his lack of perspective, and his credibility with that audience was greatly damaged. But in a world where his jury pool had been more vulnerable to prosecutorial curation, his detachment from the folks he was prosecuting wouldn't have made a dent.

Beyond who is on the jury, there's also the question of what those people have been steeped in, what they are primed to believe. I once had a prosecutor tell an elaborate story about his "Grandpa Pete" to help explain circumstantial evidence to a jury. He claimed that during an idyllic upstate summer his grandfather was seen rolling on the ground with the dog, the sound of buzzing audible in the air. Grandpa returned to the house with red welts. "It was bees, right?!" he asked the jury excitedly. They stared at him.

This was a circumstantial case in which he needed the jury to go with him on a leap; he had a partial fingerprint and a blurry video, and he needed the jury to believe his witnesses when they said that these two things implicated my client beyond a reasonable doubt. But instead of building credibility with this group of strangers, he had overestimated his sway and inextricably linked this example to the strength of his circumstantial case, not realizing that this first impression of circumstantial evidence—which he would need the jury to feel is a strong, incontrovertible tool in order to win—left gaps you could drive a truck through. Which I was lucky enough to do when my turn came.

I got up and asked the jury if anyone had ever heard of an EpiPen. They had. "That's great! Because Grandpa Pete is actually *allergic* to bees. But you have an EpiPen! You can save his life. If, of course, it was bees. But the thing is . . . you didn't *see* any bees, did you? And if it was, say, horseflies, well . . . Grandpa Pete is eighty-five years old. The epi could stop his heart. So . . . who here is *so sure* it was bees they're ready to stick that EpiPen in Grandpa Pete?"

No one raised their hand.

I had entered the world of the DA's story and undermined it, which is a small thing conversationally, but the larger effect was to break the jury's feeling of stability and certainty in relying on circumstantial evidence. I also implied the stakes. For the prosecutor, the stakes in the example were small—just a question of figuring out the right insect to go in a strange little story about his childhood. But by creating life-or-death consequences, I had pulled the circumstances in which the jury was operating back to the extremely serious consequences of the courtroom. I reminded them that their willingness to rely on circumstantial evidence would, potentially, cost my client years of his life.

We make different kinds of decisions when the stakes are very, very high. We are more cautious, as we should be. Recognizing that the key decision-makers here were ordinary people who still held the capacity to take their decision as seriously as it deserved, and whose way of looking at the facts would be inextricably tied to what they felt was on the line, I had to reset the stakes in the room, and thus reset the level of caution—and doubt—to the place where my client had a fairer chance of being heard with care.

This is the kind of opportunity that isn't usually available with a judge as a decision-maker. System stakeholders and expert legal players become inured to the high stakes around them, accustomed to sending people off to horrifying fates and then going to lunch. Which means that a jury system creates a uniquely American opportunity to reach people who are not so numbed to the worst harms of our legal system, and have their fresh perspective offer a potential lifeline to their fellow citizen. But it only really works when jurors walk in with a truly fresh perspective, one that hasn't already been fully tainted by thirty years of *Law & Order* episodes and constant repetition of police strategic communications in the media. When the jury is made up of mostly people who have experienced court only on TV and very few people whose loved ones have experienced court in real life, the priming is a mess, the real-world stakes are felt as theoretical rather than visceral, and the level of care we can expect from the jury is impacted.

———

Those real-world stakes are made even more theoretical by the rule of "jury ignorance," which dictates that jurors are not allowed to be told the punishment that may follow their verdict. This rule often surprises people when they learn about it; after all, if a jury of one's peers is supposed to sit in judgment of misconduct, it's reasonable to think they should not only weigh the evidence but also consider whether the punishment for guilt fits the crime. And if you think that sounds right, you're actually in line with history. In eighteenth-century England, for example, the death penalty abounded, but only on paper. Specific legal exceptions enabled juries to spare the life of the accused: they could render a "partial verdict," deciding that someone didn't steal 40 shillings worth of goods (death) but only 39 shillings (not death), which they did with startling regularity for ordinary community members, albeit less for career criminals and crimes that they found especially disturbing. The regularity of this practice suggests that it wasn't a series of lawbreaking juries run rampant, but rather an accepted system. Parliament put harsh punishments on the books as a deterrent, but the harsh punishments were rarely handed down in real life. And it wasn't just England. In eighteenth-century America, examples are, predictably, more puritanical: instead of trying to figure out how to find someone guilty of stealing half a sheep rather than a whole sheep, American juries were finding people guilty of "libidinous actions" instead of adultery.[34]

But then came the 1990s. In a case where the defense was insanity, and the accused person wanted the jury to know that a finding of insanity would result in his being confined to a mental hospital, the Supreme Court suddenly came up with a "principle" that "juries are not to consider the consequences of their verdicts."[35] Justice Clarence Thomas, a big fan of legal history and "originalism," decreed this principle "well established" on the basis of one other case from 1975, cited zero historical support for the idea that the sentence is exclusively the judge's job, and effectively closed the door on informed juries in America.[36]

The result is not something that most people see as just. For example, in Three Strikes–era California, jurors might convict a person of stealing a piece of pizza, thinking it was no big deal and then be horrified to learn that their decision had just cost a man the rest of his *life*. Research indicates jurors may be less likely to convict when they know the punishment will be harsh.[37] This means that a fully informed jury is not just a safeguard for the accused, but a crucial space for the public to voice their opinion on the law and public policy. With Justice Thomas's revisionist history in place, that crucial check on the system evaporated.

Jury ignorance becomes even more perverse when you take a look at it next to another standard feature of our jury selection process: death qualification. Death qualification is a unique process used in death penalty trials to ensure that only jurors who are willing to consider the death penalty are selected—essentially, all jurors are questioned about their willingness to convict with death on the line, and their willingness to impose the death penalty if they see fit, and any conscientious objectors are excluded from the jury at the outset.[38] This isn't reserved for juries that will decide only the sentence for a conviction; rather, the jurors who will decide *guilt* or *innocence* first have to affirm that they wouldn't refrain from convicting someone just because they do not want to bring about the death of their fellow citizen.[39] Unsurprisingly, early research on this practice found that death-qualified juries were significantly more prone to convict and more prosecution-friendly than regular juries.[40] The tilting by way of exclusion doesn't just impact individual trials, but can impact the continued use of the death penalty itself. When people raise challenges under the Eighth Amendment, arguing that execution is cruel and unusual, the court often considers whether the penalty is still broadly acceptable to Americans and whether it remains *usual*.[41] When everyone who objects to the death penalty is excluded from weighing in via jury service, the court's use of death penalty juries as an index of acceptability ends up just as skewed as the juries themselves.[42]

So what do we do when the system's consequences have ventured so far outside the window of human tolerance that ordinary people must be kept in ignorance or weeded out to uphold the system's ability to punish?

We inform the public.

What most people don't know is that the law largely does not allow inquiry into what happens in the jury room and cannot pry into why a person voted to convict or not to convict. Because of this protection for the deliberative process, even though the law orders jurors to convict accused people if there is evidence beyond a reasonable doubt, the law cannot prevent people from voting their conscience in court.

This is what we call jury nullification, or a jury's choice to reject a case or evidence and refuse to convict—even when there is ample evidence of guilt—simply because they think the law is, in some way, unjust. Nullification is not legal, per se, but rather a collision between what is allowed and what is possible. Jurors are not legally *allowed* to refuse to find guilt when guilt has been proved beyond a reasonable doubt. But the court process relies upon ordinary citizens, serving on juries, feeling free to make findings of fact without inappropriate pressure on their decision-making, which means that the law protects, to a large extent, the sanctity of the jury room, as well as the right of jurors to be free from interrogation about their decisions. The decision to nullify takes place not in open court but rather inside the mind and heart of the individual civilian weighing a case. So even though it's not legal, it's entirely possible, and essentially impossible to prevent.

It also becomes more relevant the further the law strays from the governing social mores and values of a community. Nullification has played this role historically. Paul Butler, a former prosecutor and strong advocate for the community voice in the criminal court system, gives the example of prosecutions for aiding and abetting slave escapes in the northern U.S. states.[43] If you were a juror on a case in 1853 where a man was accused of helping a slave escape to Canada, and you believed the prosecution had proved this man did so, would you vote to convict? If you said no, then you understand exactly what nullification is for. Over the years, nullification has been used to prevent conviction for people accused of criticizing British rule (back when we had that), selling alcohol during Prohibition, protesting the Vietnam War, and consensual sodomy cases (we often forget that sodomy laws were only rejected by the Supreme Court in 2003).[44]

Why should people be forced to *personally* advance the imposition of a law they think is unjust? And why should politicians be able to put harsh laws in place—laws so harsh that jurors might refuse to convict if they knew the full extent of their impact—and then hide the truth from the very jurors whose participation they need to impose punishment? After all, from a policy perspective, jury ignorance is a disaster.[45] It enables the people in power to put insupportable laws in place, meaning that our primary control on lawmakers—the ability to withhold our support from them when they do things we don't like—is eroded. When jurors are able to reject draconian laws, it follows that politicians should have to pass better laws instead.

This argument—that the power to nullify is the last mechanism through which ordinary people can reject bad laws and bad punishments, protecting one another from government overreach and pushing those in power to change the law—is also an inversion of a common policy argument heard in favor of bad prosecutions. Recently, some of the harshest prosecutions have been defended as an effort to highlight bad policy: "I have to impose the law to its fullest extent so that lawmakers can see what their laws really do and change them if they want to" is a common argumentative shield for ludicrous prosecutions. But in fact, the citizenry has the ability to impose the exact same—or perhaps more—power, by rejecting the prosecutions that fall into that terrifying category of fully legal but morally appalling. After all, it takes only one juror refusing to convict on a ludicrous prosecution to protect someone from a felony conviction.

Nullification sits in a weird place, legally. The Supreme Court, in a case called *Sparf v. United States,*[46] said that while jurors have the "physical power" to reject the law, they have no "moral right" to do so. So they *shouldn't,* but functionally can't be stopped, meaning that the compromise reached by the law is to essentially leave people in the dark about their ability to nullify and hope they don't poke around too much. While courts can't prevent nullification, people have still been arrested for "jury tampering" when they try to tell others about their power to nullify.[47] Are these prosecutions legitimate? Well, again, it's weird: the consensus is that telling people *generally* about nullification is protected by the First Amendment (so please don't arrest me for this book), but trying to interfere in a *specific* case could be jury tampering. But that consensus didn't prevent the arrest of advocates in Colorado[48]— the First Amendment may help you beat the rap, but you can't beat the ride.

Of course, nullification only works in one direction—it echoes our Constitutional presumption of innocence in that it gives a juror the power to *not* convict, allowing them to exert the power only to liberate, not to incapacitate or punish. Which, of course, isn't always a power that serves the disempowered; a juror can nullify charges against a police officer or corrupt politician just as readily as charges against a subway fruit seller. But the inherent mathematics of the system tend against that result, because the former are prosecuted so much less frequently than the latter.

Nullification can also just be hard to *do*. I met a woman who told me that her jury service had been one of the worst experiences of her life, something about which she still has nightmares. She had been chosen for a jury in L.A., where a young Black man, a college student, was accused of possession of a firearm while prohibited—having a gun even though there was some legal reason why he was not supposed to. The police who testified about seeing a gun in his house offered stories that didn't quite match up—one said they had seen a suitcase in the kid's room, the other said they hadn't—and she was also troubled by the manner in which this young man had been followed and surveilled by police. "Why were the police coming across the lawn, jumping out, and looking into his house? I don't want police pulling up and following *me* into my house, looking through *my* window. Is this legal? What I do in my home is what I do in my home. It seemed like very aggressive policing, like the police had an agenda here. I'm familiar with the LAPD, with Rampart. Their history of racist convictions. It seemed aggressive to me." But when it came time to deliberate, she found herself up against eleven other people who wanted to convict and go home, not sit around debating inconsistencies in the police story, or whether we, as a community, want to reject this manner of policing altogether.

"When we go in to deliberate, they make this one guy foreman, probably the tallest guy in the room. He's the biggest guy. He's got a lot of heft. I can't remember what his job was, but he was a foreman or something; he managed some construction crew or a warehouse crew or something like that. The other jurors? No Black people. So basically it was, Oh, let's just take a vote. I said, 'Can we just vote by paper or something? I'm not sure we all want to be putting our hands up at this point. We don't know each other.' He grumbled about that, and I think there were three people who said not guilty, and the rest said guilty." The other two jurors who didn't want to convict were also troubled by the police telling of events, but they were quickly reminded by others in the room that "the police are there to protect us." By the second vote within about half an hour, it was 11 to 1.

"I'm thinking this is insane in L.A., because the police department is *notoriously* corrupt. We know this from O.J. They could have convicted O.J. without tampering with the evidence, but they still tampered with it. We also know that we have mass incarceration in L.A. Black people are convicted, while there's plenty of white people who are criminals, too, who don't get pulled over."

So she held out. "As the afternoon wore on, the foreman in particular got pretty agitated that I wouldn't cave. At one point he was standing over me with his face red yelling at me, and I was terrified. But my conscience just couldn't let me do that. I was not so clear then on the whole police reliability or police unreliability. Are they there to protect us? Do they have an agenda? Are they really trustworthy in a case like this? I don't know. But I certainly had a doubt about the police. No one else in the room seemed to have any doubt."

One sticking point was that the defense hadn't really put up a strong alternate theory, while the prosecutor in the case had presented a clear accusation of weapons possession. "I was really angry that the defense lawyer didn't do his job. He wasn't a public defender. That family had coughed up some money, and he did a terrible job. There was no alternate story."

She held out for the whole first day, but by the second day she was feeling both frightened and exhausted. "I purposely chose a seat close to where I could call the bailiff. Because if that guy was standing up red-faced and yelling at me again, I was going to call the bailiff. There were times when all of them were yelling. I spent most of the day, the second day, with my head down on the table, just trying not to get berated. I was thinking, How many more weeks am I going to go with this? And no, no one offered to go get the bailiff or tell them that we couldn't reach a verdict. I didn't know what it would take to hang the jury, if it would take two weeks or two weeks more of sitting there. I had a business to run. I had to get back to work." When one of the other jurors pointed out to her that there must be a *reason* the kid in question was prevented from having a gun, that he must be a *bad person,* she couldn't shake the pressure. She found herself hoping that this college kid was secretly a bad person when she relented and voted to convict.

These days, she still has nightmares. "It goes so against the person I am, to hope someone is a bad person. This is not at all natural to me, I had to force myself into that assumption. He seemed like a clean-cut kid. He was a Black man going to college. He was beating the odds in a lot of ways too. It was a horrible moment. I did not have the tools I needed at the time to save that kid. I wish I had. But I'm not a lawyer; I didn't know what to say to end the deliberation. It took me years to unpack it and understand it to where I am today. I was sick about it. I'm still sick about it."

To be clear, this juror was betrayed by a system that never should have let her get bullied into doing something she didn't believe in. When a juror has made up their mind, it's the court's job to end the deliberation and declare a mistrial. The case can be brought again. No one should be left to be screamed at in a roomful of strangers until they assent. Yet because of the secret nature of jury proceedings, if a juror doesn't let somebody know what's going on, it can be impossible for a court to step in. Jurors are given reams of instructions before they go deliberate, but rarely if ever will a juror be instructed on what to do if they feel bullied in the deliberation room. It's not just nullification that is put on mute in America; it's also what to do with your conscience when you take on your highest duty as a citizen.

———

Our jury system has some truly beautiful aspects of potential: it is fascinating to live in a nation that trusts the citizenry with this staggering responsibility and believes in the ability of ordinary people to find truth. But right now, the system isn't using ordinary people or seeking out a jury of one's peers; it's curating the pool into its most privileged form, eliminating the kind of real-world experience that would make our juries smarter, sharper, and better able to find truth.

It's still true that very few cases go to trial. But remember earlier when I mentioned that the small jury had a bigger influence on the system as a whole than the big one? That's because wins and losses at trial fundamentally change what prosecutors do, whom they charge, and how they charge. When they are able to get a jury pool so curated as to not blink at police misconduct or unreliable witnesses, prosecutors are free to charge without restraint, enhancing their power and confidence in a way that results in greater charge stacking and more pressure on ordinary people to plead guilty.

Jurors, through their decisions, can reject whole swaths of prosecutorial overreach and politicized prosecution; they can force prosecutors to focus more on the crimes that actually matter to them and less on the low-hanging-fruit cases that ruin lives with zero benefit to public safety. Prosecutors won't bring cases they know they can't get past a jury and, if they do bring them, will offer more favorable deals to people whose cases they don't think they can win at trial. If juries were free to know the full consequences of those laws and convictions, we might have even more feedback for prosecutors on how we the people actually feel about the punishments they seek.

As it stands, the trickle-down impact of trial juries is still massively underestimated. Which means that the scale of power being stolen from Black and brown people by jury exclusion is massively underestimated as well.

Without their power and presence, the whole idea of justice in America has lost its legitimacy. As Woods put it, "The fact that people of color have no voice in the outcome of cases makes the entire system suspect to any person of color. We do not believe in the outcomes, because we are not participating. We are intentionally excluded. But if you are able to participate, if you are able to render a decision with twelve people from the community with regard to an outcome, and actually see some kind of justice done? It's absolutely transformative. It gives you some kind of faith and belief in the system. Because you're now participating."[49]

Chapter Nine

An Unwinnable Game

How Prisons—and Release—Set People Up to Fail

Many years ago, I was standing in front of the Los Angeles Twin Towers jail. It was somewhere between two and three o'clock in the morning, but the plaza was decently lit, and even though the concrete under my sneakers was getting colder every minute, I was prepared for the night. Jails, one of the most supposedly regimented places on the planet, rarely do anything on time.

I was there to help someone who had once been sentenced to life in prison. When I was working at the Three Strikes Project, helping people come home well was a crucial part of my job. Some of the best days in my life as a lawyer were days when I got to drive up to the front of a California state prison and welcome someone home with a ride and a meal. Soon, the Anti-Recidivism Coalition (ARC) one-upped me in the best way, working with the Three Strikes Project to organize the Ride Home Program, where instead of being met by their lawyer, people being released from prison hundreds of miles away from their families were offered a warm welcome by someone who had, themselves, experienced incarceration and release.[1] They were safely taken to their landing spot—the home of a loved one, or perhaps a supportive or sober living house—with a meal and some small adventure (of their choosing) on the way. Some people want to dip their toes in the ocean, like a client of mine released in Redding. Others want to visit a record shop or get a favorite hamburger. In the hours of driving, they can forge a relationship with someone who has shared this experience, who understands the difficulty of transition. And they can become part of a community of people who carry hard-won insight into this circumstance, and who choose to support one another.

As fantastic as news of a release is, it's also not what most people imagine—a dignified courtroom with a judge who orders the release and bangs a gavel and the person walks into the arms of their awaiting family. In reality, once a person is ordered released, they have to be "processed out." This means that if they're ordered released by a local judge, they still leave the courtroom in shackles and go back to the local jail where they are being held. Then they have to await endless processes on no particular timeline—paperwork, the gathering of belongings, various officials signing off. What sounds as if it should (ethically and logically) take a few hours at most can take days, or even weeks. You call the jail to ask when your client is coming out and get told that even the jail doesn't know.

When they do get around to releasing someone, they often do so with no warning, and at strange hours. Take, for example, the client of one of the best colleagues I've ever had, a lawyer who had carefully arranged a residential program for her client following his release. Instead of releasing him to the program's transportation, as she had requested, they waited until the program's intake was closed for the weekend and then left this man in a major California city, in the middle of the night, with no phone, in a paper jumpsuit.

That night at Twin Towers, I was waiting for a man who would have no idea who I was and whom I knew only by his photo. The jail refused to indicate at what time he might be released, so I showed up in the late afternoon. I asked the person at the desk about his progress, but they claimed to have no more information than I did. All I knew was which doors he was likely to come out of, so I sat by those doors and waited. Occasionally, people would come out of the doors. For a long while in the day, there were other families and friends waiting with me, receiving their loved ones as they emerged. As the night deepened, there were fewer families. At one point, a man walked out wearing hospital scrubs and a military jacket complete with epaulets. "What's up with the epaulets?" I asked one of the others who was waiting with me. "Oh, there's a donation box inside where people can take clothes if they need them. They can take whatever they want." A few minutes later, the guy in the epaulets seemed to realize that he needed something inside and went back in the doors. In the entryway, there was a conversation, and he became upset. Seconds later, he was grabbed and pulled, screaming in anguish, back inside. It was almost midnight.

Release from incarceration—or reentry, as it is often called—isn't easy. It's a difficult transition with incredibly high stakes. If we, as a people, wanted greater public safety, reentry would be handled with care. People would be released at a set time so that they could have someone waiting for them to give them a ride and a welcome home. Housing would be set up in advance, as well as access to medicines, therapies, or forms of supportive care a person needs in order to be well. No one would be released without a means of contacting help—everyone should have some amount of cash in hand, and a phone, when they set foot outside. If everyone who came home did so with a place to stay, a path to finding income, and access to medical care, we would have substantially less recidivism. If someone dumped you on a street corner with nothing—perhaps wearing humiliating paper clothing—miles from home and with no way to call loved ones, you, too, might find yourself faced with difficult choices. Do you ride the bus without paying, and risk rearrest and re-incarceration? Do you beg strangers for help even if one of them might call the police on you for harassment? Why would our system so assiduously set people up for failure?

———

Before we can fully understand reentry, though, we have to take a step back and think about what people are reentering *from*. Most people's idea of incarceration is shaped by some potpourri of media, maybe a little *Shawshank Redemption*, a smattering of *Oz*, and a wistful note of *Orange Is the New Black*. There are often notes of truth in the media, but none have managed to fully capture the combination of terror, boredom, grief, desperation, and determination that characterizes American incarceration.

For many people in hyper-policed neighborhoods (the majority of people who end up in the criminal court system in the first place), contact with the system starts young. For Malcolme Muttaqee, a teacher and aspiring PhD student, his first contact with police started when he and some other boys were joking around on the elementary school playground, putting a thumb through their fly and trying to startle people by getting them to look down. The school called the police, and had officers scare the boys about "indecent exposure" and their risk of going to jail.[2]

For Amir Chapel, now deputy program director at the Council of State Governments, that first childhood contact was terrifying. "My first experience of incarceration was at Barry J. Nidorf Juvenile Hall. There was a fight in school, and the school police officer called the LAPD. I was scared on the ride over. The officer wasn't talking to me. I didn't get to tell my mom where I was going. I didn't get to tell anybody where I was going. And I started getting cold and sweaty. I was uncomfortable sitting in the back of that police car with the hard seats and wondering what was going to happen next. Were there crazy gang members that I'm going to have to fight when I got there? I'd heard the stories. Was I going to be assaulted? I got dropped off, and went in through the double gates. They put me in this holding cell. There were two other kids in there and we were talking to each other: 'Have you been here before? What's going to happen? Do you know what's going to happen? How long are we going to be here? When can we call our moms?' Everybody wanted to call their moms."[3]

The experience of immediate criminalization isn't unique to Amir and Malcolme. For families in neighborhoods routinely surveilled by police, contact with the cops starts in childhood. In our country, as of 2019, 1.7 million students were in schools with police but no counselors, 3 million students were in schools with police but no nurses, 6 million students were in schools with police but no school psychologists, 10 million students were in schools with police but no social workers, and 14 million students were in schools with police but no counselor, nurse, psychologist, or social worker.[4] No matter how wealthy the school, schools with larger proportions of Black students are likelier to have school police, and the Black and Indigenous kids are the ones more likely to experience suspension, expulsion, or arrest at school, and that unequal exposure to law enforcement has all kinds of corollary effects on student performance.[5] Beginning as early as elementary school, teachers and school workers hand out more disciplinary infractions to Black kids than any other group, regardless of classroom context or the kids' behavior,[6] and given the overwhelming police presence in schools, the racial bias that fuels disciplinary action is also pushing children, unjustifiably, into the carceral system.[7]

This is the starting point of a system that results in about twice as much school punishment and nearly five times as much incarceration for Black children as for white children.[8] Black children are often perceived as older by police, prosecutors, judges, and other key adults in their lives, a phenomenon called adultification that leads directly to worse treatment of Black children by these systems.[9] White kids, even when arrested, are so much less likely to be booked and charged (and so much more likely to be let go with a warning) that the proportion of Black children neither booked nor cited on their first arrest is still less than that of white children on their *fourth* arrest.[10] Each little decision adds up; the higher likelihood of being stopped by police feeds into a higher likelihood of arrest and a lower likelihood of diversion from the system.[11]

Concretely, this means that Black kids are getting harsh punishments—
or even sentences—for normal childhood misbehavior like schoolyard
scuffles or pranking a teacher, when white children are not.[12] We live in
a country where kids as young as five have been injured by police in
school, and kids as young as four have felt the sensation of being handcuffed.[13]

Much of this is invisible when it's happening, because kids don't have
the right to a lawyer in school disciplinary proceedings, nor for police
contact that doesn't immediately result in arrest, nor are their parents
always alerted. As a public defender, I may meet my client on their first
arrest at sixteen years old, but police contact might have started years
before. There may be dozens of police contacts—officers pulling up on
kids walking home from school, detaining them, asking them about
their homes, family, friends, connections, taking notes, filling out "field
identification cards,"* and even, in some places over the years, quietly
entering their information into gang databases. These contacts are invisible because, although they may be time-consuming and scary for the
child involved, they don't result in arrest. They result in the creation of
police surveillance paperwork that may never see the light of day. But
if that kid gets arrested later and becomes my client, and I am able to
get discovery that includes this history, it is common to find that a child
has already experienced years of being treated, by grown-ups in uniforms, like a criminal, and their trust in the system has already been
eroded.[14]

———

* Field identification (FI) cards are pretty much what they sound like—index
cards police carry into which they can enter the personal information of anyone
they stop, including not just name but monikers and nicknames, identifying
marks, tattoos, relationships, and so on. Whether police fill out an FI card is
entirely up to them, but they are often treated as a de facto precursor to unwitting entry (even baselessly) into a gang database.

Adelaida Caballero wasn't a kid when she went to jail for the first time. She was twenty-seven years old and pregnant with her first child. She worked in the accounting department at a Safeway in Menlo Park, California, and had recently ended her relationship with her child's father. "We were in a very abusive relationship," she recalls now. "I had allowed him to steal my self-worth. My friends saw bruises at the time, saw how I would tense up around him, and they put two and two together. I was just full of shame. And I think at that point I had enough, and I said, 'I can't do this anymore; you need to leave my house.' I made him leave the apartment." A short while later, though, she found out she was pregnant.

Adelaida asked her ex to meet up with her so that she could tell him about the pregnancy and make a safe plan to co-parent. She asked him to meet her at a local restaurant, which she thought was safer because it was in public. "He wanted us to get back together. I said no. When I got home to my condo, he was lying in wait. He pushed me inside and he just tried to hit me, so I tried to run out the door. And at that time, I had really, really, really long hair. So he would grab it and get me back inside. He pushed me onto this closet door, where the knob hit my back, and I fell down." Over the next few minutes, Adelaida realized that not only was her life in danger; her baby's was as well. "He was just throwing stuff on top of me and I'm trying to crawl away. And then he grabs me again by my hair, takes me to the kitchen, and puts me in the freaking corner and gets a knife from the cutlery set and puts it to my throat. And he says, 'You're not going to have that baby if you're not with me.' He starts punching my stomach."

Describing the incident now, she doesn't remember how she fought back.

"The next thing you know, he's on the floor. I asked him to get up off my floor. And he says, I'm bleeding. I'm like, What are you talking about, from where? And I see that he was bleeding profusely. So I called 911."[15]

When the police came, Adelaida was arrested and charged with a string of felonies. She remembers the number of years of prison on the table—seventeen years for trying to protect herself and her child. Sitting in jail, unable to be released pretrial, keep her job, or fight her case from home, and with a top end that would have separated her from her child until nearly his adulthood, she accepted a plea to a strike felony and six years of incarceration.

It's often shocking to hear of instances of abuse survivors being prosecuted for fighting back against their abuser, but it's horribly common in our criminal court system. Adelaida isn't alone. It is estimated (because no national data exists) that tens of thousands of women have been in prison for defending themselves.[16] The Bureau of Justice Statistics notes that about one in five people in state prison has been a victim of physical or sexual abuse,[17] and a study found that 86 percent of women in jails have survived sexual violence.[18] One of the first cases I worked on as a legal intern—and which I've never been able to forget—involved a woman who had been abused for nearly a decade by her partner. He had been on top of her, beating her in broad daylight, on the street, in front of neighbors, when she fought back. Guess which member of that couple was charged with a felony and ended up doing several years of prison time?

Prosecutors can cite many reasons for prosecuting abuse survivors—in Adelaida's case, she remembers them asking why she didn't flee the apartment. In many cases, the abusive partner may have their own version of the facts—in Adelaida's case, she says he told police she stabbed him over a Snickers bar, a detail that attracted attention and ridicule from the press that she found deeply humiliating. Prosecutors and police are free to choose whom to believe. For many survivors of violence, that choice falls against them.

Adelaida gave birth a few months later with her ankles shackled to the hospital delivery room bed. "Cops are [in the delivery room] laughing at me when I'm in pain. After I gave birth to my son, they put him on my chest, and they took him away, and I had to go back to the prison."

She was lucky to have family who could come and pick up her baby. Many women around Adelaida had no one who could take custody of their child within forty-eight hours. "I witnessed that throughout my years in prison that folks, they will go out to medical and give birth to their baby and then come back and they're in tears because their babies were not picked up. It's just the meanest thing the state can do, to forcefully adopt out your baby. And so literally, you're just not even a person in prison. You're just this object, numbered, that they have to check off a list every day."[19] Adelaida had hoped to do a mother-infant program—which she remembers her sentencing judge recommending, and which would have allowed her to bond with her child and begin societal reintegration in a less restrictive setting than prison—but the Department of Corrections had no program available to women whose crime of conviction was violent.

No matter what age a person is, being incarcerated takes an enormous toll. Whenever I'm listening to the radio or watching a *Dateline*-style show about the horrors of incarceration in a foreign place (usually the show is talking about a country on poor diplomatic terms with the United States), the "horrors" they list as endemic to distant gulags are almost laughably familiar.[20] Freezing or heat-ravaged prisons[21] with rotten food that makes you sick[22] and no access to basic sanitation,[23] cells overrun with bugs and vermin,[24] overcrowded to the point of becoming unlivable,[25] where incarcerated people are regularly abused or threatened by their captors?[26] Places where on any given day, as many as a third of the people inside report they are victims of brutal violence, and literally 100 percent of people in one study reported witnessing violence, with 90 percent of people in another study describing prison violence as "inevitable"?[27] Set up so it's incredibly hard to get access to your lawyer or your family? Yeah, that's the good old US of A. Once behind bars in our country, nearly all people will witness or experience violence. The impact on a person's mental health is lasting—depression, anxiety, problems with emotional regulation.[28] Disconnection from family, lack of autonomy, lack of privacy, violence, unpredictability, boredom—all of these are signature aspects of any jail or prison and also factors that directly undermine a person's ability to both be well and eventually succeed in the world outside prison walls.[29]

Talking to Amir about his first time in the L.A. County Jail, you hear the exact things that studies warn us about—the dehumanization, alienation, disorientation, and overcrowding that dramatically increase instances of both hostility and suicidality:[30]

I did crazy things. I stole my auntie's credit card and her checks, and I got arrested for pawning a stolen item, using checks, credit cards, because my aunt called the cops on me. Today she regrets that. But at that time it was like tough love. And so I got arrested.

I remember going into the first big room. How did I feel? I felt like cattle. Hundreds of people in this room, just packed into this room.

And then they tell you to line up against the walls and you have to line up against the perimeter with your shoulder to the wall. They tell you to take off all your clothes and they throw a plastic bag in front of you. They tell you to take off all your clothes and put it in that plastic bag because that's going to be the property that they're going to take.

We're all standing there naked, nuts to butts basically, shoulder to the wall. . . . And they tunnel you into this shower area because they essentially want to hose you off. It felt like chattel slavery where you get off the ship and they blast you with water. There's no soap; it's just water. People have filth coming off of them to different degrees.

They give you your county roll, which is your jumpsuit, a towel, a bar of soap, a little toothbrush, and a toilet paper, and they tell you to go to the next room, which is a classification room. You're literally down there for maybe two days, waiting to get assigned up to whatever floor you go to.

I went to the dungeon floor, Denver Row. There's four tiers.

And I went to that floor, and you walk in and you're walking slowly, it's dark. You hear everybody yelling, you hear the rumbling of the concrete, you hear people slapping things, you hear all these things because everything's magnified in there. People are yelling to each other. And I'm just getting walked across the tier by a sheriff, by an L.A. County sheriff, and I'm walking past people, I'm looking at people. I'm not saying anything. I was nervous.

And these are two-people cells with six people in them. They have this thing called boats, where people are sleeping on the floor. I was thinking, I hope they don't put me in a cell where I'm going to have to be violent. I caught up to the cell, they opened the cell, everybody's standing because when a new person comes in the cell, everybody's standing with their boots on and everything.

I just tried to go to sleep. That night, it was 11:30 at night when I finally got up in there. I slept with my shoes on. I had my boots on. I was cold. The blanket doesn't fit me all the way. I'm on the top rack. I'm concerned about these people that I don't know. And just waited until chow time.

You can feel the rumble, and you have nowhere to run. You're in a cell; you can't escape. You can hear people screaming.[31]

Most people don't realize that while prisons and jails are both horrible and built to punish rather than to rehabilitate, jails are, in some ways, much worse. Prisons are built for long-term stays. As bad as they are, they are places where people are, one way or another, building a life. Jails are not. They're built for short-term stays, meaning nothing to do—no jobs, education, little programming—and poor access to things like medical care or visits. Now, because of the volume of our system, they're being used for long-term stays,[32] so the little infrastructure that was in place is destroyed by massive overcrowding.[33] To give you a sense of how bad it is, my client who was convicted of stealing plumbing supplies had been in prison for more than a decade when I got his case. After trying multiple strategies to get him out, we finally had a hearing at which I believed we would be able to win his freedom. But to go to that hearing, he'd have to leave the state prison where he had been building his life—where he had belongings and a job—and come to L.A. County Jail for two weeks so that he could be brought to court and have his hearing. A few days in, as I was preparing to come to L.A. for his hearing, he called my cellphone. He sounded shell-shocked as he told me that he wanted me to withdraw our filings, cancel the hearing, and call the whole thing off, leaving him with a life sentence. I was stunned and asked him why. "I can't do this," he told me. The jail was too hard. He felt he couldn't make it through another week in there. He just wanted to go back, and was willing to give up anything—even freedom—to avoid one more week in the county jail.

In light of this, it's unsurprising that putting people in jails seems to make it more likely that they will engage in crime in the future.[34] One study found that Black Americans' exposure to trauma makes them more likely, in the future, to be entangled in the criminal justice system.[35] People often think of "reentry" as meaning a person's return from a long prison sentence. But when you look at the numbers, even though at any given time only about half as many people are in jails as prisons, jails churned through more than seven million admissions in 2022,[36] which is roughly sixteen times as many admissions as there were to prison that year.[37] Every admission and release is a person trying to reenter their community after the incredibly difficult destabilization of having been jailed, and when we talk about "reentry" support, almost all of it is focused on people coming home from prison rather than jail.

Incarceration changes people. No, not in the way copaganda tells you; time in prison isn't "rehabilitative." America loves a good comeback story, and it feels as if most "reentry" stories are some version of a hard-won, pulling-oneself-up-by-the-bootstraps story that can sanitize prison time as something akin to a useful time-out. And yet prison time makes it harder for people to succeed in almost every way imaginable. Those who do succeed do so in spite of having been incarcerated. Not because of it.

Years of living in a highly violent environment can give people post-traumatic stress disorder, which occurs at twice the rate in formerly incarcerated people.[38] Incarceration can create hypervigilance, anxiety, problems sharing space with people, and trouble with emotional regulation, all of which are difficult to shake after a sentence is over.[39] On any given day in this country, tens of thousands of people are being held in solitary confinement,[40] locked in a cell alone, with limited to no social contact or access to religious chaplains, educators, or treatment personnel, just a correctional officer dropping food through a slot in the wall three times per day.[41] A few times a week, a person may be shackled in leg, arm, and belly chains and taken for one hour of "recreation" in a small caged area, which may or may not even be outdoors.[42] Realistically, we're talking about just concrete in natural light or concrete in artificial light.

The way we in the United States leave people in these conditions for months and years is considered torture internationally.[43] Solitary confinement is sometimes used to punish those who commit infractions in prison, which at least has a defined time span. "Administrative" segregation—when a prison puts a person in solitary supposedly for safety reasons, or for some other administrative purpose—is the true nightmare, because it can mean years rather than weeks of isolation. A study by Yale revealed that most people stay in solitary for one to three months, and in some states much longer. In Texas, for example, half of people in solitary confinement stay there for three years or more.[44] Meanwhile, researchers tell us that less than a week in these conditions can permanently alter a person's brain, creating cognitive issues and increasing the risk of suicide.[45]

It's not just the researchers who can see this reality; people in prison experience it firsthand. For Amir, worrying about how prison would change him, and who he would be—who he *could* be—afterward was consuming:

> The thing that I was most scared of was when it was time to go home. Was I going to make it? Was I going to come back here? Is my mom going to look at me differently? I only heard from her on special occasions. It was too emotional for her. I would call her periodically, but I also didn't want to get on the stress box [the phone] and call my mom because I would get emotional. And so anytime I did call, I did my best to gather myself before I turned around to go back into the world that I was in.
>
> After you get past that first fear of violence, as humans, we adapt. And so unfortunately, I normalized it. I could hear people getting sexually assaulted. You can see the sheets over people's beds, and here I am within earshot of someone getting assaulted. And I can't do anything about it. Nobody else is doing anything about it. And that's scary. That's scary. I became someone who I didn't want to be. I didn't want to be that person, but you have to be that person.
>
> And then the problem is, *When I get out of here, can I turn it off? How do I turn it off?*[46]

Even though I happen to believe that *no one* deserves to experience what Amir describes, or to be fed rotting bologna sandwiches[47] while spending three years in the torture of total isolation, I also understand that some people have different views on retribution. There is a strong vein of belief that substantial suffering is the just comeuppance of engaging in harm. The problem, though, is what the *result* is from this perspective. When the system itself takes the view that suffering is justice, it sets us all up for a worse, more crime-ridden future.

The truth is, almost no one who goes to prison or jail stays there forever, although the fastest-growing demographic in jail is currently elderly people with little to no likelihood of recidivism if released (classic system logic, locking up the people who have the lowest arrest, re-arrest, and recidivism rates across the board, but the highest medical costs, which you as a taxpayer are now paying for with zero benefit to your safety).[48]

Much attention is rightly given to sentences that result in death in prison—both life sentences and death sentences—because they are ineffective deterrents,[49] do little for public safety, and cost unconscionable sums. For one thing, the certainty of getting caught is a much more important deterrent than the severity of the punishment[50]—meaning that if we want deterrence, we should be side-eyeing low police clearance rates, not imposing longer and harsher sentences. On death sentences, your government is spending millions more. In California, for example, it cost $90,000 more per year in 2005 to house a person on death row versus the general prison population, which totaled $57.5 million back then.[51] In 2025, it would cost $149,923 more to house a person on death row.[52]

All of this is, essentially, security theater, since research tells us that almost no one commits crimes while thinking about potential sentences.[53] Even sentences that are just too long seem more likely to be criminogenic than deterrent.[54] So the more we expand the prison system, the less safety we get out of it. To put it another way, "the United States was spending roughly $33 billion on incarceration in 2000 for essentially the same level of public safety it achieved in 1975 for $7.4 billion—nearly a quarter of the cost."[55]

The theme of "doing very expensive things that don't work at all" isn't limited to life-and-death cases. And this is where most retribution-focused hot takes fail: more than 95 percent of people in prison and jail will come home.[56] So when we talk about prison policy, the vast majority of the time, the question isn't whether someone will return to society; the only question is what condition they'll be in when they return.

———

With the system we have right now, most people will be sicker, poorer, less well networked in their communities, less employable, and more heavily saddled with debt. Spending time in a prison—with high levels of exposure to violence, isolation, and stress, as well as bad food and limited medical care—has serious long-term consequences. One study found that each year in prison shaved two years off a person's life expectancy.[57] Other research suggests that time behind bars can add ten to fifteen years to a person's physiology, exposing them early to health issues that usually come with greater age.[58] Medical care in prison ranges from limited to negligent to fatally harmful.[59] In one survey of incarcerated women in California, 83 percent of respondents said that they had experienced medical abuse or neglect while in prison.[60] Hepatitis C is a great example. The CDC says that 95 percent of hepatitis C cases are curable with treatment, but in state prison 80 percent of people who have ever had hep C still have it.[61] Perhaps because our prison system draws so heavily from communities that are already struggling with access to care, people in prison are twice as likely as the general public to have asthma,[62] nearly twice as likely to have hypertension,[63] over three times as likely to have heart-related problems,[64] over twice as likely to have a stroke,[65] and nearly three times as likely to have a disability.[66] Almost half of people incarcerated in state prison have an indicated mental health concern.[67] And, of course, *all* are less likely to receive adequate care.

In the free world, where we're all struggling to pay for America's expensive, for-profit health-care system, 90 percent of the $4.1 trillion annual cost of our health-care apparatus is spent on chronic conditions and mental health disorders.[68] In California's prisons, the average cost of health care is the biggest expense behind security, accounting for about a third of the total annual cost of incarceration.[69] In the end, both the free and the carceral health-care systems are on our dime as taxpayers. Prison health care manages to be expensive without being good, and prisons send 80 percent of people home with a chronic health condition.[70] And most people are sent home without connections to health-care providers or health insurance, which may be why people on parole, probation, or with a recent arrest are only 4 percent of the adult population but make up more than 7 percent of hospital expenditures and 8.5 percent of emergency department expenditures—translating, in expenditures, to an additional $8.5 billion in hospital costs and $5.2 billion in emergency room costs.[71]

Prisons and jails also create an economic nightmare. People cannot really earn money while in prison; it's the last place where slavery is legal, so people can be compelled to work jobs that pay pennies per hour (if they are paid at all).[72] In addition, they will be charged great sums of money they do not have for the privilege of being confined.

Once in prison, people have to pay exorbitant prices for simple things like phone calls,[73] food, or even basic toiletries,[74] paying much more in prison than they would outside.[75] And there's no rule saying incarcerated people get a break from outside debt—things like child support, existing debt obligations, and other bills, which can build up while a person is serving time.[76] Making matters worse, some people with convictions are barred from vital public benefits like emergency food aid in the form of TANF and SNAP,[77] and can also be barred from unemployment benefits or small business loans.[78]

If a prison saddles a person with a ton of extra debt and pays them slave wages, what will they do when they come home? Of the forty-five thousand documented local regulations that create "collateral" consequences for a conviction—the literal forty-five thousand ways being incarcerated negatively impacts a person's life—62 percent place some kinds of limits on a person's employment eligibility.[79] Even being locked up on a misdemeanor can make a person ineligible for certain jobs or job licenses.[80] Ironically, these are often the very same jobs that they are trained to do in prison, like being a barber or cosmetologist—but these employment bars range far beyond prison jobs, too, meaning that if you were hoping to be a roofer or even a bingo operator, you're out of luck.[81]

Yet people who have work when they come home are substantially less likely to end up back in prison.[82] A great example is Colorado's Work and Gain Education and Employment Skills (WAGEES) program, which connects people to jobs on release. Of the folks who were connected with jobs, only 2.5 percent returned to prison for new crimes within two years.[83] This is compared to the 50 percent of people who usually return to prison within that time frame.[84]

Even though having work is correlated with lower recidivism,[85] we have built a system that combines huge debt burdens with banishment from many professions. Overall, being locked up cuts a person's lifetime earning potential in half, often dropping it by half a million dollars per person overall.[86] Every year, people in America are at least a cumulative $370 billion poorer because of their convictions and former incarceration.[87]

If a person has huge debts but no ability to pay, they get desperate. Debt creates stigma, forcing people to rely on their already-strained relationships and cementing a person's identity as "criminal" or "other" when they can't stand on their own two feet.[88] This spreads legal system burden across communities as the families and friends of formerly incarcerated people take on debt to support their loved ones.[89] Debt itself can cause people to be sent back to prison if paying the debt is a condition of their probation or parole,[90] and one study of young people found debt increased the likelihood of re-incarceration.[91] It is no wonder that research has documented that people put in these conditions will commit new crimes to pay back old court debts, even if they'd rather find legal work.[92] After all, the debt itself has huge ripple effects. It reduces a person's credit score,[93] which in turn can make it impossible to secure the tools one needs for a stable life: a phone, decent work, transportation, housing, or even a utility account.[94]

Malcolme experienced much of this firsthand. As a teenager, he was arrested for stealing a few hundred dollars from a weed dealer; the other kid he was with had a fake gun, and even though Malcolme didn't have a weapon, he was pressured into taking a plea deal for thirteen years. The worst part was that this deal made Malcolme a "walking lifer" in California. When he was sixteen, he had stolen candy from a store in the mall—a petty theft that became a robbery when the mall security guard jumped on his back and he tried to run away. That was his first "strike" felony, and his second plea was his second "strike," meaning that a third offense would get him a life sentence. So even though he did exemplary service in prison—fighting fires and earning college credits—and he came home and immediately set to work getting his associate's, bachelor's, and then master's in education, he was still living in fear. "California is dangerous for me, because I could be out and about and if somebody came and snatched my wife by the hair, if I grab them, I will be struck out and do life in prison for that. If I assert my human right to defend myself, I risk being in prison for the rest of my life."

It wasn't just the fear—Malcolme was also drowning financially. "I applied for an apartment. My credit score is great. My rental history is good, but the application says, 'Have you ever been convicted of a felony?' They say, 'If so, explain.' I say yes, and explained the whole story. I was nineteen; it was fifteen years ago. They respond with, 'Sorry, we don't even process the application of somebody who answers yes to that question.' What does me catching a case when I was barely out of high school have to do with me being a good tenant?"

Malcolme left California. He left his family and his social network, because he couldn't live in fear of re-incarceration, and he couldn't find affordable housing. He found a house he could afford in Ohio—a "fixer-upper," in a place where he felt he could safely bring his family and raise his three children. With his master's in education and an additional master's in counseling, he felt he'd be able to find work teaching. But when he got to Ohio and applied for a license, he was told no. "The state gets back to me and says, 'You're denied because we don't hire anybody that has a felony.' The state says, 'In order for us to give you a teacher's license, we have to do an investigation.' Then the lady tells me, 'This is a whole list of criteria, a whole list of crimes that absolutely bar somebody from getting a teacher's license if they commit them while they're a teacher.' So I replied, 'Well, I never was a teacher. I never had a license. I committed this when I was barely out of high school myself. Why are you sending me this list?'" It turned out, she was only sending him this list because of the length of time he'd spent in prison, when he was himself barely older than his prospective students.

"I paid my debt to society," Malcolme explains. "You have people working in these inner-city schools and these schools in the hood, and the people that are most qualified to reach out to these students and to connect with them, you're barring them access from the schools." At that point, he'd been waiting for five months on the outcome of the state's investigation into his past. Needing to support his family, he started looking into other options, like therapy and counseling, but ran into the same barriers to entry. After he had worked so hard to get his degrees and prepare for a meaningful career that would enable him to give back to his community and use what he had learned, it was painfully apparent that selling fentanyl would be a considerably more feasible option than trying to work in the field for which he was trained. "The university has no problem letting you study a field that you can't even actually practice. You work all of these years, you take all of these tests, you write all of these papers, only for them to tell you you're not good enough. You're not qualified, because you made a mistake when you were a kid."[95]

If a person is on probation, parole, or another form of community supervision, they can be required to find work, or risk being sent back inside.[96] Supervision, a kind of prison without walls, is its own form of nightmare. Parole—the opportunity to be released, under supervision, from a prison sentence—is a false promise in that it lures people into believing that if they behave well they could be released early, when in fact only eight out of twenty-nine states studied have parole boards that accept more than half of the applications for release that come before them (and some states reject as many as 90 percent).[97] This is, in part, because our Supreme Court has found that there is no "fundamental liberty interest" at play in parole hearings (that's right—years of your life in confinement versus freedom is not a fundamental liberty interest according to these guys, because release on parole is merely an "act of grace"),[98] so people do not have the right to a lawyer when they go before the parole board.[99]

When someone comes up before the parole board, they aren't just lawyerless; they also, in many cases, have no right to a hearing, no right to be told the criteria on which the board will decide their case, and no right to appeal.[100] Sometimes the board may not even see the person—they might make the call based solely on records provided by the prison, with complete discretion and no obligation to explain their choice.[101] This may explain why parole boards also face zero pressure—or mandate—to take into consideration real-world data on things like recidivism risk: greater age means a lower likelihood of recidivism, but parole boards are not required to factor this in,[102] and even though many states provide mechanisms for releasing people who are elderly or sick, utilization of these mechanisms remains low.[103] Parole board members are usually appointed by the governor of a state, with little oversight—in Alabama as recently as 2023, for example, a two-member board denied more than 90 percent of parole applications, including people who had been preapproved by the Department of Corrections for release to work in the community. When people are denied parole, they are sent back to continue serving their sentence—sometimes for years before their next hearing, and sometimes until the sentence is up, with no next hearing at all.[104]

Probation—a type of supervised release a person can have in lieu of a jail sentence—is also a bit of a trick, in that people often accept a yearslong probation term thinking that it will enable them to stay in the community, work, and be with their family, while the rules of probation itself tend to set people up for failure. Though viewed as a lenient sentence—or even an opportunity for extra support—probation actually extracts wealth,[105] makes people less (rather than more) employable,[106] increases the chances of eviction (around the country, public housing authorities are allowed to evict people for violations of probation),[107] and can even force people who *could* afford an apartment into homelessness anyway, because none of the places they can afford are allowable by their probation terms.[108] Knowing how bad jail conditions are, it's also understandable why a person would opt for a guilty plea that signs them up for years of personalized surveillance and requirements instead of spending another day in a cell.

What all these forms of "community supervision" have in common is that they allow someone to ostensibly be free, but subject to a whole ton of conditions. Some of them are obvious (don't commit new crimes), but others are Kafkaesque (wear this ankle monitor that you yourself have to pay for and that you have to charge for two hours a day, but also somehow find a full-time job, go to AA meetings every day, meet with a probation officer once a week . . . oh, and also refrain from driving). People under supervision are required, on average, to comply with eighteen to twenty different conditions *every day.*[109]

In practice, this looks like telling someone they can't live in a particular neighborhood, or go stay with family one county over. It looks like a requirement to maintain employment with little help finding a job, and requirements to pay fees or court costs even when you make no income—two-thirds of people on probation make less than $20,000 per year.[110] It looks like being required to complete programs that conflict with a job or school schedule and attend meetings with a supervisory officer that happen during business hours and that require time off from work and the ability to find child care. Almost all states require the person on probation to pay for their own supervision—and almost as many require people on parole, who are returning from years in prison, to do the same.[111] Supervision fees are one of the most common—and burdensome—forms of legal debt[112] with costs ranging from as much as $200 per month in supervision fees[113] to as much as $5,000 per year for the privilege of wearing an ankle monitor.[114]

There are also conditions restricting whom a person can "associate with." Often, association with anyone else who has a criminal record is banned.[115] Which might seem like a reasonable anti-criminal-conspiracy measure at first blush, but consider that more than a third of Americans have a criminal record, and that the proportion of people with a record is higher in hyper-policed communities.[116] It also ignores the realities that most people are facing, like a personal network limited by years of isolation.[117] People who have experienced incarceration themselves—and who have navigated reentry—have special insight into what a person needs when coming home, and may be some of the best connections a person could have on reentry. Los Angeles's Anti-Recidivism Coalition, for example, which provides this kind of peer-led, thoughtful support, has a three-year recidivism rate of less than 10 percent in a state where average recidivism hovers around 60 percent.[118] But if the terms of release say you can't associate with anyone who has a record, well, all these forms of help are off the table.

And if, upon reading this, anyone is still thinking, "Oh, well, people can plan ahead and work around these obligations," I'm sorry to tell you that there are also *surprise* requirements of supervision. Random drug tests, for example, require a person to drop everything they're doing and report for testing the same day, even if they're across town on their second day of a brand-new job. Or sudden visits by a supervisory officer to search a person's home, at any time of day or night, without warning. And of course, requirements to submit to a search of your person, car, or other property anytime law enforcement feels like it—because the rules of supervision often force a person to give up their Constitutional Fourth Amendment right against unreasonable searches, police and other officers can search them as unreasonably as they want, whenever they want, for the entire term of their supervision. Driving to work and don't have two hours for police to thoroughly dismantle and search the interior of your car? Too bad, better call your boss and say you won't be in on time. Lost the job? Yikes, having a job is a condition of your release, and if you violate the condition, you can be locked up again.

————

Because these requirements are numerous and hard for even the most organized person to handle, a ton of people violate one or more of these conditions. In 2020, a study estimated that 42 percent of state prison admissions were due to parole violations.[119] In twenty states, they make up more than half of state prison admissions.[120] About half of these violations are purely technical,[121] meaning that the person didn't engage in behavior that would be considered lawbreaking for a person not on supervision, like missing a meeting, being out past curfew, not showing up to school, or moving residences without permission.[122]

The idea behind this system is safety—the notion that this category of people is at high risk of committing crimes, so we have to watch them really closely and be ready to throw them back in prison at any moment. So, is this making us safer?

Ryan Sakoda is an assistant professor of law at the UC Berkeley School of Law whose research is a deep dive on these forms of supervision. In a 2023 paper, he examined a naturally occurring experiment in the state of Kansas.[123] There, people being released from a "determinate" prison sentence (a set number of years, like a five-year sentence, as opposed to an "indeterminate" sentence of five to ten years) were put on post-release supervision. He wanted to look at the utility of the supervision itself.[124]

In 2000, Kansas ditched the post-release supervision requirement for a certain subset of people released from prison, specifically people who had originally been sentenced to probation and then violated probation, got sent to prison, and are now coming home. This is a good chunk of people; about 35 percent of people coming home from prison in Kansas were originally supposed to be only on probation.

This is notable, because it means that for more than a *third* of people released from prison in Kansas, their original crime—the thing that got them into the system in the first place—was minor enough to get only probation. Prior to 2000, these folks would have had another probation-like period of post-release supervision after they returned. But from 2000 to 2013, people with original probation sentences no longer got post-release supervision in Kansas. They just came home. In 2013, though, the state reinstated the supervision—this time with a softer rebrand, reformed with the intention to result in fewer prison sentences and more helpful interventions. Did supervision 2.0 work better than supervision 1.0 in Kansas?

Professor Sakoda had a ready-made experiment in front of him: a "treatment" group impacted by the 2000 law, as well as a "control" group of people whose post-release supervision was not eliminated by law. If post-release supervision is achieving its goals—helping people succeed or, in the alternative, shuffling malfeasants back to prison—then the elimination of post-release supervision should have resulted in more crime in the community. And if the 2013 reform worked, the gentler supervision should have dropped crime and violations.

That is not at all what Professor Sakoda found. For the people relieved of supervision, the re-incarceration rate dropped—it was about 80 percent lower than it had been before.[125] And there was no increase in re-offending or new crimes. People who were now unsupervised didn't take advantage of it and engage in rampant harm in the community. Instead, ditching post-release supervision resulted in fewer people going to jail, and essentially no increase in criminal behavior.

Maybe the technical violations that people were previously being locked up for weren't such a good proxy for their risk of re-offending after all.

Unfortunately, when Kansas brought back supervision, even the kind it claimed was kinder, re-imprisonment rates popped right back up. According to Professor Sakoda, the reform "returned the one-year re-imprisonment rate to about 30 percent, which is fairly close to the pre-2000 level of 35 percent. So we see a jump up in re-imprisonment by a substantial amount, and then also looking at re-offending, there's no statistically significant change in my measures of re-offending."[126] Even though more people were being sent back to prison, Kansas didn't actually manage to reduce crime.

Community supervision, in short, is a very expensive way to send more people to prison with little to no impact on public safety.

When Adelaida came home, the only place she wanted to be was by her son's side. But there were a few hurdles: first, she was released on parole to San Mateo County, but her son was a few hours away in Stanislaus County. She needed permission to go out of county, not just to see him, but also to fight to regain custody of her child. Her parole officer wasn't interested in helping. "She was just a really mean woman, just cruel. My conditions were to take a class for a year—anger management, domestic violence abuse.[127] It's every single week for fifty-two weeks. But I just came home, and I'm broke, and the class that I had to take was $20 a week. If I didn't have the money to pay for this class, 'Oh, well, you're going to get violated.' So I had to beg people for money. And on top of that, she was looking for ways to entrap me and violate my parole. I would be at the house I was staying at, and she would come knock on the door just once and then call me and say, 'I'm here at your house and you're not here. I'm going to violate you.' Or when I wanted to see my son, because within thirty days of getting out of prison, I was served with court papers because my family was trying to take my son away from me. He was in Modesto, and I had to go to court."

When she asked for permission to go to court, her officer asked her for approval from Child Protective Services (CPS). The problem is, Child Protective Services is an agency that gets involved only in cases of abused or neglected children and Adelaida wasn't accused of abuse or neglect. She had no CPS case. "She goes, 'You have a CPS case?' 'No, I don't. My son visited the prison two times. If I had a CPS case, he wouldn't be able to see me at all.' But she would still not give me a piece of paper to go see my son."

Thankfully, Adelaida was able to fight for herself. She ultimately took records of what she was going through to her parole officer's supervisor and was reassigned. Her new officer became an ally, supporting her as she fought to regain custody of her child. "My first couple of years out of prison were really hard. I had no family support. My son and I were homeless, and I really do not know how I got out of that hole. I just know I was just being so tenacious. Keep thriving. Get out of this homeless situation, out of the transitional home. And then moving into a freaking cottage shack for eight years with no kitchen. I lived there for eight years with no kitchen! Because that's all I could afford at the time."

Work was elusive. "My first job out was a little mom-and-pop commercial door company. Before I landed that job, there were two jobs that were admin roles that I applied to. I would go through the interview process with flying colors and then get the job. And then this first job I got in 2010, I worked there for two days. By day three, they said, 'We ran your background. You cannot work here. Thank you for your time. Thank you so much for your time. Have a great day. Bye.' Another job, same thing. Went through the interview process. They loved me. Thought, Wow, you have knowledge, a relevant background in operations. You'll be great. This is amazing. I go, Cool, cool. I get excited. Go to work the first day, do the paperwork. The next day, I didn't even get to the building. They had a box of my little things. They said, 'You can't work here. We ran your background. You just cannot work here. Thank you for your time again.'

"I have no money. I have a kid. What am I going to do? I have this nasty, scarlet letter hurdle that just won't let me achieve. And I thought, How can you want me to be on parole, to reintegrate back into society, and not give me an opportunity to do so? This is just insane."[128]

Around the country, "ban the box" initiatives have urged lawmakers to prevent employers from asking about criminal records during the hiring process. Adelaida, like so many Americans, experienced the limits of such a policy: once their employer does find out about a conviction, they still have a chance to choose not to move forward if they can identify a rational reason why the conviction relates to job duties. Overall, ban the box policies have only modestly boosted employment for formerly incarcerated people. In fact, they also might have resulted in more overall discrimination, particularly against young men of color.[129] Beyond the pain of discriminatory employment policies, employers are probably also shooting themselves in the foot, because formerly incarcerated people have a lower turnover rate on the job and, according to a 2019 survey, are valued as much as, or more than, their colleagues without records, by a whopping 81 percent of business leaders.[130]

Adelaida, sick of dismissals, changed tactics, and started unpacking her whole background in interviews to avoid the repeated process of hiring followed by near-instant firing. "I thought, I'm going to just lay it all on the table. This is what I got going on." And it worked. "This one job in Hayward gave me an opportunity, and I worked with them for two years. I went to a stepping stone role where I could get more knowledge about payroll and HR. And then I left that role after a couple of years, went to San Francisco to work with at-risk youth." After another few years at a nonprofit, she wanted to find a professional home. She found it at the law school at the University of California, Berkeley. "I've always wanted to be in school. I love higher education. I love the law. So I thought, What better place to work than where I can be in the guts of a law school and read so many things, be around law students, sit in classes, sit in seminars . . . and so I applied. I immediately got the role and I accepted it."[131] Now, in the clinic space where young lawyers are honing their skills, Adelaida is sitting with them, sharing her experiences, shaping their arguments, offering ideas on public policy solutions, and bringing in knowledge that can't be learned in any school.

———

For Amir, finding safety was the single biggest stressor of his impending release. He was reading constantly—he hadn't read much before he was incarcerated, but he had become voracious—"self-help books, fantasy books, fiction books. I didn't even like fiction, but I started reading it because it allowed me to free my mind. My body was captive, but I'd be damned if they kept my mind captive." He was also thinking about the future. "I would dream about things, and things like, well, what am I going to do when I get out of here? Where am I going to live? Is anybody going to hire me? Am I smart enough to do anything? I'm a felon now. I have the scarlet letter. I have a strike. I don't know if I'm going to make it."

He was working on yard crew, getting up at 3:00 in the morning to sweep the yard. He picked up discarded cigarette butts for 31 cents per hour, and reminded himself that if he could do this for three dimes and a penny, he could do any job in the outside world. Three months before his release, he entered a pre-release program, which he hoped would give him what he needed to come home well: help planning, finding work, preparation. He wanted guidance on what to do when he felt like regressing to behavior that had been problematic in the past. Instead, they focused on things like whether he had outstanding warrants, asked him if he had an ID, and gave him a list of shelters and food pantries in L.A. County. They told him to report to parole within forty-eight hours.

Amir had a huge advantage in homecoming, which is that he had a loving mom to go home to. "I can't quantify love, and I don't know what the research is on the impact of love on somebody coming out of a facility, but I will damn sure tell you that if I didn't have that safe place to go to, I don't know if I would've succeeded."[132] The science backs up Amir's experience: the involvement of a loving family, or any other strong social ties, is vital to successful reentry.[133] These ties can improve mental health,[134] reduce reliance on substance use,[135] lower recidivism,[136] and raise the likelihood of a person finding work post-release.[137]

For Amir, that support was everything. "I can't give the system credit for changing my behavior, because it definitely didn't. It was everybody and anybody else that showed me love, support, and kindness. And when I teetered, they pushed me back up. When I was faltering, they put a hand out to me, a hand up. They didn't drive me into the ground like the system does."[138] When Amir left prison, he left as almost everyone does: broke and far from home.

Prisons provide "gate money," which is supposed to be enough funding to get home. For Amir, it was about $200, but the prison took $75 off the top for a fee they charged to drive him from the gate to the Greyhound station. Then he had to pay for a ticket home, leaving him with barely enough money to buy food along the way, let alone rent a room, had he needed to. Others aren't so lucky, finding themselves unable to navigate their way home, and end up stranded in an unfamiliar town. It's a lose-lose situation for both the released person and the community wherever they land.

Amir's mom was waiting at the Greyhound station, and took him home to her new place in Santa Monica, giving him a way to avoid his old neighborhood. "When we drove home, I was kind of silent. I was just looking around. She was kind of silent. We didn't say much. But then I came into the house, and I immediately felt like I was in a safe place. It smelled like home. It was tiny. I knew I was sleeping on the living room floor, but at that moment I would rather sleep on the living room floor at my mom's house than anywhere else."

His mom pushed him to make a plan. "Are you going to get a job? Are you going to go to school? What are you going to do? She had this very motherly kind of encouraging pressure on me to do something sooner rather than later." But she was also providing reassurance, reminding him that she would help him and support him as he got on his feet. "And so day to day, I would leave the house; I'd go fill out applications. It took me about a month and a half before I got a job. And my first job out of prison was at Krispy Kreme Doughnuts."

The job wasn't without its perils. Almost immediately, Amir had an encounter with someone whose position he recognized. "I got robbed at gunpoint at that Krispy Kreme Doughnuts. I think I was more calm than the individual who was robbing me. I told him, 'I know where you're at. I know how you're feeling, just be patient. I'm going to get you whatever you need so you can get out of here, but you're taking a risk.' That is literally what I said. You're taking a risk to do twenty years for this $60 in this register, but I understand where you're at, and if you're doing this, I know you're desperate, so just be calm. He was shaking, and he was scared. He told me to hurry up. And so I hurried up and got him what he needed."

Amir walked to that Krispy Kreme from his mom's house every day. Meanwhile, his mom drove him to the local community college to sign up for classes. "She helped me with my admissions paperwork, my FAFSA. She told me I could get free money to go to school. And I was like, *what??* She helped me through that process, and I started taking one class at a time, trying to figure out what I'm going to study. But at the same time, I was also on parole."

The parole presence was nearly overwhelming. "My parole officer had to come to my work. My parole officer had to see my school paperwork. My parole officer even wanted to come to my class, which was embarrassing. My parole officer came to my mom's house. And for my mom, that was a big deal because it's shameful that other people in the building would be able to see a law enforcement person come into her apartment." Amir didn't yet realize how lucky he was—out of all the overworked parole officers in a burnout-prone, highly carceral system, he drew an officer who chose support over punishment. Amir was doing well, but had also slipped up in his return—seeing people he shouldn't have been seeing and, one day, ending up in a car he knew he shouldn't have been in, because it was stolen. He wasn't driving, but when the driver got pulled over, he was arrested with everyone else—a clear violation of parole. "I went to the county, and that report went to my parole officer, and my parole officer came to the county jail and essentially scolded me like she was my mother. She basically said, 'Amir, I don't know what the hell's wrong with you. You're in school, you're working, like why are you doing this BS? You're forcing my hand, and you were doing so good. *I* don't want to ruin your life, and I'm not going to let *you* ruin your life.' And you know what she didn't do? She didn't violate me. She didn't submit a technical violation paperwork on me. She released the parole hold on me and told me that if I ever put her in this position again, she's going to close the book on me."

That moment of redemption was the turning point Amir needed. Given grace, he didn't step over the line again. "I faltered and I teetered, but instead of doing what I thought they would normally do, she did the opposite. She uplifted me. She took me to my mom's house. She literally picked me up from the county and took me to my mom's house and talked to my mom for an hour. And so that, for me, was a pivotal point. A conflict between how I thought the system should be versus how it normally is. She was a pivotal player in my life, and I wish I could thank her."

Because that parole agent chose not to send Amir back to prison, he deepened his studies. He became active in policy, lobbying in Sacramento to prevent the elimination of a crucial stipend for low-income students. He moved from community college to the University of New Mexico, where he focused on sociology and criminology with a minor in statistics. "I've been a data point my whole life, a booking number, a case number, arrest number, a fingerprint number, all of these data points. A risk-assessment score. I decided I need to understand this data. I felt like I could do something with it. Once when I was sitting in a cell reading a book, I came across my name, Amir, in that book. I had contraband in the form of a razor. I took my name and I cut it out of that little book, and I stuck it on the back of my ID card. I did that because, in the facility, I'm V46708. But in my mind, I'm *Amir*. I was forgetting that I was Amir. I cut my name out of that book and put it on my ID so I could remind myself who I am."

Amir went to school to find a way to humanize the numbers. "I was there all the time. I was in class there, I worked there, I was active there. It was my community. That community allowed me to think about what a career would look like. What would something that gave me economic mobility and stability look like? Even when I wrote a paper, they reviewed it meaningfully. 'Amir, have you thought about this? Do you know about this research? Do you know there's people funding research to look at this in more detail? Do you know there's a center on campus where you could go talk to some folks who are actually looking at the jails and the prisons in this state?' I didn't even know they paid people to look at this kind of thing. How does that happen? Then you learn about research grants. And you start understanding, little by little, more and more of everything that goes into the work of building new ideas."

Which is where Amir is now: at the intersection of deeply human numbers and big ideas. After spending years studying booking sheets and victimization surveys for a social science institute, Amir built a robust career in criminal justice research and analysis. I was even lucky enough to work with him for a time, and he remains one of the best colleagues I have ever known. These days, though, he's busy working for the Council of State Governments to build out new frontiers of numbers—in a system famously devoid of data, the person trying to build out new collaborations, partnerships, and initiatives across the country to track and share data on the realities of the criminal legal system is none other than Amir Chapel.

"Bureaucracies are heartless," Amir says now. "What I'm trying to do is bring the heart into bureaucracy, because in many ways the systems are going to do what they do regardless of who's running them. So I'm about changing the rules of the game. And if I have information that can change a rule, I can change a life. What I mean by that is if an unhoused person sleeping in a park is made no longer illegal, then nobody who's unhoused sleeping in a park would be in jail. Bad rules and regulations and policies got us to this in the first place. The same thing will get us out of it. We have to force these systems to change because they won't change themselves."[139]

———

Malcolme, too, is working his way toward success. Though fighting for the right to teach is a long road, he found a job at a private school teaching PE. It wasn't utilizing his expertise and education, and because he's not allowed to reveal anything about his history of incarceration at school, he also couldn't use the experience he won the hard way as a path to mentoring troubled students.

But still, it was a foothold, and an important one. It gave Malcolme enough stability to apply to a PhD program at the University of Toledo, and in the summer of 2024 he was accepted. With these pieces in place, he can keep caring for his family, and even encouraging family members to move to his new neighborhood, slowly building his community back even though he no longer lives in his home state. With the lower cost of living in his new neighborhood, he feels he has a chance to spur investment in the community and build something meaningful. As he encourages people he loves to move closer, he also wants to gather enough investments to build a youth center in his new neighborhood, which can give kids a path out of trouble. "I've been trying to encourage people to invest in something out here. So we can actually build a community that we envision. It's hard. When I was out in San Diego, I was telling people, it's hard to actually build community without having any land. You can build a theoretical community, which is good. You can have a community in faith, community in principles, community in ideals, which are good. But I think there should also be something where there's a model where people could say, 'Okay, look. This is what these people over here did. They built it up. They moved in. They built something they cared about.' I want to have a model so I can then start bringing people out and show them, Look, this is what we have going on. Let's try to replicate this."[140]

————

Back in L.A., all those years ago, in front of Twin Towers, I wasn't waiting for my own client. I had been told who to meet, but he didn't know me, and I didn't know him. His family was ready to welcome him back home, but they had small kids who needed to be in bed, and no child care, and no freedom to wait in front of the jail all night until the mysterious gears of Corrections released their loved one. So I found myself looking at every person who walked out, studying their face, and usually asking awkward questions like "Hey, are you Jimmy?"[141] Ultimately, it paid off. He walked out, alone. I found him. I called his family and told them it was time. In the wee hours, they drove downtown and brought him home. I hope he's doing well and that, unlike so many others, he managed to come home without being tripped up, entrapped, or returned to the criminal courts.

Amir, Malcolme, and Adelaida are unique and quite exceptional, particularly when you consider the fact that the Bureau of Justice Statistics says as many as 82 percent of incarcerated people are arrested within ten years and 43 percent are arrested within one year of release.[142] All three have worked incredibly hard to retain the freedom so many of us take for granted, but they've also been lucky. Much of the time, people will be funneled back into the prison system for minor missteps, but also for the crimes of desperation—and even nihilism—that emerge when attempts at a successful life are repeatedly undermined by a million slammed doors. Their talent will not be visible to us, and their potential to move us all forward will go unrealized. As Amir put it, "You've got people in there that are doing some NASA space stuff on how to make a tattoo gun with extremely limited supplies. There are people with incredible artistic abilities; there are engineers thinking about new ideas and innovations. I can imagine some of these folks going in front of the sharks on *Shark Tank*. I think part of life is about who you know, but the other part of life is about the opportunities you get, and sometimes who you know does lead to different opportunities. And so these folks, some of them have burned bridges, some of them just weren't taught, some of them haven't even lived outside of the five-block radius they grew up in. The way they see and think about the world has been kind of suppressed. Exposure, opportunity, and support are the key to unlocking all that potential. But if you don't have a safe place to go when you get out, well, it's not likely that you're going to make it. You're going to get discouraged quickly if every road you take ends in a barrier."[143]

There is a staggering amount of talent locked up inside our prisons and jails. Our legal system stacks the deck against everyone it touches, before, during, and after incarceration. There are still huge numbers of people beating the odds and contributing tremendously to our society in spite of that stacked deck. What would happen if we unleashed the broader world of talent inside by setting everyone up to succeed?

Part Two

Solutions

Toward a Better Tomorrow

In the decades since I took my first case, the stroke-inducing effect of the court system's inescapable, Orwellian inversions has remained strong. This is a system that is *consistently* doing the exact opposite of what it claims. Our "safety" systems spur cycles of arrest by using tactics that traumatize people and render them less able to find legitimate success. Our "impartial" finders of law and fact are left highly vulnerable to bias through both the structure of the system and the training (or lack thereof) offered to its stakeholders. The rules we have in place intended to foster transparency and a real adversarial testing of allegations are actually allowing concealment, and the introduction of fake science that actual scientists reject. The process is so bad that everyone gets punished in one way or another long before they're found guilty.

The good news is that we're not flying blind. We know a great deal about what creates safety, and how to lower crime. Even better, most of the things that would lower crime have a legion of other benefits—reducing public health costs while increasing community well-being, reducing unemployment while increasing economic mobility, lowering family separation while increasing positive outcomes for children and young people. The list is endless. When we talk about fighting climate change, people in favor of radical action often point out that even if we're wrong, our worst-case scenario for climate interventions is building a better, more sustainable world. The same is true for our system of justice: we know that the status quo is violent, dysfunctional, and regularly lethal. We have little to lose by trying something new, and everything to gain.

But change has been slow to come. As you've probably noticed, this is a system that makes strikingly little data available to the public, and has built a phenomenal track record of obfuscation, misdirection, and generally keeping the public in an unjustified state of fear. Often, people pushing for change have the data on their side, but a *huge* uphill battle when it comes to getting that information out to voters. Informed voters are much harder to scare and tend to make much better decisions than voters who know only what they've seen or heard on the innumerable true crime horror shows and podcasts stalking our airwaves. Movements to eliminate cash bail, reform discovery, end solitary confinement, abolish the death penalty, and prevent children from being treated as adults in the penal system, for example, are all supported by strong evidence but have been undermined by politically driven fearmongering. If we were able to wave a magic wand and get the most cutting-edge data and analysis on safety out to every voter in America, we would experience a sea change with policies people choose to support.

We don't have a magic wand. But we have these pages. So let's talk about what people ought to know about how to improve safety, accountability, and justice in America.

Chapter Ten

Redefine Success

D iversity matters. Not for optics, but for insight, life experience, and expertise. Can we really let the legal system—the judges, the lawyers, anyone admitted to practice law—remain overwhelmingly well-off and white while directing the vast majority of its surveillance and punishments toward people who aren't wealthy or white? On an individual level, of course better decisions don't *always* come from people who share lived experience with the people in their courts. But at a system scale, increasing the diversity of judges, juries, and practitioners adds greater insight—and therefore higher chances of finding truth, or something even resembling justice—to our court system.

Across the country, there are many jurists who embody what a diversity of background experiences can mean for justice. But one of them, the Honorable Leslie Harris, a Massachusetts trial court judge who spent decades overseeing the juvenile court in Boston's Suffolk County, holds a special significance for me. It is his perspective—and his choice to see potential in me at the age of sixteen—that changed the course of my life. I had no idea, when I was all alone in the courtroom that day and he asked me to approach the bench, that he wasn't just another judge from a fancy law firm or a long career in prosecution. I had no idea how deeply unusual his path to the bench had been. Years later, after I had built a life, I wrote to thank him for giving me that chance. A conversation between us began, and I learned, for the first time, about his path.

"I had worked for the juvenile division of the DA's office after I had been a public defender. But I'd also been a schoolteacher, a licensed social worker, and a camp counselor. All those things were a part of me. But I'm a project kid. And I didn't think anybody would ever make a kid from the projects in Chicago a judge.

"Our public TV station had done a special on me as a public defender," he went on, "and my father had it on VHS. An old VHS tape. He literally wore it out, he showed it so many times. So I knew he was proud of me. My father had a sixth-grade education, but he taught us so much, by example. In so many ways, I was blessed. I got opportunities that others didn't: my older brother graduated from high school in 1964 and went into the Marines—not just the Marines, Marine Recon. I graduated in '66, when colleges were looking for Black students . . . just two years' difference, but it gave me an opportunity that my older brother didn't get."

What Judge Harris had been through as a young person, I learned, continually informed his perspective on the bench. When kids who had made terrible choices came before him, he knew that he, too, could have done so. That he, too, had stood at the precipice of life-altering decisions. "I went to a conference on trauma where I was supposed to speak about the traumas that our children are going through," he said. "I listened to the experts talking, when I thought, Wait a moment, they're talking about *me*. I got stabbed twice as a kid. Cut once and shot at a few times. I never thought much of it. I *had* looked for the guy who cut me. I had never done anything to him, and yet he cut me. I kept thinking that if I had found him, my life would've been quite different. Because I would have hurt him or possibly killed him. I was blessed never to find him. There were a couple of other folks I looked for—one who had tried to rob me and another who attacked my younger brother. I ended up going off to college, not finding them, and leading a different life.

"I went to Northwestern and it wasn't a welcoming school when I got there. We were the first group of Black students there who were not on an athletic scholarship. I was going to leave. I was going home. I got on the elevated train, went back to the South Side of Chicago, and walked home. I passed my high school, I passed the pool hall, and saw friends, and stopped to talk with them. I talked with Jimmy Ferguson, who was a year older than me and one of my heroes. I told Jimmy I was leaving school to come home. And he said, 'You can't do that! I'm talking about going back to get my GED so I can be like you. You can't leave college and come back here.' Another guy said, 'If you come back here, we're going to whup your ass every day.' I looked at him, said, 'You can't whup me.' He said, 'I didn't say *I;* I said *we.*' And they all laughed. They said, 'Leslie, you are the only one who's gotten out of here. You can't do that to us.' And those are experiences I took to the bench with me. Experiences my colleagues didn't have."

Those experiences extended to the very thing he had given me that day in Suffolk County Juvenile Court—the grace of a chance. "I also know what it's like to go into court," he told me. "In Chicago, when you buy a new car, you take the plates off the old one and put them on the new one. So when I got a car, I did that. But you *don't* do that in Massachusetts. You have to go get new plates." Unfortunately, the young Leslie Harris learned this lesson the hard way, and the next thing he knew he was in court. "I was sitting there, totally at the mercy of the court." Crucially, he points out, "I don't ever forget how that felt, sitting there, wondering where my future was going to be. Those things stay with you."

It's still with him as a judge. "Standing in court, watching a stream of young Black men, primarily, some young Black women, coming to my court and feeling like they don't have a chance." He remembers one young man in particular, whom he saw looking down, especially hopeless. "He was dragging his feet, and he heard me say something and he looked up. He recognized my voice as being a Black man. And you could see the change in his face: *I might not win, but at least I've got a chance.*" The judge paused. "And I understand that feeling, because I've sat in the suburbs and small towns across Massachusetts, where I was the only Black person in the courthouse. I even got denied entrance with my robe on in two different courts, because they didn't believe I was a judge. And so I *understand.*"

I was far from the only kid Judge Harris's perspective saved. As we talked, he told me story after story of the children who had been in his court. He remembers their stories down to the most minute detail. He keeps in touch with their families. He's retired now, but he still lives in Roxbury, taking an active role in the community where he once practiced. "My belief in being a judge is that every child who comes to court is mine. I'm a father, grandfather, great-grandfather. If my child went to court, how would I want them to be treated? The challenge, I think, for judges, is to see each child as an individual. They come in with the same charges, looking the same way, talking the same way, but they're *different people.* You have to remember that you're dealing with an individual, not a group, not just some number, coming into your court. And that's a challenge."

When I was in Judge Harris's court, he told me something that never really left my mind. He said he never wanted to hear from me again unless I had done something good with my life. So years later, when I wrote to him, I told him that, thanks to the chance he had given me, I didn't lose my college admission. As a result, I had not only graduated but gone on to law school and become a public defender. I told him I was proud to have carried my own life experience into how I fought for each person I had the privilege of representing. And that none of this could have happened without him.

When I wrote to him, I didn't hear back for a long time. It wasn't until years later that I found out that at the moment I wrote him, he had just undergone the incredible trauma of losing a young person he had fought to help. The teenager had been shot to death in Boston. Later he recalled, "It was so traumatizing to me that I was getting ready to step down from the bench. I kept saying, If I can't help the neediest child, what am I doing here?" That was when he got my letter. The reminder of what giving a kid a chance could do, he told me, lifted his depression. "I said to myself, I actually did help somebody. And it helped me stay on for a few more years. I talk about that all the time—that we impact young people, but young people impact us."[1]

To me, there is only one Judge Leslie Harris. No doubt there must be a few more like him across this huge country. But if we sought to empower more jurists like him, from backgrounds that do not typically lead to law school, our system could be fundamentally changed.

But the gift of great judges is a gift we have to earn. We need to support their well-being and help them sustain the incredibly difficult task of believing in strangers, day after day, and finding hope instead of condemnation. We need to offer them the kind of training and education that can help jurists feel confident that they are doing their best work to overcome some of the innate human biases that can carry us further from justice. And we also need to build new pathways to the bench.

Some of the work to be done requires years—building stronger educational pipelines for low-income students and students of color, for example, lowering the debt burdens associated with a legal education, and increasing public service debt forgiveness programs. We need to increase resources to ensure that the system is able to pay wages that attract high-quality candidates, and, yes, this means systems should stop spending twice as much on prosecutorial teams—including prosecutor salaries, but also on quantities of staff like investigators and paralegals—as on public defenders.[2]

But not all of the changes required are slow burning. Elected officials can appoint more candidates with poverty law, civil rights, or public defense experience to the bench. Lawmakers can remove barriers to jury service for people with prior convictions, recognizing how these laws, combined with the ongoing hyper-surveillance of Black men in particular, have been used intentionally and historically to silence the Black political voice as it manifests itself in the courtroom. They can pass laws to make the exclusion of jurors for subtly race-based reasons more difficult, as California is beginning to do.[3] They can compensate jurors more appropriately, arrange free transportation for people needing to access the courthouse, or broaden whom they are calling in to serve as a matter of policy. It's not impossible: In 2024, Brendon Woods helped to convince his county to pilot a juror pay program that would increase compensation to $100 per day, with additional funding for public transportation.[4] And they can create post-conviction relief opportunities like California's Racial Justice Act, which enables people to seek a second look at their conviction when racial bias might have brought about that conviction.[5]

To Maximize Safety, We Have to See Potential

When I was sixteen and standing in front of Judge Harris, the very fact of being in court—the incredible stress of the pretrial process—provided me with a massive incentive to want to never ever be there again. Did it fix all the problems that brought me there? No, absolutely not, that took years. Could it have? Again, no, probably not. What I needed, and what I was so deeply lucky to receive, was time to recover from a bunch of trauma. I needed stability, the love and support of my family, and, crucially, someone to give me a chance to prove that I could do better.

Judge Harris gave me that chance. I do not want to skate around the layers of privilege that advantaged me in that courtroom. It's not just the fact of whiteness—I was the only white kid I saw at court that day—but also the educational privilege that meant I was walking into court with a college acceptance letter already in hand, as well as the privilege of having present, involved grown-ups in my life who not only came and got me from pretrial holding but came with me to court and made sure I was prepared (or at least as prepared as a scared, surly teenager can be). Access to these privileges is not just racialized in America, but also apportioned socioeconomically and geographically, and influenced by every system that touches our lives, from public schools to food systems to the kinds of jobs one's parents can access. Which is why so much of this book about the court system also needs to be about housing, health, income, and family unity.

As much as these factors would inevitably influence how I was perceived in court, I also walked into the courtroom of a judge who had decided that when he looked at children, he would choose to see their potential rather than focusing on the specter of threat. His difference of experience—both life experience and professional experience—showed. And because of that, he was able to choose, again and again, to do the *work* of finding each child's potential rather than treating them as flawed, dangerous, and discardable.

We have to de-carceralize our schools and neighborhoods. We need fewer police in schools and more counselors, coaches, and after-school programs. Realistically, because of our national plague of school shootings, there may be a lot of gray area here. A school cop who is extensively trained in how to stop an incident of mass violence, and who is *specifically not tasked with addressing minor misconduct,* is a value add. But a school cop whose primary utility is arresting kids for things that should have been detention-worthy is a disaster. With new research finding disparities in educational attainment potentially becoming the largest driver of inequality in prison admissions, we cannot avoid the conclusion that turning our schools into an extension of the punishment bureaucracy is a bad idea.[6]

Overall, this requires that we dramatically raise the threshold for when cases are even referred to the court system, and return to school-based disciplinary processes that keep parents, teachers, and a care-first perspective in place when kids mess up. *No one* should be talking to a cop because of marijuana, grumpy outbursts, and dumb kid choices like petty thefts, vandalism, and schoolyard scuffles.

When kids *do* engage in real harm, the type of accountability they face must account for the fact that children are not mini-adults. They are weird little creatures with biologically different brains, which means they do not make choices like grown-ups and they don't have the same kind of behavioral control that grown-ups have either. If we want the legal system to reflect biological reality, we need to do two things with our juvenile court system: First, we need to make the age of entry into the adult system higher, and keep people in the juvenile system while they have juvenile brains. The "Raise the Age" movement, which has taken root across the country, argues that people under the age of twenty-five should be evaluated by a system that recognizes the neurological realities of their behavior and decision-making processes. Such a system would be better equipped to provide educational opportunities, employment readiness, and youth-specialized care that would enable more young people to walk away from the system with their future intact.[7]

Second, we need to decide that kids are always kids, regardless of how angry they might make us or how frightened we may be of their worst behavior. This means that we have to acknowledge the reality kids face when interacting with police. When we look at exonerations by age, over a third of kids under eighteen falsely confessed, and the figure is over 86 percent for kids under fourteen.[8] More than 90 percent of kids whom police interrogate waive their *Miranda* rights and do not ask for a lawyer.[9] When you put all this together, it becomes clear that if we want to protect both our children and the integrity of our system, children should get an attorney, every single time, whether they ask or not, before they speak to police.

Part of deciding to treat kids like kids means ending laws that automatically transfer children to adult court for certain offenses or give prosecutors unilateral power to send kids out of juvenile jurisdiction. The data supports this choice. Kids who are sent to the adult system are disproportionately Black and brown, suggesting racial bias in the charging and transfer processes. They also don't end up sentenced to prison time very often, suggesting that the very "public safety" rationale that sent them out of kid court wasn't a very big factor after all.[10] Moreover, even though kids who get sent to adult court are rarely found dangerous enough to incarcerate, they still see worse long-term outcomes (including more frequent and serious recidivism) than kids who are kept in juvenile court, which suggests that exposure to the adult system itself may be causing more problems than it's solving.

Stop Gatekeeping Help

Most treatment courts, diversion programs, probationary opportunities, and other off-ramps from the legal system are usually reserved for people prosecutors see as most deserving. This makes no logical sense. A person on their first arrest might be allowed to resolve their case with a simple fine or agreement to stay out of trouble. Using system resources to make *that* person jump through more hoops, like a whole treatment program, as opposed to using those same resources to try to help a person who has been arrested several times flies in the face of what we know about how to address root causes. It's terrific to think about how we can ensure that a person who gets arrested once never gets arrested again, but it's idiotic to decide that if a person has had many problems, or if their behavior is very severe, the system should disappear the problem into a prison somewhere instead of attempting to address the root cause. Why would anyone do this? Because limiting programs to first-time arrestees makes for better optics when those prosecutors have to run for reelection.

And indeed, by the numbers, we simply can't solve mass incarceration by focusing only on first-time, nonviolent, non-upsetting cases, because about half of people in prison and jail are there for things that are categorized as violent.[11] One of the biggest problems in pushing smart reforms is that people tend to recoil from doing anything they see as "nice" for people convicted of violent crimes. I get it. I don't like being nice to creeps either, and if I didn't work in this system, I'd probably assume that most people who engage in violent crime are creeps. But because I do work here, I know that the charges a person is carrying don't actually define their full behavior, the motivations for that behavior, or what we need to do to change things.

In part, it's because of a huge categorization problem. Burglary, for example, is often categorized as a violent crime, which means that a case where a person breaks into an occupied dwelling and terrifies the residents is in the same general category as a case where a person drunkenly stumbles into an empty garage and attempts to steal some boxes. Both of these people could be convicted of burglary, and would have a violent felony on their record. Robbery is always categorized as violent, but because the elements of the crime are stretchy, the category may comprise people who robbed others at gunpoint and also people who tried to shoplift and struggled when a Target loss prevention officer leaped on them from behind. In other words, the category of violent crime encompasses a substantial amount of nonviolent behavior.

If we decide, then, as many jurisdictions have, that people accused of violent crimes aren't eligible for any restorative program, we're undermining our own path toward safety. After all, these are the crimes we probably *most want to prevent,* and to my knowledge there is no research proving that a person who steals from a garage (burglary) is less receptive to help than a person who steals from a corner store (petty theft, a nonviolent misdemeanor). If anything, restorative justice programs may be *more* effective for people with more serious misconduct, especially those involving a victim.[12]

Violent crimes might actually be scary, or they might be dumb; you have to look beyond the category. And violent crimes can also actually turn out to be drug crimes when behavior is driven by substance use. This is a crucial insight, because sometimes when ideas that focus on addressing drug crimes are proffered, they are critiqued for impacting too few people: when we look at incarceration writ large, only about one in five people in prison in 2024 were incarcerated for drug crimes.[13] But the number of people who are in prison for *drug crimes* is very different from the number of people who are *in prison because of drugs.*

As a public defender, a vast swath of my caseload was what I thought of as drug crimes once removed—not the getting high itself, but stuff people did while high. On paper, these crimes might be listed as violent—burglary, robbery, assault, carjacking, even arson. But in reality, the behavior we were addressing was something the person in question might never have done if substance use had not led them into a deeply problematic situation. Indeed, while about 5 percent of the U.S. population meets the diagnostic criteria for drug dependence or abuse, 58 percent of people in prisons and 63 percent of sentenced people in jails do, and somewhere around one-fifth of people in prisons and jails admitted that their offense was committed to get drugs or money for drugs.[14] The problem doesn't stop at the jailhouse door: overdose deaths have gone up 600 percent in prisons and 200 percent in jails from 2001 to 2018.[15] A huge chunk of nondrug charges are actually drug-involved crimes.

Kassandra Frederique, executive director of the Drug Policy Alliance, acknowledges how much more complex the interplay between substance use and harm really is. "Inside, there are a substantial number of people who meet the criteria for a substance use disorder. Addiction and its connection to harm, the way people commit offenses, violence—*all those things are connected.* Ignoring the impact of drugs in the criminal justice space and the reform space is futile. If someone committed harm because they were trying to get money for their drug use, the conversation should be, 'Okay, let's deal with their motivations for drug use because now their drug use has gotten chaotic. They need some version of treatment. What is the support for them?' "[16]

I once represented a person (let's call her Jennifer) who would go into the supply or storage areas of large buildings and steal things to resell for drug money. Now well beyond retirement age, she had been dealing with this substance use problem for several decades, and, to be honest, Jennifer was exhausted. She did not want to use anymore. She did not want to burglarize anymore. But every time I made a persuasive argument at arraignment and got her out of jail, she would relapse, and go into a building again. It was an awful cycle, and at a certain point I stopped being able to convince judges to let her go.

Logically, the right outcome was clear. Jennifer really wanted inpatient drug treatment. She had never had a chance to do inpatient treatment, because she'd never been able to afford it. With a court order, she could get a twenty-eight-day rehab stay for the first time in her life. Additionally, the root cause of *all* of these crimes was substance use; if she wasn't trying to buy drugs, she wouldn't need to steal things. The prosecutor on her case was inclined to agree, but the rules of our local drug court program said that only people accused of *drug* felonies were allowed to go to drug court. And although Jennifer's burglaries were drug-driven, they weren't technically "drug crimes." The prosecutor's supervisor refused to agree to trying the drug court. The supervisor's supervisor, and, ultimately, the elected DA of the jurisdiction, both backed up that refusal.

Jennifer sat in jail for ages. Eventually, I was able to wear every prosecutor on the case down enough that I got them to agree to let her have a shot at treatment, but only after she had spent an incredible amount of time in jail. Her cases had become a substantial drag on the system. She had several open felonies, she was incarcerated pretrial, she was older and therefore more likely to have had medical needs the jail would have to address. The underlying driver of her offense was very clear, and she was eager to make amends and get the help she needed. Yet our system was set up with overly rigid rules (only drug felonies in drug court) and incentives tending to favor punitiveness and rule following (forcing the line prosecutor to seek prison time, an even larger waste of public resources, rather than agreeing to address the root cause of the problem).

There is a huge eligibility problem here. "Problem-solving" courts have popped up everywhere,[17] but most of them include only the people prosecutors or judges see as most palatable.[18] The optics are great: judges and prosecutors can allow first-time arrestees into a program they might not really need, and get the public accolades for having sent more people to treatment instead of prison. But it's all an illusion—the first-time arrestee was never in jeopardy of prison, and the person who most needs the program is likely not on their first arrest.

A much more meaningful impact could be made by investing in deep, thoughtful, and proven treatment approaches for people like Jennifer. People with long records and a history of violent misconduct aren't *always* right for these programs, but they shouldn't be subject to a blanket ban, either. By removing arbitrary barriers to entry, we could get more care to the people who may need it most. Restorative opportunities need to be open to anyone, as a matter of law and policy, not prosecutorial discretion.

Decriminalization and Ending the Drug War

This also highlights a key problem with the way many alternative court programs arise. The system should not be wasting time forcing people through hoops who never should have been arrested in the first place. Arresting someone for being unhoused and struggling with substance use doesn't make sense, yet it's a phenomenon we see in every U.S. city and has been made substantially worse by the Supreme Court's ruling in *City of Grants Pass, Oregon v. Johnson,*[19] which now allows cities to remove and penalize unhoused residents. When we make the path to treatment for poor people rely on policing, we are asking police and prosecutors to decide who is worthy of help.[20]

None of this works if there are no resources to address underlying problems. Across the country, there are *a lot more* jail beds than staffed hospital beds—920,531 staffed hospital beds were counted in 2022 as opposed to 1,587,089 jail and prison beds, a figure that researchers report is an undercount.[21] Almost half of people who said they needed substance use or mental health care in the United States in that year said they were unable to get it.[22] Psychologists report that the need for treatment—and for more prolonged treatment, addressing more severe symptoms—is growing year over year,[23] and within a few years our country is projected to be short somewhere around 14,280 to 31,109 mental health professionals.[24]

This is not a problem that is going to go away on its own. We need to take some of the money that has poured for decades into incarceration and move it to systems that are better equipped to deal with the problems we actually face. Sometimes, that may mean expanding court-based opportunities. It's ridiculous that if you're a veteran with PTSD in Iowa, you can get access to a court program that lets you get special, trauma-informed treatment, tailored care that is responsive to your specific case, and even a dismissal of charges in Woodbury County, but more than 40,000 other vets can't get the same thing in Polk, Linn, or Scott Counties, which are the state's largest.[25] But it also means investing in non-court solutions.

Ending the drug war means, in large part, ceasing to arrest and prosecute people because of substance use. Which, for most Americans, sounds pretty unappealing, because the first thing that pops into their head is a scene we've seen in cities across the country of people using drugs openly on some chaotic street. The thing is, what we picture isn't actually the reality of most substance use; what we're picturing is the circumstances of people who have no housing, have nowhere to go, are dependent on substances (sometimes *because* they're trying to mentally survive having nowhere to go), and therefore are using in a place where you can see them.

When we think about heavily criticized efforts to step away from drug prosecution—as Oregon attempted in the early 2020s—decriminalization of drug use wasn't paired with a sufficient investment in building recovery resources. It seems obvious, but if you decriminalize drugs without investing in recovery support, you're going to have a pretty bad time.

Let's start with the decriminalization side. Taking policing and prosecution out of the equation offers massive potential benefits: It diminishes the use of "zero tolerance" or petty drug policing as a tool of mass surveillance and targeting of marginalized people and neighborhoods, removing one of the factors that allows heavy policing of minority communities.[26] It lowers the barriers to lifesaving support, making it safer and more feasible for people to access drug-testing supplies, overdose prevention medicines, supervised injection sites (things that all save lives and public dollars and reduce drug-related arrests, drug-related nuisance complaints, and the spread of communicable diseases without increasing crime).[27] Portugal, for example, which entirely decriminalized and regulated recreational drugs, achieved the lowest overdose death rate in Europe in 2017, dropping the number of people using heroin by three-quarters, and dropping HIV infection by 90 percent.[28]

But here's the thing: these gains are not the result of decriminalization. They're the result of decriminalization *when paired with supportive services.* When Portugal reduced funding for rehabilitation programs, overdose rates shot back up.[29] Investing in and maintaining the kind of care that people can utilize to reduce their substance dependence takes time and money. Without anywhere for people to get help, the general public is left to bear witness to the horrors of poverty mixed with unchecked substance dependence and a total lack of care options. No one wants to walk to the store or walk their kid to school through blocks where people are using drugs openly on the street. Which may be why, as Kassandra Frederique points out, "people have lost patience with the long-term solutions of housing and support. People are like, 'Well, if you can't build it tomorrow, what are you going to do today? 'Cause I don't want to see this person today.' "[30]

Oregon's experiment with decriminalization might have fallen prey to exactly this problem of timescale and resource allocation. Oregon's Measure 110 decriminalized all personal (not commercial) possession of drugs.[31] It also increased funding to harm reduction services and community-based organizations, but in the wake of the pandemic much of that funding went to keeping these organizations from limiting services or shutting down altogether.[32] Early results were striking: although property crimes went up slightly, homicides dropped by around 60 percent, which implies that more than seventy people were not murdered because of the reform.[33] But the issue Frederique explains above—the desire of the general public to just *not have to look at drug use*—couldn't be resolved fast enough. "That money took a while to get through," she explained, "and was really hard to implement, so the infrastructure that was packaged with decriminalization was never fully realized." Even so, "in the first nine months, we saw the percentages of people accessing treatment and housing skyrocket over 200 percent."[34]

It wasn't enough. Even though murders dropped and treatment use increased, having police stop "disappearing" the problem of drug use meant that the general public and the courts *perceived* crime as high. More than 60 percent of voters thought the measure had increased crime,[35] and it was rolled back before longer-term results could be realized. The simultaneous rise of fentanyl contamination in the drug supply didn't help.[36] With fatal overdoses going up in both criminalized and decriminalized regions, one study indicates that fentanyl's arrival in Oregon is a more plausible explanation for fatal drug overdoses in the state than Measure 110 (with some criminalized regions actually seeing more overdoses, underscoring the potential value of regulation).[37]

As negative as the perception of Measure 110 was, the law was effective *even* without sufficient investment in the necessary precursors to safety. Because of how much homicides dropped and how little other crime increased, researchers estimate that Measure 110 lowered the social cost of crime by more than $800 million per year.[38]

Holding Problem-Solving Courts More Accountable for Success

There are an incredible variety of "problem-solving" or "treatment" courts operating in America. Drug treatment, mental health court, veterans' courts, domestic violence intervention courts, DUI courts, homelessness courts, sex work courts, you name it, they have it. As a public defender, it's hard to have clearly positive or negative feelings about them all. First, they vary wildly from place to place, and are highly reflective of the judge who oversees them. A heroic judge with a deep interest in helping people recover and get what they need to succeed can create a phenomenal space where people are disentangled from the legal system and enabled to thrive. A judge who might be assigned against their preference to such a court, or who comes into such a court with little knowledge and training on the subject matter they oversee, may create a disastrous space that ticks the box of an alternative court program while functionally not helping anyone recover or avoid incarceration. I've practiced in both kinds of courts, and noted the swinging variety of services offered, attention to client needs, appropriateness of care, and general tone of hope or despair. No two are really alike.

Let's start with the positive: creating a formal acknowledgment within the legal system that crime is often driven by factors beyond a person's immediate control, and that the correct systemic action is to address the root problem, is great. On the other hand, in practice, all too often these courts become just another form of punishment. Rarely are these programs truly voluntary; people are often engaging in mental health or substance use treatment under threat of incarceration if they "fail," which is especially weird to think about when we consider how long the road to recovery can be for people in the regular world. Mental health providers will tell you that relapse is often part of recovery. That the road is long and rocky. Yet in court-ordered treatment, we often see stumbles construed as willful failure to comply and punished with jail or even prison time.

Laboring under the threat of incarceration can prolong both court and treatment processes unnecessarily. As in Jennifer's case, a defender might spend ages just fighting to get someone *admitted* to a treatment court program, and then the person may have to keep coming back to court for twelve or eighteen months to "complete" the treatment court program, tethering this individual and their family to the court system for years. Worse, research shows that people who do treatment court and are not deemed successful see longer, harsher punishments than similarly situated people who never did treatment court in the first place.[39] And on top of all of this, treatment courts may be bad at, well, treatment, providing a one-size-fits-all approach or insufficiently screening for individual needs, so that people are forced to do programs, against their will, that are not the right fit for them. At worst, treatment is administered as a stand-in for punishment, with "harsher" terms, such as inpatient care or longer program duration, applied not when medically necessary but when judges or prosecutors think the charges in the underlying case are more egregious.[40]

This isn't to say that treatment courts aren't a good thing. They are! Without them, thousands of people who don't have a strong legal defense against their charges but do have a very clear cause (and solution) to their misconduct would be facing prison time. But while courts need a *way* to offer a treatment-oriented path out of the system, that doesn't mean the system has to *personally* administer the path. Specifically, it's not clear that court-governed treatment does the best job of actually helping people recover.[41] Which means there's plenty of room for improvement, starting with what kind of treatment people can access, and how.

It is incredibly depressing, as a defender, to have a person who was motivated to recover complain that whenever they go to their program, there's no real therapy, just a bunch of guys smoking cigarettes for ten minutes, signing a form, and leaving. The treatment providers that work with courts are required to be approved by the court's appointed selector of programs (often probation or a similar department), but feedback from the actual *people* sent to these programs is rarely heard or believed. Our systems need to be accountable to the people they serve, which includes the people who stand accused and participate in programs like these. Ensuring that their feedback is not only heard, but meaningfully incorporated into how alternative courts are evaluated, is essential.

Defense teams, too, can have a huge impact on success. When the Delaware County, Pennsylvania, public defenders started working with Partners for Justice and assigned non-attorney Client Advocates to work with diversion program participants, successful completion rates increased by nearly 50 percent.[42] For many people, defense teams may be much better situated to help them find the right treatment; after all, defender-client relationships are confidential, and within that space of trust people can be more honest about their needs. Letting defense teams have a bigger voice in shaping the alternatives available to our clients, both on an individual level (help picking and evaluating programs) and on a system level (input on how alternative courts are established, whether they are offered to people before or after a guilty plea, what legal benefits people receive in exchange for participation, and so on), would make these programs stronger.

Offering more programs *before* a guilty plea would also be a useful change. Many treatment programs require participants to plead guilty up front if they want to attempt to complete the program. This makes prosecutors and judges feel as if they have more leverage—a person has already admitted to a crime and has a sentence hanging over their head like a sword of Damocles, waiting to spear them if they fail. They also have fewer legal rights, potentially giving up their right against unreasonable searches or their right to remain silent as part of their treatment deal.

The truth is, no one needs to plead guilty up front as a motivator to engage with alternative courts. The motivation for going to an alternative court and agreeing to do what the court asks is the fact of facing charges itself. A person who doesn't plead guilty up front, but tries treatment and fails to complete the program, *still* has charges to face, but is afforded the benefit of a fair trial. By not requiring a guilty plea up front, alternative courts could get more people willing to take part. They could stop weeding out people who might benefit from help but who have been overcharged, or those who do not want to give up their due process protections and right to a trial.

Chapter Eleven

Sunlight Is the Best Disinfectant

Data Access

A recurring theme in our conversation about the criminal court system is data. We have a lot of data that suggests certain things work: addressing the root causes of harm, making sure people have what they need to live healthy lives, avoiding repeating cycles of trauma and violence. But at the same time, we also have much *less* data than we should on the criminal court system. Whether any given place has, say, a clear picture of how most judges rule on specific requests for release or what sentences they impose (and when, and on which people) depends entirely on whether that jurisdiction has chosen to routinely collect that data— and whether they choose to share it.

The federal system has a stronger playbook on this, although in recent years some tracking organizations have pointed out problems with federal data releases.[1] Also, the federal criminal court system is one system (unlike the state and local courts), so it's easier to impose uniform policy, though it can be hard to implement, as evinced by patchy reporting on crime and arrests by police everywhere.[2] But the federal system is also responsible for a stark minority of cases—only about 11 percent of incarceration comes from the federal system.[3] The vast majority of criminal cases heard in America are heard in state and county courts.

The states, if you listen to the research community, are a mess. "There is no unified data infrastructure for measuring the U.S. criminal justice system, evaluating its policies, or understanding the population that interacts with it," said researchers in a 2022 paper.[4] "Despite accounting for a substantial portion of local, state, and federal budgets, our criminal justice institutions are among the least measured systems in our country," adds Measures for Justice, an organization dedicated to fixing the legal system by developing better comparative data about it.[5] There is so little data collected about misdemeanors, which make up roughly 80 percent of cases in the court system,[6] that the House Appropriations Committee felt the need to call upon the Bureau of Justice Statistics to do better back in 2022.[7]

Paul Heaton is a law professor at Penn's Carey Law School and academic director of the Quattrone Center for the Fair Administration of Justice. He's also one of the legendary researchers in the field of the criminal legal system, and one of the few who has done deep and meaningful research on public defense.[8] Remember a few chapters back when we talked about how jailing people before trial can actually cause *more* crime? Dr. Heaton is the one who figured that out.[9]

According to Dr. Heaton, "The single most significant obstacle to advancing our knowledge about how the criminal legal system actually operates is the siloing of data. We have a whole bunch of individual jurisdictions, each of which is able to control how it collects—and *whether* it collects—certain data points. To study something, there's a fair bit of legwork at the outset just to figure out what data are available in each jurisdiction you want to explore. And depending on the jurisdiction, the quality of that data will be different."

When Dr. Heaton wants to study these systems, the irregularity of data can make comparing one place to another quite difficult, which results in huge amounts of time and effort being poured into pulling data from thousands of cases and manually coding different types of charges or demographics, and that's if such data is publicly available at all. "In many jurisdictions," he explains, "if you want to get the bulk of the data, you have to go through the court system, you have to make a special application, and that requires time. It often involves having access to attorneys or other people who can negotiate the necessary data use agreements. Because of that, the process favors wealthy institutions like Penn, which have the resources to put all of that together. It disfavors newer researchers, younger researchers, people who aren't academics, and members of the public who might want to understand these issues."[10]

To build—and garner public support for—smarter, more effective strategies, this kind of large-scale public data access is critical. To paraphrase the old saying, without data, we're all just jerks with opinions. We can't know whether inequity in the system is going down, for example, without more robust data on who police are stopping, where, and for what. Whether they're being searched or let go. Whether police suggest charges, under what circumstances, and whether prosecutors actually file charges or reject the case. How long cases spend in the system, what their outcomes are, who gets diversionary outcomes, and who gets prison.

Answering these questions doesn't just help those of us who want to advocate for change. It helps people on the inside of the system recognize their own blind spots. If a person is accused of a DUI, for example, and enrolls in treatment on day one of their case, they might seem like a better bet for a restorative offer from the prosecution. But what if the people who don't enroll in treatment from day one are failing to do so because they cannot *afford* to? What if the barrier isn't intent or willpower, but just plain old dollars? This kind of wealth gap leading to disparate outcomes might not be obvious to any prosecutor in the office unless they're getting larger-scale data on whom their collective actions are advantaging and disadvantaging the most. To the line prosecutor, one case looks "better." By the numbers we see larger undercurrents at play.

Gathering more kinds of data can also open our eyes to problems with the things we currently focus on. If you talk to anyone who works in public safety, they will probably at some point bring up "recidivism," meaning the rate at which people who have been arrested previously get arrested again. It's understandable why. If we want to know whether a program or intervention works, checking out how many people get arrested again after doing that program or intervention makes sense. But the problem is, people often get arrested for reasons that have little to do with whether a program was beneficial. In a hyper-surveilled neighborhood, a program might have helped someone stop engaging in real harm, but they may still experience high rearrest rates because they are Black, male, young, and present on the street, therefore *available* for arrest. Rearrest, by itself, doesn't fully tell us whether a given program or intervention was beneficial, because it's not entirely about the individual, but also about that individual's context and community.[11] Did the individual return from a restorative and therapeutic community to a neighborhood that has been so abandoned by our public systems that success is almost impossible? Were they forced to make a (logical!) choice to engage in illegal activity to pay back court debts or support a loved one in urgent crisis? Gathering more kinds of data can free us from the reflexive habit of allowing a focus on recidivism to cloud our understanding of what happens to people when they return home.[12]

Court employees whose work would be exposed may be less than eager to be subjected to public scrutiny, particularly elected judges and prosecutors. But they are already subject to scrutiny; all of them live in some fear of being splashed across the newspapers because of a mistake they made. Certainly, one could argue that this problem is solved by appointing rather than electing our judges, removing them from the sway of the mob. But what if, in a world where we cannot immediately end all elected judicial roles, the public gave elected jurists something else to worry about? Right now, their fear operates largely in one direction—the fear of releasing someone into the community who then carries out an atrocious act (sometimes called being Willie Hortoned, after the case George H. W. Bush used as a political lever to smear his opponent in 1988).[13] Few, if any, judges and prosecutors are living in fear of being Kalief Browdered or Central Park Fived, and this is a reflection of the media and political environment in which they operate.

With more rigorous and universal data transparency, perhaps the fear of an inaccurate portrayal could lessen. With more robust data about prosecutorial and judicial decisions, for example, less pressure could be put on one high-profile case because there would exist a record of a judge or prosecutor's fair decision-making over the years instead of just a splashy headline. And when we think about whom to reelect, we could base our decision on whether their policies and practices to date reflect what we actually want from our system.

It's easy enough for me to posit the theory, but do real judges feel as though they'd be better protected from splashy headlines if data on their rulings was routinely collected? It turns out, yes. In my own conversations with judges, and also in Dr. Heaton's, it's clear that there is tremendous anxiety about being misunderstood as a jurist, but also faith in one's own ability to build a just track record. "I remember recently sitting down with a federal district judge," Dr. Heaton told me. "Someone who's had a long career, who lamented that she had always wondered how her sentencing compared to her peers'. She actually went and tried to ask the federal courts for that information, and they completely refused. . . . And she's a total insider who has *authority.* So I think we can imagine how challenging it could be for the public to get the same things."[14]

It's not just about spreadsheets. Ordinary people can, if they choose, take an active role in monitoring their own court system by doing something as simple as just showing up to watch court. Around the country, court-watching programs have sprung up, many since 2020 (sometimes with musical icon Fiona Apple leading the charge).[15] They can note how the judge is speaking to the people in the courtroom. How many people are being "stepped in" to jail, what the demographics of those people are, the types of charges that are being heard, how much bail prosecutors are asking for, the kinds of storytelling and argument the defense is able to bring. One might hope that with the public watching, system stakeholders might treat the people in these rooms with greater care. But even barring real-time change, the information these watchers can bring and share with friends, family, colleagues, and acquaintances can chip away at the (often false) governing narratives that prop up a bad system.

Open File Discovery

There really isn't a great reason not to implement universal open file discovery. If a person is accused of a crime, they should get to see *all* the evidence against them.[16] If the evidence is robust, they may be more likely to promptly agree to a plea deal. If the evidence is weak, well, we the people *should* get the benefit of having weak prosecutions tested fully by our adversarial system. If all the prosecution witnesses, for example, have received a lesser sentence in exchange for their testimony, that's something fairness dictates be revealed. If there is a fact that could be interpreted as exculpatory or inculpatory depending on who looks at it, a prosecutor alone in a room should not be the sole decider of whether it gets handed over. We built a system to test evidence, so let's allow all the evidence to be tested.

Chris Fabricant is the director of strategic litigation at the Innocence Project, and author of the book *Junk Science and the American Criminal Justice System.* According to him, the chasm between how discovery is handled in civil cases (where money is on the line) and how it's handled in criminal cases (where life and liberty are on the line) is "one of the biggest outrages about the American legal system." According to Chris, "Prosecutorial misconduct, including *Brady* violations, is one of the leading contributing factors to wrongful conviction. We see it every day, every week, a new scandal, when there is no argument that I could be aware of for shielding any information from the defense, if it is in the prosecution's control, apart from the one excuse that is always trotted out, which is witness safety. That's a credible reason to prevent a certain amount of information from being exposed. But the idea that people who are charged with crimes are regularly bumping off witnesses or intimidating them isn't—it's a *vanishingly* small number of cases where that's a real threat. Much more often, this is used as a blanket excuse not to turn over important discovery. The government should never be hiding information. If it needs to hide information to prove its case, then it's a weak case and it shouldn't be brought. Transparency in the criminal legal system can only bring more justice."[17]

Access to Experts

The same is true of access to expert witnesses. In far too many places, accused people are left to beg the court for an expert to weigh in on their case, an appeal to fairness that is regularly denied. As we have learned time and time again in the context of exonerations, juries believe experts, and when the vast majority of testifying experts are part of the larger law enforcement apparatus, juries are getting misled.[18] More information is healthy here, too. If two accredited experts in a field can disagree about a set of facts, let them! Let them state their reasons and how they formed their conclusions. We cannot both know that much of the "science" we've allowed to drive convictions in recent decades has turned out to be bunk, and also maintain a practice where wealthy defendants can hire any expert they want, but the majority of people in the system cannot afford to do the same.

There are many ways to address this, but two feasible options in the near term are political pressure and legislative action. Citizens can put pressure on lawmakers and judicial candidates to commit to funding access to experts for everyone, regardless of wealth. That pressure should be directed toward lawmakers, too, who could change the law in ways that would encourage equal access. For example, they could create a legal "presumption" in favor of accused people getting the expert they need, which is basically a legalistic way of saying that the default answer to a request for a specialist is "yes" unless you have insurmountable reasons why saying yes is an awful idea.

These are good and important solutions. But these solutions don't get us there alone. They can't, because as long as the primary place forensic science happens is inside police and prosecutor offices, we may not even *have* the experts we need in the first place.

Decoupling Science and Prosecution

Science, by its very nature, should be an equal-access practice that has no allegiance to prosecution or defense. Ideally, science has allegiance only to solid methodology, rigorous standards, and the pursuit of truth. But right now, forensic science is a field that essentially exists only in the context of criminal prosecution—no one is out there doing fingerprint analysis to develop new medicines (that I know of, anyway).

Chris Fabricant has worked on countless wrongful conviction cases where the problem comes down to lack of information, lack of expertise, or bad science (so much so that he wrote a book on it).[19] "One of the most important reforms that the National Academy of Sciences made in its seminal 2009 report[20] was separation of crime laboratories from law enforcement. And the reason is because *it's everybody's science.* There is no 'defense science' and there is no 'prosecutorial science.' The root of the problem is the prosecutorial bias that exists implicitly in this marriage between law enforcement and crime laboratories. Often they share the same *budget.* Many of the experts in those laboratories come from law enforcement backgrounds. And many view their roles not necessarily as scientists so much as crime solvers and crime fighters and crime busters. And that is a huge problem with forensics."[21]

It's not just the conflation of interests; relegating crime labs to police purview means they also have to compete with other things in the police budget for resources (and often lose out). They have substantially less oversight than clinical laboratories, and the result is "(1) no standards for many forensic identification techniques; (2) no uniformity in the certification of forensic practitioners, or in the accreditation of crime laboratories; and (3) no entity that can adequately investigate claims of negligence, incompetence, or misconduct."[22]

Instead of relegating forensic science almost entirely to the prosecution side, with no oversight and insufficient funding, a more equitable practice would be to separate these labs and experts from law enforcement entirely. Certainly, law enforcement could access these labs to have materials tested and seek expert perspective, but *also* these labs and experts could be universally available to the defense—for insight, new testing, or retesting questionable outcomes. In a world where the job of a lab is scientific accuracy and truth seeking rather than collaboration with (and advancement of) the prosecution and its interests, we'd significantly lower the chances of wrongful conviction.

Perhaps even more importantly, we'd also create opportunities for people to do good, fair science in independent labs instead of having to work in law enforcement if they want to study forensics. Right now, forensic science essentially only *exists* as a law enforcement practice, so if your job is in a criminal forensic field, the only use for your research, for the most part, is in advancing prosecutions. In other fields, there may be a massive incentive to take a contrarian perspective, challenge the popular methodology or beliefs, and publish groundbreaking work that upends the status quo and advances knowledge. But in crime science, as Chris explains, "there are almost no industries in which a forensic science expert can apply their skills, outside of the criminal legal system. Within the criminal legal system, their skills are already widely accepted, and are entered into evidence without scrutiny by criminal courts. So there's no incentive to actually do any research that might jeopardize that continued admissibility. And as it relates to experts in fields particular to the defense, there may be *no* dissenting experts within the forensic community. Because they'll lose their jobs. Because the only place that they can work is in a crime lab and on behalf of law enforcement."[23] So yes, we need to fund and legislate equal access to experts, but we also need to weed the bad incentives out of the system. Give science its own budget, its own leadership, and take it off the prosecution team so that scientific dissent, and the true testing of ideas, can move us forward and away from the junk science in which we are currently drowning.

End Barriers to Fixing Bad Convictions

Perhaps the single most prevalent falsehood about the American criminal court system is that it values justice above all. If that were the case, undoing wrongful convictions would, you'd think, be a top priority. Instead, undoing wrongful convictions is, if anything, treated as a kind of deeply unpleasant chore to be avoided at all costs. It is reasonable to have a principle of "finality" in litigation—the idea that all legal matters should have some established end point. But it's not reasonable to prioritize that principle over what most laypeople would assume is the most basic obligation of a legal system, which is some version of *getting it right.* If we want to even pretend we have a "justice" system, we have to stop letting courts stuff their fingers in their ears and yell *nyah nyah nyah* when asked to take another look at a potential wrongful conviction.

These days, that's Chris Fabricant's primary focus. "We have cases where we have probative DNA evidence. Full DNA profiles. They just need to *be tested* to see if the actual perpetrator is in prison. Before I got to the Innocence Project, I wouldn't have believed this to be true, but prosecutors say *out loud on the record* that these samples don't need to be tested, and refuse to have evidence tested that wasn't previously available, because of the principle of 'finality.' They don't want to know the truth."

This isn't a new problem, but it's a hell of a lot more visible now that we have DNA evidence. "The principle of finality has been used to saw off avenues to release innocent people for a long, long time. It wasn't such a *notable* problem until the advent of forensic DNA testing, and the establishment of the Innocence Project and similar organizations that showed what a farce the principle of finality can make of fundamental due process rights."[24]

Sometimes terms like "fundamental due process rights," legalistic as they are, can sap the true meaning from what we're talking about here. What we're talking about is each person's right to get a fair shake in a structure that's supposed to be about fairness. And when we know that the criminal court system isn't impacting people equally, the scrapping of fairness for finality is especially offensive.

Being innocent isn't enough to get your case back in court if you've been wrongly convicted and want the court to take another look at your conviction, and, if the conviction is in fact wrong, let you out of prison. Stanford Law School professor Lawrence Marshall spent much of his career litigating death penalty cases and engaging in scholarly work on how our legal system takes lives. He points out that finality is often functioning as cover for a failure to investigate a case up front: "If even a small amount of work had been done on the front side before a conviction, it may have led to the dropping of charges or an acquittal. And that would have prevented thousands and thousands of hours of work on the back side of the case, trying to move a mountain in terms of overturning convictions. The commitment to finality, at some level, is a commitment to the jury system, and to the many people who believe we're not going to get it *more* right down the road. Why do we think that today we're going to do better than was done back then? But with the advent of more advanced scientific evidence, with the advent of more intensive investigations and the like, that argument is undercut."

As resistant as the system is to hearing innocence claims, it doesn't have to be this way. Our lawmakers have the ability to roll back restrictive laws like the Antiterrorism and Effective Death Penalty Act (AEDPA), which Professor Marshall points out was perhaps enacted via an overly credulous belief that state courts didn't need too much federal double-checking: "AEDPA was driven by the Clinton administration's belief that . . . state courts no longer had to be distrusted. It's sort of like how we currently see courts saying we don't need the Voting Rights Act anymore, we don't need affirmative action anymore. It is all in that same spirit."[25] We could get rid of AEDPA, and have courts actually consider the petitions for relief that come before them.

The gold standard would be to create a more expansive right to a lawyer on appeals beyond the first direct appeal of a criminal conviction. After all, many innocence cases come to light years after a conviction happens. New technology or new evidence may emerge that unravels an entire case, but if the impacted person has no legal avenue to even get that information in front of a judge, and no ability to utilize legal service providers because they're no longer in the early stages of their case, they're likely to be shut out. Innocence Projects are amazing endeavors that continually save lives. But there will never be enough nonprofits in the world to make up for the government's failure to fully realize the right to counsel by giving people access to lawyers whenever they have a potentially viable innocence claim, no matter how long it's been since they were convicted.

John Hollway, who served as the executive director of the Quattrone Center for the Fair Administration of Justice until 2025, points out that there are some states that are doing this well, including, surprisingly, Texas. "They have both an actual innocence statute and a junk science statute. Credit where credit's due, Texas is essentially a libertarian state—they hate criminals and they hate big government and government overreach. So if you've committed a crime, we're going to come at you hard, but if you haven't committed a crime . . . get out of my kitchen." He points out that in addition to using statutes that allow people to bring innocence claims, one could have a sliding scale of finality. "If we got you for possession of an ounce of weed, and you've pled to it, and then later on you want to revisit it, no. But if it's murder, and you have a plausible claim of actual innocence, we're always going to allow that. And if it's a capital offense, we're going to allow these claims multiple times. We're never going to put it aside."[26]

Where should these claims go? Ideally, they should have multiple potential avenues. Not just federal habeas and state innocence laws, but also Conviction Integrity Units, or CIUs. CIUs are branches of a prosecutor's office whose job is to go back and double-check their work. This can circumvent the problem the law has created by prioritizing finality over justice—when the court system does not allow an individual to bring their matter back in front of a judge on a claim of innocence, prosecutors can still reopen their old cases and check their old work, and may have an easier time getting a bad conviction back in front of a judge. So if the CIU works, this can be great; prosecutor's offices may have access to information within their own files that reveals misconduct or otherwise calls convictions into question and, if they're incentivized to really go after these claims, can exonerate innocent people. Even though there were only ninety-five CIUs operating in 2022 (an appalling figure, given the fact that there are more than two thousand prosecutor's offices nationwide), they still managed to help secure 60 percent of the exonerations recorded that year, demonstrating how impactful they can be.[27]

Like so much else in this sector, though, it comes down to incentives. A CIU with several exonerations per year and openness about prior misconduct—including active participation in conversations about how to make current prosecutorial practices better—can do a lot of good. CIUs like those in Washington, D.C., and the Oneida County district attorney's office, which have had no recorded exonerations since their formation?[28] That raises some serious questions about what they're actually doing.

Police Oversight

Just as bad evidence and bad convictions should be rousted out, so should bad policing. But what is "bad" policing? Certainly, there are people in the profession of policing, as there are in any profession, who relish the opportunity to abuse their power. But there are also problems with the structure of policing itself—for example, the goal of ever-expanding surveillance, the historical and ongoing focus on Black and brown people and neighborhoods, and the decoupling of policing and safety in service of a marriage between policing and harsh enforcement. The law has allowed police to selectively target and punish people and groups they disfavor. Policing operates not in a vacuum but as just one piece of a number of legal systems, all of which have disadvantaged historically marginalized groups.[29] With this in mind, it's necessary to say at the outset that a ton of the policing reforms suggested to the public are kind of optical illusions, the sorts of things that can make people feel better about police (implicit bias training! De-escalation training! New uniforms! Baseball games with youngsters!) without actually changing the practice of policing. It's marketing, not change.

So to be clear, the best answer on how to fix police probably involves a lot of rethinking regarding which public safety professionals we rely on the most and what we invest in. But that doesn't mean we can't also do the work of creating police accountability now, working to combat the onslaught of misconduct at the same time as we invest in better alternatives.

Anyone who has ever been told that every police department might have "a few bad apples" should remember that the original saying is "a few bad apples *ruin the bunch*." Systems that hide information can hide insight into who the bad apples are and how they got that way. Which is why professions with life-or-death consequences are supposed to have measures to weed out dangerous individuals by stripping them of licensure.

Police, though, are subject only to limited forms of "decertification."[30] If a doctor is fired from a hospital because of malpractice, that will almost certainly have licensure implications for them that prevent them from practicing medicine until they have rectified whatever was dangerous about their work. But police officers, historically, have been able to "wander," meaning that even though they might have been fired for misconduct, very narrow rules in their state about what merits decertification may prevent them from being decertified.[31] So they can just move one county over and get right back to business.

Worse, one study found that these "wandering" cops tend to move to lower-resource departments in places with slightly larger populations of people of color, subjecting these communities to more misconduct-prone police (think cops who were fired for sexually abusing a young woman in their patrol car, for example).[32] Unsurprisingly, these officers were likelier to have more complaints about them in the future.[33] And that's if they're even fired—many who face termination for misconduct actually bounce back. In a look at D.C.'s police, researchers found that each year, on average, nine officers are fired and six successfully appeal their termination and get themselves rehired.[34] Sometimes, departments are forced to rehire cops for jaw-droppingly bureaucratic reasons, like the officer who was fired for attacking a shoe-store employee and had to be rehired because his department missed an arbitration deadline by a mere seven days. Police chiefs themselves have pointed out how demoralizing and toxic it is to be forced to keep bad cops in their departmental ranks.[35]

In recent years, there have been moves to strengthen decertification rules. Attempts to make certification look more like other professional licenses—with strict rules for professional compliance, recertification processes every few years, universal requirements for certification (requiring potential employers to, you know, actually check on the professional license of the candidate applying), and an expanded definition of misconduct that can result in decertification (to include, for example, standing by while other officers engage in unlawful force).[36] Still, we could do better—with more transparency with the public, stronger national registries of misconduct, and a lessening of union strangleholds on departmental personnel decisions.

Twenty states require decertification only if a police officer has been charged with a crime.[37] Prosecutors have a role to play in taking action on complaints against police—and if prosecutors don't file charges, the whole role of certification can be undermined. This, too, makes police certification different from other forms of professional licensure—a lawyer, for example, can be disbarred for failing to keep up with their continuing education requirements. But a cop may have to pick up a felony conviction in order to see the same result.

Prosecutors, though, also have other means to impact police behavior. DA's offices can disincentivize misconduct with "do not call" lists, wherein bad officers are, as a matter of policy, not used as witnesses in court, thus undercutting their utility in the field and usually de facto relegating them to desk duty. Prosecutors are also fully capable of watching the watchmen, in that they can create units that monitor police misconduct and actually prosecute officers who abuse the citizenry. Are there thorny alliances to be untangled in order to make this happen? Of course. Do all of these options involve creating the political will to defeat massively powerful police unions, who fight tooth and nail against accountability measures? Unfortunately, yes. But with a more informed public, the will can be built.

To inform the public, though, we need better distribution of information. In the context of police misconduct, far too often the records that would tell the public the truth about their law enforcement system are limited to people like me. When I prepare a case, one of the first things I do is file papers requesting any and all information relating to prior misconduct by the police officers involved. And I don't stop there. I also go check court records for civil cases filed against the officers so I know if they've ever been sued for things like violence, lying, or violating people's Constitutional rights. I can then (usually, if a judge allows me) use that information to cross examine those officers and show jurors more about the uniformed person in the witness box. The jurors can make up their own minds; the uniform, for many years, carried a great deal of credibility, and if there is also a sordid history of misconduct, to leave that information out would be to do a grave disservice to the jurors themselves. They, after all, have to live with their decision.

But whatever I do in a given case, I, as a defender, cannot readily raise the alarm for the general public. I might have seen the same cop in sixteen cases and cross examined that cop sixteen times on an instance when they assaulted someone in the community and then lied about it (or in the case of some other cops, how they've assaulted people again and again). I might go home to my family knowing that Officer So-and-So is incredibly dangerous. But I'm just one public defender. Without investment in oversight systems—like licensure, or police misconduct units that actually take action, or, yes, a civilian oversight commission for police that has the power to dismiss bad cops—the people who hold the information have no way to take real action.

We could also reconsider "qualified immunity," the judge-created legal principle that protects government actors, including law enforcement and prosecutors, from civil lawsuits. This makes it incredibly hard to hold bad actors accountable; courts often suggest that when police or prosecutors break the rules, they are held accountable because the evidence gathered illegally can be excluded from trial. But in a world where only about 5 percent of cases even go to trial,[38] and where courts have been consistently ready to accept law enforcement narratives about how their mistakes were in "good faith,"[39] it's hard to avoid the conclusion that exclusion isn't the remedy we need to actually lower misconduct.

Lawmakers, though, could make police and prosecutors just as subject to suit as other high-stakes professions, like doctors, pilots, or truck drivers, by ending qualified immunity. They could pass laws that allow citizens to hold law enforcement monetarily accountable for misconduct, including bad acts and failure to intervene when their colleagues engage in misconduct. Three states are already headed this way: Colorado passed a law limiting qualified immunity in 2020,[40] and Connecticut and New Mexico followed suit in 2020[41] and 2021,[42] respectively (though neither bill was as robust as Colorado's). By 2023, Colorado had actually seen police officers prosecuted and sued for misconduct, it had a statewide database tracking police misconduct and informing the public about their law enforcement apparatus, and body camera footage had become more readily available, all moves that earned praise even from the head of the Colorado District Attorneys' Council.[43] As of 2024, the Colorado reform is credited with increased public transparency, and the hearing of at least eighty-two claims by the citizenry that might never have made it to court without this reform.[44]

Critics from law enforcement have argued that the law has caused attrition within their departments, and there exists a real concern about what ending qualified immunity does to prosecutorial incentives. Would it, for example, cause prosecutors to be more reluctant to dismiss cases out of fear a dismissal might aid a future lawsuit? While police have been having more trouble recruiting since 2020, the issue certainly isn't limited to states that eliminated qualified immunity, and plenty of officers have pointed out that toxic culture in policing is itself a driver of attrition.[45] No impact on dismissal rates has been reported so far in Colorado.[46] If Colorado is any example, many more states could end qualified immunity—whether legislatively or through a voter-passed amendment to the state constitution—and see increased accountability for law enforcement, less misconduct, more safety from police violence, and, down the line, maybe a healthier workplace for law enforcement themselves.

Police Unions Don't Protect the Public

None of these problems are new. Let's assume that, as polling shows, most Americans don't really want police departments that go to the mat protecting their worst officers.[47] So why are we stuck with this? Why aren't we investing nearly as much money as we could be in promising alternatives? And why are we still allowing killer cops to get fired from one department and rehired one county over?

There is always a certain amount of inertia in large, complex systems. Reforms have long struggled to straddle a system that is both vast and hyperlocal. Additionally, reforms are often passed by one group of people (lawmakers) and then implemented by another group of people (those who work in the reforming system), and those two groups may have very different values, priorities, and goals. Even within individual agencies, folks on the ground—who have to implement a reform—may simply not want to, even when their boss very much does.[48] This hampers the effectiveness of a reform, because it doesn't get implemented well.

When we think about reforms in the criminal legal system, we have to confront the role of specific labor groups, specifically special interest groups that personally benefit from mass incarceration and, therefore, work constantly to block systemic reform (think private prison contractors and corporations, yes, but also correctional officers' unions, police unions, prosecutors' groups, the bail industry, and even court employees whose jobs are funded by fines and fees).[49] While I'm confident that righteous ideas can defeat even the most stubborn county clerk, there are real reasons to worry about smart, pro-safety ideas being stymied by police, prosecutorial groups (such as the California District Attorneys Association, which spent its environmental justice money on non-environmental-crime matters like, say, lobbying instead),[50] and correctional unions in particular.[51] This is especially true when you consider the fact that 98 percent of police union contracts contain at least one provision protecting police from being held accountable for misconduct.[52] Or the fact that from 2015 to 2018, prosecutors were involved in more than a quarter of criminal-system-related bills in state legislatures, where they were more than twice as likely to lobby in favor of laws that expanded criminalization and where their efforts made those bills more than twice as likely to pass.[53]

While union membership nationally may not always be high, police unions have managed to maintain higher than average membership, giving them unique political clout.[54] It makes sense: policing has been set up as a high-conflict job, with individual officers fearing the public both as a safety threat and as a reputational one in the age of cellphone cameras and citizen journalism. No one wants to be inappropriately fired from a high-stakes, high-stress job. Union protections are massively attractive.

So, like any other professional service worker union, police unions fight for their membership to retain employment. But unlike other unions, that fight to keep members on the job may carry a much steeper public cost—the cost not just of keeping a violent or corrupt officer on the job but of creating a culture in which it is known that violence and corruption will be protected rather than punished.[55] Horrifyingly, two studies of law enforcement agencies suggest that their collective bargaining rights increased violence and misconduct by those departments.[56] And that's not all: research has also pointed out that increases in collective bargaining rights for police result in a "substantial increase in non-white civilians killed by law enforcement over both the medium and the long-run. These are large effects: our findings suggest that access to collective bargaining rights accounts for 10 percent of the total non-white civilian deaths from 1959 to 1988. We find no associated increase in white civilian deaths."[57]

This extends beyond the walls of the precinct and into the legislature, where the incentive set for a union's protection of its members may cause it to fight against, for example, healthy efforts to have prosecutors go after police misconduct. Police unions have long leveraged our fear and the desire we all feel for safety, labeling those who wish to more closely scrutinize police as "soft on crime," and ultimately weakening the ability of lawmakers to hold power *and* hold police accountable.[58] They've put their money where their mouth is, too, pouring $52 million into state-level lobbying[59] and more than $83 million into federal, state, and local lawmakers (candidates and committees) from 2014 to 2024.[60]

States with the most police have the most money flowing from police unions to lawmakers, though California is truly an outlier with $38 million contributed from law enforcement groups to politicians between 2012 and 2022, dwarfing the state with the second most stuffed pockets, New York, where just shy of $10 million was contributed in those years.[61] The money works. Across the United States, bills that law enforcement interest groups don't like have been blocked, from civilian oversight boards to body-worn cameras.[62]

It's not just police. Correctional officers' unions have a vested interest in keeping prisons full so that their members have job security. Is that good for society? Probably not, given what we know about prisons and their long-term impact on not only safety but also health, families, and the economy. Yet these unions have, in the past, successfully defeated reform efforts that would have put fewer people into the prisons they guard.

They don't always win these days. In California, voters ignored the squeals of these groups and passed Propositions 47 (reducing some felonies to misdemeanors) and 57 (increasing parole eligibility). Maryland and New Jersey have both passed bail reform over the objections of law enforcement groups *and* the bail bonds industry. And since 2008 all but two states have succeeded in doing *something* to reduce reliance on incarceration.[63] A highly informed voting public can learn to see through copaganda emanating from these bodies. Because very real questions remain about what to do when a labor union's work to protect its membership directly harms the safety of millions of other people.

We aren't stuck. We don't *have* to have police unions. There are departments that very much don't want them. Camden, New Jersey, famously cracked down on its police union, fired almost the entire police force, started over, and dropped the murder rate. Is this a great example of police reform? In that they eliminated a corrupt union and lowered most violent crime by about half, sure.[64] Against union claims that police will be defunded if the grip of the union is loosened, Camden is a solid example, because it actually increased spending on police during its rehiring process.[65]

Is that great? Absolutely. But there are still concerns that this reform increased police surveillance of communities in problematic ways.[66] Regardless, Camden proves that it is entirely possible to have contractual, strong due process in the employment context, and also target and eliminate groups that have made it their mission to preserve misconduct.[67] Add to this the fact that when labor movements strike, police are more likely to protect the employers than stand with the workers. With this in mind, it becomes even more difficult to justify their inclusion in a movement they regularly stand against. Because we cannot forget that they're using their collective bargaining power to cement practices of violence against ordinary people.[68]

Chapter Twelve

Unclog the System

Whether you're a public defender, a prosecutor, or a judge, we all have one thing in common: a huge number of the cases that cross our desks every year are a waste of public resources. For every thorny, complex case, we have about ten nothingburgers of small-time, victimless crime—the kids trespassing, the person with a few unprescribed prescription pills in their pocket, the lady selling (delicious) sliced mangoes in the subway without a license.

It's difficult to overstate how extensive the impact of this system overload has been. Attorneys who don't have enough time might end up cutting corners—this may be a prosecutor failing to look into a key angle of the case that might reveal they have the wrong person, or a defender failing to notice a crucial detail in the record that demonstrates the need for a scientific expert or further investigation.

The system has almost zero safety net for these kinds of failures. It has no structure to ensure equity of investigatory or expert resources, no way for people impacted by these failures to raise a red flag for the court at the time it happens (usually their only recourse is, if convicted, on appeal), and an awful track record of normalizing overstretched, under-resourced lawyering. With judges incentivized to just get through their docket by any means necessary, slowing down to look into whether cases are actually being responsibly handled just becomes less likely. Expeditiousness drowns out justice.

It can also cause the courts to become parasitic. There are too many cases coming into these courts, and also too few resources to support even the best efforts at reform or court improvement, leaving the courts to operate on a shoestring. In many places, courts have been forced to subsist off fines and fees levied against people in both civil and criminal cases, leading the courts to treat arrests, prosecutions, and even civil debt as a valuable revenue source rather than a social ill they should work to prevent.[1]

But there *is* good news: one fix for all of the above is a solution that would also result in better emergency resources for all of us. It begins with stemming the flow of cases into the system in the first place by modifying who is responsible for responding to calls for help from the community. And it continues with what kind of response the community is empowered to offer.

Unbundle Policing

One of the most challenging contradictions in recent polling is the fact that people who are often most harmed by police are also often the most likely to support more policing.[2] Why would people who have been routinely abused, killed, and falsely arrested by police also want more police in their community? One key factor may be that people in America are rarely offered forms of safety that don't involve police—our system is set up to force an impossible choice between a person's fear of being harmed by crime and their fear of being harmed by police. Perhaps it's that binary itself; after all, it is perfectly reasonable for people to want less police brutality and negligence, but no less protection or safety. So what if they could ask for a third option—a different kind of emergency first responder?

Somewhere between one- and two-thirds of police calls are for "non-criminal" things.[3] This means that sending police to deal with those issues is probably both a waste of police effort and, more importantly, a missed opportunity to send people with the appropriate skill set. Since a ton of these noncriminal calls stem from problems like mental health crises, substance use problems, and deep poverty, sending social workers instead of police would seem like a no-brainer. We have a public dispatch system that can choose to send fire, paramedics, or police; why not add in social work or mental health crisis teams?

It turns out, that's a great idea. In Denver, for example, the Support Team Assisted Response (STAR) program is a civilian team dispatched through 911. When they get a call for a mental health crisis or substance use problem that doesn't have significant safety concerns, they send behavioral health clinicians and paramedics to the scene *instead* of police.[4] The results have been exceptional. STAR responded to 9,244 calls between 2020 and 2023.[5] About half of the people they encountered were referred to formal mental health or substance use treatment, and another third were transported to a community-based organization that could meet their needs, such as housing, mental health care, food, clothing, and transportation.[6]

Now, I'm going to pause here for a minute, because when you say stuff like this, it makes it sound easy. "Oh, they just took them to a program." In fact, getting someone into treatment—especially if they're unhoused or in crisis—can be massively difficult. Recently, a former client of mine reached out to me and told me she was in the hospital, having chosen to detox, and asked for help finding a place to go. She had previously been through hospital detox and gone to the program that the hospital recommended, but they turned her away because they didn't take her public health insurance. She had a place she could stay for one night, but after that she had zero options. Had I been on my own, I could easily have spent a day calling rehab programs throughout her area, asking them about insurance, sliding scale payments, and available beds.

As it is, because I founded a national program doing the work of connecting people with resources in about half of U.S. states (more on that in a minute), I had a team I could reach out to. But even they could only help me narrow down the resources; there was still legwork to be done finding a bed. We had found a few options and she had done the intake survey for some promising programs, but none had a bed available, and the weekend was upon us. A bed might open Monday. We had to wait. But where? She had nowhere to go, no transportation, and I was trying to help out from three thousand miles away. So we decided to get her a hotel room for a few nights, just to get her through until Monday. But even with the room prepaid, the hotel insisted that she pay $50 cash as a deposit, which, of course, she couldn't do, and I couldn't do from across the country. It took ages on the phone, getting transferred from one person to another, suggesting a million different ways that in the modern world we could get them their $50 deposit without having her present cash. Venmo? No. PayPal? No. Cash App? No. Maybe I could give them a gift card to a service they use, like a gas card, Target, Amazon, anything? I started to feel like the reverse of a scammer, begging the person on the other end of the phone to just let me buy them a gift card. Still no. I pointed out that we had paid hundreds of dollars for several nights in this hotel, and they suggested I get a refund. But a refund won't fix the problem, I insisted, which is that this person has come very far, and gone through a lot, to make it to the safety of your doors. I finally got someone on the phone who relented and let me send him a Zelle payment. This solved the problem of the next few nights—but not the uncertainty of whether there would be a bed on Monday. And even if there is a bed, will she have the right documents on arrival? Will she have all her prescriptions prefilled, since you can't leave rehab to get medicines, and many rehabs won't bring them to you?

Obviously, STAR teams aren't begging hoteliers to accept Zelle.

Instead, programs that are built into the apparatus of emergency response carry a dual benefit from their position of authority: they can network with local providers to build more streamlined, less labor-intensive or ad hoc mechanisms to get people into appropriate care, and they can also reduce the likelihood that the person will ever enter the criminal court system. STAR was so good at getting people into appropriate care that of more than a thousand clinical encounters in the first half of 2022, none resulted in an arrest or citation.[7] The overall result, in just the first six months of this program in eight precincts, was a 34 percent drop in measured crimes, preventing nearly fourteen hundred cases from entering the court system during that time.[8]

STAR is a superb example of the potential in alternative first responders, but it wasn't the first program of its kind. In Oregon, the Crisis Assistance Helping Out on the Streets (CAHOOTS) program brought mental health first responders to the scene as early as 1989. Currently, they are not only successfully diverting calls for service[9] but need police involvement in only 1 percent of calls.[10] The rest of the time, they're just getting people to appropriate care, and because the need for care is so high, public demand for the program has outstripped service availability. These days, it's not just civilians calling for CAHOOTS help, it's the police. When the police encounter a situation, often one spurred by drug or mental health issues, and they feel mental health de-escalation would be better than police force, they can call CAHOOTS and hand off the case.[11]

In Albuquerque, the same idea is showing success. Between its first outing in 2022 and the fall of 2023, Albuquerque Community Safety increased the proportion of police calls they were able to divert fourfold[12] and, like CAHOOTS, have needed to call for police backup in only 1 percent of matters.[13]

These programs have shown us what's possible and, critically, prove that a pure mental health response team can operate independently and rarely need backup from police. Their data demonstrates how overutilized police are in most places. And, excitingly, alternative first responders have been popping up all over the country, from Dallas to New York.[14] But more cities have embraced "co-response" models, where police and social workers respond to crises together. These models lack some of the benefits of a pure alternative—for example, sometimes a person in crisis will react better to a non-cop showing up than they would to a cop, because cops are coded (and visibly uniformed) as people who can take your freedom, or even your life. The risk that police pose to someone frightened and unwell makes everyone less safe, while the relatively lower threat of a civilian first responder, arguably, keeps both the first responder and the impacted person safer.[15] The fact that the alternative first responders above rarely need police backup is an excellent demonstration of the safety potential inherent in nonthreatening, care-oriented teams.

Like anything else, these alternatives vary greatly from place to place. Research on co-response found, for example, that some programs are much more effective than others—some more likely to refer to community organizations and others more likely to utilize hospital ERs—but overall it seems that co-response teams are just much better at getting people to care than police responders. They're also taking a ton of pressure off the court system, managing to route people away from arrest even when people might become violent due to their condition.[16]

Rethink How We Regulate Transportation

Traffic stops are some of the most common encounters between the public and the police,[17] and can quickly turn lethal for civilians.[18] From 2016 to 2021, police killed, on average, one unarmed motorist or passenger per week, none of whom were accused of dangerous crime, and among this group Black people were overrepresented.[19]

A solid chunk—roughly a third, in one study—of traffic stops are for violations that don't impact safety, like a broken taillight.[20] Jared Fishman is a former federal prosecutor and founder of the nonprofit Justice Innovation Lab, an organization that works with justice systems around the country to be more fair and effective. His organization analyzed traffic stops in St. Paul, where, like everywhere else, police use traffic stops as a dragnet. "They are not good at sniffing out crime. They're stopping people at random in neighborhoods that are affected, and they're seizing weapons less than 1 percent of the time," Jared explains.[21] Indeed, recent research of the practice in North Carolina showed that as few as 0.3 percent of these stops yielded actual convictions for contraband.[22]

But unlike much of the country, prosecutors and police in St. Paul ended up doing something about it. They deliberately reduced traffic stops for minor infractions, placing restrictions on when police could actually pull over a motorist. Prosecutors chose not to prosecute any case arising from a non-public-safety traffic stop, so these stops became useless as investigatory tools for police. They changed the incentives, and the result was that stops for non-safety-related things went down, and stops became more equitable for Black drivers.[23] Police seized the same number of guns before and after the change.[24]

Instead of stopping, searching, and ticketing drivers, the region opened up other programs to help people fix small problems with their car.[25] Unsurprisingly, choosing help instead of punishment has strong benefits, like reducing the number of people in the court system, reducing fatalities from police encounters, and, well, getting more taillights fixed. Now cities across the country such as Los Angeles, Philadelphia, Berkeley, and Minneapolis have begun limiting the police role in traffic stops and tapping local departments of transportation to attend to non-safety traffic violations.[26]

Similarly, programs that offer low-income people free access to public transportation eliminate cases for "failure to pay" from entering our legal system while also increasing access to jobs, services, and medical care and helping the environment by increasing transit ridership.[27] In any given arraignment shift, I might see a dozen cases that started with a transit problem. My first trial was the case of a young woman with an expired ticket whom police yanked violently off the light rail and then, predictably, accused of resisting arrest to cover up their own misconduct. Luckily, there was video. We won. The young woman is now pursuing her degree and has a successful career in the court system. But if transit issues had transit solutions, twelve citizens wouldn't have had to take a week off from work to set things right.

In New York, I would often be dealing with court-created transit arrest problems, where my clients were ordered to report to a program in another borough, but given no sustainable means to get there. If they hopped the turnstile, it didn't help that they were doing so to try to comply with a court order. In 2023 half of transit arrests came from just a handful of districts in the majority-minority Bronx and Brooklyn,[28] and about 90 percent of the people arrested for fare evasion were Black or Latin.[29]

Why are we so stingy with transit? In New York, a one-year fare-free pilot for buses showed fantastic benefits: ridership increased more than 30 percent on all routes, and assaults on bus operators on fare-free routes dropped nearly 40 percent.[30] In Massachusetts, Boston's mayor set up fare-free buses. It increased transit efficiency because the bus didn't have to stop and wait for people to tap their cards or pay the fare. Time per passenger on these routes decreased by as much as 23 percent.[31] Portland is trying out another model for reform. Instead of arresting people for fare evasion, it's giving people ninety days to pay the fare, work it off with community service, and enroll in a reduced-fare program, if eligible.[32] Though this method gets some people out of the criminal court system, it lacks some of the efficiencies and advantages of simply funding public transit for all.

Stop Manufacturing Arrests

When I was a kid, I would go over to a friend's house to see if they were home. But under New York's Clean Halls program, I could have been arrested for it; after all, if my friend wasn't home to vouch for me, I would have no way to prove I was "invited" to the building, and therefore could have gotten arrested for trespassing in the Bronx.

Sending police to troll for arrestable kids in buildings where no one called for help is a huge waste of resources and a fast way to fill the system with junk cases.[33] But even before the program was nominally ended in 2020, litigation over NYPD pedestrian enforcement practices managed to decrease trespass cases by 77 percent between 2011 and 2018.[34] When we reduce the amount of time police spend creating arrests—like going undercover as sex workers to arrest people for soliciting, or tricking a desperate substance-dependent person into buying drugs for an undercover—we can similarly refocus the legal system on what it should actually do, which is maximizing safety rather than maximizing arrest numbers.

Better Discretion

Prosecutors have the power to either choose not to pursue, or ultimately dismiss, matters that don't belong in the legal system. Obviously, having fewer matters brought to them in the first place would be massively beneficial. But even under our present circumstances, adapting their intake processes to give them better information up front could result in substantial reductions in total caseload and related reductions in how long each case needs to drag on. In 2021, Jared Fishman set to work on prosecutorial intake systems, trying to ensure that prosecutors got more of the information they need up front so that they could decide quickly if a case isn't fit to move forward.

In our Dick Wolf–soaked culture, many people assume that if an arrest is bad, it will be thrown out quickly, but as Jared Fishman acknowledges, "The reason that's not the case is, in a lot of these places, there's no one actually *looking* for bad arrests. But with a rigorous, universally applied intake system where prosecutors are actually incentivized to weed out weak or baseless cases, we could return to the original idea of a prosecutor's role at the beginning of the process—to exercise discretion and seek justice, rather than just seeking conviction on any case that comes across their desk." These measures work. In just eighteen months, these efforts removed over two hundred insufficient cases from the court system, saving taxpayers about $400,000 and eliminating over three thousand days in jail. There was no negative impact to public safety—in fact, people whose cases were dismissed were less likely to be rearrested.[35]

Early analyses of cases and needs could also make our system better at caring for survivors of crime. A 2022 report noted that 74 percent of survivors of crime got no counseling, mental health support, or other aid with recovery, and, true to that math, only one in four crime survivors surveyed felt that the justice system had offered any kind of support in that vein. That same 2022 study revealed that for about 80 percent of survivors surveyed, their crime was never even solved, and 96 percent of survivors of violent crime never got any form of victim compensation to help them move forward. Half of the people surveyed said they wanted things like therapy, legal aid, help with relocation, or job protections, and only 12 percent got any of these things.[36] This may be in part because 90 percent of these programs require victims to fully "cooperate" with law enforcement to get support, requiring time, effort, and potentially re-traumatization of survivors—perhaps for months or even years—just to secure the kind of care they need. They also commonly deny people compensation if they are seen as having "contributed" to their own victimization by engaging in illegal acts, like sex work or illegal drug activity. Overall, the way these programs are structured means that victims of human trafficking, adult sexual assault, elder abuse, child physical abuse, or stalking, as well as people who don't speak English or who come from specific marginalized groups, are less likely to apply and get the kind of help that prevents cycles of harm.[37]

Though the discourse on the courts often treats "survivor" and "perpetrator" like separate categories, high numbers of criminally accused people are, themselves, survivors of crime.[38] Ensuring stronger support for people who have been harmed is a key factor in breaking cycles of harm.

Stop Conditioning Liberty on Wealth

These days, 70 percent of people in jails are being held pretrial, not having been convicted of any crime.[39] Yes, you read that right.

In America, most people have about as much freedom as they can buy. In the context of bail, this is quite literal. Whether a person can remain free while accused of a crime, and thereby avoid some terrible life repercussions and more effectively fight the charges against them, is overtly tied, in most jurisdictions, to purchasing power. Specifically, cash bail remains the dominant form of pretrial release: a judge orders a person to pay a certain amount of money, which they can have back if and when they successfully return to court. But all too often, that amount is out of reach for the (largely very poor) people our system impacts.

In the United States, the bail bonds industry (an idea banned by England almost fifty years ago) is a $2 billion per year enterprise.[40] This cost is borne almost entirely by low-income families.[41] Conditioning freedom on the ability to pay makes people poorer, and then sicker, and then less able to succeed as they languish in jail. Luckily, though, some states are figuring this out, and testing ways to do better.

Community bail funds, which use donated dollars to bail people out and recoup those dollars when those people come back to court, have been remarkably successful. The Bail Project, a national nonprofit, has reported that 91 percent of the people it bails out come back to court.[42] By cutting into the profit margins of the bail bonds industry, community bail funds can not only bring a lot of people home but also potentially drive down the bail industry's profit-driven dominance.

Replacements for cash bail have also proven effective. Something as simple as an automated reminder for people, pinging their phone to tell them when their next court date is, can reduce failures to appear by a fifth.[43] Phone call reminders can increase appearance rates by 42 percent. A letter reminder can improve appearance rates by 33 percent.[44] And two-way text messaging apps that let people not only get notifications but ask questions and communicate with their lawyers have shown wonderful success, with one such app reporting a 95 percent court appearance rate for its users.[45] Getting people to come to court might be as simple as *telling them they have a court date* and answering their questions.

And when bail reform actually happens, it seems to work pretty well. The Brennan Center analyzed thirty-three jurisdictions and found that regions that had enacted some kind of bail reform had not seen any increase in crime.[46] An analysis from the Harvard Kennedy School similarly concluded that enacting bail reform lowered the number of people being held in jail pretrial and didn't increase crime. This isn't terribly surprising. Even when cash bail is eliminated or restricted, judges still retain large discretion to detain people they think are dangerous. Some of the studies analyzed found other benefits, like reductions in racial disparities and more people ultimately being found not guilty of their charges (in other words, they weren't being ground down into pleading guilty).[47]

There has also been interest in using algorithms to determine whether people should be released. This gives major *Minority Report* vibes and rightly so; algorithms are only as good as the data that feeds into them, and because factors like criminal history, age at first arrest, number of prior arrests, and other risk-assessment factors can be heavily influenced by race, a lot of the data feeding into these systems is *already* racially biased. A young Black man is likelier to have, for example, a younger age at first arrest because of hyper-surveillance by police and the adultification of Black children. This lets human bias filter into nonhuman systems, where the bias may be made invisible by the sanitizing optics of an algorithm.

That being said, even racist algorithms might be a little better than pure cash bail. Research on a public safety assessment tool found that its use resulted in less cash bail, lower pretrial incarceration, fewer guilty pleas, fewer convictions, and no increase in failures to appear in court. But the same tool also assigned Black people more "high risk" scores than other groups, demonstrating the impact of existing racial bias in these "neutral" systems.[48]

No matter what, more people getting out—and fewer being held in on bail—has the potential for massive downstream benefits. More people getting out means more parents home for dinner, more employees showing up for work, more rent payments being made on time, and more people housed. Lower conviction rates means more people moving forward without a criminal record, retaining the economic health of their family, not to mention the health benefits of exposing fewer people to incarceration.

Chapter Thirteen

Accountability over Punishment

If you start paying attention to the way people use the word "justice," you might notice that it's often used synonymously with "comeuppance." Justice itself can mean wildly different things to different people—there are eye-for-an-eye people and turn-the-other-cheek people, and all kinds of people in between—so engaging a highly subjective concept like justice as the core purpose of a public system creates all kinds of murkiness on what we're actually doing here.

We have a big carceral elephant in the room, since the primary cudgel of the system we've built, incarceration, doesn't seem to do much for public safety. This is bad news. The United States spends $182 billion to incarcerate about two million people each year,[1] but research tells us that incarceration has essentially no long-term effect on violence.[2] A 2021 analysis of more than one hundred studies showed that putting people into the custody of the prison system doesn't lower long-term re-offending overall, and may actually *increase* it.[3] Sure, prison may seem to temporarily incapacitate people by removing them from where they live and putting them in a highly restrictive environment, but if you look at rates of violence in prison,[4] it becomes clear that incarceration may be more a form of moving and concentrating violence rather than actually preventing or even reducing it.

This isn't a truth that only experts know. Victims of crime, for example, would prefer our system invest in prevention rather than more punishment by a more than two-to-one margin. If you ask victims of crime what they'd like to see their government invest in, they would pick schools, mental health care, community supervision, access to specialized programs, and most rehabilitative ideas over more prison, and it's not even close: most of these preferences aren't fifty-fifty, they're more like seventy-five to twenty-five.[5]

What these survivors understand much more deeply than their elected officials is what the "grandfather of restorative justice," Howard Zehr, spent fifty years trying to explain to us. "Accountability is understanding the harm you've caused and doing something to make it right."[6] Processes that focus on meting out punishment often not only ignore the primary goal of the survivor but re-traumatize them in the process of rushing to punishment.

Most states, at this point, have some kind of restorative justice program in place, often reserved for young people.[7] These programs bring together both the people who have been harmed and the people who engaged in harm, and try to find both accountability and solutions through a process of confrontation, honesty, apology, and repair.[8] These programs deserve more attention and investment, because they offer promising results. A restorative justice program in Chicago, for example, managed to substantially reduce student suspensions and even arrests, improving in-school culture and increasing the amount of instruction time kids were getting (because they weren't losing school time to bad behavior).[9] Even an incredibly broad review of "restorative justice" programs found that over 70 percent were either "effective" or "promising,"[10] which may be why one famous program in Brooklyn, Common Justice, reports that more than 90 percent of victims of crime who are given the option choose Common Justice over incarceration for the person who did them harm.[11] And the crimes involved are serious and violent—robberies and assaults[12]—underscoring the idea that restorative ideas aren't just forms of charity or kindness reserved for people with negligible offenses or records. In fact, one study of young people accused of crimes found that restorative justice program participants' recidivism rate was over a third lower than those sentenced through the normal court-ordered punishment system.[13] Not all studies have been as promising, but overall, research suggests that prisons cannot do *better* than restorative justice on recidivism, and the overall consensus is that these processes result in higher victim satisfaction and greater feelings of "procedural justice," meaning that everyone involved is happier even when outcomes are comparable.[14] In short, we can and already are doing better than the prison status quo, and if we invested more in using these programs, we might be able to not only increase the impact of our systemic response to harm but also knock out all the horrible side effects of incarceration.

Toward the North Star

It's not just that prisons haven't solved our safety problems. It's that they're actively making them worse. After all, all the trauma, destabilization, stigma, undermining of educational and professional futures, destruction of physical and mental health, and generational damage from the separation of families are factors that create not only huge costs but also higher risks of future crime. The brightest solution to this grim picture is to imagine a world without prisons—a world where we have so successfully invested in the well-being of our people and in alternatives to incarceration that incarceration itself becomes obsolete. It's an ideal long-term goal, a North Star.

But in the near term, we are still very much in the process of laying that groundwork. There are still people in our world who cannot safely be around others. As the scholar Ruth Wilson Gilmore has pointed out, "Abolition is about abolishing the conditions under which prison became the solution to problems, rather than abolishing the buildings we call prisons."[15] Part of reaching that goal is continually pushing for solutions that can provide equal or better safety impact without the same devastating downstream effects as a prison. Reforms that are not ends in themselves, but steps toward the North Star. But when we're confronted with a person who *truly* cannot engage in diversion, treatment, restorative justice, or any other alternative, and whose behavior is impacting the safety of those around them, we have to think about how to best remove that person from their current situation. Which makes the following less a set of solutions and more of an important set of ways to reduce suffering as we work toward a more just world.

There are two factors here that are incredibly difficult to disentangle from each other: time and conditions. If we have to confine people, we should confine them much more briefly, and in places that are built for success rather than punishment.

Changing Our Sense of Time

On the time front, the United States is a huge outlier in terms of sentence length.[16] Most people change over time. Who were you five years ago? Ten? Twenty? Even though very few if any of us would say we're exactly the same human being as we were a decade ago, almost 60 percent of people in U.S. prisons are serving sentences of ten years or longer,[17] an incredibly weighty "average" sentence length that explains why judges and prosecutors and even lawmakers can come to believe that stripping a human being of six or seven years of liberty is a slap on the wrist. One in seven people in prison in the United States is serving *life*,[18] which is just a death sentence in slow motion, because the state will kill you by old age instead of by lethal machines.

Meanwhile, we also have research showing that lengthy sentences don't seem to relate much to how much crime we have, because some states have managed to cut crime and imprisonment simultaneously.[19] We also know that long sentences may spur future crime,[20] and that most people age out of crime.[21] You will be unsurprised to learn that teens and young adults are most prone to the kind of impulsive behavior that can give rise to misconduct, whereas people over the age of forty-five just aren't that likely to cross the same lines, and people over sixty are too damn tired for any of this nonsense.[22]

If we wanted our sense of time in the legal system to match what neurology tells us, we would probably raise the age of criminal liability, but we would also decide most sentences should be much shorter, capping all sentences at twenty years—a long enough time period to ensure that a person has significantly aged toward safety. To the extent that prison sentences can have a deterrent effect—a limited factor, given how few people engaging in crime calculate potential sentence lengths—short to moderate terms of incarceration are deterrent, while longer sentences, according to the National Institute of Justice, "produce only a limited deterrent effect."[23] Because prisons are expensive, dangerous, and bad for public safety, they should be treated more like chemotherapy than vitamins; we should use the lowest sufficient dose.

A better system would normalize minimized sentences, treating regular reviews for release as appropriate rather than "early." Everyone should get routine reviews of their conduct and prospects, as often as every year in short sentences. These reviews should be in person, and with ample time to review materials and correct the record. They should look nothing like our present parole process, which often denies people, without counsel, based on a two-to-three-minute skimming of their record (which may be rife with errors), and almost always kicks them back into prison for another five years before their next two-to-three-minute look. Right now, prosecutors are often given a chance to opine on parole matters, but the person seeking parole has, appallingly, no right to their own lawyer to counter the government—lopsided legal resources are fundamentally unfair, and curtailing prosecutorial involvement could increase fairness. And finally, the decision-makers should have some kind of balanced expertise in safety determinations, and in evaluating plans for rehabilitation and release, rooted in either professional or lived experience. Which, at present, they almost never do.[24]

Remaking sentences to render them more accurately tied to risk means recognizing that mandatory minimums make no sense. No two people are alike, and no two crimes are identical, meaning that laws that impose more incarceration as a blanket rule are essentially prioritizing the judgment of people who know nothing about a given case (lawmakers) over people who may know a great deal about it (judges). Mandatory minimums also consolidate power in the hands of prosecutors, letting them tie a judge's hands via their choice of charges. Unsurprisingly, prosecutors bring charges with mandatory minimum sentences against Black people 65 percent more often than they do against others.[25]

Community supervision (probation, post-release supervision, and other forms of conditional release with surveillance) should also be limited. Deciding to supervise people until they achieve a particular goal—like getting stable housing, a solid job, appropriate medical care—probably makes more sense than just surveilling them for a given period of time. Supervision should end when a person achieves the agreed-upon goals. For something like this to succeed, though, incentives must be reset so that more people get a supervising officer like Amir's and no one gets a supervising officer like Adelaida's.

The ultimate crime of prioritizing optics over reality might be the death penalty. Improvements in DNA analysis over recent decades have resulted in the inescapable conclusion that our system gets it wrong *a lot,* and that a punishment as irrevocable as death is therefore unjustifiable.[26] Repeated analyses have found that there is no evidence the death penalty is actually deterring crime in states where it's used.[27] It's also wildly expensive.[28] As of 2023, more Americans think it's applied unfairly than fairly,[29] and has likely killed innocent people, is probably racist, and isn't serving a deterrent purpose.[30] There is simply no justification for its continued use, other than morbid cruelty.

Dungeons Don't Fix Problems

Maybe politicians would be more apt to release people through their extraordinary clemency powers if they had to actually spend a night in a prison. These spaces must do the work of rehabilitation and opportunity.

Lawmakers need to hold corrections systems accountable for the inhumane conditions within their facilities. Reforms in this arena would require creating feedback mechanisms for people inside these facilities to safely report on what they are experiencing. One would also need to ensure that the evaluation of these facilities—and the promotion or firing of the people who work there—is based on things like the overall health of people living there, reported well-being, communicable disease rates, food and medical audits, low rates of violence, high accessibility of (and engagement with) programs, and other indicators of actual success.

Solitary confinement is one of those inhumane conditions. There are times when a person inside a prison is not safe to be around other people. But even if a person cannot physically be with others, they can speak with others and have time in conversation or in therapy. If we chose to, we could structure the law to require that no one be left in total isolation for more than a few hours, that certain very young people and elders simply not be put in solitary, and that practices be subject to community oversight, as 2023's End Solitary Confinement Act would have done.[31]

The culture of an institution, too, must be addressed. Rich Subia has been the warden of some of California's most challenging prisons, and ultimately rose to be director of California's statewide Department of Corrections. These days, he works as an expert in evaluating dangerousness and readiness to return home for people in prisons all around the United States, and has seen his share of issues with institutional culture. "Too often, there's still a mindset among correctional staff that their job is simply to 'keep the bad guys locked away.' That attitude is fundamentally opposed to the idea of rehabilitation. If you view the people you're working with as incapable of change, how can you support their rehabilitation? Leaders need to drive a cultural shift from the top down. Everyone involved needs to believe that the system can improve and that meaningful reform is achievable."[32]

Recently, U.S. officials have started looking at Norwegian prisons as a model. These facilities are smaller, much more comfortable and dignified, with an emphasis on opportunities for rehabilitation (meaningful work, education, mental health care). Community connection is emphasized rather than curtailed. A person can live in a space that is their own, decorate with throw rugs and curtains, move down the hallways without being shackled or escorted by officers, take a shower alone and without threat of assault, and prepare their own food in a communal kitchen.[33] While we put people in far-flung prisons and replace in-person visits with cold tablets, they are letting spouses spend the night together.[34] And their two-year recidivism rate is 20 percent lower than ours.[35]

Location is another key factor. When we think about what we want to have in prisons, opportunity and community connection are top of mind.[36] When prisons are placed really far away from where people live, it's hard to get family there to visit, hard for kids to keep in touch with incarcerated parents, and hard for teachers and employers to build inroads into the prison space. San Quentin, in California, is an incredibly unique prison in its plethora of opportunities, from college courses to reentry programs that connect directly to jobs in the tech sector. This is possible in part because of leaders within the institution who have sought out these opportunities, but also possible because San Quentin is located on beautiful waterfront property in Marin, California, only about half an hour from San Francisco.

On the family side, prisons have come to treat families as adversaries—strip-searching moms and kids who try to visit Dad in prison, suspecting them of smuggling contraband, and making the visiting process a unique and lasting humiliation. But family willingness to connect substantially improves safety. Even if governments cannot make prisons closer to population centers, they should invest in free, easily available transportation to and from these facilities, and in visiting spaces that are safe, welcoming, and comfortable for kids. Instead of allowing prisons to end in-person visits and line the pockets of tablet and telecom companies, governments should insist upon policies that enhance availability: free phone calls, longer and more flexible visiting hours, more variety in the activities families can do together, increased options for families to stay with their loved one overnight.

Similarly, the role of work in prison needs to be fundamentally re-evaluated. Right now, slave labor remains legal in American prisons,[37] which is obviously a shocking and continual mechanism of oppression. But *meaningful work* isn't. Most people, given the option, would choose to have a way to spend their days, hone skills, and earn money. The problem isn't the labor. It's the lack of choice, and the lack of wages, which means that the reform necessary is to give people in prison the same freedom to choose work and the same minimum wage as the rest of us. They can save for release so that when they come home, they have a nest egg they can rely on to find a place to live and bridge them to their first post-prison job. This money can also help to foster the same community connections that we know are vital to that post-prison success.

Subia recalled how much this meant to the people living in the prison of which he was a warden: "They can utilize that money to assist their family in their community, and they still feel like they're a part of a family unit. They can send a gift, some money, a check, to a son, a daughter, a mother, a wife, who may need some assistance. They may have a child who's going to college, and the only thing they can do is send them a check for $100. I've worked a lot of jobs where I can pull an inmate trust account and see where every month or every other month he's sending money out to go to his daughter or son, to assist with something. At least he still feels a connection to the family by participating in whatever way he can. That's very important inside. Very, very important." Charity events, walkathons, volunteering, and coming together in support of outside causes have also been tremendously important connection builders, in Subia's experience. To him, they are a way of saying, "I'm still here, I'm still participating in this community, and so I'm still a *part* of this community," which is a vital bulwark against the kind of terminal isolation, stigma, sense of abandonment, and even shame that otherwise accompanies time in confinement.[38]

Chapter Fourteen

A Budget Is a
Statement of Values

When the slogan "Defund the Police" was ubiquitous in the year following the murder of George Floyd, I heard a common refrain from people who found the call to action unnerving: "We can't just *not have* police. Who will I call if something is going wrong?" Yes, there's a perspective in that question—the feeling that police bring more safety than danger. And certainly there are different perspectives on the relative value and threat of police, but that doesn't mean we can sidestep the question. Big changes take big coalitions, and addressing this concern head-on is crucial to building the kind of consensus that brings about real transformation.

And the answer is what you'd expect: no one is trying to build a world where there's no one to call when something bad is happening. Instead, we are currently living in a world where the number of bad things that happen requiring an armed and potentially lethal response (active shooter in a mall) is relatively small,[1] and the number of bad things that happen that require a level head, de-escalation, and social work skills (people having mental health crises at home or in public, drug-related crises, unarmed disputes and scuffles, kids being small jerks on loud dirt bikes) is pretty high. Responding to *all* of these events with a team whose skill set is geared toward violence is not just unhelpful but demonstrably dangerous. Daily news alerts remind us of this. So, having more appropriate, varied, and expert responses is both urgent and plain common sense. The answer to the question isn't "Sorry, Karen, you're on your own"; it's "Actually, Karen, you don't need the police for *everything,* and the vast majority of police calls would be better handled by teams with different training and skill sets."

The fact that Americans have a hard time imagining anyone other than police responding to any type of emergency reveals how much we have overinvested in one public safety strategy, at the expense of developing solutions that work better and have stronger evidence in their favor.

Investing in solutions that make places feel not just observed (like with surveillance cameras) but *cared for* can be notably effective at lowering crime. For example, research connected streetlights, painted crosswalks, public transit, and parks with 76 percent decreased odds of *all* juvenile homicide in a Philadelphia neighborhood.[2] For comparison, a recent study showed that, on average, it would take ten to seventeen additional police officers to prevent just *one* homicide per year,[3] meaning that a onetime investment in public space may be substantially more effective and less costly than incurring the annual expense of increased police salaries.

We should absolutely spend money on safety, and plenty of it. But safety funding doesn't equate to police funding. Another study in Philadelphia found that investing in cleaning up and fixing up vacant lots in poor neighborhoods was associated with a 29 percent drop in gun violence.[4] In New York, adding streetlights to public housing led to a 36 percent drop in street crime after dark.[5]

It's not just about buildings and lots. You know what really drops crime? *Trees.* Just trees. In Baltimore, a 10 percent increase in tree canopies was tied to a 12 percent decrease in crime (and yes, they controlled for other socioeconomic factors).[6] In Washington state, they studied residential neighborhoods and found that there were fewer property crimes when houses had more trees and vegetation in and around the property (a finding that's kind of weird, because you'd think it would be easier to burglarize a house hidden by trees, and actually some argue that small trees are bad for crime but large trees are good, following this logic). In Portland, too, having more trees in the public thoroughfare was associated with lower crime.[7] Even more intriguing, another study found that among public housing buildings, those with more nearby trees and greenery had fewer reports of domestic violence *inside* the housing.[8] In Chicago, a study found that people in public housing who had more trees around them reported 25 percent fewer instances of violence toward partners than people with fewer trees.[9] Another notable study in Chicago found that public housing with greenery had 56 percent fewer violent crimes (and 48 percent fewer property crimes) than other buildings with less greenery. This was a study that looked at a whole bunch of different factors, and found that the amount of plant life around the property was one of the most important housing characteristics tested.[10] If you want to be safer both inside and outside your house, your dollars may be better spent on a nice row of maples instead of more cops.

Similarly, projects that make people's living environments better seem to drop crime. Fixing up low-income homes in Philadelphia was associated with a 22 percent drop in total crime,[11] and crime seems to be lower when residential areas are mixed income and low-income housing is not isolated.[12] Lack of isolation has a number of beneficial effects. In Flint, Michigan, for example, creating opportunities for the residents of a community to clean up vacant lots and plant greenery in them was tied to a 40 percent decrease in assaults and violent crimes (compared with lots that weren't maintained by the neighborhood), and this was even after controlling for socioeconomic factors and prior rates of violent crime.[13] In Philadelphia, the Pennsylvania Horticultural Society spent ten years trying to make vacant lots more cared for, buying fencing, benches, plants, and more, which was associated with a 29 percent drop in gun violence, as well as a 30 percent drop in nuisances like loitering and vandalism.[14]

More Housing and Less Debt Help Everyone

Access to safe and affordable housing lowers recidivism, and also lowers the likelihood that a person will be criminally accused in the first place.[15] States that spend more on housing have lower incarceration rates,[16] meaning that you can choose to put your dollars into prisons or homes, but you have to pay for one or the other.

Studies back this up. In L.A., researchers found that getting unhoused people housed reduced the chance they would commit a crime by 80 percent.[17] In Denver, people in supportive housing had 34 percent less police contact and 40 percent fewer arrests than similarly situated people not in the program.[18] In Washington state, having housing dropped new convictions by 14 percent and dropped the chance of a person returning to prison by 19 percent.[19] If you're into people doing well and not engaging in crime, you should be very into programs that get people housed.

But we also can (and must) focus on initiatives that help people make ends meet in other, more nuanced ways. The court system itself, as you recall, is massively expensive, imposing fees for everything from the conviction itself to the privilege of being jailed, and often increasing fees as a punishment for, you guessed it, being too poor to pay the original fees.[20] So initiatives that prevent these costs in the first place are a tremendous step toward making people more able to access the pro-safety things we want them to have—like housing.

This means, for example, eliminating court system fees that drive people into debt. The scale of court debt is staggering. The Fines and Fees Justice Center analyzed only the fourteen states that were able to provide complete data and eleven more with incomplete data, and with that alone uncovered more than $27 billion in court debt burdening American families.[21] Some communities studied have spent "more than 41 cents of every dollar of revenue they raise from fees and fines on in-court hearings and jail costs alone," which is "121 times what the Internal Revenue Service spends to collect taxes and many times what the states themselves spend to collect taxes. One New Mexico county spends at least $1.17 to collect every dollar of revenue it raises through fees and fines, meaning that it loses money through this system."[22] Relieving families of this debt so that their dollars can go to their kids' needs, flow back into local economies, and increase overall stability for low-income families is not just crucial but sensible.

It's not just the fines and fees. We should also stop letting the government rob its citizens through the process of civil asset forfeiture. In practice, this looks like police seizing almost $1,000 from a man they accused of selling drugs, only to find out that the pills he had were his own prescription, and dropping the charges but never returning the cash.[23] Or a nursing student having *two* of her cars seized because police claimed her ex-boyfriend was a petty drug dealer. We can eliminate this. New Mexico did and saw no uptick in crime.[24] What's more, to do so could be a political coup, since people across the political spectrum truly detest this practice.[25]

Where Can the Kids Go?

Giving kids good places to go after school can have surprisingly strong effects. It can be *very simple.* Take Lift Zones, which gave about six million people access to Wi-Fi across more than a thousand locations, half of whom said they wouldn't have had internet access otherwise. In places with Lift Zones, kids got arrested up to 17 percent less.[26]

These effects peaked in the after-school hours, because after-school hours are when kids are most at risk of making awful choices. After-school programs (ASPs) seem like the natural solution, because they reduce the amount of unsupervised time kids have at loose ends. In programs that work, the results are fantastic: a program called Becoming a Man did a randomized controlled trial of its after-school program results and found that it reduced arrests by as much as 35 percent, reduced violent crime arrests by up to 50 percent, and ultimately increased graduation rates by 12–19 percent. Because the program had such impressive results and wasn't that costly to implement, the study suggested a cost-benefit ratio of up to thirty to one.[27] Another landmark study looking at L.A.'s BEST program found, again, that crime among kids drops by as much as 50 percent when they have something healthy to do with their time, and also that kids in the program "develop better relationships with adults and peers, have better conflict resolution skills, have higher aspirations towards their future and indicate a desire to finish high school and go on to college."[28] These results are consistent with another study of twelve California districts' ASPs that found that kids who went to the ASP had vandalism rates that were two-thirds lower, violent crime rates that were 50 percent lower, and overall arrest rates that were 50 percent lower than those of kids who didn't. The kids even did better in school, with suspensions, expulsions, and detentions going down by a third.[29]

Public Defense Is Part of the Safety, Health, and Economic Mobility Infrastructure

All these investments look at the horizon, but do not help the people who are sitting in jail *right now.* When we think about dismantling the harm of the legal system as it currently operates, we have to attend to the right now just as much as we attend to the distant horizon. And when it comes to where dollars can do the most good right now, one of the most under-attended spaces for serious benefit is public defense.

First of all, we need more public defenders. Until we can successfully reduce the volume of cases pouring into the courts, we need to address the fact that there is no attorney so talented that they can withstand caseloads that have become typical in public defense. One friend of mine practicing in Louisiana had, when he *started* as a young defender, around four hundred in-custody felony cases. Another attorney I spoke with recently in the Southwest was laboring under more than five hundred open treatment court cases. The under-resourcing and overburdening of defense has become commonplace in this country.[30]

Our role is to make things happen for our clients—investigating, catching errors, fighting governmental abuses, holding prosecutors and police accountable, protecting people's rights, and doing the legwork to secure phenomenal outcomes in cases. We can't do that if we're crushed under an impossible workload. To lower the workload, we need more people to take these jobs in the first place, which means we need governments to invest in their defenders, creating resource parity with prosecution (not just paying defenders as much as prosecutors, but also providing the same kind of investigatory and forensic support). An adversarial system cannot even pretend to be fair if just one side gets the vast majority of funding and staffing power.

But it's not just about expanding the number of defenders nationwide. It's also about changing *how* defenders do the job. The strongest near-term intervention to amp up the power of the defense to better protect people against the harms detailed in this book? Changing how we define "defense" altogether, and ensuring that poor people get a style of legal representation that's much closer to what rich people can afford.

As you can tell, a huge number of the reforms relate to policing and prosecution. But public defenders have tremendous access to the impacted public. Eighty percent of people in the criminal court system are represented by public defenders,[31] and because the system is now so huge that it has touched nearly half of *all* Americans,[32] one can do the math and conclude that about a third of us have had a loved one represented by a public defender.[33] Defenders are also upstream in a system with horrifying downstream effects; most of the time, they're assigned automatically, shortly after a person has been arrested. There's no barrier to entry. A person who needs a defender *will* have a defender, meaning that, unlike other service access points, defenders may be more available and easy to utilize. What's more, they have special protection by law. A person's conversation with their lawyer is privileged and confidential, allowing anyone to be fully honest with their defender and not have to worry about reprisal or punishment. A defender is legally obligated to be loyal only to the person they represent. Unlike any other actor in the legal system, public defenders don't punish. Their only role is to protect. At its best, this relationship is the ultimate safe space.

A safe harbor is important when a person is in crisis. And everyone who has been arrested, one way or another, is in crisis. After I had spent nearly a decade as a public defender, meeting people in lockup and hearing about all the intersecting crises that had brought them there, I started thinking about what more we could do. The Bronx Defenders is a "holistic" defense agency, meaning that they are funded, staffed, and equipped to provide help to their clients on issues beyond the criminal case—to fight for families in family court, to fight for housing in housing court, to sign people up for benefits, and to help those seeking immigration asylum. Their results are spectacular, including reducing the chance their clients would be incarcerated by 16 percent compared with "traditional" defense, and shortening sentence lengths by about a quarter.[34] But that isn't the norm—or it wasn't, back when I was thinking about this problem.

To me, a defender's job could not stop at the courthouse doors. If we're being honest, it already doesn't. For all the credit given to treatment programs and diversion, usually the person fighting to get an individual into such a program, and figuring out what type of program will be the best fit, and making sure they have what they need to successfully complete the program isn't a prosecutor, a judge, or even a probation officer. It's their defender. We're the ones sometimes paying out of pocket to get a client a ride to a court date they must not miss, or getting on the phone with a school counselor to explain why our young client needs to be able to come to court *and* make up their math exam. Our clients' problems do not exist neatly packed in vacuoles, arranged by subject matter, so why should our defense? My client's arrest may be driven by the fact that they lost access to their benefits and couldn't keep seeing a doctor they needed, leading to an unraveling that cost them their job. If they were rich, and paying me $1,000 per hour to defend them, they would expect that I would be thinking about how this legal matter intersects with their personal, familial, and economic well-being. So why are most public defenders set up without resourcing for this work, asking poor people to sacrifice that quality of counsel?

They shouldn't. Which is why, in 2017, I got together with Rebecca Solow, a close friend from childhood who had spent her career in the private sector working as a management consultant and helping governments and nonprofits do better work. Nothing bothers her more than a bad system. So I invited her to brunch and told her some of what you've read here, and she was, as you might expect, outraged and appalled enough to jump in with both feet. Together, we started Partners for Justice, an organization designed to transform the very definition of public defense.

No one who has a public defender, we found, has just one issue. PFJ's experience in the field demonstrates that defender client needs range from two to seven separate issues they're struggling with (simultaneously!) outside their case, many of which influence how their case will turn out and how that outcome will impact their lives.[35] Together with our team, we came up with collaborative defense, a system that could rework what defenders can do. It's different from holistic defense, focusing more on the client's actual needs and less on what a perfect public defense office should look like—the next iteration of how defense could evolve. To advance the collaborative defense approach, we created a fellowship to embed sharp new professionals—often people whose own lived experiences bring them to this work—with defenders around the country, and trained these "Client Advocates" to work on finding housing, jobs, educational opportunities, medicines, benefits, transportation, and more. They are the go-to problem solvers walking side by side with impacted people through that grind of criminal court, guiding them through the shoals, and shielding them from harm whenever possible.

The model worked. First of all, Client Advocates are able to carry out the tasks their clients ask of them over 80 percent of the time, and, second, and perhaps more importantly, they are able to pour the knowledge of their clients' needs, work, and achievements into what prosecutors and judges are told about the person and their case. Suddenly, instead of seeing the accused person in a dehumanizing "criminal" framework, prosecutors and judges receive the information they need to see *whole* human lives. Incarceration dropped. By 2023, we were able to look at our work in Delaware (where our model had grown to be statewide) and see that when Advocates not only performed services, but also told the story of that person and their work in court, we ended cases with zero prison or jail sentences 87 percent of the time.[36]

In public defense, we spend a lot of time knowing how we could do better (I cite, as evidence, this whole damn book), but fearing that no one will listen, or feeling beaten down by a professional life lived in a system that seems impermeable to change. If you asked me how I felt ten years ago, that might have been me. But since starting Partners for Justice, I've seen an extraordinary appetite for change. We began the program in two locations: Wilmington, Delaware, and Oakland, California. We started it up on philanthropic dollars, with a few true believers giving us the seed money we needed to get the program off the ground. In just six years, we grew from those two locations to more than forty places around the nation, impacting defense in twenty-one states, and, crucially, we didn't do it on donated dollars alone.

Governments began to notice our results and realized that they had underestimated their public defenders. They hadn't previously understood that defenders can be public health workers (preventing the health hit of incarceration, yes, but also connecting people to treatment programs that are well suited to their needs, and getting people the benefits coverage to pay for care). They hadn't realized that public defenders spur economic mobility (clearing people's past convictions to make them more employable, or holding out for a plea deal that preserves someone's clean record, or even negotiating with someone's boss to prevent them from being fired for coming to court). They had profoundly underestimated the impact of equipping an upstream, low-barrier, confidential system resource with the power to do good—and when they saw what was possible, they started to make different budget decisions.

Around the United States, governments have started to invest more deeply in their defenders. We are at the beginning of a very long road; public defense is not one system but a distributed network of more than 5,900 agencies, nonprofits, government entities, and individual practitioners spread over America's 3,144 counties.[37] But in just a handful of years, our collaborative defense movement went from fully philanthropically funded to over 70 percent government funded, by proving the incredible value of public defense and eliminating more than eight thousand years of exposure to incarceration.[38] By 2024, nearly half of people who received both services and powerful in-court storytelling had their cases dismissed or were on track to resolve them entirely without a conviction.[39]

Let the People Innovate

Investing in the expansion and transformation of public defense is a solution that impacts people who are sitting in jail right now. Near-term strategies like this are an essential part of the puzzle because the people sitting in jail right now cannot afford to wait for long-term solutions to reduce harm. They need a way home. Investing strongly in defense is one such way home, but there are many, many others. Brilliant innovations are springing up around the United States, aimed at preventing harm and bringing people home.

On the prevention of harm front, it's hard to overstate how hyperlocal solutions need to be. Every community is unique, and that uniqueness means that one-size-fits-all solutions are harder to implement than locally rooted innovations. This also means that some of the most effective interventions have been ones that follow an established, tested idea, but iterate on it to make it properly suited to the community in which it will operate. When they work, they really work. One study estimated that every ten community-based organizations working on lowering crime and improving life in a city with at least 100,000 residents "leads to a 9 percent reduction in the murder rate, a 6 percent reduction in the violent crime rate, and a 4 percent reduction in the property crime rate."[40]

Collaborative defense is one such example. We have principles that we know work, but how these principles manifest themselves in each neighborhood we serve is defined by the people who live there. This means the services provided in Pablo, Montana, may be different from those offered in Compton, California, or Chester, Virginia. It works: each community gets what they *actually* need, instead of being told by an outsider about what they *should* need.

Participatory defense is another such idea. Born in Silicon Valley about twenty years ago, this model of community organizing, which trains the families and loved ones of system-impacted people to act as change makers in their own right, has shown stunningly decarceral results. The National Participatory Defense Network consists of a series of "hubs" around the country that are trained to help families become active participants in their loved one's case—writing mitigation, dissecting police reports, assisting in defense strategies, gathering letters of support, and filling courtrooms with friends and neighbors whose very presence emphasizes, to judges and prosecutors, how much the accused person matters.[41] As of 2023, they estimate they have eliminated 25,869 years of incarceration in the last decade-plus.[42]

Community violence interruption (CVI) is another solution, which upstreams all these forms of defense because, unlike our entire legal system, it actually *prevents* violence. CVI takes a public health approach to harm that would otherwise end up in the legal system.[43] CVI largely focuses on gun violence, treating it as the epidemic that it is, and recognizing how gun violence moves like a contagion through groups of people. These programs train violence interrupters to identify which people might be at highest risk of engaging in gun violence and contact them before they do—working in hospitals to speak with victims of gun violence about (and prevent) retaliation, or working with community elders and leaders who figure out which kids in the neighborhood are having a hard time and develop relationships with those kids that can lift them out of harm's way. Interrupters—who are sometimes called peacekeepers or neighborhood change agents—are, crucially, *from the community*, and are often themselves people who have lost loved ones to gun violence. Because of this credibility, they can be enormously effective. Cities across the United States that have adopted CVIs have seen homicides drop 20–30 percent, saving both lives and money, because CVI can generate about $20 in savings for every $1 spent on the program.[44] In one Detroit hospital-based program, as of 2021 zero program participants had been seriously reinjured, and of those who were previously unemployed or did not finish high school, "more than 80 percent have either enrolled in an educational program or obtained employment."[45]

Looking at those results, one wishes that CVI models would spread further beyond gun violence. But there are plenty of profoundly promising initiatives that invest in community members to prevent bad things from happening. My favorite is the Dads on Duty program, which popped up in Louisiana in 2021 at a school that had a problem with fighting among students. These dads started spending time at the school, spreading good vibes, resolving problems between kids, and shooting "the look" (you know the look, the dad look) at kids who were headed toward misbehavior. Fights in the school dropped, which meant that arrests and police contact for kids dropped, too, preventing the trauma and disengagement from school that follow a police encounter.[46]

The program is new, and small, and developing, but already showing promising reductions in minor misconduct like vaping, and also in referrals to police in schools, in those places where it has been replicated.[47] When we ask ourselves how to make schools safer, the answer may be "more present, trusted grown-ups who love these kids" and not necessarily "blanketing the school with cops." This is especially true when we consider the mixed findings of research on school police officers, who may have some positive safety effects, but may also generate endless low-level (disorderly conduct) arrests, spike the rates of suspension and expulsion, and ultimately cause fewer kids to graduate.[48] Even if the nonpolice grown-ups are just lessening the frequency of students interacting with school police or school resource officers, it's a win for safety and student achievement.

As a parent, I think about this a lot. When I drive by my daughter's school, I think of the twenty-one people killed in Uvalde, Texas, and about the police who not only didn't do their jobs but prevented parents from trying to save their children.[49] When my daughter was in kindergarten, there was a threat to our local schools, with a man one county over having been accused of a school-related shooting plot, and a local police officer was stationed outside my daughter's Montessori. He was young, maybe early twenties. To me, he also looked like a kid. *What would you do?* I thought to myself. There are heroic police officers who can, and have, run into harm's way and put their lives on the line to save others. There are also police officers who are human, and scared, and unready to take the risks this job imparts. How was he trained? What is his character? What was he ready to do? Not all police officers are antagonistic or dangerous, but also not all of them are heroes, which is why I wish we had a wider variety of grown-ups, with a wider variety of commitments and skills, protecting our kids.

When I was in elementary school, I was the kid in the school with an active shooter. I had been taking an informal science class with friends at Van Allen Hall, a University of Iowa building, when a graduate student entered the building and went on to execute several of his professors, a dean, and a fellow student.[50] It wasn't the police who got us out. It was my mom, who ran past a police barricade and up several flights of stairs to gather the children and rush us out of the building and into her car. She had tried to get the police to go in—when she arrived at the building, she told them there was a group of elementary school students upstairs, but they didn't believe her, because we weren't on their building manifest. "I dropped them off myself twenty minutes ago," she remembers saying, but none of the officers in front of the building would listen. So she ran past them.

Was that the right thing to do? There's no way to know. Obviously she took a huge risk. She might have been putting us at greater risk. But, at the same time, I'm here and alive and telling you this story, and she got us out before the gunman made it to our floor (where he was headed, we later found out) while the police were not entering the building. The point isn't "parents are better at handling school shootings," but, rather, parents—and other grown-ups who are deeply committed to these kids—are willing to do things, and have insights that allow them to do things, that police sometimes cannot or will not do. This is an example of terrifying and complicated crisis response, but the previously mentioned dads are doing equally heroic work upstream, preventing the crises from happening in ways school police simply cannot.

Community groups, too, are filling in where our institutions have failed to help people return from prison. You would think that prisons would be tasked with spending real time helping people return from incarceration, because, well, they should. In an ideal world, prisons would dedicate months if not the full year prior to a person's expected release ensuring that they have the means to strengthen their social network, arrange a place to live, apply for jobs they can begin when they come home, file paperwork to reconnect with health insurance or other vital benefits, and get their driver's license back. All things that would be easy to do slowly pre-release but are exceptionally hard to do alone, post-release. Unfortunately, most institutions have utterly failed to invest in this level of pre-release support and planning, so it's up to innovators like the Anti-Recidivism Coalition to do the work on the back end. From providing housing to finding jobs to offering rides home to creating bonding experiences, ARC's work to help people succeed means that 3 percent or fewer of their members go back to prison, which is astonishing in California, a state that funnels people back into the system at a rate of around 60 percent.[51]

Other groups around the country are doing similar work, investing in people who have experienced prison firsthand, working on clearing barriers to success for their membership, and using their knowledge to impact policy. After Michigan's successful Michigan Prisoner Reentry Initiative (which had dropped recidivism rates 25 percent in its early years) was ended, a group of formerly incarcerated people founded Nation Outside, a grassroots organization that uses peer-led reentry coaching and high-level policy work to change both the processes and the perception of reentry.[52] Antoniese Gant was the co–executive director of Nation Outside, and credits a combination of coaching and direct employment for their success: "I know what I faced once I was released and the biggest thing I faced was trying to get a simple job. So we are working with business leaders and employers to figure out what the biggest fear is. What is the biggest fear of hiring people with a criminal record? Within our organization, we tend to hire people with criminal records, so we can take the folk that nobody else wants to hire and train them, get them professionally developed, give them a really good job with the hope that they'll move on somewhere else to a better job. But also, we've created this peer reentry idea, so when we take people who will struggle to get a professional job and we train them and give them a professional job, we also create a benefit to the people that are being released, in that they have somebody right there with lived experience that can help them through the transition of reentry."[53]

One of the most satisfying things, to me, is watching organizations and ideas that no one thought possible even ten years ago take off. When I was representing people sentenced to Three Strikes life sentences in California, there was a program at San Quentin teaching men who might have never seen a cellphone how to code apps. Another lawyer and I were talking about it and he scoffed a bit, incredulous at the idea that these guys could ever compete for jobs in the tech sector. A few years later, though, one of the men I had the honor of representing, Chrisfino Kenyatta Leal, came home, got a tech job, and, after seeing how more training would benefit his peers, became the executive director of Next Chapter, an organization creating a pipeline from prison to Silicon Valley. "Our work leverages the power of technology and education to open doors that were once closed, transforming lives and challenging societal perceptions," he told me. It's working. Over 90 percent of Next Chapter graduates find a job in the tech sector within a year of finishing their apprenticeship, with an average base salary of more than $100,000. "In 2024, 95 percent of our program participants are expected not to return to jail or prison on a new conviction within twelve months of completing the program," Kenyatta says.[54] With companies like Slack, PayPal, and Asana getting on board, the fight for more inclusive hiring practices can gain momentum.

Post-release access to employment is obviously vital, and while there are superb programs working on finding jobs for people, these efforts would be greatly aided by real occupational licensing reform. No one should spend years in prison training to do a job—from barbering to electrical work to firefighting—that they cannot be licensed to do on the outside. States that have heavier restrictions on who can get a license to do a job have higher recidivism, and states that lower these restrictions see recidivism go down.[55]

There is no way to list the full spectrum of organizations whose work will lead us into the future, because there are too many, and that is great news for us as a country. It means that if we can inspire those around us with means and power to invest in fixing things instead of breaking them, we have a great deal of hope.

Personally, I have hope. As grim and complex as the problem of our criminal court system is, there are lines of clarity in how we replace it. The data leads to an unavoidable conclusion that helping people is good; the knowledge that people can and do change, often much more readily and rapidly than our system expects; the exciting evidence that the changes that make our world more beautiful also make it safer.

There are plenty of problems facing us, as a society, that we do not yet know how to fix. But in this sector, we should be thrilled that we know how to do better. We are not searching for solutions—they're here, and they're working.

What we're searching for is the political will to overcome resistance to change. The necessary will cannot be produced by one or two powerful people, but has to arise from each of us, from our voices and our votes, demanding better. From better information about the true state of affairs and the availability—and efficacy—of known solutions. From cantankerous Thanksgiving dinners where someone finally takes on Uncle Frank's claims about "felons." From the testaments of employers who love their system-impacted star employees. From judges who are ready to call for change and politicians who push their peers to invest in new ideas instead of burning money in the furnace of the status quo.

Our safety is collective. As you read this, there is a person sitting in a county jail who cannot afford to wait for change. On their behalf, neither can we.

Acknowledgments

This book represents the insights, experiences, hard work, and good ideas of so many people, to whom I am deeply indebted. To begin with, the phenomenal individuals who have appeared in its pages, lending their knowledge to all of us and guiding us through the morass of our legal infrastructure. It is a rare joy to write a book wherein one can constantly engage, interview, and late-night text with people one admires tremendously.

This book (and my brain writ large) are only possible because of my incredible teachers, mentors, and the people who generally honed my sense of justice and reality: the late Barbara Babcock, Judge Ed Davila, Michelle De La Isla, Anne Devereaux, Daniel Donoghue, Geralyn Dreyfous, Marjorie Garber, Judge Nancy Gertner, James Gilligan, Stephen Graham, Judge Mary Greenwood, Judge Thelton Henderson, Gene M. Heyman, Daniel Ho, Mark Kelman, Robert Kirshner, Larry Kramer, Justice Margaret Marshall, Barry Mazur, David Mills, Judge Robin Rosenberg, Robert Scanlan, Elaine Scarry, Norman Spaulding,

Marcus Stern, Jim and Susan Swartz, Laurence Tribe, Davis Weinstock, Robert Weisberg, and, of course, Brendon Woods.

I am also grateful for a chance, here, to thank the people who helped me along and refined my thinking: Khalid Alexander, Cecilia Boyers, Eric Budin, Susan Champion, Amir Chapel, Chloe Cockburn, Amelia Cogan, Laney Ellisor, Jared Fishman, Jason Flom, Ricardo Garcia, Scott Hechinger, Ben Heineman, Carissa Byrne Hessick, Emily Hughes, Andrea James, Raj Jayadev, Vida B. Johnson, Daniel Khalastchi, Chrisfino Kenyatta Leal, Galit Lipa, Rachel Marshall, Ann Mathews, Sarah Mayeux, Al Menaster, Jason Mendelson, Ann Miller, Amy Nelson, Sarah Obenauer, Mel Ochoa, Jimmy Parr, D. A. Powell, Mike Romano, Maybell Romero, Rebecca Rukeyser, Porsha-Shaf'on Venable, Alana Sivin, Larry South, Dyjuan Tatro, Stacey Walker, Carlie Ware, Frank Williams, Whitney Williams, and David Menschel, without whom this book may never have come to be.

There are also so many people without whom I might not have the combination of frustration, passion, grief, and indelible hope that made this writing possible: James Galvin, the late Richard Borgmann, Joanna Klink, Shirley Lily, Jane Miller, Brighde Mullins, Nola Naughton, Mary Szybist, and Peter Sacks.

There are also people without whom nothing I have helped to build would have been possible. Thanks, in particular, to my partner in transforming public defense, Rebecca Solow, whose genius is a joy to be near every day. Ten years ago, I got her really pissed off about the state of affairs in our criminal legal system, and she hasn't quit dismantling toxic systems and replacing them with powerful, more effective structures since.

Additional thanks to the national team at PFJ, who are a bunch of wild true believers, all of whom jumped on board with an insurgent start-up and agreed to tackle the staggeringly audacious goal of system-scale transformation. Thanks to each and every public defender who has agreed to take on collaborative defense as a core part of their practice, and to the defender leaders who leapt into the future with us. And thanks, of course, to every Client Advocate who has moved through the PFJ program, whose labor has utterly changed what we know is possible inside public defense.

Lifelong gratitude to my husband, Alvaro Almanza, whose brilliance and fearlessness as a lawyer spur me to constantly sharpen my skills, and who also spent a lot of time making avocado sandwiches and doing thousand-piece puzzles with our six-year-old so that her mother had time to write. And also to my daughter, for whom, I hope, this book is one day obsolete.

Finally, thanks to research goddess Liz Deichmann, whose tireless rigor profoundly strengthened these pages. To my wonderful agent, Ian Bonaparte, who saw value in this project when it was but a wee kernel and breathed life into it, and to my patient editor, Aubrey Martinson, who refined these pages and brought the idea to fruition.

And to my mother, Jorie Graham, who read every word and told me *exactly* what she thought. Thank you.

Notes

Chapter 1: Outsiders on the Inside

1. As of 2019, 45 percent of Americans have had a loved one locked up. Because 80 percent of accused people are represented by public defenders, 80 percent of that 45 percent, or 36 percent of all of us, have had a free lawyer assigned by the courts. The figure is calculated by multiplying the percentage of Americans with a loved one incarcerated by the percentage of people represented by public defenders. Susan Kelley, "Study: Nearly Half of Americans Have Had a Family Member Jailed, Imprisoned," *Cornell Chronicle,* March 4, 2019, news.cornell .edu/stories/2019/03/study-nearly-half-americans-have-had-family-member -jailed-imprisoned; Caroline Wolf Harlow, "Defense Counsel in Criminal Cases," U.S. Department of Justice, Office of Justice Programs, Bureau of Justice Statistics, Nov. 2000, bjs.ojp.gov/content/pub/pdf/dccc.pdf.
2. "You Have the Right to a Lawyer," Sixth Amendment Center, n.d., 6ac.org/.
3. Harlow, "Defense Counsel in Criminal Cases," notes that "over 80% of felony defendants charged with a violent crime in the country's largest counties" are assigned counsel, and it remains one of the better estimates available (in a system with a notorious lack-of-data problem) of overall proportion of cases assigned to free lawyers.
4. *Gideon v. Wainwright,* 372 U.S. 335 (1963).
5. Mortimer D. Schwartz, Susan L. Brandt, and Patience Milrod, "Clara Shortridge Foltz: Pioneer in the Law," *Hastings Law Journal* 27 (1976): 545–64;

Barbara Babcock, *Woman Lawyer: The Trials of Clara Foltz* (Stanford University Press, 2011).

6. Babcock, *Woman Lawyer*.

7. Schwartz, Brandt, and Milrod, "Clara Shortridge Foltz"; Beth Mora, "The First Female Lawyer in California: Clara S. Foltz," Contra Costa County Bar Association, Nov. 2016, www.cccba.org/article/the-first-female-lawyer-in -california-clara-s-foltz/.

8. Schwartz, Brandt, and Milrod, "Clara Shortridge Foltz."

9. Mora, "First Female Lawyer in California"; Schwartz, Brandt, and Milrod, "Clara Shortridge Foltz."

10. Sara Mayeux, *Free Justice: A History of the Public Defender in Twentieth-Century America* (University of North Carolina Press, 2020).

11. Clara Shortridge Foltz, "Public Defender: Rights of Persons Accused of Crime," World's Columbian Exposition, Chicago, Aug. 8, 1893, speakingwhilefemale .co/law-foltz/.

12. Mayeux, *Free Justice*.

13. Barbara Babcock, *Fish Raincoats: A Woman Lawyer's Life* (Quid Pro Books, 2016).

14. "Time-in-Cell 2019: A Snapshot of Restrictive Housing," Correctional Leaders Association and the Arthur Liman Center for Public Interest Law at Yale Law School, Sept. 2020, law.yale.edu/sites/default/files/area/center/liman/document/ time-in-cell_2019.pdf.

15. Saul M. Kassin, "False Confessions: Causes, Consequences, and Implications for Reform," *Current Directions in Psychological Science* 17, no. 1 (2008): 249–53.

16. Miriam Aroni Krinsky and Norman L. Reimer, "Children Deserve Protections That Too Many Aren't Getting in the US Justice System," *USA Today*, March 8, 2022; "Age and Mental Status of Exonerated Defendants Who Confessed," National Registry of Exonerations, accessed Nov. 4, 2024, https:// disabilityandguardianship.org/age-and-mental-status.pdf.

17. "Confined and Costly," Council of State Governments, June 2019, csgjusticecenter.org/wp-content/uploads/2020/01/confined-and-costly.pdf.

18. "ACLU of Pennsylvania Sues the Commonwealth over Inadequate Public Defense System," ACLU Pennsylvania, June 13, 2024, www.aclupa.org/en/ press-releases/aclu-pennsylvania-sues-commonwealth-over-inadequate-public -defense-system; Debra Cassens Weiss, "Prosecutors and Public Defenders Strike for Higher Pay in This California County," *ABA Journal*, Aug. 27, 2024, www .abajournal.com/news/article/prosecutors-and-public-defenders-strike-for -higher-pay-in-this-california-county; Jonah E. Bromwich, "Hundreds Have Left N.Y. Public Defender Offices over Low Pay," *New York Times*, June 9, 2022; Nicholas M. Pace, Malia N. Brink, and Stephen F. Hanlon, "National Public Defense Workload Study," RAND Corporation, July 27, 2023, www.rand.org/ pubs/research_reports/RRA2559-1.html; Richard A. Oppel Jr. and Jugal K.

Patel, "One Lawyer, 194 Felony Cases, and No Time," *New York Times,* Jan. 31, 2019.

19. Andrea Miller, Briana Paige, and Allison Trochesset, "Collateral Consequences of Criminal Records," *Caseload Highlights: Special Issue,* Court Statistics Project, Nov. 12, 2021, https://nationalcenterforstatecourts.box.com/shared/static/qtvqmprvjy3lhel7ev6o02lci9uxc1k9.docx.

20. Where it has been necessary to mention a prior experience to explain a point or perspective, but I have been unable to reach the person whose case gave rise to that experience, any anecdote has been fully anonymized.

Chapter 2: All Rise

1. "Testimonials from Inmates Incarcerated at Orleans Parish Prison During Hurricane Katrina," ACLU of Louisiana, Jan. 11, 2006, assets.aclu.org/live/uploads/document/asset_upload_file182_23418.pdf.

2. "Chief Justice Roberts Statement—Nomination Process," U.S. Courts, accessed May 16, 2024, www.uscourts.gov/educational-resources/educational-activities/chief-justice-roberts-statement-nomination-process.

3. "Prison Conditions," Equal Justice Initiative, accessed Nov. 5, 2024, eji.org/issues/prison-conditions/.

4. Ruth Delaney, Alison Shames, and Nicholas Turner, "Examining Prisons Today," Vera Institute of Justice, Sept. 2018, www.vera.org/reimagining-prison-web-report/examining-prisons-today; Mariel A. Marlow et al., "Foodborne Disease Outbreaks in Correctional Institutions—United States, 1998–2014," *American Journal of Public Health* 107, no. 7 (2017): 1150–56, doi.org/10.2105/AJPH.2017.303816.

5. Natalie Neysa Alund, " 'Eaten Alive by Insects': Atlanta Man Found Dead in Jail Cell Infested with Bed Bugs, Coroner Says," *USA Today,* April 13, 2023; Manny Ramos, "Cells at Illinois Prison Intake Facility in Joliet Infested with Vermin, Lawsuit Says," *Chicago Sun Times,* Feb. 18, 2022.

6. Lauren-Brooke Eisen, "The Violence Against People Behind Bars That We Don't See," *Time,* Sept. 1, 2020; Carrie Johnson, "Senate Probe Found Some Federal Prison Staff Abused Female Inmates Without Discipline," NPR, Dec. 14, 2022; Timothy Williams, "Mentally Ill Inmates Are Routinely Physically Abused, Study Says," *New York Times,* May 12, 2015.

7. Meghan A. Novisky and Robert L. Peralta, "Gladiator School: Returning Citizens' Experiences with Secondary Violence Exposure in Prison," *Victims & Offenders* 15, no. 5 (2020): 594–618, doi.org/10.1080/15564886.2020.1721387.

8. Peter Wagner and Wanda Bertram, "State of Phone Justice 2022: The Problem, the Progress, and What's Next," Prison Policy Initiative, Dec. 2022, www.prisonpolicy.org/phones/state_of_phone_justice_2022.html; "MFIA Wins

Access to Records Showing if Maine Jail Recorded Attorney-Client Calls," Yale
Law School, Sept. 25, 2023, law.yale.edu/yls-today/news/mfia-wins-access
-records-showing-if-maine-jail-recorded-attorney-client-calls; Chelsia Rose
Marcius, "Over 1,500 Private Phone Calls Between NYC Jail Inmates and Legal
Advisers Wrongly Recorded, Audits Show," *Daily News,* March 21, 2021, www
.nydailynews.com/2021/03/20/over-1500-private-phone-calls-between-nyc-jail
-inmates-and-legal-advisers-wrongly-recorded-audits-show/.

9. Juliana Kim, "Heart Transplant Recipient Dies After Being Denied Meds in Jail;
ACLU Wants an Inquiry," NPR, June 3, 2023.

10. Jill Curran et al., "Estimated Use of Prescription Medications Among
Individuals Incarcerated in Jails and State Prisons in the US," *JAMA Health
Forum* 4, no. 4 (2023): e230482, doi.org/10.1001/jamahealthforum.2023.0482.

11. Julie Wertheimer and Tracy Velázquez, "Jail Admissions Have Fallen, but Average
Length of Stay Is Up, Study Shows," Pew Charitable Trusts, Jan. 12, 2022, www
.pewtrusts.org/en/research-and-analysis/articles/2022/01/12/jail-admissions
-have-fallen-but-average-length-of-stay-is-up-study-shows.

12. "The State of New York City Jails: One Year of Measuring Jail Operations
and Management on the Comptroller's DOC Dashboard," Office of the New
York City Comptroller, Aug. 2023, comptroller.nyc.gov/wp-content/uploads/
documents/The-State-of-New-York-City-Jails.pdf.

13. Erik Ortiz, "New Report Reveals over 122K Are Held in Solitary Confinement
in U.S. Prisons and Jails," NBC News, May 23, 2023.

14. Chase Montagnet, Jennifer Peirce, and David Pitts, "Mapping U.S. Jails' Use
of Restrictive Housing," Vera Institute of Justice, Sept. 2021, www.vera.org/
downloads/publications/mapping-us-jails-use-of-restrictive-housing.pdf.

15. Jennifer Gonnerman, "Kalief Browder, 1993–2015," *New York Times,* June 7,
2015.

16. Kayla James and Elena Vanko, "The Impacts of Solitary Confinement," Vera
Institute of Justice, April 2021, www.vera.org/downloads/publications/the
-impacts-of-solitary-confinement.pdf.

17. Leah Wang, "Rise in Jail Deaths Is Especially Troubling as Jail Populations
Become More Rural and More Female," Prison Policy Initiative, June 23, 2021,
www.prisonpolicy.org/blog/2021/06/23/jail_mortality/.

18. Carissa Byrne Hessick, *Punishment Without Trial: Why Plea Bargaining Is a Bad
Deal* (Harry N. Abrams, 2021).

19. Nick Petersen, "Do Detainees Plead Guilty Faster? A Survival Analysis of
Pretrial Detention and the Timing of Guilty Pleas," *Criminal Justice Policy
Review* 31, no. 7 (2020): 1015–35, doi.org/10.1177/0887403419838020.

20. Paul Heaton, Sandra G. Mayson, and Megan Stevenson, "The Downstream
Consequences of Misdemeanor Pretrial Detention," *Stanford Law Review* 69,
no. 3 (2017): 711–94, www.stanfordlawreview.org/print/article/the-downstream
-consequences-of-misdemeanor-pretrial-detention/.

21. Will Dobbie, Jacob Goldin, and Crystal S. Yang, "The Effects of Pretrial Detention on Conviction, Future Crime, and Employment: Evidence from Randomly Assigned Judges," *American Economic Review* 108, no. 2 (2018): 201–40, doi.org/10.1257/aer.20161503.

22. Pamela R. Metzger et al., "Ending Injustice: Solving the Initial Appearance Crisis," Deason Criminal Justice Reform Center, Sept. 2021, www.smu.edu/-/media/site/law/deason-center/publications/public-defense/initial-appearance-campaign/ending-injustice-solving-the-initial-appearance-crisis-final.pdf.

23. *13th* (Netflix, 2016), www.youtube.com/watch?v=krfcq5pF8u8; Michelle Alexander, *The New Jim Crow: Mass Incarceration in the Age of Colorblindness* (New Press, 2012).

24. U.S. Constitution, amend. XIII, § 1.

25. A. E. Raza, "Legacies of the Racialization of Incarceration: From Convict-Lease to the Prison Industrial Complex," *Journal of the Institute of Justice and International Studies* 11 (2011): 159–70; Elizabeth Hinton, LeShae Henderson, and Cindy Reed, "An Unjust Burden: The Disparate Treatment of Black Americans in the Criminal Justice System," Vera Institute of Justice, May 2018, www.vera.org/downloads/publications/for-the-record-unjust-burden-racial-disparities.pdf.

26. Christopher Muller and Alexander F. Roehrkasse, "Falling Racial Inequality and Rising Educational Inequality in US Prison Admissions for Drug, Violent, and Property Crimes," ed. Paul DiMaggio, *PNAS* 122, no. 4 (2025), doi.org/10.1073/pnas.2418077122.

27. Amanda Agan, Jennifer Doleac, and Anna Harvey, "Misdemeanor Prosecution," National Bureau of Economic Research, March 2021, doi.org/10.3386/w28600.

28. To calculate figure, remove occupations with missing data, sort occupations by white percentage of total employed, identify lawyers, and divide the number of occupations equal to or greater than white percentage of total employed for lawyer by total occupations. "Table 11: Employed Persons by Detailed Occupation, Sex, Race, and Hispanic or Latino Ethnicity," U.S. Bureau of Labor Statistics, Jan. 26, 2024, www.bls.gov/cps/cpsaat11.htm.

29. *Profile of the Legal Profession 2023* (American Bar Association, 2023), www.americanbar.org/content/dam/aba/administrative/news/2023/potlp-2023.pdf.

30. Reflective Democracy Campaign, "Tipping the Scales: Challengers Take On the Old Boys' Club of Elected Prosecutors," Women Donors Network, Oct. 2019, wholeads.us/wp-content/uploads/2019/10/Tipping-the-Scales-Prosecutor-Report-10-22.pdf.

31. "The Demographics of Jobs from 1991–2021," National Association for Law Placement, March 2023, www.nalp.org/0323research; Marisa Manzi and Nina Totenberg, "'Already Behind': Diversifying the Legal Profession Starts Before the LSAT," NPR, Dec. 22, 2020.

32. Jennifer Hunter, "Economic Justice, Judges, and the Law" (Alliance for Justice, 2022), afj.org/wp-content/uploads/2022/08/LaborJudgesReport_Final.pdf.

33. Harlow, "Defense Counsel in Criminal Cases"; "Indigent Defense," OJP Fact Sheet, Office of Justice Programs, Dec. 2011, www.ojp.gov/sites/g/files/xyckuh 241/files/archives/factsheets/ojpfs_indigentdefense.html.

34. Emily Ekins, "Policing in America: Understanding Public Attitudes Toward Police. Results from a National Survey," Cato Institute, Dec. 7, 2016, www.cato .org/survey-reports/policing-america-understanding-public-attitudes-toward -police-results-national; Kim Eckart, "How a Police Contact by Middle School Leads to Different Outcomes for Black, White Youth," *UW News,* Dec. 3, 2020, www.washington.edu/news/2020/12/03/how-a-police-contact-by-middle-school -leads-to-different-outcomes-for-black-white-youth/; "Report to the United Nations on Racial Disparities in the U.S. Criminal Justice System," American Civil Liberties Union and the Sentencing Project, July 14, 2022, www.sentencing project.org/app/uploads/2022/10/07-14-2022_CERD-Shadow-Report-Draft _with-endnotes.pdf.

35. Hinton, Henderson, and Reed, "Unjust Burden"; Eddie Kim, "The Case for Defunding Police Is in Our Affluent White Suburbs," *MEL,* 2020, melmagazine .com/en-us/story/the-case-for-defunding-police-is-in-our-white-affluent -suburbs.

36. Cydney Schleiden et al., "Racial Disparities in Arrests: A Race Specific Model Explaining Arrest Rates Across Black and White Young Adults," *Child and Adolescent Social Work Journal* 37, no. 1 (2020): 1–14, doi.org/10.1007/s10560 -019-00618-7.

37. Wendy Sawyer, "How Race Impacts Who Is Detained Pretrial," Prison Policy Initiative, Oct. 9, 2019, www.prisonpolicy.org/blog/2019/10/09/pretrial_race/.

38. "Homelessness and Racial Disparities," National Alliance to End Homelessness, Dec. 2023, source no longer available online.

39. "Labor Force Characteristics by Race and Ethnicity, 2022," U.S. Bureau of Labor Statistics, Nov. 2023, www.bls.gov/opub/reports/race-and-ethnicity/ 2022/home.htm; Kyle K. Moore, "State Unemployment by Race and Ethnicity," Economic Policy Institute, accessed Nov. 4, 2024, www.epi.org/indicators/state -unemployment-race-ethnicity/.

40. "Post 5: Racial Differences in Educational Experiences and Attainment," U.S. Department of the Treasury, June 9, 2023, home.treasury.gov/news/featured -stories/post-5-racial-differences-in-educational-experiences-and-attainment; Linda Darling-Hammond, "Unequal Opportunity: Race and Education," Brookings Institute, March 1, 1998, www.brookings.edu/articles/unequal -opportunity-race-and-education/.

41. Muller and Roehrkasse, "Falling Racial Inequality and Rising Educational Inequality in US Prison Admissions for Drug, Violent, and Property Crimes."

42. Attempts to replace human decision-making with supposedly neutral algorithms—to determine future dangerousness, for example—can create even more racially biased outcomes. Tom Simonite, "Algorithms Were Supposed to Fix the Bail System. They Haven't," *WIRED,* Feb. 19, 2020; Julia Dressel and Hany Farid, "The Accuracy, Fairness, and Limits of Predicting Recidivism," *Science Advances* 4, no. 1 (2018): eaao5580, doi.org/10.1126/sciadv.aao5580; Erin Collins, "Punishing Risk," *Georgetown Law Journal* 107 (2018): 57–108; Danielle Kehl, Priscilla Guo, and Samuel Kessler, "Algorithms in the Criminal Justice System: Assessing the Use of Risk Assessments in Sentencing," Berkman Klein Center for Internet & Society, Harvard Law School, July 2017, dash .harvard.edu/bitstream/handle/1/33746041/2017-07_responsivecommunities _2.pdf.

43. Pat K. Chew and Robert E. Kelley, "The Realism of Race in Judicial Decision Making: An Empirical Analysis of Plaintiffs' Race and Judges' Race," *Harvard Journal on Racial & Ethnic Justice* 28 (2012): 91–115, journals.law.harvard.edu/ wp-content/uploads/sites/92/2012/11/HBK1021.pdf; Raquel Muñiz, "A Theory of Racialized Judicial Decision-Making," *Michigan Journal of Race and Law* 28, no. 2 (2023): 345–415; Jason Silverstein, "I Don't Feel Your Pain," *Slate,* June 27, 2013, slate.com/technology/2013/06/racial-empathy-gap-people-dont -perceive-pain-in-other-races.html; Joan Y. Chiao and Vani A. Mathur, "Intergroup Empathy: How Does Race Affect Empathic Neural Responses?," *Current Biology* 20, no. 11 (2010): R478–80, doi.org/10.1016/j.cub.2010.04 .001; Julia Angwin et al., "Machine Bias: There's Software Used Across the Country to Predict Future Criminals. And It's Biased Against Blacks," ProPublica, May 23, 2016, www.propublica.org/article/machine-bias-risk -assessments-in-criminal-sentencing.

44. The passage relating to Ken Oliver comes from his court transcripts and his conversation with the author on August 9, 2023. Jenna Greene, "From Prisoner to Philanthropist, the Remarkable Journey of Ken Oliver," Reuters, Dec. 9, 2021.

45. John H. Wilson, *Hot House Flowers* (BookSurge, 2006).

46. Glenn R. Schmitt, Louis Reedt, and Kevin Blackwell, "Demographic Differences in Sentencing: An Update to the 2012 *Booker* Report," U.S. Sentencing Commission, Nov. 2017, www.ussc.gov/sites/default/files/pdf/research-and -publications/research-publications/2017/20171114_Demographics.pdf.

47. Alma Cohen and Crystal S. Yang, "Judicial Politics and Sentencing Decisions," *American Economic Journal: Economic Policy* 11, no. 1 (2019): 160–91, doi.org/ 10.1257/pol.20170329.

48. Justin D. Levinson, Mark W. Bennett, and Koichi Hioki, "Judging Implicit Bias: A National Empirical Study of Judicial Stereotypes," *Florida Law Review* 69 (2017): 63–113.

49. Colleen M. Berryessa, Itiel E. Dror, and Chief Justice Bridget McCormack,

"Prosecuting from the Bench? Examining Sources of Pro-Prosecution Bias in Judges," *Legal and Criminological Psychology* 28, no. 1 (2023): 1–14, doi.org/10.1111/lcrp.12226.

50. Clark Neily, "Are a Disproportionate Number of Federal Judges Former Government Advocates?," Cato Institute, May 27, 2021, www.cato.org/study/are-disproportionate-number-federal-judges-former-government-advocates.

51. "Behind the Bench: Professional Diversity & State Supreme Courts," State Law Research Initiative, May 2023, state-law-research.org/professional-diversity/; "Unprotected: Analyzing Judicial Protection of Constitutional Rights," Scrutinize, Sept. 2024, static1.squarespace.com/static/635986ea4e3869 168261490b/t/66e6cde13267a967de6969c3/1726402018002/unprotected -report.pdf.

52. Allison P. Harris and Maya Sen, "How Judges' Professional Experience Impacts Case Outcomes: An Examination of Public Defenders and Criminal Sentencing," Dec. 5, 2024, scholar.harvard.edu/sites/scholar.harvard.edu/files/harris-sen-public -defenders.pdf.

53. Oded Oren and Chad Topaz, Unpublished research report, Feb. 19, 2024. On file with author.

54. For more information on how police overtime payments are spurred by low-quality or baseless arrests, see this thread on X: twitter.com/GalvinAlmanza/status/1272254871664766976?s=20.

55. Harris and Sen, "How Judges' Professional Experience Impacts Case Outcomes."

56. David Roodman, "The Impacts of Incarceration on Crime," Open Philanthropy Project, Sept. 2017, www.openphilanthropy.org/files/Focus_Areas/Criminal _Justice_Reform/The_impacts_of_incarceration_on_crime_10.pdf.

57. Kate Berry, "How Judicial Elections Impact Criminal Cases," Brennan Center for Justice, Dec. 2, 2015, www.brennancenter.org/our-work/research-reports/how-judicial-elections-impact-criminal-cases.

58. Shai Danziger, Jonathan Levav, and Liora Avnaim-Pesso, "Extraneous Factors in Judicial Decisions," *Proceedings of the National Academy of Sciences* 108, no. 17 (2011): 6889–92, doi.org/10.1073/pnas.1018033108.

59. Barbara Benoliel, "Public Humiliation as a Mitigator in Criminal Sentencing" (PhD diss., Walden University, 2006), scholarworks.waldenu.edu/cgi/view content.cgi?article=1387&context=dissertations.

60. Ben Bryant, "Judges Are More Lenient After Taking a Break, Study Finds," *Guardian,* April 11, 2011.

61. Ozkan Eren and Naci Mocan, "Emotional Judges and Unlucky Juveniles," National Bureau of Economic Research, Sept. 2016, doi.org/10.3386/w22611.

62. Greene, "From Prisoner to Philanthropist, the Remarkable Journey of Ken Oliver."

Chapter 3: The Grind

1. Brian J. Ostrom et al., "Timely Justice in Criminal Cases: What the Data Tells Us," National Center for State Courts, 2020, https://www.researchgate.net/publication/344888868_Timely_Justice_in_Criminal_Cases_What_the_Data_Tells_Us.

2. *Allen v. City of Oakland*, 3:00-cv-04599 (N.D. Cal. Dec. 17, 2000); Christine Schiavo, "Finding 'Significant Cultural Problems' in Oakland Police Department, Federal Judge Tells Parties to Find Solution," Oakland North, Jan. 25, 2023, oaklandnorth.net/2023/01/25/oakland-police-misconduct-federal-judge-disappointed/.

3. Even when reports include more than a single sentence, police might have been encouraged (and sometimes explicitly told) to include misrepresentations and exaggerations to ensure that they were perceived as justified in their actions (or even as victims themselves). Haven Orecchio-Egresitz, "Police Officers Are Trained to Frame Their Police Reports to Deceive, Former Cop Turned Academic Says," *Business Insider*, June 22, 2021, www.insider.com/former-police-trained-cops-to-frame-reports-to-deceive-2021-6; Stanley Z. Fisher, "Just the Facts, Ma'am: Lying and the Omission of Exculpatory Evidence in Police Reports," *New England Law Review* 28 (1993): 1–62, scholarship.law.bu.edu/faculty_scholarship/906.

4. Huge thanks to Ken Klippenstein for aiding me in accessing the notorious Shake Shack police report.

5. Minyvonne Burke, "Shake Shack Manager Accused of Poisoning Shakes Sues NYPD Officers, Union for Defamation," NBC News, June 15, 2021.

6. Don Stemen, "The Prison Paradox: More Incarceration Will Not Make Us Safer," Vera Institute of Justice, 2017, www.vera.org/downloads/publications/for-the-record-prison-paradox_02.pdf.

7. Anonymous, conversation with the author, Nov. 29, 2023, and Feb. 22, 2024.

8. Beth Schwartzapfel, Abbie VanSickle, and Annaliese Griffin, "The Truth About Trials," Marshall Project, Nov. 4, 2020, www.themarshallproject.org/2020/11/04/the-truth-about-trials; *2018 Annual Report and Sourcebook of Federal Sentencing Statistics* (U.S. Sentencing Commission, 2018), www.ussc.gov/sites/default/files/pdf/research-and-publications/annual-reports-and-sourcebooks/2018/2018-Annual-Report-and-Sourcebook.pdf; John Gramlich, "Fewer Than 1% of Federal Criminal Defendants Were Acquitted in 2022," Pew Research Center, June 14, 2023, www.pewresearch.org/short-reads/2023/06/14/fewer-than-1-of-defendants-in-federal-criminal-cases-were-acquitted-in-2022/.

9. "Indeed, only 10 states uniformly provide counsel at the first bail and pretrial release judicial determination that typically is conducted within 24–48 hours of arrest. In contrast, 10 states continue to deny counsel at the initial bail hearing. The remaining 30 states decide representation at the pretrial release

hearing on a county-by-county basis." "Urging the Recognition of Right to Counsel at Initial Appearance," National Association of Criminal Defense Lawyers, Feb. 19, 2012, www.nacdl.org/Content/Urging-the-Recognition-of -Right-to-Counsel-at-Init.

10. Hessick, *Punishment Without Trial*.

11. Carissa Byrne Hessick, Ronald F. Wright, and Jessica Pishko, "The Prosecutor Lobby," *Washington and Lee Law Review* 80 (2023): 143–227, scholarlycommons.law.wlu.edu/wlulr/vol80/iss1/5.

12. *The Trial Penalty: The Sixth Amendment Right to Trial on the Verge of Extinction and How to Save It* (National Association of Criminal Defense Lawyers and Foundation for Criminal Justice, 2018), www.nacdl.org/getattachment/95b7 f0f5-90df-4f9f-9115-520b3f58036a/the-trial-penalty-the-sixth-amendment -right-to-trial-on-the-verge-of-extinction-and-how-to-save-it.pdf.

13. Allan Fong, "Interrogations and False Confessions: How the Innocent Are Made Guilty," *Southern California Review of Law and Social Justice* 30 (2020): 363–89, gould.usc.edu/students/journals/rlsj/issues/assets/docs/volume30/spring2021/ Fong.pdf.

14. Fong, "Interrogations and False Confessions"; Melissa B. Russano et al., "Investigating True and False Confessions Within a Novel Experimental Paradigm," *Psychological Science* 16, no. 6 (2005): 481–86, doi.org/10.1111/j .0956-7976.2005.01560.x; Mark Costanzo, Netta Shaked-Schroer, and Katherine Vinson, "Juror Beliefs About Police Interrogations, False Confessions, and Expert Testimony," *Journal of Empirical Legal Studies* 7, no. 2 (2010): 231–47, doi.org/10.1111/j.1740-1461.2010.01177.x.

15. The total number of exonerations in which false confessions were a contributing factor (452) was divided by the total number of exonerations from 1989 to 2024 (3,582). This is a point-in-time count that is subject to change as new exonerations are added to the registry. "Exonerations in the United States," National Registry of Exonerations, 2024, https://exonerationregistry.org/ exonerations-contributing-factor.

16. Megan Crane, Laura Nirider, and Steven A. Drizin, "The Truth About Juvenile False Confessions," *Insights on Law & Society* 16, no. 2 (2016): 10–15.

17. Krinsky and Reimer, "Children Deserve Protections That Too Many Aren't Getting in the US Justice System."

18. Kassin, "False Confessions."

19. Allison D. Redlich et al., "The Influence of Confessions on Guilty Pleas and Plea Discounts," *Psychology, Public Policy, and Law* 24, no. 2 (2018): 147–57, doi.org/10.1037/law0000144.

20. Madison G. Gallimore, "Jurors' Perceptions of False Confessions" (master's thesis, West Virginia University, 2021), doi.org/10.33915/etd.10200.

21. Metzger et al., "Ending Injustice"; Michael Mrozinski and Claire Buetow, "Access to Counsel at First Appearance: A Key Component of Pretrial Justice,"

National Legal Aid & Defender Association, Feb. 2020, www.nlada.org/sites/default/files/NLADA%20CAFA.pdf.

22. Jannell Spikes, conversation with the author, Dec. 22, 2023.

23. Margit Wiesner, Deborah M. Capaldi, and Hyoun K. Kim, "Arrests, Recent Life Circumstances, and Recurrent Job Loss for At-Risk Young Men: An Event-History Analysis," *Journal of Vocational Behavior* 76, no. 2 (2010): 344–54, doi.org/10.1016/j.jvb.2009.10.004.

24. Though the numbers of hearings, continuances, and other court events vary, a person might have to show up at court more than ten times before even being convicted of anything. Ostrom et al., "Timely Justice in Criminal Cases."

25. "Resources & Services: Orders of Protection," New York City Police Department, accessed Nov. 5, 2025, www.nyc.gov/site/nypd/services/victim-services/resources-services-orders-protection.page.

26. This is a common enough occurrence that New York has a specific hearing (called a Forman Hearing) to address housing and property loss resulting from a restraining order. *People v. Carrington,* 105 A.D.3d 970, 964 N.Y.S.2d 546, 2013 N.Y. Slip Op. 2587 (N.Y. App. Div. 2013).

27. Eli Hager and Anna Flagg, "How Incarcerated Parents Are Losing Their Children Forever," Marshall Project, Dec. 12, 2018, www.themarshallproject.org/2018/12/03/how-incarcerated-parents-are-losing-their-children-forever.

28. Spikes, conversation with the author, Dec. 22, 2023.

29. Alexandra Natapoff, *Punishment Without Crime: How Our Massive Misdemeanor System Traps the Innocent and Makes America More Unequal* (Basic Books, 2018).

30. Here, too, incentives matter. When police are rewarded for solving problems and engaging with the community they serve in a prosocial manner, crime goes down. Nadine M. Connell, Kristen Miggans, and Jean Marie McGloin, "Can a Community Policing Initiative Reduce Serious Crime? A Local Evaluation," *Police Quarterly* 11, no. 2 (2008): 127–50, doi.org/10.1177/1098611107306276.

31. Anonymous, conversation with the author, Nov. 29, 2023, and Feb. 22, 2024.

32. Hessick, *Punishment Without Trial;* Amy Bach, *Ordinary Injustice: How America Holds Court* (Picador, 2010).

33. Reuven Blau, "The City: Demand Grows to Make Rikers Island Death Reports Public," New York City Council, Aug. 28, 2023, council.nyc.gov/carlina-rivera/2023/09/06/the-city-demand-grows-to-make-rikers-island-death-reports-public/.

34. Miller, Paige, and Trochesset, "Collateral Consequences of Criminal Records."

35. In a world where about 96 percent of employers use background checks on job applicants, and as many as a third of those background checks may be incorrect or incomplete (based on case records that don't even have a listed disposition or outcome), tons of American employers are judging candidates based on incomplete information, or even arrest records alone. It's also notable that although much research has been done on the impact of a criminal record on job prospects, not nearly enough has been done on the impact an open—and

long-pending—case can have on employability. Becki R. Goggins and Dennis A. DeBacco, "Survey of State Criminal History Information Systems, 2016: A Criminal Justice Information Policy Report," Office of Justice Programs, Feb. 2018, www.ojp.gov/pdffiles1/bjs/grants/251516.pdf.

36. Mitali Nagrecha et al., "Fees, Fines, and the Funding of Public Services: A Curriculum for Reform," Yale Law School Arthur Liman Center for Public Interest Law; Harvard Law School Criminal Justice Policy Program; UC Berkeley School of Law Fines & Fees Justice Center, Aug. 2020, law.yale.edu/sites/default/files/area/center/liman/document/fees_fines_and_the_funding_of_public_services.pdf.
37. Beatrix Lockwood and Annaliese Griffin, "The Ins and Outs of Bail," Marshall Project, Oct. 28, 2020, www.themarshallproject.org/2020/10/28/the-ins-and-outs-of-bail.
38. Kate Weisburd, "Electronic Prisons: The Operation of Ankle Monitoring in the Criminal Legal System," George Washington University Law School, 2021, issuu.com/gwlawpubs/docs/electronic-prisons-report?fr=sOGI5NDcxODg3.
39. "Public Benefits Access and the Criminal System," Partners for Justice, March 2023, www.partnersforjustice.org/evidence/public-benefits-access-and-the-criminal-system.
40. "Under Pressure: How Fines and Fees Hurt People, Undermine Public Safety, and Drive Alabama's Racial Wealth Divide," Alabama Appleseed Center for Law and Justice, University of Alabama at Birmingham Treatment Alternatives for Safer Communities, Greater Birmingham Ministries, Legal Services Alabama, 2018, www.alabamaappleseed.org/wp-content/uploads/2018/10/AA1240-FinesandFees-10-10-FINAL.pdf.
41. Karin D. Martin et al., "Monetary Sanctions: Legal Financial Obligations in US Systems of Justice," *Annual Review of Criminology* 1, no. 1 (2018): 471–95, doi.org/10.1146/annurev-criminol-032317-091915.
42. Kylie McGivern, "Pay to Stay: Florida Inmates Charged for Prison Cells Long After Incarceration," WFTS ABC News, April 3, 2024, www.abcactionnews.com/news/local-news/i-team-investigates/pay-to-stay-florida-inmates-charged-for-prison-cells-long-after-incarceration.
43. "Under Pressure."
44. "Across the nation, children and teens who commit crimes are routinely ordered to pay their victims restitution for damaged property, lost wages and medical bills, leaving many saddled with a financial burden that can follow them long into adulthood. Just a half-dozen states cap these payments, which often reach into the tens of thousands of dollars, according to a Marshall Project review of five years of cases in 10 states that collect data on juvenile restitution. As a result, young people like McMullan can find themselves homeless and in debt, paying off victims many years after they've served their sentences." Eli Hager, "Punishing

Kids with Years of Debt," Marshall Project, June 11, 2019, www.themarshall
project.org/2019/06/11/punishing-kids-with-years-of-debt.

45. Jodi S. Cohen and Jennifer Smith Richards, "The Price Kids Pay: Schools
and Police Punish Students with Costly Tickets for Minor Misbehavior,"
ProPublica, April 28, 2022, www.propublica.org/article/illinois-school-police
-tickets-fines.

46. "Under Pressure."

47. Stemen, "Prison Paradox"; Heaton, Mayson, and Stevenson, "Downstream
Consequences of Misdemeanor Pretrial Detention."

48. Matthew DeMichele, Ian Silver, and Ryan Labrecque, "Locked Up and Awaiting
Trial: A Natural Experiment Testing the Criminogenic and Punitive Effects of
Spending a Week or More in Pretrial Detention," SSRN, June 2, 2023, doi.org/
10.2139/ssrn.4467619.

49. "Pretrial Criminal Justice Research," Laura and John Arnold Foundation, Nov.
2013, https://cjcc.doj.wi.gov/sites/default/files/subcommittee/LJAF-Pretrial-CJ
-Research-brief_FNL.pdf.

50. Matthew DeMichele et al., "The Benefits of Early Release from Pretrial
Detention," Advancing Pretrial Policy and Research and RTI International,
June 2023, advancingpretrial.org/story/the-benefits-of-early-release-from-pretrial
-detention/.

51. "Know Your Rights: Housing and Arrests or Criminal Convictions," Bronx
Defenders, Oct. 2, 2010, www.bronxdefenders.org/housing-and-arrests-or
-criminal-convictions/.

52. "Collateral Consequences of Criminal Convictions: Judicial Bench Book,"
American Bar Association, March 2018, www.ojp.gov/pdffiles1/nij/grants/
251583.pdf.

53. "FAQs: Excluding the Use of Arrest Records in Housing Decisions," Office of
Public and Indian Housing, 2015, web.archive.org/web/20240224202136/
https://www.hud.gov/sites/documents/FAQ_EXCLUDE_ARREST_RECORDS
.PDF.

54. "Know Your Rights: Housing and Arrests or Criminal Convictions"; *Statement
of Policies 2016/2017* (Minneapolis Public Housing Authority, 2017), www
.mphaonline.org/wp-content/uploads/2016/10/FY2017-Low-Income-Statement
-of-Policies-ACOP.pdf.

55. Maia M. Cole, "Permanently Excluded," *New York University Law Review* 95,
no. 4 (2020): 1062–104.

56. Batya Ungar-Sargon, "NYCHA Questioned on Policy of Banning Arrested
Residents," *City Limits,* June 2, 2015, citylimits.org/2015/06/02/nycha
-questioned-on-policy-of-banning-arrested-residents/.

57. Manny Fernandez, "Barred from Public Housing, Even to See Family," *New York
Times,* Oct. 1, 2007.

58. *People v. Carrington,* 105 A.D.3d 970, 964 N.Y.S.2d 546, 2013 N.Y. Slip Op. 2587 (N.Y. App. Div. 2013).

59. Linda Morris and Sandra Park, "A Disturbing Number of Missouri Towns Evict Residents for Calling the Police," American Civil Liberties Union, Jan. 24, 2019, www.aclu.org/news/womens-rights/disturbing-number-missouri-towns -evict-residents-calling.

60. Christopher O'Donnell, Ian Hodgson, and Nathaniel Lash, "Tampa Police Called for Hundreds to Be Evicted. Entire Families Lost Their Homes," *Tampa Bay Times,* Sept. 17, 2021, www.tampabay.com/investigations/2021/09/15/ tampa-police-called-for-hundreds-to-be-evicted-entire-families-lost-their -homes/.

61. Mary Hansen, "With Crime-Free Rules, Tenants Evicted After Overdose Calls," St. Louis Public Radio, May 9, 2019, news.stlpublicradio.org/2019-05-09/with -crime-free-rules-tenants-evicted-after-overdose-calls#stream/0.

62. Jeremy Kohler, "St. Louis Can Banish People from Entire Neighborhoods. Police Can Arrest Them If They Come Back," ProPublica, Dec. 1, 2022, www .propublica.org/article/st-louis-can-banish-people-from-entire-neighborhoods.

63. "Low Turnover and Higher Rental Prices in 2017 Driving Profitable and Attractive Market for Landlords," TransUnion, April 19, 2017, newsroom.trans union.com/low-turnover-and-higher-rental-prices-in-2017--driving-profitable -and-attractive-market-for-landlords/; Demetria L. McCain, "Implementation of the Office of General Counsel's Guidance on Application of Fair Housing Act Standards to the Use of Criminal Records by Providers of Housing and Real Estate–Related Transactions," Office of Fair Housing and Equal Opportunity, June 10, 2022, www.hud.gov/sites/dfiles/FHEO/documents/Implementation %20of%20OGC%20Guidance%20on%20Application%20of%20FHA %20Standards%20to%20the%20Use%20of%20Criminal%20Records%20 -%20June%2010%202022.pdf.

64. Anonymous, conversation with the author, Nov. 29, 2023, and Feb. 22, 2024.

65. Spikes, conversation with the author, Dec. 22, 2023.

Chapter 4: Bad Incentives in a Bad System

1. Frank Edwards, Hedwig Lee, and Michael Esposito, "Risk of Being Killed by Police Use of Force in the United States by Age, Race–Ethnicity, and Sex," *Proceedings of the National Academy of Sciences* 116, no. 34 (2019): 16793–98, doi.org/10.1073/pnas.1821204116.

2. Black people are more than three times as likely to die at the hands of police as white people. Gabriel L. Schwartz and Jaquelyn L. Jahn, "Mapping Fatal Police Violence Across U.S. Metropolitan Areas: Overall Rates and Racial/Ethnic Inequities, 2013–2017," ed. Jonathan Jackson, *PLOS ONE* 15, no. 6 (2020):

e0229686, doi.org/10.1371/journal.pone.0229686; "Fatal Police Violence by Race and State in the USA, 1980–2019: A Network Meta-Regression," *Lancet* 398, no. 10307 (2021): 1239–55, doi.org/10.1016/S0140-6736(21)01609-3.

3. Keith L. Alexander, Steven Rich, and Hannah Thacker, "The Hidden Billion-Dollar Cost of Repeated Police Misconduct," *Washington Post,* March 9, 2022; Vida B. Johnson, "Whom Do Prosecutors Protect?," *Boston University Law Review* 104, no. 2 (2024): 289–344.

4. Johnson, "Whom Do Prosecutors Protect?"; Jennifer Jenkins et al., "Fatal Force," *Washington Post,* April 4, 2024.

5. Johnson, "Whom Do Prosecutors Protect?"; German Lopez, "Police Officers Are Prosecuted for Murder in Less Than 2 Percent of Fatal Shootings," *Vox,* April 2, 2021, www.vox.com/21497089/derek-chauvin-george-floyd-trial-police-prosecutions-black-lives-matter.

6. Alex S. Vitale, conversation with the author, May 8, 2024.

7. Jeff Asher and Ben Horwitz, "How Do the Police Actually Spend Their Time?," *New York Times,* June 9, 2020.

8. Vitale, conversation with the author, May 8, 2024.

9. The majority of the 1.1 million arrests for drug/narcotic offenses in 2020 were for "drug possession or use rather than for sale or manufacturing. Drug arrests continue to give residents of over-policed communities criminal records . . . [and are] a defining feature of the federal prison system." Wendy Sawyer and Peter Wagner, "Mass Incarceration: The Whole Pie 2024," Prison Policy Initiative, March 14, 2024, www.prisonpolicy.org/reports/pie2024.html#datasection; Jan Hoffman, "Harsh New Fentanyl Laws Ignite Debate over How to Combat Overdose Crisis," *New York Times,* June 21, 2023; Ryan S. King and Marc Mauer, "Distorted Priorities: Drug Offenders in State Prisons," Sentencing Project, Sept. 2002, www.prisonpolicy.org/scans/sp/distorted_priorities.pdf.

10. George Hunter, "Detroit Police Overtime Up 136% over 5 Years," *Detroit News,* March 21, 2018, www.detroitnews.com/story/news/local/detroit-city/2018/03/21/detroit-police-overtime-costs/33132469/; Vitale, conversation with the author, May 8, 2024.

11. Kavahn Mansouri, "Independence Had No Limits on Overtime and One Police Officer Got Paid for 2,800 Hours," KCUR, Feb. 9, 2022, www.kcur.org/2022-02-09/independence-had-no-limits-on-overtime-and-one-police-officer-got-paid-for-2-800-hours.

12. Sean Philip Cotter, "Boston Police Overtime Spending Bounced Back Up to Record High in 2022," *Boston Herald,* March 3, 2023, www.bostonherald.com/2023/03/03/boston-police-overtime-spending-shot-back-up-in-2022/; Nami Sumida, "S.F.'s Top-Paid Employee Makes $640K. Here's What Every City Worker Gets Paid," *San Francisco Chronicle,* Aug. 14, 2023; Jenny Gathright and Aarushi Sahejpal, "These D.C. Police Officers Work So Much Overtime They Out-Earn the Mayor," DCist, Oct. 25, 2023, dcist.com/story/23/10/25/dc

-police-top-overtime-earners/; Mike McPhate, "California Today: Hefty Paychecks for Police Officers and Firefighters," *New York Times,* March 2, 2017.

13. "Port Authority Unloads Big Overtime for Cops," Empire Center, Nov. 21, 2023, www.empirecenter.org/publications/port-authority-unloads-big-overtime -for-cops/; "2022 Payroll Information," Port Authority NY NJ, accessed Nov. 5, 2024, www.panynj.gov/corporate/en/transparency/payroll.html.

14. Melissa Klein, "This Port Authority Cop Makes More Than the President," *New York Post,* May 30, 2020, nypost.com/2020/05/30/this-port-authority-cop-makes -more-than-the-president/.

15. Heather Cherone and Jared Rutecki, "Chicago Spent $524M on Overtime in 2023, Including $293M for Police, Setting New Records," WTTW, March 12, 2024, news.wttw.com/2024/03/12/chicago-spent-524m-overtime-2023-including -293m-police-setting-new-records.

16. "Police Overtime: A Curated Collection of Links," Marshall Project, Oct. 3, 2024, www.themarshallproject.org/records/4241-police-overtime.

17. Roger Pryzbylski et al., "The Impact of Long Sentences on Public Safety: A Complex Relationship," *Federal Sentencing Reporter* 36, no. 1–2 (2023): 81–87, doi.org/10.1525/fsr.2023.36.1-2.81; *The Growth of Incarceration in the United States: Exploring Causes and Consequences* (National Academies Press, 2014), doi .org/10.17226/18613; Oliver Roeder, Lauren-Brooke Eisen, and Julia Bowling, "What Caused the Crime Decline?," Brennan Center for Justice, Feb. 12, 2015, www.brennancenter.org/our-work/research-reports/what-caused-crime -decline.

18. *Harlow v. Fitzgerald,* 457 U.S. 800, 818 (1982).

19. Kathryn McKelvey et al., "Exploratory Analysis of Nix the 6 Law Enforcement Collective Bargaining Agreements (CBAs)," Campaign Zero, Oct. 2022, campaignzero.org/wp-content/uploads/2024/04/NT6CBAs_043024.pdf.

20. Aaron L. Nielson and Christopher J. Walker, "A Qualified Defense of Qualified Immunity," *Notre Dame Law Review* 93, no. 5 (2018): 1853–85.

21. Laurie Udesky, "New Book Explores How Qualified Immunity Protects Police in Brutality and Wrongful Death Cases," *ABA Journal,* Oct. 1, 2023.

22. Joanna C. Schwartz, "How Governments Pay: Lawsuits, Budgets, and Police Reform," *UCLA Law Review* 63 (2016): 1144–269; Marc L. Miller and Ronald F. Wright, "Secret Police and the Mysterious Case of the Missing Tort Claims," *Buffalo Law Review* 52, no. 3 (2004): 757–91.

23. Kallie Cox and William Freivogel, "Police Misconduct Records Secret, Difficult to Access," Pulitzer Center, Jan. 24, 2022, pulitzercenter.org/stories/police -misconduct-records-secret-difficult-access.

24. Johnson, "Whom Do Prosecutors Protect?"; Katey Rusch and Casey Smith, "This Is the Secret System That Covers Up Police Misconduct—and Ensures

Problem Officers Can Get Hired Again," *San Francisco Chronicle,* Sept. 18, 2024; Ben Grunwald and John Rappaport, "The Wandering Officer," *Yale Law Journal* 129, no. 6 (2020): 1676–782.

25. Johnson, "Whom Do Prosecutors Protect?"

26. Johnson, "Whom Do Prosecutors Protect?"

27. Keith, Rich, and Thacker, "Hidden Billion-Dollar Cost of Repeated Police Misconduct"; Amelia Thomson-DeVeaux, Laura Bronner, and Damini Sharma, "Cities Spend Millions on Police Misconduct Every Year. Here's Why It's So Difficult to Hold Departments Accountable," Fivethirtyeight and Marshall Project, Feb. 22, 2021, fivethirtyeight.com/features/police-misconduct-costs -cities-millions-every-year-but-thats-where-the-accountability-ends/?itid=lk _inline_enhanced-template.

28. Johnson, "Whom Do Prosecutors Protect?"; Philip Matthew Stinson Sr. et al., "Police Integrity Lost: A Study of Law Enforcement Officers Arrested," Bowling Green State University, Jan. 2016, www.ojp.gov/pdffiles1/nij/grants/249850 .pdf.

29. Kimberly A. French and Keaton A. Fletcher, "Officer-Involved Domestic Violence: A Call for Action Among I-O Psychologists," *Industrial and Organizational Psychology* 15, no. 4 (2022): 604–8, doi.org/10.1017/iop .2022.74.

30. Vitale, conversation with the author, May 8, 2024.

31. Cassie Miller, "Civil Asset Forfeiture: Unfair, Undemocratic, and Un-American," Southern Poverty Law Center, Oct. 2017, www.splcenter.org/sites/default/files/ com_policybrief_civil_asset_forfeiture_web.pdf; Wex Definitions Project, "Civil Forfeiture," Legal Information Institute, Cornell Law School, Aug. 2022, www .law.cornell.edu/wex/civil_forfeiture.

32. Vitale, conversation with the author, May 8, 2024.

33. Mike Baker and Nicholas Bogel-Burroughs, "How a Common Air Freshener Can Result in a High-Stakes Traffic Stop," *New York Times,* April 17, 2021.

34. Lisa Knepper et al., "Policing for Profit: The Abuse of Civil Asset Forfeiture," Institute for Justice, Dec. 2020, ij.org/wp-content/uploads/2020/12/policing -for-profit-3-web.pdf; Dick M. Carpenter II, "Generating Revenue Through Civil Forfeiture," *New York University Law Review* 98 (2023): 205–24.

35. Jefferson E. Holcomb, Tomislav V. Kovandzic, and Marian R. Williams, "Civil Asset Forfeiture, Equitable Sharing, and Policing for Profit in the United States," *Journal of Criminal Justice* 39, no. 3 (2011): 273–85, doi.org/10.1016/j.jcrimjus .2011.02.010; Marian R. Williams, "Civil Asset Forfeiture: Where Does the Money Go?," *Criminal Justice Review* 27, no. 2 (2002): 321–29, doi.org/10 .1177/073401680202700207; Nagrecha et al., "Fees, Fines, and the Funding of Public Services."

36. This figure includes criminal forfeiture as well as noncriminal seizures. Knepper

et al., "Policing for Profit"; Ian MacDougall, "Police Say Seizing Property Without Trial Helps Keep Crime Down. A New Study Shows They're Wrong," ProPublica, Dec. 14, 2020, www.propublica.org/article/police-say-seizing -property-without-trial-helps-keep-crime-down-a-new-study-shows-theyre -wrong.

37. Like many areas in the law, there is a dearth of data on civil asset forfeitures including convictions, but existing data suggests that forfeiture without conviction is a regular occurrence. For example, convictions accompanied approximately 70 percent of forfeitures in Pennsylvania in 2018. Knepper et al., "Policing for Profit."

38. Johnson, "Whom Do Prosecutors Protect?"

39. Stephanos Bibas, "Plea Bargaining Outside the Shadow of Trial," *Harvard Law Review* 117, no. 8 (2004): 2463–547.

40. Johnson, "Whom Do Prosecutors Protect?"

41. Johnson, "Whom Do Prosecutors Protect?"; Erwin Chemerinsky, "The Role of Prosecutors in Dealing with Police Abuse: The Lessons of Los Angeles," *Virginia Journal of Social Policy & the Law* 8 (2001): 305–21.

42. Johnson, "Whom Do Prosecutors Protect?"; Paul Butler, "How Can You Prosecute Those People?," in *How Can You Represent Those People?*, ed. Abbe Smith and Monroe H. Freedman (Palgrave Macmillan, 2013), 15–27, doi.org/ 10.1057/9781137311955_2.

43. Johnson, "Whom Do Prosecutors Protect?"; Stinson Sr. et al., "Police Integrity Lost."

44. Johnson, "Whom Do Prosecutors Protect?"; Justin Jouvenal and Rachel Weiner, "Prosecutors Won't Pursue Marijuana Possession Charges in 2 Northern Va. Counties," *Washington Post,* Jan. 2, 2020.

45. Johnson, "Whom Do Prosecutors Protect?"; Jouvenal and Weiner, "Prosecutors Won't Pursue Marijuana Possession Charges in 2 Northern Va. Counties."

46. Kate Levine, "Who Shouldn't Prosecute the Police," *Iowa Law Review* 101 (2016): 1447–96.

47. Levine, "Who Shouldn't Prosecute the Police"; Emma Tucker, Mark Morales, and Priya Krishnakumar, "Why It's Rare for Police Officers to Be Convicted of Murder," CNN, April 21, 2021.

48. Johnson, "Whom Do Prosecutors Protect?"; Jasmine B. Gonzales Rose, "Racial Character Evidence in Police Killing Cases," *Wisconsin Law Review* 3 (2018): 369–439.

49. In 2022, Colorado became the only state to legislatively mandate "peace officer credibility disclosures." "Policies for Peace Officer Credibility Disclosures," S.21-174, 2021 Cong. (2022), leg.colorado.gov/bills/sb21-174; Rachel Moran, "Brady Lists," *Minnesota Law Review* 107 (2022): 657–733; Steve Reilly and Mark Nichols, "Hundreds of Police Officers Have Been Labeled Liars. Some Still Help Send People to Prison," *USA Today,* Dec. 16, 2019.

50. *Berghuis v. Thompkins,* 560 U.S. 370 (2010).
51. *State v. Demesme,* 228 So. 3d 1206 (La. 2017).
52. Johnson, "Whom Do Prosecutors Protect?"; Alexander, *New Jim Crow;* Rachel E. Barkow, "Institutional Design and the Policing of Prosecutors: Lessons from Administrative Law," *Stanford Law Review* 61, no. 4 (2009): 869–921; John Pfaff, *Locked In: The True Causes of Mass Incarceration—and How to Achieve Real Reform* (Basic Books, 2017); Renee McDonald Hutchins, "Policing the Prosecutor: Race, the Fourth Amendment, and the Prosecution of Criminal Cases," *Criminal Justice Review* 14 (Fall 2018), digitalcommons.law.udc.edu/fac _journal_articles/61/.
53. *Terry v. Ohio,* 392 U.S. 1 (1968).
54. Johnson, "Whom Do Prosecutors Protect?"
55. *Berghuis v. Thompkins,* 563 U.S. 452 (2011).
56. Johnson, "Whom Do Prosecutors Protect?"; *Kentucky v. King,* 563 U.S. 452 (2011).
57. *Town of Newton v. Rumery,* 480 U.S. 386 (1987).
58. Johnson, "Whom Do Prosecutors Protect?"
59. Grunwald and Rappaport, "Wandering Officer"; Amir Vera, "There's a Database Whose Mission Is to Stop Problematic Police Officers from Hopping Between Departments. But Many Agencies Don't Know It Exists," CNN, May 16, 2021; Kerry Breen, "Settlements for Police Misconduct Lawsuits Cost Taxpayers from Coast to Coast," CBS News, Sept. 27, 2023.
60. Joseph Goldstein, "Promotions, Not Punishments, for Officers Accused of Lying," *New York Times,* March 19, 2018; Christopher Slobogin, "Testilying: Police Perjury and What to Do About It," *University of Colorado Law Review* 67, no. 4 (1996): 1037–60; "Fear and Silence: How Culture, Policy, and the 'Win at All Costs' Mentality Allows Police Testifying to Thrive," Chicago Appleseed Center for Fair Courts & Chicago Council of Lawyers, Jan. 2023, www .chicagoappleseed.org/wp-content/uploads/2023/01/2023_01_10_Police-Perjury -Report-FINAL.4.pdf.

Chapter 5: What We Talk About When We Talk About Crime

1. "New Analysis Shows 8% Increase in U.S. Domestic Violence Incidents Following Pandemic Stay-at-Home Orders," Council on Criminal Justice, Feb. 24, 2021, counciloncj.org/new-analysis-shows-8-increase-in-u-s-domestic -violence-incidents-following-pandemic-stay-at-home-orders/; Alex R. Piquero et al., "Domestic Violence During the COVID-19 Pandemic—Evidence from a Systematic Review and Meta-Analysis," *Journal of Criminal Justice* 74 (May 2021): 101806, doi.org/10.1016/j.jcrimjus.2021.101806.
2. The author received permission to reuse Gallup's copyrighted material. Lydia

Saad, "Local Crime Deemed Worse This Year by Americans," *Gallup News,* Nov. 10, 2021, news.gallup.com/poll/357107/local-crime-deemed-worse-year-americans.aspx.

3. Ken Dilanian, "Most People Think the U.S. Crime Rate Is Rising. They're Wrong," NBC News, Dec. 16, 2023; John Gramlich, "What the Data Says About Crime in the U.S.," Pew Research Center, April 24, 2024, www.pewresearch.org/short-reads/2024/04/24/what-the-data-says-about-crime-in-the-us/.

4. Jennifer Kavanagh and Michael D. Rich, "Truth Decay: An Initial Exploration of the Diminishing Role of Facts and Analysis in American Public Life," RAND Corporation, Jan. 16, 2018, www.rand.org/pubs/research_reports/RR2314 .html; Christopher St. Aubin and Jacob Liedke, "News Platform Fact Sheet," Pew Research Center, Sept. 17, 2024, www.pewresearch.org/journalism/fact -sheet/news-platform-fact-sheet/.

5. The degree that crime fell in 2023 is incredible: Violent crime and property crime dropped by almost 3 percent. Homicides fell by 11.6 percent, which one analyst called "the largest year-to-year decline since national record-keeping began in 1960." Burglaries also declined by 7 percent and larceny by 4.4 percent. Experts (even the Attorney General) say these "historic" trends continued into 2024. Tom Costello and Corky Siemaszko, "New FBI Stats Show 'Historic' Declines in Violent Crime Rate, with Murder Showing Sharpest Drop," NBC News, June 1, 2024; "Attorney General Merrick B. Garland Statement on FBI's Quarterly Uniform Crime Report," U.S. Department of Justice, June 10, 2024, www.justice.gov/opa/pr/attorney-general-merrick-b-garland-statement-fbis -quarterly-uniform-crime-report.

6. Dilanian, "Most People Think the U.S. Crime Rate Is Rising"; Taylor Wilson, "The Excerpt: Crime Stats Show Improvement. Why Do So Many Believe It's Never Been Worse?," *USA Today,* Feb. 22, 2024.

7. Ken Dowler, Thomas Fleming, and Stephen L. Muzzatti, "Constructing Crime: Media, Crime, and Popular Culture," *Canadian Journal of Criminology and Criminal Justice* 48, no. 6 (2006): 837–50, doi.org/10.3138/cjccj.48.6.837; Sara Sun Beale, "The News Media's Influence on Criminal Justice Policy: How Market-Driven News Promotes Punitiveness," *William and Mary Law Review* 48, no. 2 (2006): 397–481.

8. Philip Bump, "Crime Is Down, Though Fox News Viewers Might Not Be Aware," *Washington Post,* Dec. 18, 2023.

9. Mylan Denerstein, "Sixteenth Report of the Independent Monitor," Gibson Dunn, May 16, 2022, www.nyc.gov/assets/nypd/downloads/pdf/monitor -reports/federal-monitor-16th-report.pdf.

10. Becca Cadoff, Preeti Chauhan, and Erica Bond, "Misdemeanor Enforcement Trends Across Seven U.S. Jurisdictions," Data Collaborative for Justice at John Jay College, Oct. 2020, datacollaborativeforjustice.org/wp-content/uploads/ 2020/10/2020_20_10_Crosssite-Draft-Final.pdf; Terry Gross, " 'Punishment

Without Crime' Highlights the Injustice of America's Misdemeanor System," NPR, Jan. 2, 2019.

11. John Gramlich and Kirsten Eddy, "The Link Between Local News Coverage and Americans' Perceptions of Crime," Pew Research Center, Aug. 29, 2024, www.pewresearch.org/short-reads/2024/08/29/the-link-between-local-news-coverage-and-americans-perceptions-of-crime/.

12. Daniel Romer, Kathleen Hall Jamieson, and Sean Aday, "Television News and the Cultivation of Fear of Crime," *Journal of Communication* 53, no. 1 (2003): 88–104, doi.org/10.1111/j.1460-2466.2003.tb03007.x.

13. *Illinois v. Wardlow,* 528 U.S. 119 (2000).

14. Johnson, "Whom Do Prosecutors Protect?"

15. Johnson, "Whom Do Prosecutors Protect?"; Andrea Wang, "*Illinois v. Wardlow* and the Crisis of Legitimacy: An Argument for a Real Cost Balancing Test," *Minnesota Journal of Law & Inequality* 19, no. 1 (2001): 1–30.

16. *Illinois v. Wardlow,* 528 U.S. 119 (2000).

17. Johnson, "Whom Do Prosecutors Protect?"

18. Jeounghee Kim and Skye Allmang, "Wage Theft in the United States: A Critical Review," Center for Women and Work, Rutgers, June 2020, smlr.rutgers.edu/sites/default/files/Documents/Centers/CWW/Publications/wage_theft_in_the_united_states_a_critical_review_june_2020.pdf.

19. David Cooper and Teresa Kroeger, "Employers Steal Billions from Workers' Paychecks Each Year," Economic Policy Institute, May 10, 2017, www.epi.org/publication/employers-steal-billions-from-workers-paychecks-each-year/.

20. Chris Hacker et al., "Wage Theft Often Goes Unpunished Despite State Systems Meant to Combat It," CBS News, June 30, 2023, www.cbsnews.com/news/owed-employers-face-little-accountability-for-wage-theft/.

21. Kim and Allmang, "Wage Theft in the United States."

22. Andrew Bowen, "Despite Racial Disparities in Tickets, Jaywalking Will Remain a Crime in California," KPBS, Oct. 18, 2021, www.kpbs.org/news/local/2021/10/18/despite-racial-disparities-in-tickets-jaywalking-will-remain-a-crime-in-california.

23. Megan Cassidy, "Audit Finds State District Attorney Group Misspent Millions Allocated for Environmental Cases," *San Francisco Chronicle,* Jan. 15, 2021, www.sfchronicle.com/bayarea/article/Audit-finds-state-district-attorney-group-15868701.php.

24. Lisa Friedman, "New Top Cop at the E.P.A. Aims to Get Enforcement Back on Track," *New York Times,* Aug. 17, 2023; Joshua Ozymy and Melissa L. Jarrell, "Does the Criminal Enforcement of Federal Environmental Law Deter Environmental Crime? The Case of the U.S. Resource Conservation and Recovery Act," *Environmental and Earth Law Journal* 11, no. 1 (2021): 65–88; Syrena Shirley, "Crime and Punishment: Corporate Criminal Prosecution and Corporate Misconduct," Columbia Business School, Nov. 2023, business

.columbia.edu/sites/default/files-efs/imce-uploads/Burton%202023/Crime %20and%20Punishment%20-%20Corporate%20Criminal%20Prosecution %20and%20Corporate%20Misconduct.pdf.

25. Shirley, "Crime and Punishment."

26. Dorothy S. Lund and Natasha Sarin, "Corporate Crime and Punishment: An Empirical Study," *Texas Law Review* 100, no. 2 (2021).

27. Stephen Murray, conversation with the author, Feb. 7, 2024.

28. Travis L. Dixon and Daniel Linz, "Overrepresentation and Underrepresentation of African Americans and Latinos as Lawbreakers on Television News," *Journal of Communication* 50, no. 2 (2000): 131–54, doi.org/10.1111/j.1460-2466 .2000.tb02845.x; Travis L. Dixon and Daniel Linz, "Race and the Misrepresentation of Victimization on Local Television News," *Communication Research* 27, no. 5 (2000): 547–73, doi.org/10.1177/009365000027005001; Travis L. Dixon, Cristina L. Azocar, and Michael Casas, "The Portrayal of Race and Crime on Television Network News," *Journal of Broadcasting & Electronic Media* 47, no. 4 (2003): 498–523, doi.org/10.1207/s15506878jobem4704_2; Eileen E. S. Bjornstrom et al., "Race and Ethnic Representations of Lawbreakers and Victims in Crime News: A National Study of Television Coverage," *Social Problems* 57, no. 2 (2010): 269–93, doi.org/10.1525/sp.2010.57.2.269.

29. Dr. Matthew Guariglia pointed out that the idea of showing mug shots at all is historically fraught; originally, people were appalled at the idea that a person's photograph could be hung in a "rogues' gallery" and have their future and employability impacted by a photograph taken at the moment of *accusation* rather than *conviction*. Turns out there are a number of ways in which we are substantially more punitive now than we were in the days of Butch Cassidy and the Hole in the Wall gang. "Innocent Until Proven Guilty? A Look at Media Coverage of Criminal Defendants in the U.S.," Global Strategy Group, 2021, globalstrategygroup.com/wp-content/uploads/2012/07/GSG_Report_Innocent _Until_Proven_Guilty.pdf.

30. Nikki Goth Itoi, "How Social Media Shapes Our Perceptions About Crime," Stanford University, Feb. 27, 2023, hai.stanford.edu/news/how-social-media -shapes-our-perceptions-about-crime.

31. Michael O'Hear, "Violent Crime and Media Coverage in One City: A Statistical Snapshot," *Marquette Law Review* 103, no. 3 (2020), scholarship.law.marquette .edu/mulr/vol103/iss3/14.

32. Yuning Wu, Ivan Y. Sun, and Ruth A. Triplett, "Race, Class or Neighborhood Context: Which Matters More in Measuring Satisfaction with Police?," *Justice Quarterly* 26, no. 1 (2009): 125–56, doi.org/10.1080/07418820802119950; Yuning Wu, "Race/Ethnicity and Perceptions of the Police: A Comparison of White, Black, Asian, and Hispanic Americans," *Policing and Society* 24, no. 2 (2014): 135–57, doi.org/10.1080/10439463.2013.784288.

33. Jake Horowitz, "Making Every Encounter Count: Building Trust and Confidence

in the Police," *National Institute for Justice,* Feb. 1, 2007, web.archive.org/web/
20250104131217/nij.ojp.gov/topics/articles/making-every-encounter-count
-building-trust-and-confidence-police; Juliana Menasce Horowitz, Anna Brown,
and Kiana Cox, "Race in America 2019," Pew Research Center, April 9, 2019,
www.pewresearch.org/social-trends/2019/04/09/race-in-america-2019/;
Christopher Muller and Daniel Schrage, "Mass Imprisonment and Trust in the
Law," *Annals of the American Academy of Political and Social Science* 651, no. 1
(2014): 139–58, doi.org/10.1177/0002716213502928.

34. Nancy La Vigne, Jocelyn Fontaine, and Anamika Dwivedi, "How Do People
in High-Crime, Low-Income Communities View the Police?," Urban
Institute, Feb. 2017, www.urban.org/sites/default/files/publication/88476/
how_do_people_in_high-crime_view_the_police.pdf; Hunter M. Boehme,
Deanna Cann, and Deena A. Isom, "Citizens' Perceptions of Over- and
Under-Policing: A Look at Race, Ethnicity, and Community Characteristics,"
Crime & Delinquency 68, no. 1 (2022): 123–54, doi.org/10.1177/00111287
20974309.

35. Kingston Farady, conversation with the author, May 7, 2024.

36. Khalil Gibran Muhammad, *The Condemnation of Blackness: Race, Crime, and the
Making of Modern Urban America* (Harvard University Press, 2019).

37. "U.S. Diplomacy and Yellow Journalism, 1895–1898," Office of the Historian,
Foreign Service Institute, U.S. Department of State, accessed Nov. 5, 2024,
history.state.gov/milestones/1866-1898/yellow-journalism; Nicholas Lemann,
"Paper Tigers," *New Yorker,* April 6, 2009; Karen Campbell, "How KCUR
Reporters Collaborate for Better, More Empathetic Crime Coverage," KCUR,
Jan. 26, 2024, www.kcur.org/inside-kcur/2024-01-26/how-kcur-reporters
-collaborate-for-better-more-empathetic-crime-coverage.

38. Dr. Matthew Guariglia, interview with the author, May 7, 2024.

39. Fola Akinnibi and Raeedah Wahid, "Fear of Rampant Crime Is Derailing New
York City's Recovery," Bloomberg, July 29, 2022, www.bloomberg.com/
graphics/2022-is-nyc-safe-crime-stat-reality/; O'Hear, "Violent Crime and
Media Coverage in One City"; Robert Reiner, Sonia Livingstone, and Jessica
Allen, "From Law and Order to Lynch Mobs: Crime News Since the Second
World War," in *Criminal Visions: Media Representations of Crime and Justice,* ed.
Paul Mason (Willan, 2003), 13–32.

40. Jarret S. Lovell, "Media Power & Information Control: A Study of Police
Organizations & Media Relations," National Criminal Justice Reference Service,
Oct. 24, 2002, www.ojp.gov/pdffiles1/nij/grants/197060.pdf.

41. Drew Shenkman and Kelli Slade, "Police Reports Shouldn't Set the News
Agenda: A Guide to Avoiding Systemic Racism in Reporting," American Bar
Association, Jan. 22, 2021, www.americanbar.org/groups/communications_law/
publications/communications_lawyer/fall2020/police-reports-shouldnt-set-news
-agenda-guide-avoiding-systemic-racism-reporting/; Ari Shapiro, Jason Fuller,

and Christopher Intagliata, "Police Reports Are Biased. What Can Journalists Do to Better Cover Policing?," NPR, May 28, 2021.

42. Johnson, "Whom Do Prosecutors Protect?"

43. Faye Elkins, "Managing Your Message: How to Work with the News Media," *Dispatch* 12, no. 11 (2019), web.archive.org/web/20250103043500/cops.usdoj .gov/html/dispatch/12-2019/news_media.html.

44. Lovell, "Media Power & Information Control"; Melissa Motschall and Liqun Cao, "An Analysis of the Public Relations Role of the Police Public Information Officer," *Police Quarterly* 5, no. 2 (2002): 152–80, doi.org/10.1177/10986 1102129198084; Maya Lau, "Police PR Machine Under Scrutiny for Inaccurate Reporting, Alleged Pro-Cop Bias," *Los Angeles Times,* Aug. 30, 2020; Alexandria Neason, " 'Officials Say . . . ': In Chicago and Elsewhere, Police Departments Plant Misinformation in the Press," *Columbia Journalism Review,* Dec. 3, 2019, www.cjr.org/special_report/officials-say-chicago-police-joshua-beal.php.

45. Alec Karakatsanis, "Police Departments Spend Vast Sums of Money Creating 'Copaganda,' " *Jacobin,* July 20, 2022, jacobin.com/2022/07/copaganda-police -propaganda-public-relations-pr-communications.

46. Neason, " 'Officials Say . . . ' "; Julia Craven, "The Media Is Finally Addressing Its Police Report Problem," *Slate,* April 23, 2021, slate.com/business/2021/04/ george-floyd-initial-police-report-false-journalism.html.

47. Kelly McBride, "AP Stylebook's New Chapter on Crime Is a Glimpse into the Future," Poynter, June 4, 2024, www.poynter.org/commentary/2024/ap-style book-new-criminal-justice-entry/; Nazgol Ghandnoosh, "Media Guide: 10 Crime Coverage Dos and Don'ts," Sentencing Project, July 9, 2024, www .sentencingproject.org/fact-sheet/media-guide-10-crime-coverage-dos-and -donts/.

48. The perspective of these medical professionals has been substantially hampered by the fact that the U.S. DEA itself has put out misinformation about fentanyl as recently as 2016, claiming it could cause adverse health effects via touch alone. Brandon del Pozo et al., "Can Touch This: Training to Correct Police Officer Beliefs About Overdose from Incidental Contact with Fentanyl," *Health & Justice* 9, no. 1 (2021): 34, doi.org/10.1186/s40352-021-00163-5.

49. Athina Morris, "Florida Cop Treated for Overdose After Possible Fentanyl Exposure, Police Say," WFLA, Dec. 15, 2022, www.wfla.com/news/florida/video -florida-cop-treated-for-overdose-after-possible-fentanyl-exposure-police-say/; Brooke Wolford, "Cop Saved from Fentanyl Overdose in Dramatic California Video. 'Not Gonna Let You Die,' " *Sacramento Bee,* Jan. 27, 2022, www.sacbee .com/news/california/article253325223.html; Artemis Moshtaghian, "Police Officer Overdoses After Brushing Fentanyl Powder off His Uniform," CNN, May 16, 2017, www.cnn.com/2017/05/16/health/police-fentanyl-overdose -trnd/index.html.

50. del Pozo et al., "Can Touch This"; Jonathan Jarry, "You Won't Die from Touching Fentanyl," McGill University, Oct. 13, 2023, www.mcgill.ca/oss/article/medical-critical-thinking/you-wont-die-touching-fentanyl.

51. Dennis Romero, "Viral Video of San Diego Deputy's Fentanyl Exposure Raises Questions," NBC, Aug. 2, 2021.

52. Amanda Hernández, "States Stiffen Penalties for Fentanyl, Despite Public Health Concerns," Stateline, July 23, 2023, stateline.org/2023/07/20/states-stiffen-penalties-for-fentanyl-despite-public-health-concerns/; Hoffman, "Harsh New Fentanyl Laws Ignite Debate over How to Combat Overdose Crisis"; Gabe Stern, James Pollard, and Geoff Mulvihill, "State Lawmakers Consider Harsher Penalties for Fentanyl Possession," PBS News, March 20, 2023, www.pbs.org/newshour/nation/state-lawmakers-consider-harsher-penalties-for-fentanyl-related-crimes.

53. Adam Gelb et al., "More Imprisonment Does Not Reduce State Drug Problems," Pew Charitable Trusts, March 18, 2018, www.pewtrusts.org/en/research-and-analysis/issue-briefs/2018/03/more-imprisonment-does-not-reduce-state-drug-problems; Doug McVay, Vincent Schiraldi, and Jason Ziedenberg, "Treatment or Incarceration? National and State Findings on the Efficacy and Cost Savings of Drug Treatment Versus Imprisonment," Justice Policy Institute, March 2004, www.opensocietyfoundations.org/uploads/bc64a0f5-caa4-46a8-894a-e9ecf18f6198/treatment1.pdf.

54. Shima Baradaran Baughman, "How Effective Are Police? The Problem of Clearance Rates and Criminal Accountability," *Alabama Law Review* 72, no. 1 (2020): 47–112.

55. Gramlich, "What the Data Says About Crime in the U.S."

56. Hady Mawajdeh, "Police Are Solving Fewer Crimes. Why?," *Vox,* Dec. 23, 2023, www.vox.com/2023/12/23/24012514/police-crime-data-solve-rate-eddie-garcia-today-explained.

57. Baughman, "How Effective Are Police?"

58. "Crimes and Clearances," Open Justice, California Department of Justice, Office of the Attorney General, accessed Nov. 5, 2024, openjustice.doj.ca.gov/exploration/crime-statistics/crimes-clearances.

59. Eliott C. McLaughlin, "Ex-Deputy Accused of Planting Drugs on Florida Drivers Is Arrested," CNN, July 11, 2019; Ryan J. Foley, "Video Evidence Increasingly Disproves Police Narratives," AP News, June 9, 2020, apnews.com/article/us-news-ap-top-news-mn-state-wire-pa-state-wire-police-a172fb01bdb74b4159b39da390d9e79e; Neil Vigdor, Daniel Victor, and Christine Hauser, "Buffalo Police Officers Suspended After Shoving 75-Year-Old Protester," *New York Times,* Feb. 23, 2021.

60. Grace Manthey, Frank Esposito, and Amanda Hernandez, "Despite 'Defunding' Claims, Police Funding Has Increased in Many US Cities," ABC News, Oct. 16,

2022; Mathis Ebbinghaus, Nathan Bailey, and Jacob Rubel, "The Effect of the 2020 Black Lives Matter Protests on Police Budgets: How 'Defund the Police' Sparked Political Backlash," *Social Problems,* March 15, 2024, spae004, doi.org/10.1093/socpro/spae004.

61. Annelise Finney, conversation with the author, April 11, 2024.
62. Henry L. Roediger III, John H. Wixted, and K. Andrew Desoto, "The Curious Complexity Between Confidence and Accuracy in Reports from Memory," in *Memory and Law,* ed. Lynn Nadel and Walter P. Sinnott-Armstrong (Oxford University Press, 2012), 84–117, doi.org/10.1093/acprof:oso/9780199920754.003.0004; Michael D. Robinson, Joel T. Johnson, and David A. Robertson, "Process Versus Content in Eyewitness Metamemory Monitoring," *Journal of Experimental Psychology: Applied* 6, no. 3 (2000): 207–21, doi.org/10.1037/1076-898X.6.3.207.
63. Finney, conversation with the author, April 11, 2024.
64. Guariglia, interview with the author, May 7, 2024.

Chapter 6: A Game of Telephone

1. *Brady v. Maryland,* 373 U.S. 83 (1963).
2. Anonymous, conversation with the author, Nov. 29, 2023, and Feb. 22, 2024.
3. *Strickler v. Greene,* 527 U.S. 263 (1999).
4. *Wardius v. Oregon,* 412 U.S. 470 (1973).
5. *Weatherford v. Bursey,* 429 U.S. 545, 97 S. Ct. 837, 51 L. Ed. 2d 30 (1977) (emphasis added).
6. *Miller v. Schwartz,* 72 N.Y.2d 869, 532 N.Y.S.2d 354, 528 N.E.2d 507 (N.Y. 1988).
7. "Discovery in the States," Strengthening the Sixth, accessed Nov. 5, 2024, www.strengthenthesixth.org/Discovery/States/States.
8. Cal. Penal Code § 1054.1.
9. "Rule 5: Disclosure in Criminal Cases," Court Rules, South Carolina Judicial Branch, www.sccourts.org/courtReg/displayRule.cfm?ruleID=5.0&subRuleID&ruleType=CRM.
10. Schwartzapfel, VanSickle, and Griffin, "Truth About Trials"; *2018 Annual Report and Sourcebook of Federal Sentencing Statistics;* Gramlich, "Fewer Than 1% of Federal Criminal Defendants Were Acquitted in 2022."
11. "Rule 26. Duty to Disclose; General Provisions Governing Discovery," Legal Information Institute, Cornell Law School, www.law.cornell.edu/rules/frcp/rule_26.
12. Ion Meyn, "Why Civil and Criminal Procedure Are So Different: A Forgotten History," *Fordham Law Review* 86, no. 2 (2017): 697–736.

13. John G. Roberts, "Federal Rules of Civil Procedure," April 29, 2015, www
.supremecourt.gov/orders/courtorders/frcv15(update)_1823.pdf.

14. *Hickman v. Taylor,* 329 U.S. 495 (1947).

15. Meyn, "Why Civil and Criminal Procedure Are So Different."

16. A. Holtzoff, "Reform of Federal Criminal Procedure," *George Washington Law
Review* 12, no. 2 (1944): 119–30.

17. "The CalGang Criminal Intelligence System," California State Auditor,
Aug. 2016, voiceofsandiego.org/wp-content/uploads/2016/08/CalGangs-audit
.pdf.

18. Daryl Khan, "New York City's Gang Database Is 99% People of Color, Chief of
Detectives Testifies," Juvenile Justice Information Exchange, June 14, 2018, jjie
.org/2018/06/14/new-york-citys-gang-database-is-99-people-of-color-chief-of
-detectives-testifies/; "An Investigation into NYPD's Criminal Group Database,"
Office of the Inspector General for the NYPD, April 2023, www.nyc.gov/assets/
doi/reports/pdf/2023/16CGDRpt.Release04.18.2023.pdf.

19. "Contrary to California Case Law, Gang Injunctions Infringe Targets' Right to
Familial Association," *Harvard Civil Rights–Civil Liberties Law Review,* March
18, 2017, journals.law.harvard.edu/crcl/contrary-to-california-case-law-gang
-injunctions-infringe-targets-right-to-familial-association/; *Vasquez v. Rackauckas,*
734 F.3d 1025 (9th Cir. 2013).

20. Mary Prosser, "Reforming Criminal Discovery: Why Old Objections Must Yield
to New Realities," *Wisconsin Law Review* 2006, no. 2 (2006): 541–614.

21. Prosser, "Reforming Criminal Discovery."

22. "DNA Exonerations in the United States (1989–2020)," Innocence Project,
accessed Nov. 5, 2024, innocenceproject.org/dna-exonerations-in-the-united
-states/.

23. James S. Liebman, "An 'Effective Death Penalty'? AEDPA and Error Detection
in Capital Cases," *Brooklyn Law Review* 67, no. 2 (2001): 411–28.

24. Richard H. Fallon et al., *Hart and Wechsler's The Federal Courts and the Federal
System,* 7th ed., University Casebook Series (Foundation Press, 2015).

25. *Lockyer v. Andrade,* 538 U.S. 63 (2003).

26. *Shinn v. Ramirez,* 142 S. Ct. 1718 (2022).

27. Schwartzapfel, VanSickle, and Griffin, "Truth About Trials"; *2018 Annual Report
and Sourcebook of Federal Sentencing Statistics;* Gramlich, "Fewer Than 1% of
Federal Criminal Defendants Were Acquitted in 2022."

28. *McCleskey v. Zant,* 499 U.S. 467 (1991).

29. J. William Brennan, "Criminal Prosecution: Sporting Event or Quest for
Truth?," *Washington University Law Review* 3 (1963): 279–95.

30. Prosser, "Reforming Criminal Discovery."

31. Indeed, the lobbying resources of prosecutors are often fairly substantial and
effective. Hessick, Wright, and Pishko, "Prosecutor Lobby"; Prosecutors and

Politics Project, "Prosecutor Lobbying in the States, 2015–2018," University of North Carolina School of Law, June 2021, law.unc.edu/wp-content/uploads/2021/06/Prosecutor-Lobbying-in-the-States-2015-2018.pdf.

32. Samantha Luna and Allison Redlich, "Unintelligent Decision-Making? The Impact of Discovery on Defendant Plea Decisions," *Wrongful Conviction Law Review* 1, no. 3 (2020): 314–35, doi.org/10.29173/wclawr24.

33. Bromwich, "Hundreds Have Left N.Y. Public Defender Offices over Low Pay."

34. Samantha Michaels, "The Alternative to Police That Is Proven to Reduce Violence," *Mother Jones,* June 2, 2022, www.motherjones.com/criminal-justice/2022/06/mental-health-san-francisco-street-crisis-response-team-cahoots-police-violence/.

35. Thomas S. Dee and Jaymes Pyne, "A Community Response Approach to Mental Health and Substance Abuse Crises Reduced Crime," *Science Advances* 8, no. 23 (2022): eabm2106, doi.org/10.1126/sciadv.abm2106.

36. Jonah E. Bromwich and Grace Ashford, "New York City Prosecutors Suddenly Flip on Change to Evidence Law," *New York Times,* April 27, 2023.

37. "The Impact of Discovery Reform Implementation in New York," Chief Defenders Association of New York, New York State Defenders Association, NYS Association of Criminal Defense Lawyers, NYS Office of Indigent Legal Services, March 28, 2022, cdn.ymaws.com/www.nysda.org/resource/resmgr/bail_and_discovery_/NYS_Discovery_Reform_Defense.pdf.

38. "Expanded Discovery in Criminal Cases: A Policy Review," Justice Project, 2007, www.pewtrusts.org/~/media/legacy/uploadedfiles/wwwpewtrustsorg/reports/death_penalty_reform/expanded20discovery20policy20briefpdf.pdf.

Chapter 7: Weird Science

1. Jim Hilbert, "The Disappointing History of Science in the Courtroom: Frye, Daubert, and the Ongoing Crisis of 'Junk Science' in Criminal Trials," *Oklahoma Law Review* 71 (2019): 759–821.

2. *McCormick v. Talcott,* 61 U.S. 402, 409 (1857); Hilbert, "Disappointing History of Science in the Courtroom."

3. *Winans v. New York & Erie Railroad Co.,* 62 U.S. 88 (1858); Hilbert, "Disappointing History of Science in the Courtroom."

4. Judge William Foster (1897) as cited in Hilbert, "Disappointing History of Science in the Courtroom."

5. *Frye v. United States,* 293 F. 1013 (D.C. Cir. 1923).

6. *Daubert v. Merrell Dow Pharmaceuticals Inc.,* 509 U.S. 579 (1993).

7. Sophia I. Gatowski et al., "Asking the Gatekeepers: A National Survey of Judges

on Judging Expert Evidence in a Post-*Daubert* World," *Law and Human Behavior* 25, no. 5 (2001): 433–58, doi.org/10.1023/A:1012899030937.

8. "Trial judges have an incentive, however much they try to prevent its subconscious effect on their decisions, to clear their crowded dockets of cases that are likely to be time-consuming and, given the technicality of the evidence, tedious. A virtually unreviewable opportunity to shed cases that the judge thinks of doubtful merit must be a powerful temptation." Michael H. Gottesman, "From *Barefoot* to *Daubert* to *Joiner:* Triple Play or Double Error?," *Arizona Law Review* 40, no. 3 (1998): 753–80.

9. Brandon L. Garrett and M. Chris Fabricant, "The Myth of the Reliability Test," *Fordham Law Review* 86, no. 4 (2018): 1559–99.

10. Laurel Gilbert, "Sharpening the Tools of an Adequate Defense: Providing for the Appointment of Experts for Indigent Defendants in Child Death Cases Under *Ake v. Oklahoma*," *San Diego Law Review* 50, no. 2 (2013): 469–515; J. Herbie DiFonzo, "The Crimes of Crime Labs," *Hofstra Law Review* 34, no. 1 (2005): 1–11; Jennifer L. Groscup et al., "The Effects of *Daubert* on the Admissibility of Expert Testimony in State and Federal Criminal Cases," *Psychology, Public Policy, and Law* 8, no. 4 (2002): 339–72, doi.org/10.1037/1076-8971.8.4.339.

11. Similarly, jurors are much more likely to convict in cases where any DNA evidence is presented, even if they later admit that they did not understand that evidence during the trial. Gilbert, "Sharpening the Tools of an Adequate Defense"; DiFonzo, "Crimes of Crime Labs"; Jane Goodman-Delahunty and Lindsay Hewson, "Enhancing Fairness in DNA Jury Trials," *Trends & Issues in Crime and Criminal Justice* 392 (March 2010), www.researchgate.net/publication/242775287_Enhancing_fairness_in_DNA_jury_trials.

12. Eric S. Lander, "Fixing Rule 702: The PCAST Report and Steps to Ensure the Reliability of Forensic Feature-Comparison Methods in the Criminal Courts," *Fordham Law Review* 86, no. 4 (2018): 1661–79.

13. Alison Guernsey, email to the author, Feb. 22, 2024.

14. William J. Gorta, "Expert Pimp Gets a 'Ho No,'" *New York Post,* Nov. 22, 2011, nypost.com/2011/11/22/expert-pimp-gets-a-ho-no/.

15. Committee on Identifying the Needs of the Forensic Sciences Community, National Research Council, *Strengthening Forensic Science in the United States: A Path Forward* (National Academies Press, 2009), www.ojp.gov/pdffiles1/nij/grants/228091.pdf.

16. Jules Epstein, "The National Commission on Forensic Science: Impactful or Ineffectual?," *Seton Hall Law Review* 48, no. 3 (2018): 743–71.

17. President's Council of Advisors on Science and Technology, *Forensic Science in Criminal Courts: Ensuring Scientific Validity of Feature-Comparison Methods,* Executive Office of the President of the United States, Sept. 2016,

obamawhitehouse.archives.gov/sites/default/files/microsites/ostp/PCAST/pcast
_forensic_science_report_final.pdf.

18. "Cases Where DNA Revealed That Bite Mark Analysis Led to Wrongful Arrests and Convictions," Innocence Project, Jan. 31, 2007, innocenceproject.org/cases -where-dna-revealed-that-bite-mark-analysis-led-to-wrongful-arrests-and -convictions/.

19. President's Council of Advisors on Science and Technology, *Forensic Science in Criminal Courts.*

20. "FBI Testimony on Microscopic Hair Analysis Contained Errors in at Least 90 Percent of Cases in Ongoing Review," Federal Bureau of Investigation, April 20, 2015, www.fbi.gov/news/pressrel/press-releases/fbi-testimony-on -microscopic-hair-analysis-contained-errors-in-at-least-90-percent-of-cases-in -ongoing-review; Hilbert, "Disappointing History of Science in the Courtroom."

21. Hilbert, "Disappointing History of Science in the Courtroom"; "How Santae Tribble's Wrongful Conviction Prompted Review of the FBI's Use of Hair Analysis and Inspired the Innocence Project's Research," Innocence Project, July 15, 2020, https://innocenceproject.org/news/santae-tribble-inspired-hair -analysis-review-work/.

22. "FBI Testimony on Microscopic Hair Analysis Contained Errors in at Least 90 Percent of Cases in Ongoing Review."

23. Stephanie L. Damon-Moore, "Trial Judges and the Forensic Science Problem," *New York University Law Review* 92, no. 5 (2017): 1532–70.

24. Maia Szalavitz, "The Shaky Science of Shaken Baby Syndrome," *Time,* Jan. 17, 2012.

25. Deborah Tuerkheimer, *Flawed Convictions: "Shaken Baby Syndrome" and the Inertia of Injustice* (Oxford University Press, 2015).

26. Sue Luttner, "Dr. Norman Guthkelch, Still on the Medical Frontier," *On Shaken Baby* (blog), Feb. 20, 2013, onsbs.com/2013/02/20/dr-norman-guthkelch-still -on-the-medical-frontier/.

27. Joesph Shapiro, "Rethinking Shaken Baby Syndrome," NPR, June 29, 2011.

28. Randy Papetti, Paige Kaneb, and Lindsay Herf, "Outside the Echo Chamber: A Response to the 'Consensus Statement on Abusive Head Trauma in Infants and Young Children,'" *Santa Clara Law Review* 59, no. 2 (2019): 299–366.

29. Jennifer L. Mnookin, "Fingerprints: Not a Gold Standard," *Issues in Science and Technology* 20, no. 1 (Fall 2003), issues.org/mnookin-fingerprints-evidence/.

30. The figure does not include "inconclusive examinations." If they are included, the error rate is 3.0 percent. Igor Pacheco, Brian Cerchiai, and Stephanie Stoiloff, "Miami-Dade Research Study for the Reliability of the ACE-V Process: Accuracy & Precision in Latent Fingerprint Examinations," Dec. 2014, www.ojp .gov/pdffiles1/nij/grants/248534.pdf.

31. Jonathan J. Koehler and Shiquan Liu, "Fingerprint Error Rate on Close Non-

Matches," *Journal of Forensic Sciences* 66, no. 1 (2021): 129–34, doi.org/10 .1111/1556-4029.14580.

32. President's Council of Advisors on Science and Technology, *Forensic Science in Criminal Courts.*

33. Mnookin, "Fingerprints."

34. R. Austin Hicklin et al., "Accuracy and Reproducibility of Conclusions by Forensic Bloodstain Pattern Analysts," *Forensic Science International* 325 (Aug. 2021), doi.org/10.1016/j.forsciint.2021.110856; "Study Assesses the Accuracy and Reproducibility of Bloodstain Pattern Analysis," National Institute of Justice, Dec. 14, 2022, nij.ojp.gov/topics/articles/study-assesses-accuracy-and -reproducibility-bloodstain-pattern-analysis.

35. Carrie Leonetti, "The History of Forensic-Science Evidence in Criminal Trials and the Role of Early 'Success' in Establishing Its Putative Reliability," *St. Mary's Law Journal* 54, no. 4 (2023): 1061–94.

36. Leora Smith, "How a Dubious Forensic Science Spread Like a Virus," ProPublica, Dec. 13, 2018, features.propublica.org/blood-spatter-analysis/ herbert-macdonell-forensic-evidence-judges-and-courts/.

37. Smith, "How a Dubious Forensic Science Spread Like a Virus."

38. Alex Kozinski, "Preface: Criminal Law 2.0," *Georgetown Law Journal's Annual Review of Criminal Procedure* 44 (2015): iii–xliv.

39. David Grann, "Trial by Fire," *New Yorker,* Aug. 31, 2009.

40. Rachel Dioso-Villa, "Scientific and Legal Developments in Fire and Arson Investigation Expertise in *Texas v. Willingham*," *Minnesota Journal of Law, Science & Technology* 14, no. 2 (2013): 817–48.

41. Dioso-Villa, "Scientific and Legal Developments in Fire and Arson Investigation Expertise in *Texas v. Willingham*"; "Cameron Todd Willingham's Wrongful Execution Gains New Attention After Netflix's *Trial by Fire* Release," Sept. 13, 2010 (updated Apr. 2, 2025), innocenceproject.org/cameron-todd-willingham -wrongfully-convicted-and-executed-in-texas/.

42. Arthur E. Cote and Percy Bugbee, *Principles of Fire Protection,* 2nd ed. (Jones & Bartlett, 1988); Marc Price Wolf, "Habeas Relief from Bad Science: Does Federal Habeas Corpus Provide Relief for Prisoners Possibly Convicted on Misunderstood Fire Science?," *Minnesota Journal of Law, Science & Technology* 10, no. 1 (2009): 213.

43. Wolf, "Habeas Relief from Bad Science"; Richard L. P. Custer, "Considerations for Arson Investigations in NFPA 921—Guide for Fire and Explosion Investigations," in *Proceedings of the International Symposium on the Forensic Aspects of Arson Investigations* (George Mason University, 1995), archive.org/details/proceedings oftheinternationalsymposiumontheforensicaspectsofarsoninvestigations/page/ n7/mode/2up.

44. Wolf, "Habeas Relief from Bad Science."

45. Maurice Possley, "Arson Myths Fuel Errors: Debunked Theories Plague Fire

Probes, Lead to Wrongful Arrests, Prosecutions," *Chicago Tribune,* Oct. 18, 2004.

46. Gilbert, "Sharpening the Tools of an Adequate Defense."

47. Even when a lab is technically independent, "forensic labs get the vast majority of their business from prosecutors and law enforcement, potentially creating a sense that success on the job means finding a match and getting a conviction." Damon-Moore, "Trial Judges and the Forensic Science Problem"; Hilbert, "Disappointing History of Science in the Courtroom"; David E. Bernstein, "The Unfinished *Daubert* Revolution," *Engage* 10, no. 1 (2009): 35–38.

48. Ross Miller, Paul Heaton, and Haley Sturges, "Guilty Until Proven Innocent," Quattrone Center for the Fair Administration of Justice, University of Pennsylvania, Dec. 2023, www.law.upenn.edu/live/files/12890-fdt-guilty-until -proven-innocent.

49. Emma Ockerman, "Nothing's Happening to the Officer Who Misidentified Bird Shit as Cocaine in the Arrest of a Young Black Man," *Vice,* Nov. 12, 2019, www.vice.com/en/article/zmj9gx/nothings-happening-to-the-officer-who -misidentified-bird-shit-as-cocaine-in-the-arrest-of-a-young-black-man.

50. Laurel Wamsley, "Florida Man Awarded $37,500 After Cops Mistake Glazed Doughnut Crumbs for Meth," NPR, Oct. 16, 2017.

51. Schwartzapfel, VanSickle, and Griffin, "Truth About Trials"; *2018 Annual Report and Sourcebook of Federal Sentencing Statistics;* Gramlich, "Fewer Than 1% of Federal Criminal Defendants Were Acquitted in 2022."

52. Miller, Heaton, Sturges, "Guilty Until Proven Innocent."

53. Gilbert, "Sharpening the Tools of an Adequate Defense"; DiFonzo, "Crimes of Crime Labs."

54. Hilbert, "Disappointing History of Science in the Courtroom" (internal quotations omitted).

55. Hilbert, "Disappointing History of Science in the Courtroom"; Madeleine Baran, "Troubled St. Paul Crime Lab Problems Even Worse Than First Thought, Probe Reveals," MPR News, Feb. 14, 2013, www.mprnews.org/story/2013/02/14/ troubled-st-paul-crime-lab-problems-even-worse-than-first-thought-probe -reveals.

56. Hilbert, "Disappointing History of Science in the Courtroom."

57. David Hanners, "St. Paul Crime Lab Woes First Recognized in 2006," *Twin Cities Pioneer Press,* Aug. 30, 2012, www.twincities.com/2012/08/30/st-paul -crime-lab-woes-first-recognized-in-2006/.

58. Ken Otterbourg, "Massachusetts 2017," National Registry of Exonerations, Sept. 23, 2022; Garrett Quinn, "Disgraced Crime Lab Chemist Annie Dookhan Released from Prison," *Boston Magazine,* April 12, 2016, www.boston magazine.com/news/2016/04/12/annie-dookhan-released-prison/.

59. "Colorado Bureau of Investigation Releases Findings from Internal Affairs Probe into Laboratory Testing," Colorado Bureau of Investigation, accessed Nov. 6,

2024, cbi.colorado.gov/news-article/colorado-bureau-of-investigation-releases -findings-from-internal-affairs-probe-into.

60. *Times Union* Editorial Board, "Editorial: Sunshine in the Courtroom," *Times Union,* Nov. 29, 2023, www.timesunion.com/opinion/article/editorial-sunshine -courtroom-18520083.php; Oded Oren and Rachael Fauss, "Open Criminal Courts: New York Criminal Court Decisions Should Be Public," Scrutinize and Reinvent Albany, Nov. 2023, static1.squarespace.com/static/635986ea4e386 9168261490b/t/655e2700a92fba51d0a5d431/1700669188026/opencriminal courtsreport.pdf.

Chapter 8: Finders of Fact

1. Valerie P. Hans, "Jury Systems Around the World," *Annual Review of Law and Social Science* 4, no. 1 (2008): 275–97, doi.org/10.1146/annurev.lawsocsci.4 .110707.172319.

2. Simon Jenkins, "Our Justice System Is in Crisis, So Why Not Abolish Jury Trials?," *Guardian,* Jan. 22, 2021, www.theguardian.com/commentisfree/2021/ jan/22/justice-system-crisis-abolish-jury-trials-covid; Ethan J. Leib, "A Comparison of Criminal Jury Decision Rules in Democratic Countries," *Ohio State Journal of Criminal Law* 5 (2007): 629–44.

3. Larry D. Kramer, *The People Themselves: Popular Constitutionalism and Judicial Review,* new ed. (Oxford University Press, 2006).

4. Craig S. Lerner, "Reasonable Suspicion and Mere Hunches," *Vanderbilt Law Review* 59, no. 2 (2006): 407–73; Seth W. Stoughton et al., "Policing Suspicion: Qualified Immunity and 'Clearly Established' Standards of Proof," *Journal of Criminal Law and Criminology* 112, no. 1 (2022): 37–78.

5. Sandhya Dirks, "Stories About Crime Are Rife with Misinformation and Racism, Critics Say," LAist, Nov. 9, 2022, laist.com/news/stories-about-crime -are-rife-with-misinformation-and-racism-critics-say; Alexia Fernández Campbell and Joe Yerardi, "Ripping Off Workers Without Consequences," Center for Public Integrity, May 4, 2021, publicintegrity.org/inequality-poverty-opportunity/ workers-rights/cheated-at-work/ripping-off-workers-with-no-consequences/; Cooper and Kroeger, "Employers Steal Billions from Workers' Paychecks Each Year."

6. Also, law nerds, yes, prosecutors can indict misdemeanors, but this is supposed to be a guided tour for outsiders around our disastrous, byzantine world, and there's a lot of disaster to cover, so I'm simplifying a little.

7. What does he mean by "being punished for it"? He means the "trial penalty," in which prosecutors seek more punishment against people who insist on their Constitutional right to trial. Brendon Woods, conversation with the author, Nov. 21, 2023.

8. Saul M. Kassin and Christina T. Fong, " 'I'm Innocent!': Effects of Training on Judgments of Truth and Deception in the Interrogation Room," *Law and Human Behavior* 23, no. 5 (1999): 499–516, doi.org/10.1023/A:1022330011811; Kassin, "False Confessions."

9. Melanie D. Wilson, "An Exclusionary Rule for Police Lies," *American Criminal Law Review* 47, no. 1 (2010): 1–80.

10. She's not alone. Across the United States, lower trust in police in the community results in fewer convictions. Race is a huge factor in this conversation, with Black and brown Americans who have more lived experience with over-policing expressing less faith in law enforcement and being more attuned to police misconduct. Amy Farrell, Liana Pennington, and Shea Cronin, "Juror Perceptions of the Legitimacy of Legal Authorities and Decision Making in Criminal Cases," *Law & Social Inquiry* 38, no. 4 (2013): 773–802; Mona Lynch and Emily V. Shaw, "Downstream Effects of Frayed Relations: Juror Race, Judgment, and Perceptions of Police," *Race and Justice,* May 30, 2023, doi.org/10.1177/21533687231178322.

11. Mark Motivans, "Federal Justice Statistics, 2015—Statistical Tables," Bureau of Justice Statistics, Dec. 2020, bjs.ojp.gov/content/pub/pdf/fjs15st.pdf.

12. Bradley Campbell, "England Abolished Grand Juries Decades Ago Because They Didn't Work," *World,* Dec. 4, 2014, theworld.org/stories/2014/12/04/england-abolished-grand-jury-system-decades-ago-because-it-didnt-work; Andrew D. Leipold, "Why Grand Juries Do Not (and Cannot) Protect the Accused," *Cornell Law Review* 80 (1995): 260–324.

13. Ben L. Trachtenberg, "No, You 'Stand Up': Why Prosecutors Should Stop Hiding Behind Grand Juries," *Missouri Law Review* 80, no. 4 (2015), scholarship.law.missouri.edu/mlr/vol80/iss4/12.

14. Ashley Payne, conversation with the author, Nov. 26, 2023.

15. "Voir Dire," in *The American Heritage Dictionary of the English Language* (HarperCollins, n.d.), www.ahdictionary.com/word/search.html?q=voir%20dire; Patricia T. O'Conner and Stewart Kellerman, "Voir Dire," *Grammarphobia* (blog), April 29, 2014, www.grammarphobia.com/blog/2014/04/voir-dire.html.

16. Woods, conversation with the author, Nov. 21, 2023.

17. Emmanuel Felton, "Many Juries in America Remain Mostly White, Prompting States to Take Action to Eliminate Racial Discrimination in Their Selection," *Washington Post,* Dec. 23, 2021.

18. Latin and Black adults are approximately three times as likely as white adults to lack a driver's license. Almost a quarter of Hispanic adults (24 percent) and roughly a fifth of Black adults (21 percent) don't have a driver's license, as opposed to 8 percent of white respondents. Michael J. Hanmer and Samuel B. Novey, "Who Lacked Photo ID in 2020? An Exploration of the American National Election Studies," Center for Democracy and Civic Engagement,

University of Maryland, March 13, 2023, www.voteriders.org/wp-content/uploads/2023/04/CDCE_VoteRiders_ANES2020Report_Spring2023.pdf.

19. Matt DeRienzo, "How a Jim Crow–Era Strategy Blocked 4.6 Million People from Voting in 2022," Center for Public Integrity, Dec. 8, 2022, publicintegrity .org/politics/elections/who-counts/how-a-jim-crow-era-strategy-blocked-4-6 -million-people-from-voting-in-2022/.

20. "14 states have not raised fees since 2000 when the cost of living was 39% less than today. Three states have not done so since the 1970s, and Washington State has not done so since 1957." Brendan W. Clark, "Juror Compensation in the United States," National Center for State Courts, April 2022, originally published by National Center for State Courts and available online, https://www .linkedin.com/posts/brendanwclark_ncsc-juror-compensation-report-activity -6926689538241171456-2qJf?utm_source=share&utm_medium=member _desktop&rcm=ACoAAEDO3jIB2o6TwJuLD-ECcC_tHoIRnLAjeqI.

21. Woods, conversation with the author, Nov. 21, 2023.

22. Ariel Gelrud Shiro et al., "Stuck on the Ladder: Intragenerational Wealth Mobility in the United States," Brookings Institution, June 2022, www.brookings .edu/wp-content/uploads/2022/06/2022_FMCI_IntragenerationalWealth Mobility_FINAL.pdf.

23. Mona Lynch and Craig Haney, "Mapping the Racial Bias of the White Male Capital Juror: Jury Composition and the 'Empathic Divide,'" *Law & Society Review* 45, no. 1 (2011): 69–102, doi.org/10.1111/j.1540-5893.2011.00428.x; Tara L. Mitchell et al., "Racial Bias in Mock Juror Decision-Making: A Meta-Analytic Review of Defendant Treatment," *Law and Human Behavior* 29, no. 6 (2005): 621–37, doi.org/10.1007/s10979-005-8122-9; Jennifer S. Hunt, "Race, Ethnicity, and Culture in Jury Decision Making," *Annual Review of Law and Social Science* 11, no. 1 (2015): 269–88, doi.org/10.1146/annurev-lawsocsci -120814-121723.

24. Liana Peter-Hagene, "Jurors' Cognitive Depletion and Performance During Jury Deliberation as a Function of Jury Diversity and Defendant Race," *Law and Human Behavior* 43, no. 3 (2019): 232–49, doi.org/10.1037/lhb0000332.

25. Michael Barba, "California to Allow People with Felony Convictions on Juries Beginning 2020," *San Francisco Examiner,* Dec. 29, 2019, www.sfexaminer.com/ archives/california-to-allow-people-with-felony-convictions-on-juries-beginning -2020/article_92c6bfa4-0615-533b-b484-172632ec27f0.html.

26. Ginger Jackson-Gleich, "Rigging the Jury: How Each State Reduces Jury Diversity by Excluding People with Criminal Records," Prison Policy Initiative, Feb. 18, 2021, www.prisonpolicy.org/reports/juryexclusion.html.

27. Jonathan M. Warren, "Hidden in Plain View: Juries and the Implicit Credibility Given to Police Testimony," *DePaul Journal for Social Justice* 11, no. 2 (2018): 1–32.

28. "Public Enemy," *Harper's Magazine,* Sept. 2017, harpers.org/archive/2017/09/public-enemy/.

29. Lau, "Police PR Machine Under Scrutiny for Inaccurate Reporting, Alleged Pro-Cop Bias."

30. *Batson v. Kentucky,* 476 U.S. 79 (1986).

31. "Illegal Racial Discrimination in Jury Selection: A Continuing Legacy," Equal Justice Initiative, Aug. 2010, eji.org/wp-content/uploads/2019/10/illegal-racial-discrimination-in-jury-selection.pdf.

32. Woods, conversation with the author, Nov. 21, 2023.

33. *Profile of the Legal Profession 2023.*

34. Daniel Epps and William Ortman, "The Informed Jury," *Vanderbilt Law Review* 75, no. 3 (2023): 823–90.

35. *Shannon v. United States,* 512 U.S. 573 (1994).

36. There are some limited exceptions. For example, in a death penalty case, if the prosecutor argues that a death sentence is necessary because an individual may be dangerous in the future, jurors must also be informed that the person could be held for life without parole. *Simmons v. South Carolina,* 512 U.S. 154, 114 S. Ct. 2187, 129 L. Ed. 2d 133 (1994).

37. Epps and Ortman, "Informed Jury."

38. Susan D. Rozelle, "Loading the Dice for Death: Structural Problems in Capital Punishment," *Texas Tech Law Review* 51 (2018): 45–56.

39. Craig Haney, Eileen L. Zurbriggen, and Joanna M. Weill, "The Continuing Unfairness of Death Qualification: Changing Death Penalty Attitudes and Capital Jury Selection," *Psychology, Public Policy, and Law* 28, no. 1 (2022): 1–31, doi.org/10.1037/law0000335.

40. Haney, Zurbriggen, and Weill, "Continuing Unfairness of Death Qualification."

41. *Atkins v. Virginia,* 536 U.S. 304 (2002).

42. Haney, Zurbriggen, and Weill, "Continuing Unfairness of Death Qualification."

43. Paul Butler, "In Defense of Jury Nullification," *Litigation* 31, no. 1 (2004): 46–49.

44. *Lawrence v. Texas,* 539 U.S. 558 (2003).

45. Epps and Ortman, "Informed Jury."

46. *Sparf and Hansen v. United States,* 156 U.S. 51 (1895).

47. Naomi Gilens, "It's Perfectly Constitutional to Talk About Jury Nullification," ACLU, Jan. 22, 2019, www.aclu.org/news/free-speech/its-perfectly-constitutional-talk-about-jury-nullification.

48. Noelle Phillips, "Denver Activists File Federal Lawsuit over Jury Nullification Arrests," *Denver Post,* April 22, 2016, www.denverpost.com/2015/08/17/denver-activists-file-federal-lawsuit-over-jury-nullification-arrests/; Janet Oravetz, "Colorado Supreme Court Sides with 2 Men Accused of Jury Tampering," KUSA-TV, Sept. 26, 2019, www.9news.com/article/news/local/

colorado-supreme-court-jury-tampering-ruling/73-5e6ad145-4c86-4265-8433
-d4f3712cbc81.

49. Woods, conversation with the author, Nov. 21, 2023.

Chapter 9: An Unwinnable Game

1. "Ride Home Program," Three Strikes Project, accessed Nov. 11, 2024, law
.stanford.edu/three-strikes-project/the-ride-home-program/.

2. Malcolme Muttaqee, conversation with the author, Jan. 18, 2024.

3. Amir Chapel, conversation with the author, May 22, 2024.

4. Many states reported not just more cops than counselors, but *two to three times*
as many police officers in schools as social workers. Another five states reported
more police officers in schools than school nurses. Amir Whitaker et al., "Cops
and No Counselors: How the Lack of School Mental Health Staff Is Harming
Students," American Civil Liberties Union, March 4, 2019, www.aclu.org/
publications/cops-and-no-counselors.

5. Whitaker et al., "Cops and No Counselors"; Sagen Kidane and Emily Rauscher,
"Unequal Exposure to School Resource Officers, by Student Race, Ethnicity,
and Income," Urban Institute, April 6, 2023, www.urban.org/research/
publication/unequal-exposure-school-resource-officers-student-race-ethnicity
-and-income.

6. Laura S. Abrams, Matthew L. Mizel, and Elizabeth S. Barnert, "Correction To:
The Criminalization of Young Children and Overrepresentation of Black Youth
in the Juvenile Justice System," *Race and Social Problems* 16, no. 1 (2024): 165,
doi.org/10.1007/s12552-021-09324-5; U.S. Department of Education,
"Suspensions and Expulsions in Public Schools," 2017–18 Civil Rights Data
Collection, Aug. 2022, civilrightsdata.ed.gov/assets/downloads/Suspensions_and
_Expulsion_Part2.pdf.

7. Kidane and Rauscher, "Unequal Exposure to School Resource Officers by
Student Race, Ethnicity, and Income"; Russell J. Skiba, Mariella I. Arredondo,
and Natasha T. Williams, "More Than a Metaphor: The Contribution of
Exclusionary Discipline to a School-to-Prison Pipeline," *Equity & Excellence in
Education* 47, no. 4 (2014): 546–64, doi.org/10.1080/10665684.2014.958965;
Paul Hemez, John J. Brent, and Thomas J. Mowen, "Exploring the School-to-
Prison Pipeline: How School Suspensions Influence Incarceration During
Young Adulthood," *Youth Violence and Juvenile Justice* 18, no. 3 (2020): 235–55,
doi.org/10.1177/1541204019880945.

8. Michael Rocque and Raymond Paternoster, "Understanding the Antecedents of
the 'School-to-Jail' Link: The Relationship Between Race and School Discipline,"
Journal of Criminal Law and Criminology 101, no. 2 (2011): 633–65; Josh Rovner,

"Black Disparities in Youth Incarceration," Sentencing Project, Dec. 2023, www.sentencingproject.org/app/uploads/2023/12/Black-Disparities-in-Youth -Incarceration.pdf.

9. "Study Shows Contact with Police May Be Detrimental to Health, Well-Being of Black Youth," Johns Hopkins Medicine, Sept. 7, 2021, www.hopkins medicine.org/news/newsroom/news-releases/study-shows-contact-with-police -may-be-detrimental-to-health-well-being-of-black-youth; Kenneth B. Nunn, "The Child as Other: Race and Differential Treatment in the Juvenile Justice System," *DePaul Law Review* 51, no. 3 (2002): 679–714.

10. Steven Raphael and Sandra V. Rozo, "Racial Disparities in the Acquisition of Juvenile Arrest Records," *Journal of Labor Economics* 37, no. S1 (2019): S125–59, doi.org/10.1086/701068.

11. Development Services Group Inc., "Racial and Ethnic Disparity (R/ED) in Juvenile Justice Processing," Office of Juvenile Justice and Delinquency Prevention, 2022, ojjdp.ojp.gov/model-programs-guide/literature-reviews/racial -and-ethnic-disparity.

12. Kristin N. Henning, "Criminalizing Normal Adolescent Behavior in Communities of Color: The Role of Prosecutors in Juvenile Justice Reform," SSRN, Aug. 15, 2012, doi.org/10.2139/ssrn.2128857; U.S. Department of Education, "Student Discipline and School Climate in U.S. Public Schools," 2020–21 Civil Rights Data Collection, Nov. 2023, www.ed.gov/sites/ed/files/ about/offices/list/ocr/docs/crdc-discipline-school-climate-report.pdf.

13. Corey Mitchell, Joe Yerardi, and Susan Ferriss, "Criminalizing Kids: When Schools Call Police on Kids," Center for Public Integrity, Sept. 8, 2021, publicintegrity.org/education/criminalizing-kids/police-in-schools-disparities; Abigail Kramer, "NYC Schools Handcuff and Haul Away Kids in Emotional Crisis," ProPublica and THE CITY, May 4, 2023, www.propublica.org/article/ nyc-schools-students-police-emotional-crisis-nypd.

14. Victor M. Rios, "The Hyper-Criminalization of Black and Latino Male Youth in the Era of Mass Incarceration," *Souls* 8, no. 2 (2006): 40–54, doi.org/10.1080/ 10999940600680457.

15. Adelaida Caballero, conversation with the author, June 9, 2024.

16. Mrozinski and Buetow, "Access to Counsel at First Appearance."

17. Caroline Wolf Harlow, "Prior Abuse Reported by Inmates and Probationers," Bureau of Justice Statistics, April 1999, bjs.ojp.gov/content/pub/pdf/parip.pdf.

18. Elizabeth Swavola, Kristine Riley, and Ram Subramanian, "Overlooked: Women and Jails in an Era of Reform," Vera Institute of Justice, Aug. 2016, www.vera .org/publications/overlooked-women-and-jails-report; Shannon M. Lynch et al., "Women's Pathways to Jail: The Roles & Intersections of Serious Mental Illness & Trauma," U.S. Department of Justice, Bureau of Justice Assistance, Sept. 2012, https://www.ojp.gov/ncjrs/virtual-library/abstracts/womens-pathways-jail -roles-intersections-serious-mental-illness.

19. Caballero, conversation with the author, June 9, 2024.

20. For more details on how our own prisons meet or exceed the horror of foreign prisons, just look at these recent detailed reports on state prison conditions: "Investigation of Georgia Prisons," U.S. Attorney's Offices for the Northern, Middle, and Southern Districts of Georgia, Oct. 1, 2024, www.justice.gov/crt/media/1371406/dl?utm_medium=email&utm_source=govdelivery; "Investigation of Alabama's State Prisons for Men," U.S. Attorney's Offices for the Northern, Middle, and Southern Districts of Alabama, April 2, 2019, www.splcenter.org/sites/default/files/documents/doj_investigation_of_alabama_state_prisons_for_men.pdf.

21. "Do Prisons Have Air Conditioning?," *Kent Online Degrees Blog* (blog), March 30, 2022, onlinedegrees.kent.edu/blog/do-prisons-have-air-conditioning.

22. "Overcrowding and Other Threats to Health and Safety," ACLU, accessed Nov. 6, 2024, www.aclu.org/issues/prisoners-rights/cruel-inhuman-and-degrading-conditions/overcrowding-and-other-threats-health; Leslie Soble, Kathryn Stroud, and Marika Weinstein, "Eating Behind Bars: Ending the Hidden Punishment of Food in Prison," Impact Justice, 2020, impactjustice.org/wp-content/uploads/IJ-Eating-Behind-Bars.pdf; Jessica Carns and Sam Weaver, "Two Cups of Broth and Rotting Sandwiches: The Reality of Mealtime in Prisons and Jails," ACLU, Nov. 23, 2022, www.aclu.org/news/prisoners-rights/the-reality-of-mealtime-in-prisons-and-jails.

23. "ACLU Seeks Court Order Against L.A. County over Horrific Conditions at Jail Facility," ACLU, Sept. 8, 2022, www.aclu.org/press-releases/aclu-seeks-court-order-against-la-county-over-horrific-conditions-jail-facility.

24. "Investigation of Alabama's State Prisons for Men"; Alund, " 'Eaten Alive by Insects' "; Ramos, "Cells at Illinois Prison Intake Facility in Joliet Infested with Vermin, Lawsuit Says."

25. "ACLU Seeks Court Order Against L.A. County over Horrific Conditions at Jail Facility"; "Investigation of Alabama's State Prisons for Men"; Zhen Zeng, "Jail Inmates in 2022—Statistical Tables," Bureau of Justice Statistics, Dec. 2023, bjs.ojp.gov/document/ji22st.pdf.

26. Eisen, "Violence Against People Behind Bars That We Don't See"; Johnson, "Senate Probe Found Some Federal Prison Staff Abused Female Inmates Without Discipline"; Williams, "Mentally Ill Inmates Are Routinely Physically Abused, Study Says."

27. Ian O'Donnell and Kimmett Edgar, "Fear in Prison," *Prison Journal* 79, no. 1 (1999): 90–99, doi.org/10.1177/0032885599079001006; Novisky and Peralta, "Gladiator School."

28. Novisky and Peralta, "Gladiator School."

29. Katie Rose Quandt and Alexi Jones, "Research Roundup: Incarceration Can Cause Lasting Damage to Mental Health," Prison Policy Initiative, May 13, 2021, www.prisonpolicy.org/blog/2021/05/13/mentalhealthimpacts/;

Timothy G. Edgemon and Jody Clay-Warner, "Inmate Mental Health and the Pains of Imprisonment," *Society and Mental Health* 9, no. 1 (2019): 33–50, doi .org/10.1177/2156869318785424; A. Goomany and T. Dickinson, "The Influence of Prison Climate on the Mental Health of Adult Prisoners: A Literature Review," *Journal of Psychiatric and Mental Health Nursing* 22, no. 6 (2015): 413–22, doi.org/10.1111/jpm.12231; Christine H. Lindquist and Charles A. Lindquist, "Gender Differences in Distress: Mental Health Consequences of Environmental Stress Among Jail Inmates," *Behavioral Sciences & the Law* 15, no. 4 (1997): 503–23, doi.org/10.1002/(SICI)1099-0798 (199723/09)15:4<503::AID-BSL281>3.0.CO;2-H.

30. "The mean predicted probability (.28) of suicide is 96% higher in minimum-security prisons with values one-half or more standard deviation units above the overcrowding mean compared to their counterparts at the other extreme (.01)." In other words, the probability of suicidality rises as overcrowding goes up. Meredith P. Huey and Thomas L. Mcnulty, "Institutional Conditions and Prison Suicide: Conditional Effects of Deprivation and Overcrowding," *Prison Journal* 85, no. 4 (2005): 490–514, doi.org/10.1177/0032885505282258; Edgemon and Clay-Warner, "Inmate Mental Health and the Pains of Imprisonment."

31. Chapel, conversation with the author, May 22, 2024.

32. Zeng, "Jail Inmates in 2022—Statistical Tables"; Melanie Close et al., "Understanding Trends in Jail Populations, 2014 to 2019: A Multi-Site Analysis," Data Collaborative for Justice at John Jay College, Dec. 2021, datacollaborativeforjustice.org/wp-content/uploads/2021/12/2021_12_12_DCJ -Cross-site-FINAL.pdf; Jake Horowitz and Tracy Velázquez, "Small but Growing Group Incarcerated for a Month or More Has Kept Jail Populations High," Pew Charitable Trusts, June 23, 2020, www.pewtrusts.org/en/research -and-analysis/articles/2020/06/23/small-but-growing-group-incarcerated-for-a -month-or-more-has-kept-jail-populations-high.

33. Zeng, "Jail Inmates in 2022—Statistical Tables"; Close et al., "Understanding Trends in Jail Populations, 2014 to 2019"; Chris Mai et al., "Broken Ground: Why America Keeps Building More Jails and What It Can Do Instead," Vera Institute of Justice, Nov. 2019, safetyandjusticechallenge.org/wp-content/uploads/2021/06/MacArthur-Jail-Construction_layout_FINAL2_111519_reduced-file -size.pdf.

34. Stemen, "Prison Paradox"; Heaton, Mayson, and Stevenson, "Downstream Consequences of Misdemeanor Pretrial Detention."

35. Lena J. Jäggi et al., "The Relationship Between Trauma, Arrest, and Incarceration History Among Black Americans: Findings from the National Survey of American Life," *Society and Mental Health* 6, no. 3 (2016): 187–206, doi.org/10.1177/2156869316641730.

36. The number of annual jail admissions includes multiple admissions of some individuals; it does not mean seven million unique individuals cycling through

jails in a year. Zeng, "Jail Inmates in 2022—Statistical Tables"; Sawyer and Wagner, "Mass Incarceration."

37. The total number of jail admissions (7,300,000) was divided by the total number of people admitted to prison (469,200) in 2022. Zeng, "Jail Inmates in 2022—Statistical Tables"; E. Ann Carson and Rich Kluckow, "Prisoners in 2022—Statistical Tables," Bureau of Justice Statistics, Nov. 2023, bjs.ojp.gov/document/p22st.pdf.

38. Leah Wang, "Chronic Punishment: The Unmet Health Needs of People in State Prisons," Prison Policy Initiative, June 2022, www.prisonpolicy.org/reports/chronicpunishment.html; Sharyn Adams, Jaclyn Houston-Kolnik, and Jessica Reichert, "Trauma-Informed and Evidence-Based Practices and Programs to Address Trauma in Correctional Settings," Illinois Criminal Justice Information Authority, July 25, 2017, icjia.illinois.gov/researchhub/articles/trauma-informed-and-evidence-based-practices-and-programs-to-address-trauma-in-correctional-settings; "Table 2. 12-Month Prevalence of DSM-IV/WMH-CIDI Disorders by Sex and Cohort," Department of Health Care Policy, Harvard Medical School, July 19, 2007, www.hcp.med.harvard.edu/ncs/ftpdir/NCS-R_12-month_Prevalence_Estimates.pdf.

39. Novisky and Peralta, "Gladiator School."

40. "Restricted Housing," Federal Bureau of Prisons, accessed June 30, 2024, www.bop.gov/about/statistics/statistics_inmate_shu.jsp; Montagnet, Peirce, and Pitts, "Mapping U.S. Jails' Use of Restrictive Housing."

41. Anna Conley, "Torture in US Jails and Prisons: An Analysis of Solitary Confinement Under International Law," *Vienna Journal on International Constitutional Law* 7, no. 4 (2013): 415–53.

42. Conley, "Torture in US Jails and Prisons"; "Restrictive Housing in the U.S.: Issues, Challenges, and Future Directions," National Institute of Justice, Nov. 2016, perma.cc/YK5Y-9MXZ.

43. Conley, "Torture in US Jails and Prisons"; Montagnet, Peirce, and Pitts, "Mapping U.S. Jails' Use of Restrictive Housing"; Andreea Matei, "Solitary Confinement in US Prisons," Urban Institute, Aug. 2022, www.urban.org/sites/default/files/2022-08/Solitary%20Confinement%20in%20the%20US.pdf; "The United Nations Standard Minimum Rules for the Treatment of Prisoners (the Nelson Mandela Rules)," United Nations Office on Drugs and Crime, n.d., www.unodc.org/documents/justice-and-prison-reform/Nelson_Mandela_Rules-E-ebook.pdf.

44. Dan Nolan and Chris Amico, "Solitary: By the Numbers," *Frontline*, April 18, 2017, apps.frontline.org/solitary-by-the-numbers/.

45. James and Vanko, "Impacts of Solitary Confinement"; Lauren Brinkley-Rubinstein et al., "Association of Restrictive Housing During Incarceration with Mortality After Release," *JAMA Network Open* 2, no. 10 (2019), doi.org/10.1001/jamanetworkopen.2019.12516.

46. Chapel, conversation with the author, May 22, 2024.

47. Carns and Weaver, "Two Cups of Broth and Rotting Sandwiches"; "Cold, Rotten, and Moldy Meals: Food Oppression in Orange County Jails," Stop the Musick Coalition, accessed via www.stopthemusick.net/wp-content/uploads/2021/12/Food-Conditions.pdf, Dec. 15, 2021 (website inactive as of this writing).

48. "Older people make up five times as much of the prison population as they did three decades ago." Emily Widra, "The Aging Prison Population: Causes, Costs, and Consequences," Prison Policy Initiative, Aug. 2, 2023, www.prisonpolicy.org/blog/2023/08/02/aging/.

49. Ashley Nellis and Savannah En, "No End in Sight: America's Enduring Reliance on Life Sentences," Sentencing Project, Feb. 17, 2021, www.sentencingproject.org/reports/no-end-in-sight-americas-enduring-reliance-on-life-sentences/; Damon M. Petrich et al., "Custodial Sanctions and Reoffending: A Meta-Analytic Review," *Crime and Justice* 50, no. 1 (2021): 353–424, doi.org/10.1086/715100; "Five Things About Deterrence," National Institute of Justice, May 2016, www.ojp.gov/pdffiles1/nij/247350.pdf.

50. "Five Things About Deterrence."

51. Rone Tempest, "Death Row Often Means a Long Life," *Los Angeles Times,* March 6, 2005, www.latimes.com/archives/la-xpm-2005-mar-06-me-deathpen6-story.html; "Final Report," California Commission on the Fair Administration of Justice, 2008, digitalcommons.law.scu.edu/cgi/viewcontent.cgi?article=1000&context=ncippubs.

52. "CPI Inflation Calculator," Bureau of Labor Statistics, accessed Nov. 6, 2024, data.bls.gov/cgi-bin/cpicalc.pl.

53. Nellis and En, "No End in Sight"; Petrich et al., "Custodial Sanctions and Reoffending"; "Five Things About Deterrence."

54. Petrich et al., "Custodial Sanctions and Reoffending"; Francis T. Cullen, Cheryl Lero Jonson, and Daniel S. Nagin, "Prisons Do Not Reduce Recidivism: The High Cost of Ignoring Science," supplement, *Prison Journal* 91, no. 3 (2011): 48S–65S, doi.org/10.1177/0032885511415224.

55. Stemen, "Prison Paradox."

56. Timothy Hughes and Doris James Wilson, "Reentry Trends in the United States," Bureau of Justice Statistics, April 14, 2004, bjs.ojp.gov/content/pub/pdf/reentry.pdf.

57. Evelyn J. Patterson, "The Dose–Response of Time Served in Prison on Mortality: New York State, 1989–2003," *American Journal of Public Health* 103, no. 3 (2013): 523–28, doi.org/10.2105/AJPH.2012.301148.

58. Novisky and Peralta, "Gladiator School"; Leah Wang and Wendy Sawyer, "New Data: State Prisons Are Increasingly Deadly Places," Prison Policy Initiative, June 8, 2021, www.prisonpolicy.org/blog/2021/06/08/prison_mortality/.

59. Andrew P. Wilper et al., "The Health and Health Care of US Prisoners: Results of a Nationwide Survey," *American Journal of Public Health* 99, no. 4 (2009): 666–72, doi.org/10.2105/AJPH.2008.144279; Solomon Moore, "Using Muscle to Improve Health Care for Prisoners," *New York Times,* Aug. 27, 2007.

60. Christine Mitchell and Amber Akemi Piatt, "From Crisis to Care: Ending the Health Harm of Women's Prisons," Human Impact Partners, Feb. 2023, humanimpact.org/wp-content/uploads/2023/02/HIP-From-Crisis-to-Care-02 -2023.pdf.

61. Wang, "Chronic Punishment"; "Clinical Overview of Hepatitis C," U.S. Centers for Disease Control and Prevention, Nov. 7, 2023, www.cdc.gov/hepatitis-c/ hcp/clinical-overview/index.html.

62. Wang, "Chronic Punishment."

63. Emily A. Wang et al., "Cardiovascular Disease in Incarcerated Populations," *Journal of the American College of Cardiology* 69, no. 24 (2017): 2967–76, doi .org/10.1016/j.jacc.2017.04.040.

64. The percentage of prisoners with heart-related problems (9.8 percent) was divided by the percentage of the population with heart-related problems (2.9 percent). Wang et al., "Cardiovascular Disease in Incarcerated Populations."

65. The percentage of prisoners who had a stroke (1.8 percent) was divided by the percentage of the population who had a stroke (0.7 percent). Wang et al., "Cardiovascular Disease in Incarcerated Populations."

66. The percentage of prisoners with disabilities (38 percent) was divided by the percentage of the population with disabilities (12.8 percent). Laura M. Maruschak, Jennifer Bronson, and Mariel Alper, "Disabilities Reported by Prisoners," Bureau of Justice Statistics, March 2021, bjs.ojp.gov/content/pub/ pdf/drpspi16st.pdf; W. Erickson, S. von Schrader, and C. Lee, "2016 Disability Status Report: United States," Cornell University, Yang-Tan Institute on Employment and Disability, Feb. 6, 2018, advancingstates.org/index.php/hcbs/ article/2016-disability-status-report-united-states.

67. Wang, "Chronic Punishment"; Laura M. Maruschak, Jennifer Bronson, and Mariel Alper, "Indicators of Mental Health Problems Reported by Prisoners," Bureau of Justice Statistics, June 2021, bjs.ojp.gov/sites/g/files/xyckuh236/files/ media/document/imhprpspi16st.pdf.

68. "Fast Facts: Health and Economic Costs of Chronic Conditions," U.S. Centers for Disease Control and Prevention, July 12, 2024, www.cdc.gov/chronic-disease/ data-research/facts-stats/?CDC_AAref_Val=www.cdc.gov/chronicdisease/about/ costs/index.htm.

69. The average annual cost of health care was divided by the total average annual cost to incarcerate a person. "How Much Does It Cost to Incarcerate an Inmate? California's Annual Costs to Incarcerate an Inmate in Prison," Legislative Analyst's Office, accessed Jan. 2022, lao.ca.gov/PolicyAreas/CJ/6_cj_inmatecost.

70. Kristie B. Hadden et al., "Health Literacy Among a Formerly Incarcerated Population Using Data from the Transitions Clinic Network," *Journal of Urban Health* 95, no. 4 (2018): 547–55, doi.org/10.1007/s11524-018-0276-0.

71. Joseph W. Frank et al., "Increased Hospital and Emergency Department Utilization by Individuals with Recent Criminal Justice Involvement: Results of a National Survey," *Journal of General Internal Medicine* 29, no. 9 (2014): 1226–33, doi.org/10.1007/s11606-014-2877-y.

72. "Captive Labor: Exploitation of Incarcerated Workers," ACLU and the University of Chicago Law School Global Human Rights Clinic, June 15, 2022, www.aclu.org/publications/captive-labor-exploitation-incarcerated-workers?redirect=captivelabor.

73. Wagner and Bertram, "State of Phone Justice 2022."

74. Stephen Raher, "The Company Store: A Deeper Look at Prison Commissaries," Prison Policy Initiative, May 2018, www.prisonpolicy.org/reports/commissary.html; Elizabeth Weill-Greenberg and Ethan Corey, "Locked In, Priced Out: How Prison Commissary Price-Gouging Preys on the Incarcerated," *Appeal,* April 17, 2024, theappeal.org/locked-in-priced-out-how-much-prison-commissary-prices/; Amanda Rabines, "Rising Commissary Prices in Florida Prisons Lead to Boycotts, Outcry," *Tampa Bay Times,* Oct. 23, 2023, www.tampabay.com/news/crime/2023/10/23/florida-prison-commissary-price-increase-snack-food-toiletries-sold-keefe/.

75. Bianca Tylek, email to the author, July 15, 2024.

76. Annie Harper et al., "Debt, Incarceration, and Re-Entry: A Scoping Review," *American Journal of Criminal Justice* 46, no. 2 (2021): 250–78, doi.org/10.1007/s12103-020-09559-9.

77. Darrel Thompson and Ashley Burnside, "No More Double Punishments: Lifting the Ban on SNAP and TANF for People with Prior Felony Drug Convictions," Center for Law and Social Policy, April 19, 2022, www.clasp.org/publications/report/brief/no-more-double-punishments/.

78. 13 C.F.R. § 124.108(a)(4)(ii).

79. Marina Duane et al., "Criminal Background Checks," Urban Institute, Nov. 2017, www.urban.org/sites/default/files/publication/88621/2001174_criminal_background_checks_impact_on_employment_and_recidivism_2.pdf.

80. Terry-Ann Craigie et al., "Conviction, Imprisonment, and Lost Earnings: How Involvement with the Criminal Justice System Deepens Inequality," Brennan Center for Justice, Sept. 15, 2020, www.brennancenter.org/our-work/research-reports/conviction-imprisonment-and-lost-earnings-how-involvement-criminal.

81. Michelle Natividad Rodriguez and Beth Avery, "Unlicensed & Untapped: Removing Barriers to State Occupational Licenses for People with Records," National Employment Law Project, April 2016, www.nelp.org/app/uploads/2016/06/Unlicensed-Untapped-Removing-Barriers-State-Occupational-Licenses.pdf.

82. Mark T. Berg and Beth M. Huebner, "Reentry and the Ties That Bind: An Examination of Social Ties, Employment, and Recidivism," *Justice Quarterly* 28, no. 2 (2011): 382–410, doi.org/10.1080/07418825.2010.498383; John M. Nally et al., "Post-Release Recidivism and Employment Among Different Types of Released Offenders," *International Journal of Criminal Justice Sciences* 9, no. 1 (2014): 16–34.

83. Chelsea Thomson et al., "Investing Justice Resources to Address Community Needs: Lessons Learned from Colorado's Work and Gain Education and Employment Skills (WAGEES) Program," Urban Institute, Feb. 2018, www.urban.org/sites/default/files/publication/96341/investing_justice_resources_to_address_community_needs.pdf.

84. Kim Steven Hunt and Robert Dumville, "Recidivism Among Federal Offenders: A Comprehensive Overview," U.S. Sentencing Commission, March 2016, www.ussc.gov/sites/default/files/pdf/research-and-publications/research-publications/2016/recidivism_overview.pdf; Leonardo Antenangeli and Matthew R. Durose, "Recidivism of Prisoners Released in 24 States in 2008: A 10-Year Follow-Up Period (2008–2018)," Bureau of Justice Statistics, Sept. 2021, bjs.ojp.gov/sites/g/files/xyckuh236/files/media/document/rpr24s0810yfup0818.pdf.

85. Christy Visher, Sara Debus, and Jennifer Yahner, "Employment After Prison: A Longitudinal Study of Releasees in Three States," Urban Institute, Oct. 2008, www.urban.org/sites/default/files/publication/32106/411778-Employment-after-Prison-A-Longitudinal-Study-of-Releasees-in-Three-States.pdf.

86. Craigie et al., "Conviction, Imprisonment, and Lost Earnings."

87. Ames Grawert and Terry-Ann Craigie, "Economic Struggles Worsened Under COVID-19 Already Existed Under Mass Incarceration," *USA Today*, Oct. 29, 2020.

88. Breanne Pleggenkuhle, "The Financial Cost of a Criminal Conviction: Context and Consequences," *Criminal Justice and Behavior* 45, no. 1 (2018): 121–45, doi.org/10.1177/0093854817734278.

89. "Under Pressure"; Thomas J. Mowen, Richard Stansfield, and John H. Boman IV, "Family Matters: Moving Beyond 'If' Family Support Matters to 'Why' Family Support Matters During Reentry from Prison," *Journal of Research in Crime and Delinquency* 56, no. 4 (2019): 483–523, doi.org/10.1177/0022427818820902.

90. Karin D. Martin et al., "Monetary Sanctions: Legal Financial Obligations in US Systems of Justice," *Annual Review of Criminology* 1, no. 1 (2018): 471–95, doi.org/10.1146/annurev-criminol-032317-091915.

91. Alex R. Piquero and Wesley G. Jennings, "Research Note: Justice System–Imposed Financial Penalties Increase the Likelihood of Recidivism in a Sample of Adolescent Offenders," *Youth Violence and Juvenile Justice* 15, no. 3 (2017): 325–40, doi.org/10.1177/1541204016669213.

92. "Under Pressure."

93. Pleggenkuhle, "Financial Cost of a Criminal Conviction."

94. Martin et al., "Monetary Sanctions"; Annie Harper, Tommaso Bardelli, and Stacey Barrenger, " 'Let Me Be Bill-Free': Consumer Debt in the Shadow of Incarceration," *Sociological Perspectives* 63, no. 6 (2020): 978–1001, doi.org/10 .1177/0731121420968124.

95. Muttaqee, conversation with the author, Jan. 18, 2024.

96. Leah Wang and Wanda Bertram, "New Data on Formerly Incarcerated People's Employment Reveal Labor Market Injustices," Prison Policy Initiative, Feb. 8, 2022, www.prisonpolicy.org/blog/2022/02/08/employment/.

97. Emmett Sanders, "No Release: Parole Grant Rates Have Plummeted in Most States Since the Pandemic Started," Prison Policy Initiative, Oct. 16, 2023, www.prisonpolicy.org/blog/2023/10/16/parole-grants/; Mariel E. Alper, "By the Numbers: Parole Release and Revocation Across 50 States," University of Minnesota Robina Institute of Criminal Law and Criminal Justice, 2016, perma .cc/Q9ZL-9MHY.

98. Beth Schwartzapfel, "Nine Things You Probably Didn't Know About Parole," Marshall Project, July 10, 2015, www.themarshallproject.org/2015/07/10/nine -things-you-probably-didn-t-know-about-parole.

99. Kimberly Thomas and Paul Reingold, "From Grace to Grids: Rethinking Due Process Protections for Parole," *Journal of Criminal Law & Criminology* 107, no. 2 (2017): 213–51.

100. Thomas and Reingold, "From Grace to Grids"; "ACLU Finds Parole Nearly Impossible for Prisoners Who Committed Serious Crimes as Youth," ACLU, Nov. 29, 2016, www.aclu.org/press-releases/aclu-finds-parole-nearly-impossible -prisoners-who-committed-serious-crimes-youth; "Frequently Asked Questions," U.S. Parole Commission, Aug. 23, 2023, www.justice.gov/uspc/frequently-asked -questions.

101. Schwartzapfel, "Nine Things You Probably Didn't Know About Parole."

102. "ACLU Finds Parole Nearly Impossible for Prisoners Who Committed Serious Crimes as Youth."

103. Gina Barton, "Release Programs for Sick and Elderly Prisoners Could Save Millions. But States Rarely Use Them," *Milwaukee Journal Sentinel,* April 18, 2018, projects.jsonline.com/news/2018/4/18/release-programs-for-sick-elderly -prisoners-could-save-millions.html.

104. "Parole Watch Report," ACLU Alabama, 2023, static1.squarespace.com/static/ 5ff49b04c6eb3c3de1ae3d62/t/6509f6ee0c9f4018aba7044b/1695151897728/ Parole+Watch+Report+2023.pdf.

105. "50 State Survey: Probation and Parole Fees," Fines and Fees Justice Center & Reform Alliance, May 2022, finesandfeesjusticecenter.org/content/uploads/ 2022/05/Probation-and-Parole-Fees-Survey-Final-2022-.pdf; Shalia Dewan,

"Probation May Sound Light, but Punishments Can Land Hard," *New York Times,* Aug. 2, 2015.

106. Dewan, "Probation May Sound Light, but Punishments Can Land Hard"; Ronald P. Corbett Jr., "The Burdens of Leniency: The Changing Face of Probation," *Minnesota Law Review* 99 (2015): 1697–732.

107. 42 USC §1437d.

108. "Under 18 U.S.C. § 3563(b)(13), the court may provide that the defendant 'reside in a specified place or area, or refrain from residing in a specified place or area.'" "Chapter 3: Location Monitoring (Probation and Supervised Release Conditions)," U.S. Courts, accessed Nov. 6, 2024, www.uscourts.gov/services -forms/location-monitoring-probation-supervised-release-conditions; Wes Vaughan, "How Parole Conditions Trapped Me in Homelessness," *Appeal,* May 9, 2023, theappeal.org/parole-post-prison-supervision-homelessness/.

109. Corbett, "Burdens of Leniency"; "Press Release: National Examination of Probation & Parole Fees Finds Widespread Imposition in Nearly All 50 States," Fines and Fees Justice Center, May 10, 2022, finesandfeesjusticecenter.org/ 2022/05/10/press-release-national-examination-of-probation-parole-fees-finds -widespread-imposition-in-nearly-all-50-states/.

110. "Press Release: National Examination of Probation & Parole Fees Finds Widespread Imposition in Nearly All 50 States."

111. "Press Release: National Examination of Probation & Parole Fees Finds Widespread Imposition in Nearly All 50 States"; Nathan W. Link, "Criminal Justice Debt During the Prisoner Reintegration Process: Who Has It and How Much?," *Criminal Justice and Behavior* 46, no. 1 (2019): 154–72, doi.org/10 .1177/0093854818790291.

112. Link, "Criminal Justice Debt During the Prisoner Reintegration Process."

113. "50 State Survey: Probation and Parole Fees."

114. Weisburd, "Electronic Prisons."

115. "Overview of Probation and Supervised Release Conditions," Administrative Office of the United States Courts, July 2024, www.uscourts.gov/sites/ default/files/overview_of_probation_and_supervised_release_conditions _0.pdf.

116. Sawyer and Wagner, "Mass Incarceration"; "Criminal Records and Reentry Toolkit," *The National Conference of State Legislatures* (blog), March 31, 2023, www.ncsl.org/civil-and-criminal-justice/criminal-records-and-reentry-toolkit; Matthew Friedman, "Just Facts: As Many Americans Have Criminal Records as College Diplomas," Brennan Center for Justice, Nov. 17, 2015, www.brennan center.org/our-work/analysis-opinion/just-facts-many-americans-have-criminal -records-college-diplomas.

117. Quandt and Jones, "Research Roundup: Incarceration Can Cause Lasting Damage to Mental Health."

118. "ARC 2023 Impact Report," Anti-Recidivism Coalition, 2023, antirecidivism .org/wp-content/uploads/2024/05/ARC-Report-ver_FINAL.pdf.

119. Jessica Saunders et al., "More Community, Less Confinement," Council of State Governments, Sept. 2021, csgjusticecenter.org/publications/more-community -less-confinement/national-report/.

120. "Confined and Costly," Council of State Governments, June 2019, csgjustice center.org/wp-content/uploads/2020/01/confined-and-costly.pdf.

121. "Confined and Costly."

122. Leah Wang, "Punishment Beyond Prisons 2023: Incarceration and Supervision by State," Prison Policy Initiative, May 2023, www.prisonpolicy.org/reports/ correctionalcontrol2023.html.

123. Ryan Sakoda, "Abolish or Reform? An Analysis of Post-Release Supervision for Low-Level Offenders," SSRN, Dec. 20, 2023, doi.org/10.2139/ssrn.4670939.

124. Jennifer Doleac, "Ryan Sakoda," *Probable Causation,* accessed Nov. 11, 2024, www.probablecausation.com/podcasts/episode-106-ryan-sakoda.

125. Ryan Sakoda, email to the author, Feb. 29, 2024.

126. Doleac, "Ryan Sakoda."

127. Notably, Adelaida isn't referring to a class for survivors of violence; she was required to take a class that treated her as if she had been the abuser.

128. Caballero, conversation with the author, June 9, 2024.

129. Michael Hartman, "Ban the Box: Policy Snapshot," National Conference of State Legislatures, June 2021, documents.ncsl.org/wwwncsl/Criminal-Justice/ Ban-the-Box-Policy-Snapshot.pdf.

130. "2021 Getting Talent Back to Work Report," Charles Koch Institute, SHRM, and SHRM Foundation, 2021, www.gettingtalentbacktowork.org/wp-content/ uploads/2021/05/2021-GTBTW_Report.pdf.

131. Caballero, conversation with the author, June 9, 2024.

132. Chapel, conversation with the author, May 22, 2024.

133. Christy A. Visher and Shannon M. E. Courtney, "One Year Out: Experiences of Prisoners Returning to Cleveland," Urban Institute, April 2007, www.urban .org/sites/default/files/publication/43021/311445-One-Year-Out-Experiences-of -Prisoners-Returning-to-Cleveland.pdf.

134. Danielle Wallace et al., "Examining the Role of Familial Support During Prison and After Release on Post-Incarceration Mental Health," *International Journal of Offender Therapy and Comparative Criminology* 60, no. 1 (2016): 3–20, doi.org/ 10.1177/0306624X14548023.

135. Mowen, Stansfield, and Boman, "Family Matters."

136. Jennifer E. Cobbina, Beth M. Huebner, and Mark T. Berg, "Men, Women, and Postrelease Offending: An Examination of the Nature of the Link Between Relational Ties and Recidivism," *Crime & Delinquency* 58, no. 3 (2012): 331–61, doi.org/10.1177/0011128710382348; John H. Boman IV and Thomas J. Mowen, "Building the Ties That Bind, Breaking the Ties That Don't:

Family Support, Criminal Peers, and Reentry Success," *Criminology & Public Policy* 16, no. 3 (2017): 753–74, doi.org/10.1111/1745-9133.12307.

137. Berg and Huebner, "Reentry and the Ties That Bind."
138. Chapel, conversation with the author, May 22, 2024.
139. Chapel, conversation with the author, May 22, 2024.
140. Muttaqee, conversation with the author, Jan. 18, 2024.
141. Obviously, that is not his real name—I'm a lawyer.
142. Antenangeli and Durose, "Recidivism of Prisoners Released in 24 States in 2008."
143. Chapel, conversation with the author, May 22, 2024.

Chapter 10: Redefine Success

1. Leslie Harris, conversation with the author, Aug. 28, 2024.
2. Gabriel Petek, "Assessing the Provision of Criminal Indigent Defense," Legislative Analyst's Office, Sept. 2022, lao.ca.gov/Publications/Report/4623.
3. Shirley Weber, "Juries: Peremptory Challenges," Pub. L. No. AB-3070, § 231.7, Code of Civil Procedure, relating to juries (2020), leginfo.legislature.ca.gov/faces/billTextClient.xhtml?bill_id=201920200AB3070.
4. Paul T. Rosynsky, "Jurors to Receive Increased Compensation for Service," Superior Court of California, County of Alameda, Aug. 29, 2024, www.alameda.courts.ca.gov/news/jurors-receive-increased-compensation-service.
5. Hoang Pham and Amira Dehmani, "The California Racial Justice Act of 2020, Explained," *Stanford Center for Racial Justice* (blog), April 22, 2024, law.stanford.edu/2024/04/22/the-california-racial-justice-act-of-2020-explained.
6. Muller and Roehrkasse, "Falling Racial Inequality and Rising Educational Inequality in US Prison Admissions for Drug, Violent, and Property Crimes."
7. Amanda Hernández, "Greater Focus on Crime Sparks Another Wave of Juvenile Justice Bills," Stateline, May 31, 2024, stateline.org/2024/05/31/greater-focus-on-crime-sparks-another-wave-of-juvenile-justice-bills/; Cary London, "Out with the Old Law: Why Criminal Responsibility Should Start at 25," *New York Law Journal,* March 20, 2023, www.law.com/newyorklawjournal/2023/03/20/out-with-the-old-law-why-criminal-responsibility-should-start-at-25/?slreturn=20241028114745.
8. "Age and Mental Status of Exonerated Defendants Who Confessed"; Krinsky and Reimer, "Children Deserve Protections That Too Many Aren't Getting in the US Justice System."
9. Kassin, "False Confessions."
10. Lisa Pilnik and Marcy Mistrett, "If Not the Adult System Then Where? Alternatives to Adult Incarceration for Youth Certified as Adults," 2019. On file with author.

11. Sawyer and Wagner, "Mass Incarceration."

12. Lawrence W. Sherman and Heather Strang, "Restorative Justice: The Evidence," Smith Institute, 2007, www.iirp.edu/images/pdf/RJ_full_report.pdf.

13. Sawyer and Wagner, "Mass Incarceration."

14. Jennifer Bronson et al., "Drug Use, Dependence, and Abuse Among State Prisoners and Jail Inmates, 2007–2009," Bureau of Justice Statistics, 2017, bjs .ojp.gov/content/pub/pdf/dudaspji0709.pdf.

15. Beth Schwartzapfel and Jimmy Jenkins, "Overdose Deaths in State Prisons Have Jumped Dramatically Since 2001," NPR, July 15, 2021.

16. Kassandra Frederique, conversation with the author, Aug. 7, 2024.

17. Erin Collins, "The Problem of Problem-Solving Courts," SSRN, Dec. 9, 2019, doi.org/10.2139/ssrn.3492003.

18. Richard C. Boldt, "Problem-Solving Courts," in *Pretrial and Trial Processes,* ed. Erik Luna (Arizona State University, 2017), 273–304, law.asu.edu/sites/default/ files/pdf/academy_for_justice/Reforming-Criminal-Justice_Vol_3.pdf.

19. *City of Grants Pass v. Johnson,* 603 U.S. 520 (2024).

20. Alex S. Vitale, *The End of Policing* (Verso, 2017).

21. The American Hospital Association reported 920,531 staffed hospital beds in 2022. In 2022, there were a total of 915,900 jail beds, and the total number of beds prisons held was 671,189 for a total of 1,587,089 beds. Twenty-two states did not provide the rated capacity of prisons, so the total count of beds is an underestimate. Carson and Kluckow, "Prisoners in 2022—Statistical Tables"; "Fast-Facts on U.S. Hospitals, 2022," American Hospital Association, accessed Nov. 7, 2024, www.aha.org/system/files/media/file/2022/01/fast-facts-on-US -hospitals-2022.pdf; Zeng, "Jail Inmates in 2022—Statistical Tables."

22. Harris Poll, "2022 Access to Care Survey Results," National Council for Mental Wellbeing, May 11, 2022, www.thenationalcouncil.org/resources/2022-access -to-care-survey-results/.

23. "Psychologists Reaching Their Limits as Patients Present with Worsening Symptoms Year After Year," American Psychological Association, accessed Nov. 7, 2024, www.apa.org/pubs/reports/practitioner/2023-psychologist-reach-limits.

24. Anand Satiani et al., "Projected Workforce of Psychiatrists in the United States: A Population Analysis," *Psychiatric Services* 69, no. 6 (2018): 710–13, doi.org/10 .1176/appi.ps.201700344; Stacy Weiner, "A Growing Psychiatrist Shortage and an Enormous Demand for Mental Health Services," Association of American Medical Colleges, Aug. 9, 2022, www.aamc.org/news/growing-psychiatrist -shortage-enormous-demand-mental-health-services.

25. Special thanks to my student Cassidy Rea, who highlighted this disparity for me in her research. National Treatment Court Resource Center, "Treatment Court Maps," Dec. 31, 2023, ntcrc.org/maps/interactive-maps/.

26. Brandon del Pozo et al., "Beyond Decriminalization: Ending the War on Drugs Requires Recasting Police Discretion Through the Lens of a Public Health

Ethic," *American Journal of Bioethics* 21, no. 4 (2021): 41–44, doi.org/10.1080/15265161.2021.1891339.

27. Aaron Chalfin, Brandon del Pozo, and David Mitre-Becerril, "Overdose Prevention Centers, Crime, and Disorder in New York City," *JAMA Network Open* 6, no. 11 (2023), doi.org/10.1001/jamanetworkopen.2023.42228; Chloé Potier et al., "Supervised Injection Services: What Has Been Demonstrated? A Systematic Literature Review," *Drug and Alcohol Dependence* 145 (Dec. 2014): 48–68, doi.org/10.1016/j.drugalcdep.2014.10.012; Timothy W. Levengood et al., "Supervised Injection Facilities as Harm Reduction: A Systematic Review," *American Journal of Preventive Medicine* 61, no. 5 (2021): 738–49, doi.org/10.1016/j.amepre.2021.04.017.

28. "Drug Consumption Rooms: An Overview of Provision and Evidence," European Monitoring Centre for Drugs and Drug Addiction, July 6, 2018, www.euda.europa.eu/publications/pods/drug-consumption-rooms_en; Maura McGinnity, "What Should the US Learn from New York's and Portugal's Approaches to the Opioid Crisis?," *AMA Journal of Ethics* 26, no. 7 (2024): 509–90.

29. McGinnity, "What Should the US Learn from New York's and Portugal's Approaches to the Opioid Crisis?"; Gregory Shea, "Is Portugal's Drug Decriminalization a Failure or Success? The Answer Isn't So Simple," *Knowledge at Wharton*, Sept. 5, 2023, knowledge.wharton.upenn.edu/article/is-portugals-drug-decriminalization-a-failure-or-success-the-answer-isnt-so-simple/.

30. Frederique, conversation with the author, Aug. 7, 2024.

31. Liam Sigaud et al., "Drug Decriminalization, Public Health, and Crime: Evidence from Oregon," SSRN, May 31, 2024, doi.org/10.2139/ssrn.4849348.

32. Kellen Russoniello et al., "Decriminalization of Drug Possession in Oregon: Analysis and Early Lessons," *Drug Science, Policy, and Law* 9 (Jan. 2023), doi.org/10.1177/20503245231167407.

33. Sigaud et al., "Drug Decriminalization, Public Health, and Crime."

34. Frederique, conversation with the author, Aug. 7, 2024.

35. Sigaud et al., "Drug Decriminalization, Public Health, and Crime."

36. Russoniello et al., "Decriminalization of Drug Possession in Oregon"; Michael J. Zoorob et al., "Drug Decriminalization, Fentanyl, and Fatal Overdoses in Oregon," *JAMA Network Open* 7, no. 9 (2024), doi.org/10.1001/jamanetworkopen.2024.31612.

37. Zoorob et al., "Drug Decriminalization, Fentanyl, and Fatal Overdoses in Oregon"; Charles Fain Lehman, "Drug Policing in the 21st Century: Concepts and Strategies for Policing the New Drug Crisis," Manhattan Institute, May 2024, media4.manhattan-institute.org/wp-content/uploads/drug-policing-in-the-21st-century.pdf#page=18.

38. Sigaud et al., "Drug Decriminalization, Public Health, and Crime."

39. Boldt, "Problem-Solving Courts"; Eric L. Sevigny, Brian K. Fuleihan, and Frank V. Ferdik, "Do Drug Courts Reduce the Use of Incarceration? A Meta-Analysis,"

Journal of Criminal Justice 41, no. 6 (2013): 416–25, doi.org/10.1016/j.jcrimjus
.2013.06.005.

40. Boldt, "Problem-Solving Courts."
41. Collins, "Problem of Problem-Solving Courts."
42. Kenny Cooper, "A Group of 20-Somethings in Delco Is Sparking a 'Public
Defense Renaissance,'" WHYY, March 4, 2024, whyy.org/articles/delaware
-county-public-defenders-partners-for-justice-diversion-improvements/.

Chapter 11: Sunlight Is the Best Disinfectant

1. Wendy Sawyer, "Since You Asked: Is It Me, or Is the Government Releasing Less
Data About the Criminal Justice System?," Prison Policy Initiative, Nov. 14,
2019, www.prisonpolicy.org/blog/2019/11/14/criminal-justice-data/.
2. Sawyer and Wagner, "Mass Incarceration"; Weihua Li and Jasmyne Ricard, "4
Reasons We Should Worry About Missing Crime Data," Marshall Project, July 13,
2023, www.themarshallproject.org/2023/07/13/fbi-crime-rates-data-gap-nibrs.
3. The number of people incarcerated in federal prisons and jails (208,000) was
divided by the total number of incarcerated people (1,935,000). Sawyer and
Wagner, "Mass Incarceration."
4. Keith Finlay, Michael Mueller-Smith, and Jordan Papp, "The Criminal Justice
Administrative Records System: A Next-Generation Research Data Platform,"
Scientific Data 9, no. 1 (2022): 562, doi.org/10.1038/s41597-022-01620-y.
5. "The Power and Problem of Criminal Justice Data: A Twenty-State Review,"
Measures for Justice, June 2021, measuresforjustice.org/research-publications/
the-power-and-problem-of-criminal-justice-data-a-twenty-state-review/.
6. "America's Massive Misdemeanor System Deepens Inequality," Equal Justice
Initiative, Jan. 9, 2019, eji.org/news/americas-massive-misdemeanor-system
-deepens-inequality/; Gross, "'Punishment Without Crime' Highlights the
Injustice of America's Misdemeanor System."
7. Tom Rich and Kevin M. Scott, "Data on Adjudication of Misdemeanor
Offenses: Results from a Feasibility Study," Bureau of Justice Statistics, Nov.
2022, bjs.ojp.gov/sites/g/files/xyckuh236/files/media/document/damorfs.pdf.
8. Full disclosure dictates that I tell you he's also studying our work at Partners for
Justice, conducting an external evaluation on the impact of collaborative
defense.
9. Heaton, Mayson, and Stevenson, "Downstream Consequences of Misdemeanor
Pretrial Detention."
10. Paul Heaton, conversation with the author, Aug. 14, 2024.
11. Heaton, conversation with the author, Aug. 14, 2024; James Anderson, Maya
Buenaventura, and Paul Heaton, "The Effects of Holistic Defense on Criminal
Justice Outcomes," *Harvard Law Review* 132, no. 3 (2018): 819–93.

12. Maurice Chammah, "The Future of Prisons?," Marshall Project, Sept. 26, 2024, www.themarshallproject.org/2024/09/26/south-carolina-prisons-restoring -promise-units.

13. Beth Schwartzapfel and Bill Keller, "Willie Horton Revisited," Marshall Project, May 13, 2015, www.themarshallproject.org/2015/05/13/willie-horton-revisited.

14. Scrutinize, a New York–based nonprofit, and the Center on Race, Inequality, and the Law at New York University conducted an analysis on New York judges' excessive sentences. It's the tip of the iceberg, but this information has already allowed other community organizations like the Center for Community Alternatives to persuade the state not to reappoint a judge who the data said was a substantial outlier in terms of punitiveness. Ale Perri, David Siffert, and Paco Poler, "Excessive Sentencers: Using Appellate Decisions to Enhance Judicial Transparency," Scrutinize and the Center on Race, Inequality, and the Law, New York University, March 2024, static1.squarespace.com/static/ 635986ea4e3869168261490b/t/6601c13043eff859122c78ad/1711391 024971/excessive-sentencers-pdf_full_report_final.pdf; Hurubie Meko, "N.Y. Criminal Justice Group to Push for More Scrutiny of Judges," *New York Times,* April 30, 2024; John Annese and Graham Rayman, "Longtime Brooklyn Judge Vincent Del Giudice Retiring amid Pressure from Advocacy Groups, Questions About Extreme Sentences, Reversals," *Daily News,* May 27, 2024, www.nydailynews.com/2024/05/27/longtime-brooklyn-judge-vincent-del -giudice-retiring-amid-pressure-from-advocacy-groupstions-about-extreme -sentences-reversals/.

15. Katie Mettler, "Courtwatchers, Fiona Apple Fight Against 'Assembly Line of Injustice,'" *Washington Post,* Feb. 16, 2023.

16. There can, of course, be safety exceptions. If a person's life may be at risk from having their address revealed, for example, one can easily not reveal that address while still handing over the contents of the witness's statement. Often when discussing open file discovery, one comes across the straw man of the dangerous revelation—which isn't hard at all to deal with, since redaction of certain details is already part of the discovery process in many places.

17. M. Chris Fabricant, conversation with the author, Aug. 7, 2024.

18. Valerie P. Hans and Michael J. Saks, "Improving Judge & Jury Evaluation of Scientific Evidence," *Daedalus* 147, no. 4 (2018): 164–80, doi.org/10.1162/ daed_a_00527; Paul C. Giannelli and Kevin C. McMunigal, "Prosecutors, Ethics, and Expert Witnesses," *Fordham Law Review* 76, no. 3 (2007): 1493–537; Michael J. Saks and Jonathan J. Koehler, "The Coming Paradigm Shift in Forensic Identification Science," *Science* 309, no. 5736 (2005): 892–95, doi.org/10.1126/science.1111565.

19. M. Chris Fabricant, *Junk Science and the American Criminal Justice System* (Akashic Books, 2022).

20. Committee on Identifying the Needs of the Forensic Sciences Community,

National Research Council, *Strengthening Forensic Science in the United States: A Path Forward* (National Academies Press, 2009).

21. Fabricant, conversation with the author, Aug. 7, 2024.
22. Craig M. Cooley, "Nurturing Forensic Science: How Appropriate Funding and Government Oversight Can Further Strengthen the Forensic Science Community," *Texas Wesleyan Law Review* 17, no. 4 (2011): 441–79, doi.org/10.37419/TWLR.V17.I4.3.
23. Fabricant, conversation with the author, Aug. 7, 2024.
24. Fabricant, conversation with the author, Aug. 7, 2024.
25. Lawrence Marshall, conversation with the author, Aug. 27, 2024.
26. John Hollway, conversation with the author, Aug. 28, 2024.
27. "Wrongful Convictions," Equal Justice Initiative, accessed Nov. 7, 2024, eji.org/issues/wrongful-convictions/; "Conviction Integrity Units," National Registry of Exonerations, June 25, 2024, https://exonerationregistry.org/conviction-integrity-units.
28. "Conviction Integrity Units."
29. Paul Butler, "The System Is Working the Way It Is Supposed To: The Limits of Criminal Justice Reform," *Freedom Center Journal* 2019, no. 1 (2020): 81–140.
30. "Developments in Law Enforcement Officer Certification and Decertification," National Conference of State Legislatures, Feb. 17, 2023, www.ncsl.org/civil-and-criminal-justice/developments-in-law-enforcement-officer-certification-and-decertification.
31. Dorothy Moses Schulz, "Wandering Cops: How States Can Keep Rogue Officers from Slipping Through the Cracks," Manhattan Institute, March 2022, manhattan.institute/article/wandering-cops-how-states-can-keep-rogue-officers-from-slipping-through-the-cracks.
32. Grunwald and Rappaport, "Wandering Officer"; Kimbriell Kelly, Wesley Lowery, and Steven Rich, "Fired/Rehired," *Washington Post,* Aug. 3, 2017.
33. Grunwald and Rappaport, "Wandering Officer."
34. Mackenzie Mathews, Abigail Edwards, and Ingrid Drake, "36 Fired MPD Officers Reinstated; Receive $14 Million in Back Pay," Office of the District of Columbia Auditor, Oct. 6, 2022, dcauditor.org/report/mpd-personnel-settlement-report/.
35. Kelly, Lowery, and Rich, "Fired/Rehired."
36. "Developments in Law Enforcement Officer Certification and Decertification."
37. Grunwald and Rappaport, "Wandering Officer."
38. Schwartzapfel, VanSickle, and Griffin, "Truth About Trials"; Gramlich, "Fewer Than 1% of Federal Criminal Defendants Were Acquitted in 2022"; *2018 Annual Report and Sourcebook of Federal Sentencing Statistics.*
39. This 2023 paper demonstrates how ready courts are to give cops a pass on misconduct by excusing their misconduct as having been in good faith, finding

that "the current good faith exception blocks any meaningful remedy for several core violations of the Fourth Amendment, including those targeted by the Framers of the Constitution. It motivates judges to avoid addressing substantive Fourth Amendment questions and contributes to the stagnation of Constitutional law. It introduces arbitrariness and inequity into Constitutional remedies, insulating discretionary police behavior from review in a manner likely to harm groups disproportionately targeted by the police. And it implicates separation of powers values, preventing the judiciary from acting as an effective structural check on executive or legislative overreach." Matthew J. Tokson and Michael Gentithes, "The Reality of the Good Faith Exception," SSRN, April 27, 2023, doi.org/10.2139/ssrn.4414248.

40. SB20-217 Enhance Law Enforcement Integrity, 78th General Assembly (Colo. 2020), leg.colorado.gov/bills/sb20-217.

41. HB-6004 An Act Concerning Police Accountability, 2020 session (Conn. 2020), www.cga.ct.gov/asp/cgabillstatus/cgabillstatus.asp?selBillType=Bill& which_year=2020&bill_num=6004.

42. HB-2021-04 New Mexico Civil Rights Act, 55th Legislature (N.M. 2021), www.nmlegis.gov/Legislation/Legislation?Chamber=H&LegType=B&LegNo=4 &year=21.

43. Elise Schmelzer and Seth Klamann, "3 Years After Colorado's Landmark Police Accountability Bill, What's Changed? And Has Push for Further Reform Slowed?," *Denver Post,* July 2, 2023, www.denverpost.com/2023/07/02/colorado -police-reform-body-cameras-george-floyd/.

44. Colin Cowperthwaite, "Searching for Judges Who Hear: Analyzing the Effects of Colorado's Abolition of Qualified Immunity on Civil Rights Litigation," *Columbia Journal of Law and Social Problems* 57 (2024): 1–28.

45. Amanda Hernández, "Some Police Officers Leave Big Cities for Smaller Towns to Avoid Heightened Scrutiny," Stateline, July 12, 2024, stateline.org/2024/07/ 12/some-police-officers-leave-big-cities-for-smaller-towns-to-avoid-heightened -scrutiny/.

46. While there has been no reporting on a qualified-immunity-related dismissal boom as of 2024, one county that does report its case dispositions (Boulder) reported that felony dismissals remained steady, and misdemeanor dismissals actually increased in 2020. "Case Resolution," Twentieth Judicial District Attorney (Boulder County, Colo.), accessed Nov. 7, 2024, data.dacolorado.org/ 20th/case_resolution.

47. Sixty-six percent of those surveyed said they "need to have the power to sue police officers in order to hold them accountable for excessive use of force or misconduct," while only 32 percent said "officers need to be protected against lawsuits that may be brought accusing them of excessive force or misconduct." Of course, Americans' views on police reform differ substantially by race. About

eight in ten Black adults (86 percent) favor permitting citizens to sue police officers to hold them accountable for misconduct, as do 75 percent of Hispanic adults, compared with 60 percent of white adults. "Majority of Public Favors Giving Civilians the Power to Sue Police Officers for Misconduct," Pew Research Center, July 2020, www.pewresearch.org/politics/wp-content/uploads/sites/4/2020/07/PP_2020.07.09_Qualified-Immunity_FINAL.pdf.

48. Matt Allen, "Obstacles to the Implementation of Criminal Justice Reform" (PhD diss., University of Southern Mississippi, 2021), aquila.usm.edu/cgi/view content.cgi?article=3084&context=dissertations.

49. Katherine Beckett, "The Politics, Promise, and Peril of Criminal Justice Reform in the Context of Mass Incarceration," *Annual Review of Criminology* 1, no. 1 (2018): 235–59, doi.org/10.1146/annurev-criminol-032317-092458.

50. Cassidy, "Audit Finds State District Attorney Group Misspent Millions Allocated for Environmental Cases"; "Overview of State Funding and Audit of CDAA," Legislative Analyst's Office, May 13, 2021, lao.ca.gov/handouts/crimjust/2021/CDAA-Audit-and-Overview-051321.pdf.

51. Zoë Robinson and Stephen Rushin, "The Law Enforcement Lobby," *Minnesota Law Review* 107 (2023): 1966–2037.

52. McKelvey et al., "Exploratory Analysis of Nix the 6 Law Enforcement Collective Bargaining Agreements."

53. Prosecutors and Politics Project, "Prosecutor Lobbying in the States, 2015–2018," University of North Carolina School of Law, June 2021, law.unc.edu/wp-content/uploads/2021/06/Prosecutor-Lobbying-in-the-States-2015-2018.pdf.

54. Noam Scheiber, Farah Stockman, and J. David Goodman, "How Police Unions Became Such Powerful Opponents to Reform Efforts," *New York Times,* April 2, 2021; Marshall Cohen et al., "Police Unions Dig in as Calls for Reform Grow," CNN, June 8, 2020; Benjamin Levin, "What's Wrong with Police Unions?," *Columbia Law Review* 120 (2020): 1333–402, openscholarship.wustl.edu/cgi/viewcontent.cgi?article=1382&context=law_scholarship; Catherine L. Fisk and Song Richardson, "Police Unions," *George Washington Law Review* 85 (2017): 712–99.

55. Dylan Matthews, "How Police Unions Became So Powerful—and How They Can Be Tamed," *Vox,* June 24, 2020, www.vox.com/policy-and-politics/212909 81/police-union-contracts-minneapolis-reform; Sam Blum, "Police Unions Wield Massive Power in American Politics—for Now," *Rolling Stone,* July 7, 2020.

56. Abdul Rad, "Police Institutions and Police Abuse: Evidence from the US," SSRN, Oct. 6, 2018, doi.org/10.2139/ssrn.3246419; Dhammika Dharmapala, Richard H. McAdams, and John Rappaport, "Collective Bargaining Rights and Police Misconduct: Evidence from Florida," *Journal of Law, Economics, and Organization* 38, no. 1 (2021): 1–41, doi.org/10.1093/jleo/ewaa025; Jamein Cunningham, Donna Feir, and Rob Gillezeau, "Collective Bargaining Rights,

Policing, and Civilian Deaths," SSRN, March 30, 2021, doi.org/10.2139/ssrn
.3813635.

57. Cunningham, Feir, and Gillezeau, "Collective Bargaining Rights, Policing, and
Civilian Deaths."

58. Scheiber, Stockman, and Goodman, "How Police Unions Became Such
Powerful Opponents to Reform Efforts."

59. Filtered on "selected years" (2014–24). Followthemoney.org., "State-Level
Lobbyist Spending by Police Unions & Associations Spenders," Nov. 6, 2024,
www.followthemoney.org/show-me?dt=3&lby-y=2024,2023,2022,2021,2020,
2019,2018,2017,2016,2015,2014&lby-f-ccb=453&lby-f-fc=2#[%7B1%7Cgro
=lby-s,lby-y.

60. *The Guardian*'s investigation of police unions in New York, Los Angeles, and
Chicago found their local and state donation spending totaled $82 million. At
the federal level, police unions spent "$47.3m on campaign contributions and
lobbying." Tom Perkins, "Revealed: Police Unions Spend Millions to Influence
Policy in Biggest US Cities," *Guardian,* June 23, 2020, www.theguardian.com/
us-news/2020/jun/23/police-unions-spending-policy-reform-chicago-new
-york-la. Filtered on "selected years" (2014–24) and "search for data within"
(federal, state, and local). Followthemoney.org, "Police Unions & Associations
Contributions to Candidates and Committees in Elections," Nov. 6, 2024, www
.followthemoney.org/show-me?dt=1&y=2024,2023,2022,2021,2020,2019,
2018,2017,2016,2015,2014&f-fc=1,2,3&d-ccb=453#[%7B1%7Cgro=y,f-s,d
-eid,c-t-id.

61. Srijita Datta, "Police Unions Spend Millions Lobbying to Retain Their Sway
over Big US Cities and State Governments," OpenSecrets, June 16, 2022, www
.opensecrets.org/news/2022/06/police-unions-spend-millions-lobbying-to-retain
-their-sway-over-big-us-cities-and-state-governments/.

62. Robinson and Rushin, "Law Enforcement Lobby"; Karl Evers-Hillstrom, "DC
Police Union Hired Lobbyists in Effort to Overturn Crime Bills," *Hill,* March
14, 2023, thehill.com/lobbying/3899331-dc-police-union-hired-lobbyists-in
-effort-to-overturn-crime-bills/.

63. Beckett, "Politics, Promise, and Peril of Criminal Justice Reform in the Context
of Mass Incarceration."

64. Nathan E. Enfield, "The Logic and Limits of Chapter 9: The Case of Police,"
University of Chicago Legal Forum (2016): 739–68.

65. David Alan Sklansky, "Police Reform in Divided Times," *American Journal of
Law and Equality* 2 (2022): 3–35, doi.org/10.1162/ajle_a_00036.

66. Jillian Aldebron and Rodney Green, "Changing the Illusion of Police Reform
Under Capitalism," in *The Routledge History of Police Brutality in America,* ed.
Thomas Aiello (Routledge, 2023); Joseph Goldstein and Kevin Armstrong,
"Could This City Hold the Key to the Future of Policing in America?," *New
York Times,* July 12, 2020.

67. Maya Dukmasova, "From Soldier to Worker," *Chicago Reader,* June 10, 2020, chicagoreader.com/news-politics/from-soldier-to-worker/.

68. Dukmasova, "From Soldier to Worker."

Chapter 12: Unclog the System

1. Norman W. Spaulding, "The Ideal and the Actual in Procedural Due Process," *Hastings Constitutional Law Quarterly* 42, no. 2 (2021): 261–96.

2. Linda Balcarová et al., "On the Robustness of Black Americans' Support for the Police: Evidence from a National Experiment," *Journal of Criminal Justice* 92 (May 2024), doi.org/10.1016/j.jcrimjus.2024.102186.

3. Amos Irwin and Betsy Pearl, "The Community Responder Model: How Cities Can Send the Right Responder to Every 911 Call," Center for American Progress, Oct. 2020, www.americanprogress.org/wp-content/uploads/sites/2/2020/10/Alternatives911-report.pdf; Asher and Horwitz, "How Do the Police Actually Spend Their Time?"; Maren M. Spolum et al., "Police Violence: Reducing the Harms of Policing Through Public Health–Informed Alternative Response Programs," *American Journal of Public Health* 113, no. S1 (2023): S37–42, doi.org/10.2105/AJPH.2022.307107.

4. "Support Team Assisted Response (STAR) Program," City and County of Denver, accessed Nov. 7, 2024, denvergov.org/Government/Agencies-Departments-Offices/Agencies-Departments-Offices-Directory/Public-Health-Environment/Community-Behavioral-Health/Behavioral-Health-Strategies/Support-Team-Assisted-Response-STAR-Program.

5. Thomas S. Dee and Jaymes Pyne, "A Community Response Approach to Mental Health and Substance Abuse Crises Reduced Crime," *Science Advances* 8, no. 23 (2022), doi.org/10.1126/sciadv.abm2106.

6. Sarah Gillespie, Will Curran-Groome, and Amy Rogin, "Evaluating Alternative Crisis Response in Denver's Support Team Assisted Response (STAR) Program: Interim Findings," Sept. 2024, https://www.urban.org/research/publication/evaluating-alternative-crisis-response-denvers-support-team-assisted-response; "Support Team Assisted Response (STAR): 2022 Mid-Year Report," Denver Public Safety, 2022, https://denvergov.org/files/assets/public/v/1/public-health-and-environment/documents/cbh/2022_midyear_starreport_accessible.pdf&sa=D&source=docs&ust=1730148292920397&usg=AOvVaw3MPTeJ1P6jlR7tg01y29Wf.

7. "Support Team Assisted Response (STAR): 2022 Mid-Year Report."

8. Dee and Pyne, "Community Response Approach to Mental Health and Substance Abuse Crises Reduced Crime."

9. The figure includes public calls for service that "are not traditionally law

enforcement calls and would likely not be dispatched to police." The calls for service are counted in the figure because they represent needs in the community that require emergency assistance. "CAHOOTS Program Analysis 2021 Update," Eugene Police Department Crime Unit Analysis, May 17, 2022, www.eugene-or.gov/DocumentCenter/View/66051/CAHOOTS-program-analysis-2021-update.

10. "We [CAHOOTS] request backup from police who are not already on scene in less than 1 percent of calls." Justin Madeira, conversation with the author's research team, Sept. 17, 2024.

11. Jackson Beck, Melissa Reuland, and Leah Pope, "Case Study: Cahoots," Vera Institute of Justice, Nov. 2020, www.vera.org/behavioral-health-crisis-alternatives/cahoots.

12. "Two Years of Service from Community Safety First Responders," City of Albuquerque Community Safety Department, Sept. 2023, www.cabq.gov/mayor/documents/redefining-public-safety_acs-2-year-anniversary.pdf.

13. "Quarterly Report: FY24-Q2," City of Albuquerque Community Safety Department, Jan. 2024, www.cabq.gov/acs/documents/acs-quarterly-report-fy24-q2-final.pdf.

14. Mari Bayer, Melissa McKee, and Ashtan Towles, "Emerging Practices to Elevate and Replicate Community Responder Programs Nationwide," Council of State Governments, May 2024, csgjusticecenter.org/publications/emerging-practices-to-elevate-and-replicate-community-responder-programs-nationwide/; Office of Integrated Public Safety Solutions, City of Dallas, accessed Nov. 7, 2024, dallascityhall.com/departments/OIPSS/Pages/default.aspx; "Re-Imagining New York City's Mental Health Emergency Response," City of New York's Mayor's Office of Community Mental Health, accessed Nov. 7, 2024, mentalhealth.cityofnewyork.us/b-heard.

15. Vitale, *End of Policing*.

16. G. K. Shapiro et al., "Co-Responding Police–Mental Health Programs: A Review," *Administration and Policy in Mental Health and Mental Health Services Research* 42, no. 5 (2015): 606–20, doi.org/10.1007/s10488-014-0594-9.

17. Asher and Horwitz, "How Do the Police Actually Spend Their Time?"; Susannah N. Tapp and Elizabeth J. Davis, "Contacts Between Police and the Public, 2020," Bureau of Justice Statistics, Nov. 2022, bjs.ojp.gov/media/document/cbpp20.pdf.

18. David D. Kirkpatrick et al., "Why Many Police Traffic Stops Turn Deadly," *New York Times,* Nov. 30, 2021; "2024 Police Violence Report," Mapping Police Violence, n.d., policeviolencereport.org/.

19. Kirkpatrick et al., "Why Many Police Traffic Stops Turn Deadly"; Sam McCann, "Low-Level Traffic Stops Are Ineffective—and Sometimes Deadly. Why Are They Still Happening?," Vera Institute of Justice, March 29, 2023, www.vera

.org/news/low-level-traffic-stops-are-ineffective-and-sometimes-deadly-why-are
-they-still-happening.

20. Seleeke Flingai et al., "An Analysis of Racial Disparities in Police Traffic Stops
    in Suffolk County, Massachusetts, from 2010 to 2019," Vera Institute of
    Justice, June 2022, vera-institute.files.svdcdn.com/production/downloads/
    publications/analysis-of-racial-disparities-police-traffic-stops-suffolk-county-ma
    .pdf.

21. Jared Fishman, conversation with the author, July 31, 2024.

22. McCann, "Low-Level Traffic Stops Are Ineffective—and Sometimes Deadly."

23. Rory Pulvino et al., "Traffic Stop Policy in Ramsey County, MN," Justice
    Innovation Lab, June 7, 2023, knowledgehub.justiceinnovationlab.org/reports/
    traffic-stop-policy-ramsey-county.

24. Fishman, conversation with the author, July 31, 2024.

25. Kyeland Jackson, "St. Paul Reports Safety Improvements After Years of Revised
    Traffic Policing," *Minnesota Star Tribune,* June 7, 2023, www.startribune.com/st
    -paul-reports-safety-improvements-after-year-of-revised-traffic-policing/
    600280937.

26. "Investing in Evidence-Based Alternatives to Policing: Non-Police Responses to
    Traffic Safety," Vera Institute of Justice, Aug. 2021, www.vera.org/downloads/
    publications/alternatives-to-policing-traffic-enforcement-fact-sheet.pdf;
    McCann, "Low-Level Traffic Stops Are Ineffective—and Sometimes Deadly."

27. Phineas Baxandall, "The Dollars & Sense of Free Buses," Massachusetts Budget
    & Policy Center, March 24, 2021, massbudget.org/2021/03/24/the-dollars
    -sense-of-free-buses/.

28. In the Bronx, Transit District 11 accounted for 11.9 percent (531) and Transit
    District 12 for 20.8 percent (928) of total fare evasion arrests in 2023. In
    Brooklyn, Transit District 33 accounted for 17.2 percent (767) of total fare
    evasion arrests in 2023. The count of arrests for each transit district was summed
    for the year and divided by the total number of arrests for fare evasion. New
    York City Police Department, "Subway Fare Evasion Reports," n.d., www.nyc
    .gov/site/nypd/stats/reports-analysis/subway-fare-evasion.page; U.S. Census
    Bureau, U.S. Department of Commerce, "ACS Demographic and Housing
    Estimates," 2023, American Community Survey, ACS 5-Year Estimates Data
    Profiles, Table DP05, 2023, data.census.gov/table/ACSDP5Y2023.DP05?q
    =Brooklyn+borough,+Kings+County,+New+York; U.S. Census Bureau, U.S.
    Department of Commerce, "ACS Demographic and Housing Estimates," 2023,
    American Community Survey, ACS 5-Year Estimates Data Profiles, Table DP05,
    2023, accessed March 9, 2025, data.census.gov/table/ACSDP5Y2023.DP05?q
    =Bronx+borough,+Bronx+County,+New+York.

29. 2023 "Fare Evasion Arrests" include the count of arrests by race in each quarter.
    The count of arrests by race was summed for the year and divided by the total
    number of arrests for fare evasion. New York City Police Department, "Subway

Fare Evasion Reports," n.d., www.nyc.gov/site/nypd/stats/reports-analysis/subway-fare-evasion.page.

30. "Fare-Free Bus Pilot Evaluation," Metro Transit Authority, July 29, 2024, new.mta.info/document/147096.

31. Nathaniel Meyersohn, "These Cities Are Ending Fares on Transit. Here's Why," CNN, July 8, 2023.

32. Kelly Kenoyer, "TriMet Fare Evasion Citations Become a Little More Fair," *Portland Mercury,* July 3, 2018, www.portlandmercury.com/news/2018/07/03/21031365/trimet-fare-evasion-citations-become-a-little-more-fair; TriMet, "Fares and Fare Enforcement on TriMet," n.d., trimet.org/fares/fareisfair.htm.

33. Ali Bauman, "An Unconstitutional Overreach? CBS2 Investigates NYPD Continuing Banned Practice of Patrolling Private Buildings," CBS News, May 18, 2023; Denerstein, "Sixteenth Report of the Independent Monitor."

34. Luke Scrivener et al., "Tracking Enforcement Trends in New York City: 2003–2018," Data Collaborative for Justice at John Jay College, Sept. 2020, datacollaborativeforjustice.org/wp-content/uploads/2020/09/2020_08_31_Enforcement.pdf.

35. Fishman, email to the author, June 4, 2025.

36. "Crime Survivors Speak: National Survey of Victims' Views on Safety and Justice," Alliance for Safety and Justice, 2022, allianceforsafetyandjustice.org/wp-content/uploads/2022/09/Alliance-for-Safety-and-Justice-Crime-Survivors-Speak-September-2022.pdf.

37. Jeanette Hussemann et al., "National Study of Victim Compensation Programs," NORC at the University of Chicago and Urban Institute, Aug. 2024, www.norc.org/content/dam/norc-org/pdf2024/G259_Victim-Comp-Findings-and-Recs-Brief_Final.pdf.

38. Other examples of historical violence exposure among incarcerated persons include the conclusion that between 39 and 50 percent of incarcerated persons experience abuse during childhood and one-third are victims of crime prior to coming to prison in general. Caitlin Delong and Jennifer Reichert, "The Victim-Offender Overlap: Examining the Relationship Between Victimization and Offending," Illinois Criminal Justice Information Authority, Jan. 9, 2019, icjia.illinois.gov/researchhub/articles/the-victim-offender-overlap-examining-the-relationship-between-victimization-and-offending.

39. Zeng, "Jail Inmates in 2022—Statistical Tables."

40. Andrew Davis, "How Bail Keeps People Locked Up for Being Poor, and Led to a $2 Billion Private Industry," CNBC, Nov. 14, 2019.

41. Saneta DeVuono-Powell et al., "Who Pays? The True Cost of Incarceration on Families," Ella Baker Center, Forward Together, Research Action Design, Sept. 2015, ellabakercenter.org/wp-content/uploads/2022/09/Who-Pays-FINAL.pdf.

42. Tara Watford, "Unlocking the Truth: A Closer Look at Cash Bail Data," Bail Project, Sept. 25, 2023, bailproject.org/data/unlocking-the-truth/.

43. Alex Chohlas-Wood et al., "Automated Court Date Reminders Reduce Warrants for Arrest: Evidence from a Text Messaging Experiment," n.d., 5harad.com/papers/court-reminders.pdf.

44. Megan Stevenson and Sandra G. Mayson, "Pretrial Detention and Bail," in Luna, *Pretrial and Trial Processes,* 21–47; "Smart Justice—Ending Cash Bail," American Civil Liberties Union Pennsylvania, accessed Nov. 7, 2024, www.aclupa.org/en/smart-justice-ending-cash-bail.

45. Chuck Haling, email with the author's research team, Sept. 11, 2024.

46. Terry-Anne Craigie and Ames Grawert, "Bail Reform and Public Safety," Brennan Center for Justice, Aug. 15, 2024, www.brennancenter.org/our-work/research-reports/bail-reform-and-public-safety.

47. Isabella Jorgensen and Sandra Susan Smith, "The Current State of Bail Reform in the United States: Results of a Landscape Analysis of Bail Reforms Across All 50 States," HKS Faculty Research Working Paper Series, Dec. 2021.

48. Cindy Redcross et al., "Evaluation of Pretrial Justice System Reforms That Use the Public Safety Assessment: Effects in Mecklenburg County, North Carolina," Mecklenburg County Series, MDRC Center for Criminal Justice Research, March 2019, www.mdrc.org/sites/default/files/PSA_Mecklenburg_Brief1.pdf.

Chapter 13: Accountability over Punishment

1. The estimate does not reflect the full cost of incarceration because it does not include expenses, like fines and fees, and does not account for inflation. Sawyer and Wagner, "Mass Incarceration."

2. David J. Harding, "Do Prisons Make Us Safer?," *Scientific American,* June 21, 2019, www.scientificamerican.com/article/do-prisons-make-us-safer.

3. Petrich et al., "Custodial Sanctions and Reoffending"; Nicholas Turner, "Research Shows That Long Prison Sentences Don't Actually Improve Safety," Vera Institute of Justice, Feb. 13, 2023, www.vera.org/news/research-shows-that-long-prison-sentences-dont-actually-improve-safety.

4. Emily Widra, "No Escape: The Trauma of Witnessing Violence in Prison," Prison Policy Initiative, Dec. 2, 2020, www.prisonpolicy.org/blog/2020/12/02/witnessing-prison-violence/; Nancy Wolff et al., "Sexual Violence Inside Prisons: Rates of Victimization," *Journal of Urban Health* 83, no. 5 (2006): 835–48, doi.org/10.1007/s11524-006-9065-2; Nancy Wolff et al., "Physical Violence Inside Prisons: Rates of Victimization," *Criminal Justice and Behavior* 34, no. 5 (2007): 588–99, doi.org/10.1177/0093854806296830.

5. "Crime Survivors Speak."

6. Jerusalem Demsas, "The Promise—and Problem—of Restorative Justice," *Vox,* March 23, 2023, www.vox.com/22979070/restorative-justice-forgiveness-limits-promise.

7. "The Conservative Case for Restorative Justice," *Annie E. Casey Foundation* (blog), Jan. 10, 2024, www.aecf.org/blog/the-conservative-case-for-restorative-justice.

8. Development Services Group Inc., "Restorative Justice," Office of Juvenile Justice and Delinquency Prevention, Nov. 2010, www.ojjdp.gov/mpg/litreviews/Restorative_Justice.pdf.

9. Anjali Adukia, Benjamin Feigenberg, and Fatemeh Momeni, "From Retributive to Restorative: An Alternative Approach to Justice," SSRN, Sept. 9, 2023, doi.org/10.2139/ssrn.4566132.

10. The National Institute of Justice rates the quality of evaluation studies based on the strength of evidence of a program's or practice's effect. A rating of "effective" means there is "strong evidence of a positive effect" and a rating of "promising" means there is "moderate evidence of a positive effect" of programs. To calculate the figures above, the numbers of "effective" (96) and "promising" (425) programs and practices were each divided by the total number of programs and practices (717). I use quotation marks here because programs include treatment courts, too, arguably muddling the categories a little bit. "Restorative Justice—Rated Programs and Practices," National Institute of Justice, accessed Nov. 7, 2024, crimesolutions.ojp.gov/topics/victims-victimization/subtopic/Restorative%20justice.

11. Danielle Sered, "Common Justice: Stories from Our Work," Common Justice, 2016, d3n8a8pro7vhmx.cloudfront.net/commonjustice/pages/453/attachments/original/1615395220/Common_Justice_Case_Portraits_2016_small_file_version_%281%29_%281%29.pdf?1615395220.

12. "Common Justice Model," Common Justice, accessed Nov. 7, 2024, www.commonjustice.org/common_justice_model.

13. William R. Nugent et al., "Participation in Victim-Offender Mediation and Reoffense: Successful Replications?," *Research on Social Work Practice* 11, no. 1 (2001): 5–23, doi.org/10.1177/104973150101100101.

14. Lindsay Fulham et al., "The Effectiveness of Restorative Justice Programs: A Meta-Analysis of Recidivism and Other Relevant Outcomes," *Criminology & Criminal Justice,* Nov. 30, 2023, doi.org/10.1177/17488958231215228.

15. "Covid-19, Decarceration, and Abolition: An Evening with Ruth Wilson Gilmore," moderated by Naomi Murakawa, virtual discussion, April 16, 2020, posted April 28, 2020, by Haymarket Books, YouTube, 1:37:28, www.youtube.com/watch?v=hf3f5i9vJNM&t=199s.

16. Lila Kazemian, "Long Sentences: An International Perspective," Council on Criminal Justice, Dec. 2022, assets.foleon.com/eu-central-1/de-uploads-7e3kk3/41697/international_comparison_-_kazemian.e64a9058586b.pdf; Michael

Tonry, "Punishments, Politics, and Prisons in Western Countries," *Crime and Justice* 51 (2022): 7–57, doi.org/10.1086/721278.

17. Figure as of 2020. "Long Sentences by the Numbers," Council on Criminal Justice, accessed Nov. 7, 2024, counciloncj.foleon.com/tfls/long-sentences-by -the-numbers/.

18. Nellis and En, "No End in Sight"; Turner, "Research Shows That Long Prison Sentences Don't Actually Improve Safety."

19. Adam Gelb and Jacob Denney, "National Prison Rate Continues to Decline amid Sentencing, Re-Entry Reforms," Pew Charitable Trusts, Jan. 16, 2018, www.pewtrusts.org/en/research-and-analysis/articles/2018/01/16/national -prison-rate-continues-to-decline-amid-sentencing-re-entry-reforms.

20. David Roodman, "The Impacts of Incarceration on Crime," Open Philanthropy Project, Sept. 2017, www.openphilanthropy.org/files/Focus_Areas/Criminal _Justice_Reform/The_impacts_of_incarceration_on_crime_10.pdf; *Growth of Incarceration in the United States.*

21. "The Older You Get: Why Incarcerating the Elderly Makes Us Less Safe," Families for Justice Reform, n.d., famm.org/wp-content/uploads/2021/10/ Aging-out-of-crime-FINAL.pdf.

22. "Older You Get"; Matthew R. Durose and Leonardo Antenangeli, "Recidivism of Prisoners Released in 34 States in 2012: A 5-Year Follow-Up Period (2012–2017)," Bureau of Justice Statistics, July 2021, bjs.ojp.gov/sites/g/files/ xyckuh236/files/media/document/rpr34s125yfup1217.pdf; Kim Steven Hunt and Billy Easley II, "The Effects of Aging on Recidivism Among Federal Offenders," U.S. Sentencing Commission, Dec. 2017, www.ussc.gov/sites/ default/files/pdf/research-and-publications/research-publications/2017/ 20171207_Recidivism-Age.pdf.

23. "Five Things About Deterrence."

24. Edward E. Rhine, Joan Petersilia, and Kevin R. Reitz, "The Future of Parole Release," *Crime and Justice* 46, no. 1 (2017): 279–338, doi.org/10.1086/ 688616; Katherine Barrett and Richard Greene, "To Work on Parole Boards, No Experience Necessary," *Governing,* Aug. 31, 2016, www.governing.com/ archive/gov-parole-boards-hiring-decisions.html.

25. Alison Siegler, "End Mandatory Minimums," Brennan Center for Justice, Oct. 18, 2021, www.brennancenter.org/our-work/analysis-opinion/end -mandatory-minimums.

26. Editors, "Evidence Does Not Support the Use of the Death Penalty," *Scientific American,* March 19, 2024, www.scientificamerican.com/article/evidence-does -not-support-the-use-of-the-death-penalty; Samuel R. Gross et al., "Rate of False Conviction of Criminal Defendants Who Are Sentenced to Death," *Proceedings of the National Academy of Sciences* 111, no. 20 (2014): 7230–35, doi.org/10 .1073/pnas.1306417111.

27. "Five Things About Deterrence"; Tomislav V. Kovandzic, Lynne M. Vieraitis, and Denise Paquette Boots, "Does the Death Penalty Save Lives? New Evidence from State Panel Data, 1977 to 2006," *Criminology & Public Policy* 8, no. 4 (Nov. 2009): 803–43, doi.org/10.1111/j.1745-9133.2009.00596.x.

28. Tempest, "Death Row Often Means a Long Life."

29. Megan Brenan, "New 47% Low Say Death Penalty Is Fairly Applied in U.S.," Gallup, Nov. 6, 2023, news.gallup.com/poll/513806/new-low-say-death-penalty-fairly-applied.aspx.

30. "Most Americans Favor the Death Penalty Despite Concerns About Its Administration," Pew Research Center, June 2, 2021, www.pewresearch.org/politics/2021/06/02/most-americans-favor-the-death-penalty-despite-concerns-about-its-administration/.

31. "H.R. 4972–118th Congress (2023-2024) End Solitary Confinement Act," Congress.gov, July 27, 2023, www.congress.gov/bill/118th-congress/house-bill/4972/text.

32. Rich Subia, conversation with the author, July 15, 2024.

33. Ariel Bleicher, "Norway's Humane Approach to Prisons Can Work Here Too," *UCSF Magazine* (Summer 2021), magazine.ucsf.edu/norways-humane-approach-prisons-can-work-here-too; Erwin James, "The Norwegian Prison Where Inmates Are Treated Like People," *Guardian,* Feb. 25, 2014, www.theguardian.com/society/2013/feb/25/norwegian-prison-inmates-treated-like-people.

34. Victor L. Shammas, "Pains of Imprisonment," in *The Encyclopedia of Corrections,* ed. Kent R. Kerley (Wiley, 2017), 1–5, doi.org/10.1002/9781118845387.wbeoc020; "Halden Prison," *Kriminalomsorgen,* n.d., www.kriminalomsorgen.no/halden-fengsel.5024512-237612.html.

35. Denis Yukhnenko, Leen Farouki, and Seena Fazel, "Criminal Recidivism Rates Globally: A 6-Year Systematic Review Update," *Journal of Criminal Justice* 88 (Sept.–Oct. 2023), doi.org/10.1016/j.jcrimjus.2023.102115.

36. Boman and Mowen, "Building the Ties That Bind, Breaking the Ties That Don't"; Berg and Huebner, "Reentry and the Ties That Bind"; Mowen, Stansfield, and Boman, "Family Matters."

37. "Captive Labor."

38. Subia, conversation with the author, July 15, 2024.

Chapter 14: A Budget Is a Statement of Values

1. Rare on the scale of all crime. Because America has Constitutionally enshrined the right to bear arms, and the Supreme Court has construed that right in an incredibly expansive way, the number of mass shootings we have is massively larger than anywhere else in the world. So on a global scale, mass shootings are

relatively common here. But compared with all crime experienced by people in America on a day-to-day basis, mass shootings are relatively uncommon. From 2016 to 2018, for example, mass shootings accounted for less than 0.2 percent of firearms deaths and 0.4 percent of all homicides. This is not to say they are unimportant; addressing gun violence is one of the most crucial steps our nation will have to take to move toward greater public safety. As a parent, and a researcher and practitioner who understands the numbers on these events, I would still hesitate to send my small child to school in a gun-heavy state. But when we think about the criminal court system itself, one must point out that these incidents, as terrifying and in need of urgent action as they are, are not the primary driver of system dysfunction. "Mass Shootings in the United States," in *Contemporary Issues in Gun Policy: Essays from the RAND Gun Policy in America Project* (RAND Corporation, 2021), www.rand.org/pubs/research_reports/RRA 243-2.html.

2. Hanna Love, "Want to Reduce Violence? Invest in Place," Brookings Institution, Nov. 16, 2021, www.brookings.edu/articles/want-to-reduce-violence-invest-in -place/; Alison J. Culyba et al., "Modifiable Neighborhood Features Associated with Adolescent Homicide," *JAMA Pediatrics* 170, no. 5 (2016): 473, doi.org/ 10.1001/jamapediatrics.2015.4697.

3. Aaron Chalfin et al., "Police Force Size and Civilian Race," *American Economic Review: Insights* 4, no. 2 (2022): 139–58, doi.org/10.1257/aeri.20200792; Shaila Dewan, " 'Re-Fund the Police'? Why It Might Not Reduce Crime," *New York Times,* June 22, 2023.

4. Love, "Want to Reduce Violence?"; Charles C. Branas et al., "Citywide Cluster Randomized Trial to Restore Blighted Vacant Land and Its Effects on Violence, Crime, and Fear," *Proceedings of the National Academy of Sciences* 115, no. 12 (2018): 2946–51, doi.org/10.1073/pnas.1718503115.

5. Aaron Chalfin et al., "Reducing Crime Through Environmental Design: Evidence from a Randomized Experiment of Street Lighting in New York City," *Journal of Quantitative Criminology* 38, no. 1 (2022): 127–57, doi.org/10.1007/ s10940-020-09490-6.

6. Austin Troy, J. Morgan Grove, and Jarlath O'Neil-Dunne, "The Relationship Between Tree Canopy and Crime Rates Across an Urban–Rural Gradient in the Greater Baltimore Region," *Landscape and Urban Planning* 106, no. 3 (2012): 262–70, doi.org/10.1016/j.landurbplan.2012.03.010.

7. "Crime & Public Safety," Green Cities: Good Health, University of Washington College of the Environment, Aug. 6, 2018, depts.washington.edu/hhwb/Thm _Crime.html; Geoffrey H. Donovan and Jeffrey P. Prestemon, "The Effect of Trees on Crime in Portland, Oregon," *Environment and Behavior* 44, no. 1 (2012): 3–30, doi.org/10.1177/0013916510383238.

8. "Crime & Public Safety."

9. "Crime & Public Safety"; Frances E. Kuo and William C. Sullivan, "Aggression and Violence in the Inner City: Effects of Environment via Mental Fatigue," *Environment and Behavior* 33, no. 4 (2001): 543–71, doi.org/10.1177/0013 9160121973124.

10. "Crime & Public Safety."

11. Love, "Want to Reduce Violence?"; Eugenia C. South, John MacDonald, and Vincent Reina, "Association Between Structural Housing Repairs for Low-Income Homeowners and Neighborhood Crime," *JAMA Network Open* 4, no. 7 (2021), doi.org/10.1001/jamanetworkopen.2021.17067.

12. John MacDonald, "Community Design and Crime: The Impact of Housing and the Built Environment," *Crime and Justice* 44, no. 1 (2015): 333–83, doi.org/10 .1086/681558.

13. Justin E. Heinze et al., "Busy Streets Theory: The Effects of Community-Engaged Greening on Violence," *American Journal of Community Psychology* 62, no. 1–2 (2018): 101–9, doi.org/10.1002/ajcp.12270.

14. Charles C. Branas et al., "A Difference-in-Differences Analysis of Health, Safety, and Greening Vacant Urban Space," *American Journal of Epidemiology* 174, no. 11 (2011): 1296–306, https://pmc.ncbi.nlm.nih.gov/articles/PMC3224254/.

15. Leah A. Jacobs and Aaron Gottlieb, "The Effect of Housing Circumstances on Recidivism: Evidence from a Sample of People on Probation in San Francisco," *Criminal Justice and Behavior* 47, no. 9 (2020): 1097–115, doi.org/10.1177/00 93854820942285; Eric Martin and Marie Garcia, "Reentry Research at NIJ: Providing Robust Evidence for High-Stakes Decision-Making," *NIJ Journal,* no. 284 (Dec. 2022), www.ojp.gov/pdffiles1/nij/300988.pdf; Kimberly Burrowes, "Can Housing Interventions Reduce Incarceration and Recidivism?," *Housing Matters* (blog), Feb. 27, 2019, housingmatters.urban.org/articles/can -housing-interventions-reduce-incarceration-and-recidivism.

16. "Housing and Public Safety," Justice Policy Institute, Nov. 1, 2007, justicepolicy .org/wp-content/uploads/justicepolicy/documents/07-11_rep _housingpublicsafety_ac-ps.pdf.

17. Elior Cohen, "Housing the Homeless: The Effect of Placing Single Adults Experiencing Homelessness in Housing Programs on Future Homelessness and Socioeconomic Outcomes," *American Economic Journal: Applied Economics* 16, no. 2 (2024): 130–75, doi.org/10.1257/app.20220014.

18. Mary K. Cunningham et al., "Breaking the Homelessness-Jail Cycle with Housing First: Results from the Denver Supportive Housing Social Impact Bond Initiative," Urban Institute, July 15, 2021, www.urban.org/research/ publication/breaking-homelessness-jail-cycle-housing-first-results-denver -supportive-housing-social-impact-bond-initiative.

19. Faith E. Lutze, Jeffrey W. Rosky, and Zachary K. Hamilton, "Homelessness and

Reentry: A Multisite Outcome Evaluation of Washington State's Reentry Housing Program for High Risk Offenders," *Criminal Justice and Behavior* 41, no. 4 (2014): 471–91, doi.org/10.1177/0093854813510164.

20. Aravind Boddupalli et al., "How Fines and Fees Impact Family Well-Being," Tax Policy Center, Aug. 14, 2024, www.taxpolicycenter.org/sites/default/files/publication/166004/how_fines_and_fees_impact_family_well-being.pdf.

21. Briana Hammons, "Tip of the Iceberg: How Much Criminal Justice Debt Does the U.S. Really Have?," Fines & Fees Justice Center, April 28, 2021, finesandfeesjusticecenter.org/content/uploads/2021/04/Tip-of-the-Iceberg_Criminal_Justice_Debt_BH1.pdf.

22. Matthew Menendez et al., "The Steep Costs of Criminal Justice Fees and Fines," Brennan Center for Justice, Nov. 21, 2019, www.brennancenter.org/our-work/research-reports/steep-costs-criminal-justice-fees-and-fines.

23. Jolie McCullough, Acacia Coronado, and Chris Essig, "Texas Police Can Seize Money and Property with Little Transparency. So We Got the Data Ourselves," *Texas Tribune,* June 7, 2019, apps.texastribune.org/features/2019/texas-civil-asset-forfeiture-counties-harris-webb-reeves-smith/.

24. Knepper et al., "Policing for Profit."

25. Nick Sibilla, "Poll: Most Americans Want Congress to Abolish Civil Forfeiture," *Forbes,* Nov. 16, 2020, www.forbes.com/sites/nicksibilla/2020/11/12/poll-most-americans-want-to-defund-civil-forfeiture/.

26. George Zuo and Taylor J. Landon, "From Hotspots to Safe Spots: The Impacts of WiFi-Connected Community Centers on Youth Crime," SSRN, June 25, 2024, doi.org/10.2139/ssrn.4874212.

27. Sara Heller et al., "Thinking, Fast and Slow? Some Field Experiments to Reduce Crime and Dropout in Chicago," National Bureau of Economic Research, May 2015, doi.org/10.3386/w21178.

28. Pete Goldschmidt, Denise Huang, and Marjorie Chinen, "The Long-Term Effects of After-School Programming on Educational Adjustment and Juvenile Crime: A Study of the LA's BEST After-School Program," University of California, Los Angeles, June 2007, lasbest.org/wp-content/uploads/2018/05/CRESST-2007-LASBEST_DOJ_Final-Report.pdf.

29. "After-School Programs Can Prevent Crime," Fight Crime: Invest in Kids California, n.d., sedn.senate.ca.gov/sites/sedn.senate.ca.gov/files/2pgr_-_as_2015.pdf.

30. Oppel and Patel, "One Lawyer, 194 Felony Cases, and No Time"; Pace, Brink, and Hanlon, "National Public Defense Workload Study"; "ACLU of Pennsylvania Sues the Commonwealth over Inadequate Public Defense System," ACLU, June 13, 2024, www.aclupa.org/en/press-releases/aclu-pennsylvania-sues-commonwealth-over-inadequate-public-defense-system.

31. Harlow, "Defense Counsel in Criminal Cases."

32. Kelley, "Study: Nearly Half of Americans Have Had a Family Member Jailed, Imprisoned."

33. Kelley, "Study: Nearly Half of Americans Have Had a Family Member Jailed, Imprisoned"; Harlow, "Defense Counsel in Criminal Cases."

34. "New Study by Paul Heaton and RAND Co-Authors Finds Holistic Defense Effective in Reducing Mass Incarceration," University of Pennsylvania Carey Law School, Nov. 12, 2018, www.law.upenn.edu/live/news/8644-new-study-by -paul-heaton-and-rand-co-authorsfinds.

35. Learning for Action. 2019, "Partners for Justice: Baseline Comparison Study Alameda County, California," Partners for Justice client data collected June 21, 2018–April 12, 2019, and analyzed for internal purposes only.

36. Partners for Justice, "Client Services Data" (unpublished, 2018–24).

37. "The Right to Counsel in America Today," Sixth Amendment Center, accessed Nov. 9, 2024, 6ac.org/.

38. Partners for Justice, "Organization Budget" (unpublished, 2018–24); Partners for Justice, "Client Services Data."

39. Partners for Justice, "Client Services Data."

40. Patrick Sharkey, Gerard Torrats-Espinosa, and Delaram Takyar, "Community and the Crime Decline: The Causal Effect of Local Nonprofits on Violent Crime," *American Sociological Review* 82, no. 6 (2017): 1214–40, doi.org/10 .1177/0003122417736289.

41. "About," Participatory Defense, accessed Nov. 9, 2024, www.participatory defense.org/about.

42. "Time Saved," Participatory Defense, accessed Nov. 9, 2024, www.participatory defense.org/timesaved.

43. "Community Violence Intervention," Center for Gun Violence Solutions, accessed Nov. 9, 2024, publichealth.jhu.edu/center-for-gun-violence-solutions/ solutions/community-violence-intervention.

44. "Community Violence Intervention Programs, Explained," Vera Institute of Justice, Sept. 2021, www.vera.org/inline-downloads/community-violence -intervention-programs-explained-report.pdf; "The Evidence of Effectiveness," Cure Violence Global, Aug. 2022, cvg.org/wp-content/uploads/2022/09/Cure -Violence-Evidence-Summary.pdf; Jason Corburn and Amanda Fukutome-Lopez, "Outcome Evaluation of Advance Peace Sacramento, 2018–19," University of California, Berkeley, Institute of Urban and Regional Development, March 2020, www.advancepeace.org/wp-content/uploads/2020/04/Corburn-and-F -Lopez-Advance-Peace-Sacramento-2-Year-Evaluation-03-2020.pdf.

45. Melvin Washington II, "Beyond Jails: Community-Based Strategies for Public Safety," Vera Institute of Justice, Nov. 2022, www.vera.org/beyond-jails -community-based-strategies-for-public-safety; "Hospitals Against Violence Case Study: Detroit Life Is Valuable Everyday (DLIVE)," American Hospital

Association, July 2018, www.aha.org/system/files/media/file/2020/06/hospitals-against-violence-case-study-detroit-life-is-valuable-everyday-dlive.pdf.

46. BBC World Service, "The Dads Spreading Love to Stop Fights in School," YouTube, 2:53, Jan. 4, 2023, www.youtube.com/watch?v=mNz_L2TioU0.

47. Brittany Misencik, "What Is Pine Forest High School's 'Dads on Duty' Program and How Is It Improving Behavior?," *Pensacola News Journal,* May 17, 2023, www.pnj.com/story/news/education/2023/05/17/dads-on-duty-at-pine-forest-high-school-is-a-success-in-first-year/70211137007/.

48. Kayla Susalla, "School Resource Officers: Is Police Presence in Schools Doing More Harm Than Good?," *Cato Institute* (blog), July 24, 2023, www.cato.org/blog/school-resource-officers-police-presence-schools-doing-more-harm-good; Kidane and Rauscher, "Unequal Exposure to School Resource Officers by Student Race, Ethnicity, and Income."

49. Acacia Coronado and Jim Vertuno, "Parents, Onlookers Urged Police to Charge into Uvalde Elementary School," KSAT, June 3, 2022, www.ksat.com/news/2022/05/25/gunman-kills-19-children-2-adults-in-texas-school-rampage/; Zach Despart, "'Systemic Failures' in Uvalde Shooting Went Far Beyond Local Police, Texas House Report Details," *Texas Tribune,* July 17, 2022, www.texastribune.org/2022/07/17/law-enforcement-failure-uvalde-shooting-investigation/; Chelsea Torres, "Mom Who Saved Her Kids from Uvalde School Shooting Says Police Are Targeting Her," CBS News, June 27, 2022, cbsaustin.com/news/nation-world/mom-who-saved-her-kids-from-uvalde-school-shooting-says-police-are-targeting-her-texas-robb-elementary-gunman-salvador-ramos-law-enforcement-response-angeli-rose-gomez-first-responders-who-is-pete-arredondo-town-square-protests-elementary-school-massacre.

50. Mike Kilen, "Nov. 1, 1991: The Day a University Shooting Rampage Shocked Iowa," *Des Moines Register,* Oct. 28, 2016, www.desmoinesregister.com/story/news/2016/10/28/nov-1-1991-day-university-shooting-rampage-shocked-iowa/92053548/.

51. "ARC 2023 Impact Report"; Carlos Cervantes, conversation with the author's research team, Aug. 18, 2024.

52. John Bae, "Building Reentry Ecosystems," Bureau of Justice Assistance, April 2023, web.archive.org/web/20250201185405/bja.ojp.gov/doc/building-reentry-ecosystems.pdf.

53. Antoniese Gant, conversation with the author, Aug. 1, 2024.

54. Chrisfino Kenyatta Leal, conversation with the author, Aug. 13, 2024.

55. Stephen Slivinski, "Turning Shackles into Boot Straps: Why Occupational Licensing Reform Is the Missing Piece of Criminal Justice Reform," Center for the Study of Economic Liberty at Arizona State University, Nov. 7, 2016, csel.asu.edu/sites/default/files/2019-09/csel-policy-report-2016-01-turning-shackles-into-bootstraps.pdf.

Index

Guernsey, Alison, 123
guilt, assumption of, 113
guilty pleas
    disclosure of evidence and, 112
    elimination of cash bail and, 259
    pretrial detentions/releases and, 21
    right to appeal and, 113
Guthkelch, Norman, 126

hair analysis, 125
Harris, Leslie, 3–4, 25, 207–11
Harvard Kennedy School, 259
health
    care after reentry, 183
    care during incarceration, 19–20,
        182–83, 335n69
    effects of incarceration, 15, 182,
        335nn64–66
    need for more hospital beds for
        substance use or mental health care,
        219–20
    public dispatch system for mental
        health crisis teams, 271–72
Hearst, William Randolph, 89
Heaton, Paul, 227, 228, 230
Henderson, Thelton, 25
Hessick, Carissa, 21
Hoffman, Shelby, 58
Hollway, John, 237
Holtzoff, Alexander, 103–4
homelessness
    arrests without conviction and, 59
    contact with police and, 59–60
    drug use and, 85
    probation and, 188, 339n108
    "protective orders" and, 49, 303n26
    race and, 26
    removal of unhoused residents,
        219
    restitution payments and, 304n44
Hurricane Katrina, 18
Hurst, Gerald, 131

Illinois v. Wardlow (2000), 81
incarceration
    conditions as inhumane, 11–12, 20,
        179–80, 267
    correctional officers' unions, 346
    cost of, 181, 183, 261, 354n1
    debt as cause of, 184
    for drug/narcotic use, 216, 217
    effect on violence of, 261–62
    of elderly people, 181, 334n48
    in federal system, 227
    health effects of, 15, 182,
        335nn64–66
    historical exposure to violence of
        individuals in, 353n38
    individual paying cost of, 57–58
    inmates' finances during, 183
    number of beds available for, 219,
        342n21
    post-traumatic stress disorder and, 179
    rehabilitation and, 267–68
    release from. *See* reentry
    violence as normal in, 180
    See also jails; prisons; sentences
indemnification agreements/statutes, 68
innocence, presumption of
    at arraignments, 23
Innocence Projects, 231, 235–36, 237

jails
    admissions, 178, 332n36, 333n37
    conditions in, 19–20, 175–77
    long-term stays in, 177–78
    number of beds in, 342n21
    overdose deaths in, 217
    percent in, not convicted, 258
    pretrial detention lengths in, 20
    suicides in, 20, 21, 332n30
Johnson, Vida B., 68–69, 72, 75
judges/justices
    backgrounds of, 26, 31, 32–33
    election of, 33, 229

About the Author

EMILY GALVIN ALMANZA is the co-founder and executive director of Partners for Justice, a nonprofit creating a new collaborative model of public defense designed to empower defenders nationwide. Prior to founding PFJ, Emily fought for clients inside the L.A. County Public Defender's Office, the County of Santa Clara Public Defender's Office, and the Bronx Defenders, and with the Stanford Three Strikes Project. Her writing has appeared in *The Atlantic, The Washington Post, Newsweek, Teen Vogue,* and *Time,* among other publications.